Critical Approaches to Young Adult Literature

KATHY H. LATROBE and JUDY DRURY

Neal-Schuman Publishers, Inc.

New York   London

Published by Neal-Schuman Publishers, Inc.
100 William St., Suite 2004
New York, NY 10038

Printed and bound in the United States of America.

The paper used in this publication meets the minimum requirements of American National Standard for Information Sciences—Permanence of Paper for Printed Library Materials, ANSI Z39.48-1992.

Library of Congress Cataloging-in-Publication Data

Latrobe, Kathy Howard.
    Critical approaches to young adult literature / Kathy H. Latrobe, Judy Drury.
        p. cm.
    Includes bibliographical references and index.
    ISBN 978-1-55570-564-0 (alk. paper)
    1. Young adult literature—History and criticism. 2. Young adult literature—Study and teaching. 3. Teenagers—Books and reading. I. Drury, Judy. II. Title.

PN1009.A1L38 2009
809'.89282—dc22

                                                                            2008055760

Contents

Part III: Critical Theories

List of Figures

Preface

The importance of turning those between the ages of 12 and 18 into lifelong readers and participants in the eternal power of stories is the foundation of *Critical Approaches to Young Adult Literature*. There's nothing more inherent to lifelong success than reading; stories are powerful because they engage the emotions, demand critical thinking, inspire independent reading, and free the imagination to visit the past, live differently in the present, and envision the future.

The power of the story can intertwine the heart and the mind, the emotions and the intellect. Existing first for pleasure and second for knowledge and understanding, story supports and links the affective and cognitive domains. Whether heard or read, story is a creative, sense-making experience that also becomes an emotional experience, inspiring deeper levels of sense-making and more reflective responses. Reflection on a story after the book is closed is a continuation of its reading, and the continuation may be an individual or a community endeavor, provoking divergent points of view or disparate emotions. And it is often the shared reflection in a community endeavor that can most refine a reading.

OUR SCOPE AND AUDIENCE

We define young adult (YA) literature as whatever young adults are reading—from classic literature to poems to graphic novels. Our audience for this book is anyone who seeks to help YAs hone their skills as readers and their love of reading. Prime among those for whom we're writing are pubic librarians, secondary school librarians, language arts and English teachers, university students of YA literature, parents, and school counselors who

- engage in conversations with YAs about books;
- delight in reading YA literature;
- understand YA readers and YA characters (cognitively, socially, psychologically, historically, culturally);

- develop appealing and purposeful literature programs and activities;
- encourage critical perspectives; and
- share the structures of literature with YAs, thus providing multiple approaches to any text and deepening understandings that enrich literacy skills.

By tapping the power of story for YAs' knowledge, critical thinking, creativity, and deeper understandings, these adults' lasting contribution is to ensure that YA reading is a lifelong pleasure able to sustain an ever-developing, lifelong literacy. Thus, the purpose of this work is to assist adults as they work with YAs and their literature.

ORGANIZATION

Critical Approaches to Young Adult Literature features 12 chapters organized in three parts.

Part I, "Young Adult Literature and Young Adults," consists of three chapters:

- Chapter 1, "Young Adult Literature, Young Adult Literacy," presents the literary and educational structures, theories, and competencies that guide and support YA literacy programming that emphasizes reading for pleasure and knowledge. These structures, theories, and competencies address the American Association of School Librarians' (AASL) *Standards for the 21st-Century Learner.*
- Chapter 2, "The YA, Theoretically Speaking," identifies and describes theories and stages relevant to YA readers in their development across cognitive, psychosocial, social, and ethical dimensions that guide their journeys to adulthood. These theories, which relate not only to YA readers but also to adolescent characters in young adult literature, suggest questions for YA readers' reflection and discussion.
- Chapter 3, "Reading Continues as Readers Respond," suggests avenues through which adults can promote YA reading and response and can encourage YAs to share their creative responses as peer recommendations for reading.

Part II, "Genre," features one comprehensive chapter:

- Chapter 4, "Genre Criticism," one of the first ways that young people categorize or structure literature, describes critical ways to approach contemporary realistic fiction, historical fiction, mysteries, biography, information books, picture books, poetry, short stories, and speculative fiction.

Part III, "Critical Theories," includes eight chapters:

- Chapter 5, "New Criticism/Formal Criticism," presents the critical approach that emphasizes the importance of the literary elements of plot, character, setting, mode, style, theme, tone, and point of view and discusses how the combined effect of these eight elements creates a successful and unified literary work.

- Chapter 6, "Psychological Criticism," applies science to the study of the artistic and creative process of writing, to consideration of the influence of an author's life on works created, and to the analysis of realistic characters.
- Chapter 7, "Sociological Criticism," analyzes a literary work in light of the economy in which the author worked, the social class to which the author belonged, the nature of the author's audience, and the literary tradition of the culture in which the work was created.
- Chapter 8, "Historical Criticism," discusses an approach relevant to any aspect of criticism. It focuses on the basic elements of text, author, reader, and context for the purpose of understanding the work as it was written.
- Chapter 9, "Gender Criticism," presents a method of criticism closely related to sociological criticism, differing most in that it focuses on the gender issues that affect fictional characters' options and choices, the characters' potential for conflict with others, the expectations that characters have for one another, their freedom to be independent of expectations, and the acceptance that they achieve in society.
- Chapter 10, "Archetypal/Mythological Criticism," presents a form of criticism developed from the field of psychology that emphasizes the elements and patterns used in traditional literature. Archetypes are strong images (e.g., characters, plot episodes, settings, situations, themes, symbols, and rituals) that have affective or emotional significance to human beings.
- Chapter 11, "Popular Culture and Literacy," presents criticism at the level of distributed mass media communication messages; it involves the study of media (e.g., television, movies, comics) with attention given to media literacy, visual literacy, and sociological criticism.
- Chapter 12, "Reader-Response Criticism," addresses the critical approach developed by Louise Rosenblatt, whose view of reading accepts the reader as actively and creatively transacting with the text for a unique understanding.

BOOKS FEATURED

Chapters 2–12 all provide background information on literary principles and concepts, suggest questions for leading YAs into critical discussions about a text, and annotations of books relevant to the chapter. The annotations provide brief descriptions of content and literary craft and suggest ways to engage young people in critical responses. The books annotated include a variety of genres, formats, and works (some award winners) that especially demonstrate specific literary principles and concepts. The books are in library collections, and they should suggest other works with similar plots, characters, and literary elements currently in YA collections of school and public libraries or being considered for acquisition. However, their inclusion here is not necessarily a general recommendation; adult readers of this work should reflect on the set of annotations for their specific usefulness in the application of literary principles and concepts with the long-term goal of developing collections and programming that support YAs' deep reading and critical discussions.

OUR PURPOSE

We hope that the adults who read our book will come away with the understanding that literature touches all subjects of interest to humankind. Adults working with YAs value collaboration across disciplines and genuine dialogue. In support of these values, the purpose of *Critical Approaches to Young Adult Literature* is to assist adults as they

- function as agents of change;
- apply and support inquiry learning;
- promote collaboration among those who teach and learn with young adults;
- accept each reader as one who holds values, beliefs, and knowledge that contribute to a unique and personal meaning of a text;
- devise learning activities that utilize multiple intelligences;
- encourage students to build connections to personal experiences and prior knowledge;
- teach, while understanding that knowledge is never fixed within an individual, community, or society;
- motivate reading within and across disciplines;
- promote books and materials (e.g., through the use of booktalking, readers theatre, graphics and art, and performance) in traditional and digital formats;
- participate in the literature that YAs enjoy;
- use an understanding of YA development (needs and characteristics) to inform selection and reading decisions;
- apply an understanding of culture, gender, history, and socioeconomic status to inform selection and programming decisions and to encourage deep reading;
- protect the reading rights of YAs;
- create literature programs that foster reading for pleasure;
- infuse literature programs with opportunities for critical reading and critical responses;
- design programming that motivates creative responses that readers share;

- strengthen democratic skills by encouraging critical reading and thoughtful, inclusive discussions; and
- apply established literary structures and theories in YA programming to engender a coherent and enduring approach to reading and responding to literature.

We hope that the concepts and examples covered in the pages that follow will better equip and inspire librarians, teachers, and others who foster reading and learning to connect YAs and literature.

Part I

Young Adult Literature and Young Adults

Chapter 1

Young Adult Literature, Young Adult Literacy

INTRODUCTION TO YOUNG ADULTS, YOUNG ADULT LITERATURE, AND YOUNG ADULT LITERACY

This chapter focuses on young adults (YAs), YA literature, and YA literacy and on their relationship to literary criticism. Although *Critical Approaches to Young Adult Literature* emphasizes literary criticism, the topics of YAs, YA literature, and YA literacy hold the justification for and the application of literary criticism to YA literature. Useful to this discussion are the following explanations:

- *Literary criticism* is the study of literary works.
- *YA literacy* is a set of skills that develop in the brief time between childhood and adulthood, a time in the life of YAs when, ideally, they have access to literature of interest to them and supportive, informed adults to facilitate the development of their skills. A social imperative, literacy skills are necessary to lifelong learning and, thus, to emotional, social, economic, and physical well-being if not survival. The American Library Association's division of the American Association of School Librarians (2008) identifies four aspects of literacy in its *Standards for the 21st-Century Learner* (which are expanded upon later in the chapter):
    1. Inquire, think critically, and gain knowledge.
    2. Draw conclusions, make informed decisions, apply knowledge to new situations, and create new knowledge.
    3. Share knowledge and participate ethically and productively as members of our democratic society.
    4. Pursue personal and aesthetic growth.
- *YA literature* is what YAs are reading. What they read is often a changing and overlapping set of works from picture books to graphic novels to adult fiction and nonfiction. The literature they choose or have access to may or

may not include the full range of subjects, genres, and reading levels that could meet their needs for pleasure and for personal, academic, and career information.

- *YAs* are students in secondary schools within grade levels 6–12. For this discussion, they are not defined by their literacy skills or by the works they read and enjoy. The most important point about YAs in the context of this book is that they typically begin secondary education as child readers and should emerge as adult readers. It is the tumultuous time of adolescent physical, cognitive, social, and psychological development. For the adults who link YAs and YA literature, the important goals are that young people experience the pleasure of reading, grow in the understanding of their world and of themselves, and develop a foundational knowledge of the structures and elements of literature. These goals support YAs' lifelong reading for pleasure and understanding and ensure that they have a literary voice in shaping their literature in the marketplace and in the library. These goals also shape YA literature.

MULTIDISCIPLINARITY IN SUPPORT OF LITERACY

The goal that young people's literacy skills continue to develop throughout secondary education is often shared among individuals who have interests in literacy, literary criticism, adolescent development, and YA literature. Such individuals are often boundary spanners who have interdisciplinary backgrounds (in this case, for example, those who typically combine elements of the humanities with those of the social sciences). These individuals include public and secondary school librarians, language arts and English teachers, school counselors, reading specialists, university students of YA literature, and maybe even parents who read and discuss YA literature with their children. Also included, although their desig- nated roles may be less directly related to YAs, are publishers and editors who define and market YA books, authors of YA books, reviewers who determine age/grade recommendations for YA books, and professional organizations that include, for example, the International Reading Association (IRA), the National Council of Teachers of English (NCTE), and two divisions of the American Library Association (ALA)—the American Association of School Librarians (AASL) and the Young Adult Library Services Association (YALSA). In regard to literary criticism, YA literacy, YA literature, and YAs, most of these groups have interests in YAs' values and dispositions; entertainments; socioeconomic status; developmental stages, needs, and tasks; popular culture and lifestyles; cognitive abilities; skill competencies; modes of learning; and social interactions.

When adults introduce YAs to criticism of YA literature, they rely on multiple disciplines in order to teach and facilitate the YAs' literacy development. For example, the field of *human development*, which provides a theoretical under-standing of YA abilities, natures, needs, motivations, and culture, is useful when applied by adults to YA behavior and by YAs to the behaviors of literary characters. Students' literacy skills are certainly improved by having access to books and materials but also to teachers who plan and implement learning activities that are created to be engaging and productive through well-planned applications of *instruction design and development*, including the construction of student learning objectives. When introducing a specific literary criticism and its principles, *guided inquiry learning* can promote YAs' engagement in questions and discussion. Furthermore, a major aspect of learning how to learn occurs through metacog-nition (the ability to assess and improve learning and thinking) as demonstrated by David Krathwohl's (2002) adaptation of Benjamin Bloom's (1956) *Taxonomy of Educational Objectives*, which is based in educational psychology.

YAs begin to learn to focus diverse academic perspectives on their reading and literary needs when they enter secondary education. Those who would assume that YA literacy will continue to develop without thoughtful interventions by adults may also assume that YAs have reading skills gained in primary grades to carry them through secondary levels. Although the abilities to decode words on a page, distinguish fact from fiction, explain the concept of an author creator, read visual information, and accept that different readers can have different understandings of a text are important skills, they are not the full range of skills required for adult literacy. As Moore (1999) explains in *Adolescent Literacy: A Position Statement*, when literacy skills continue to develop in grades 6–12, YAs "increase their reading fluency and adjust their reading speed according to their reasons for reading. They discern the characteristics of different types of fiction and nonfiction materials. They refine their tastes in reading and their responses to literature" (pp. 3–4). Thus, secondary students continue to develop skills that support deep reading.

LITERARY CRITICISM IN SUPPORT OF LITERACY

One avenue for supporting and developing deep reading is to approach literature with a conceptual scaffolding that supports structured, critical thinking and creates a shared understanding for discussion. One such scaffolding is the traditional view that considers a literary work from four perspectives: the text, the author, the reader, and the context in which the work is written or disseminated. These four perspectives are basic to adult literacy. Examinations of the text, author, reader, and context can contribute to YAs' development of understandings and applica-tions of critical theories, principles, and concepts reached by abstract thought rather than by concrete experience. Figure 1.1 provides a visual display of the four traditional literary perspectives. The four perspectives are often combined in

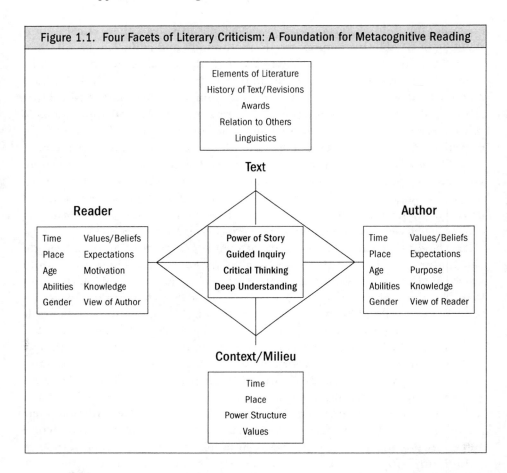

Figure 1.1. Four Facets of Literary Criticism: A Foundation for Metacognitive Reading

Elements of Literature
History of Text/Revisions
Awards
Relation to Others
Linguistics

Text

Reader

Time	Values/Beliefs
Place	Expectations
Age	Motivation
Abilities	Knowledge
Gender	View of Author

Power of Story
Guided Inquiry
Critical Thinking
Deep Understanding

Author

Time	Values/Beliefs
Place	Expectations
Age	Purpose
Abilities	Knowledge
Gender	View of Reader

Context/Milieu

Time
Place
Power Structure
Values

the consideration of a literary work and are not mutually exclusive. Thus, various approaches to literary criticism focus on one dimension or combine two or more of the dimensions. However, as a set, they form an easily understood and shared structure for advancing to higher levels of literacy by prompting new and engaging YA responses to reading and to potential follow-up activities.

The *text* is typically the primary consideration of a reading. Readers may first notice the visual appearance of a text. It may have a distinctive shape (e.g., that of poetry, nonfiction with sidebars, technical writing with ordered sequences, or fiction with imaginatively titled chapters). The narrative conventions of Peter Rabinowitz (1987) that we set forth in Chapter 12 are functions of the text. Other functions of the text include elements of literature (plot, point of view, character, setting, theme, mode, style, and tone), which are the sole focus of formalism (discussed in Chapter 5). Text also includes genre criticism (see Chapter 4) and textual history, which focuses on revisions, awards, time in print, and the relation of one text to another (see Chapter 8). An understanding of the concept of text is one of the first literacy skills acquired by young children, who demonstrate awareness of texts when they ask, for example, for another "once upon a time story" or as YAs do when they ask for a book about a specific nonfiction subject or a collection of science fiction stories.

A second facet in the structure of literature is that of the *author*, who can be a central subject in literary criticism (e.g., biographical or psychological criticism). Readers hold a natural curiosity about the authors of their favorite books, and information about those authors can extend the meaning of a text. For example, meaning is added when the reader knows the author's age (e.g., teenage authors, such as S.E. Hinton and Christopher Paolini), educational background, health, values and beliefs, intended audience, and special training. For example, Richard Peck was an English teacher; Chris Crutcher, a social worker; and Robert Cormier, a newspaper editor.

In the past 40 years, YAs have had rich information resources about their authors, including published biographies for YA readers (e.g., of Robert Cormier, M.E. Kerr, and Richard Peck) and autobiographies (e.g., by Chris Crutcher and Paul Zindel); *Something About the Author*, a 180-volume series published by Thomson Gale (Detroit); the award acceptances of Newbery Award authors (e.g., Russell Freedman), Coretta Scott King Award authors (e.g., Jacqueline Woodson), and Michael Printz Award authors (e.g., Walter Dean Myers); videos produced for commercial and marketing purposes; videos and other author information on the Internet at author and publisher Web sites; and subscription online resources about authors and their books (e.g., www.teachingbooks.com). These many and varied resources are valuable because they enrich reading, address the needs and interests of YAs, support analytical learning activities, and introduce YAs to the authors whose works they have read or may read. As many adults have experienced, studies of authors have been a traditional activity across educational levels.

A literary work's *context* includes the political, economic, and cultural setting in which the work was written. Neither a book's author nor its audience can be separated from the values and beliefs of a specific setting, which determines what the text "implicitly or explicitly promotes" (Kennedy and Gioia, 1998: 719). In realistic literature, some critics maintain that literary characters cannot be separated from the time and place in which they were created. Sociological criticism (see Chapter 7) is tightly focused on the context's relationship with the author or the audience, and some literary critics who employ sociological criticism maintain that characters in realistic fiction have no "specific individuality" that can "be separated from the context in which they were created" (Kennedy and Gioia, 1998: 720). Thus, literature is shaped by its context—by a culture's art, value systems, and power structures.

Each *reader* is a unique and integral part of a literary work. That is, readers contribute meaning to an author's words through many avenues. Like the author, the reader creatively interprets a text through a unique set of individual experiences, memories, knowledge, associations, social circles, developmental stages, family traditions, values, beliefs, health, reading environments, and motivations for reading. This book, written for adults who relate to YAs and their reading, emphasizes the creative role of the YA reader in a literary work and, in Chapters 3 and 12, focuses on YA readers' responses to literature.

READER-RESPONSE CRITICISM IN SUPPORT OF LITERACY

Reader response, as a critical theory, gave authenticity to the YA literary voice by acknowledging the reader to be an active participant in and contributor to a literary text. Young people, themselves, may not enter middle school understanding that a literary work is incomplete without the reader; however, the reader has become an element of literature through influential critical works such as Louise Rosenblatt's (1978) *The Reader, the Text, the Poem: The Transactional Theory of the Literary Work.* Through the concept of a reader transacting with the text to create meaning and emotional interpretation came an understanding that the reader creatively contributes to the text as did its author.

On a personal level, adults can think back to times in their lives when they reread a work, and if years of living intervened between the readings, they are often surprised the second time by a new view and a different understanding. Nancy Drew books and children's classics like *Where the Wild Things Are* (Sendak, 1963) are good tests for this experience as are adult works, such as Tennessee Williams' *The Glass Menagerie* (1945), if first experienced as an adolescent. However, there are shorter time frames for changing one's view of a text. Book discussions, for example, bring forth multiple points of view that can immediately alter an individual's interpretation and understanding of a literary work. Although critics debate the dimensions and nature of the transaction between the reader and the text, there is little disagreement that readers understand and react to texts in widely different and often unpredictable ways. Furthermore, young people who accept the concept of the reader as a learning and changing element of the text will approach reading from a flexible stance different from those who see literature as one fixed reading or as a book on the shelf. Readers who recognize themselves to be transacting hold another level of literacy; they are at the center of their learning, not on the periphery, waiting to be told a text's prescribed meaning. Such readers also understand that their reading continues when they interact with other readers, sharing and defending their interpretations of the text.

Although in the second half of the twentieth century formalist criticism, with its singular focus on text, largely dominated the teaching of literature in high schools and colleges, reader-response criticism gained respectability especially among secondary English teachers who responded to the call for relevance in the curriculum, recognized the birth of YA literature, discussed reader-response theory in high school English departments, and attempted to revise curricula. Teachers who were aware of reader-response theory did not did necessarily apply it or understand its roots; yet, by the 1980s the theory was well presented in professional English education publications by respected critics such as Robert Probst (1984).

PROFESSIONAL STANDARDS FOR LEARNERS

The 1980s were also a time when professional associations began to emphasize not inputs for student learning but rather outcomes of student learning. Setting indicators (standards, competencies, skills) for student learning was articulated in library and information studies (LIS) by the AASL (1988), which developed *Information Power: Guidelines for School Library Media Programs*: The statement (AASL, 1988: 6) that "[t]he mission of the library media program is to ensure that students and staff are effective users of ideas and information" reshaped the organization's professional guidelines. The student was at the center of educational endeavors, and the guidelines were promoted with the phrase: "Because Student Achievement IS the Bottom Line" (AASL, 2002). The mission remained the same in the AASL's 1998 guidelines, *Information Power: Building Partnerships for Learning*. However, *Standards for the 21st-Century Learner* (AASL, 2007) added the dimensions of skills, dispositions, responsibilities, and self-assessment strategies to four standards, extending learner outcomes beyond an emphasis on information seeking and use to include reading for pleasure and reading fluently. Thus, as indicated, the current AASL standards are compatible with reader-response critical theory. The four major 2007 AASL standards are the following:

1. **Inquire, think critically, and gain knowledge.** Like the outcomes listed for this standard, reader-response and other theories also emphasize the application of prior knowledge and experiences to learning experiences; development of questions that seek new understanding; evaluation of social and cultural contexts; ability to read, view, and listen in any format; identification of misconceptions, points of view, and bias; collaboration and discussion to increase understanding; independent choices in selection of resources; creativity; maintenance of a critical stance; flexibility in changing the inquiry; emotional resilience; contribution to the exchange of ideas; respect for divergent perspectives; management of one's own learning; and willingness to ask questions.
2. **Draw conclusions, make informed decisions, apply knowledge to new situations, and create new knowledge.** As in the objectives identified with this

standard, reader-response and other literary theories also emphasize synthesis and the construction of new knowledge; collaboration—the exchange of ideas and solutions to problems; the writing process and creation of new products and responses; testing of opinions against evidence (the text or other readers); connection of the real world to understanding; consideration of diverse perspectives; reflection on ethical decisions; use of the options one has to "accept, reject, and modify" new information; and determination of new inquiries.

3. **Share knowledge and participate ethically and productively as members of our democratic society.** Reflecting the intent of this standard, critical theories, including reader-response theory, also emphasize the sharing of and reflecting on new knowledge; collaboration among learners; application of writing and speaking skills; leadership and confidence, for example, in taking and defending a position; responsibility to contribute to group learning experiences; group productivity; the value of multiple viewpoints and of individual differences; identification of shared concerns; creation of relevant products, such as creative responses to literature; democratic principles and values; respect for intellectual freedom; reflection on other learning strategies; the quality of the learning product; and the ability to work with others.

4. **Pursue personal and aesthetic growth.** Reader-response and other literary theories support this standard by also emphasizing reading for pleasure and for personal growth; an awareness of the world (context) and of previous reading (texts); importance of creative expression in response to literature; reflection on previous knowledge and experiences; involvement in social networks; use of art and creativity to communicate ideas; importance of curiosity as a motivation for learning; resilience and flexibility of thought (e.g., revising understanding as others contribute to the discussion); ability to manage productively divergent and changing opinions; freedom to choose reading material; freedom to read for pleasure; interest in multiple literary genres; participation in electronic and face-to-face dialogue; recognition of purpose of a text; pursuit of aesthetic growth; ability to identify one's own interests; recognition of limits to one's own knowledge and perspective; interpretation of cultural and social context (milieu); ability to weigh the communication of one's ideas; and ability to select reading resources attuned to one's interests and needs.

Thus, the AASL 2007 standards and the literacy competencies that can be gained through reading for pleasure and for understanding, reading deeply and critically, and participating in the social exchange of ideas and knowledge are compatible.

EDUCATIONAL THEORIES AND PRACTICE IN SUPPORT OF LITERACY: CONSTRUCTIVISM, GUIDED INQUIRY, AND EDUCATIONAL OBJECTIVES

There has been a seemingly inevitable compatibility between reader-centered literary approaches and student-centered teaching approaches, which developed along with the acceptance of constructivism, an educational theory that learners construct their own understanding of the world. The constructivist movement accepts the principles of cognitive development as a function of age and social interaction, and it reflects the view that emotions are motivators of thoughts and actions. These concepts are the products of theorists such as John Dewey, Jean Piaget, Jerome Bruner, and Lev Vygotsky. Reflecting constructivism within English and reading education have been theoretical approaches, such as reader-response theory, that valued student-centered processes, critical and reflective thinking, democratic ideals, a commitment to dialogue and social interaction, and the outcome of deep understanding.

In addition to its application of constructivism, the AASL's (2007) *Standards for the 21st-Century Learner* explicitly emphasizes the use of inquiry learning, which is also an element in reader-response criticism. Within LIS, inquiry learning shares theoretical foundations with significant information theories. For example, within LIS, Carol Kuhlthau grounded her early research in the constructivist approach as she studied the information-seeking process of secondary students. The product of her research endeavors is one of the most respected information search process (ISP) models in the field. Her ISP model tracks individual feelings, thoughts, and actions across the ISPs of initiation, selection, exploration, formulation, collection, presentation, and assessment (Kuhlthau, Maniotes, and Caspari 2007: 19). Kuhlthau's ISP model patterns Dewey's (1903) stages of reflective thinking in that each model begins with *feelings* of doubt and uncertainty, includes *thinking* that becomes increasingly focused, and concludes with physical *actions* that resolve uncertainty.

Kuhlthau and coauthors (2007: 6) set forth the principles and foundations in *Guided Inquiry: Learning in the 21st Century*, explaining that "Guided Inquiry creates an environment that motivates students to learn by providing opportunities for them to construct their own meaning and develop deep understanding" and emphasizing that young people gain a "sense of their own learning process" and develop "strategies and skills" for "lifelong learning." Among the recognized characteristics of guided inquiry learning noted by Kuhlthau and coauthors (2007: 6) are

- integration "into content areas" of the curriculum,
- transferability of "information concepts,"
- "involvement of students in every stage of the learning,"

- connectedness of the curriculum "to the students' world,"
- "community of learners working together,"
- collaboration of "[s]tudents and teachers," and
- "emphasis on process and product."

Inquiry learning is emphasized in this chapter because it supports lifelong literacy and ensures that young people have a voice in their learning that can extend to their voice in literacy and literature. However, for this work, inquiry learning is especially valued because it builds on positive motivation that is inherent in the intellectual and emotional power of story.

One way to conceptualize how the theories, practices, and standards discussed in this chapter can be integrated into purposeful learning activities and literature programming is through Bloom's (1956) *Taxonomy of Educational Objectives* as it has been revised by David Krathwohl (2002), who renamed the first two cognitive dimensions (previously *knowledge* and *comprehension*), reversed the placement of the last two (previously *synthesis* and *evaluation*), and laid the six cognitive dimensions over four previously nonexistent knowledge domains: factual knowledge, procedural knowledge, conceptual knowledge, and metacognitive knowledge. Krathwohl's revision and its application to this work are shown in Figure 1.2.

Metacognition in the knowledge domain may seem to be a useful application for YAs' consideration; however, the entire chart can be a metacognitive experience for adults and YAs alike. Furthermore, the use of the chart by adults can ensure that a variety of literature activities are available to YAs.

SUMMARY

This chapter begins and concludes with discussion about the relationship between YAs and their literature. To value YA literature is to value YAs' literary voices—their critical responses to reading texts. Furthermore, within YA responses is the adult pleasure of reading YA literature and the joy of sharing it with YAs. However, to value, read, and share literature responsibly with YAs requires a professional commitment to foster YA literacy and literary development. Fostering "literacy and literary development" requires planning and implementation efforts, but it is an endeavor that increases literary pleasure (book by book) and builds the foundation for lifelong learning (discussion by discussion). It is not, however, an endeavor one accomplishes alone or by happenstance. Those who serve YAs well draw inspiration and expertise from professional organizations, multiple disciplines, the power and motivation inherent in good stories, and the energy, curiosity, and questions of young people.

Figure 1.2. Taxonomy Table Applied to Literary Responses				
Cognitive Process	**Knowledge Dimension**			
	Factual Knowledge (terminology, specific details and elements)	**Conceptual Knowledge** (classifications, categories, principles, theories)	**Procedural Knowledge** (subject-specific skills, techniques, and methods and criteria for procedures)	**Metacognitive Knowledge** (self-knowledge and knowledge about cognitive tasks, including contexts and conditions)
Remember (recall, list, describe, recite, name, locate, recognize)	List three characters or conflicts in a work.	Identify three shared characteristics within a set of gothic romances.	Describe methods that an author can use to develop a character.	Identify the first book one personally enjoyed reading.
Understand (interpret, summarize, explain, infer)	Explain the purpose of denouement in a plot's structure.	Interpret the principles of psychological criticism.	Summarize the techniques that an author may use to create believability in a fantasy.	Compare your personal reactions to plots with open and closed endings.
Apply (execute, attribute, use, show, choose, dramatize)	Role-play the opening scene of a novel.	Categorize a set of picture books by literary genre.	Using the conventions of booktalking, introduce a book to peers.	After a group book discussion, explain how and why personal views may have been modified.
Analyze (organize, attribute, categorize, select, point out)	Point out how a main character determines a work's events and how the events illuminate the character.	Interpret the principles of psychological criticism.	Analyze the usefulness of plot conflict in developing a booktalk or a readers theatre script.	Ascertain the effect of an author's tone on personal reactions to a work.
Evaluate (check, test, judge, criticize, appraise)	Defend five attributes that support a work's protagonist as a round character.	Appraise the concept of genre as a system of categories.	Judge a specific literary theory as a potential one to guide the critique of a work.	Use an audience's verbal and non-verbal feedback to evaluate one's success in delivering a booktalk.
Create (generate, plan, invent, compose, design, develop)	Design a literary map to portray a work's setting.	Produce a set of categories to use in structuring the issues addressed in contemporary realistic novels.	Generate a set of criteria appropriate for the evaluation of speculative fiction.	After a group discussion of individual research on a specific topic, construct a more efficient and effective research strategy.
Source: Adapted from Krathwohl, 2002: 216; applied by K. Latrobe and J. Drury.				

REFERENCES AND SUGGESTIONS FOR FURTHER READING

American Association of School Librarians. 1988. *Information Power: Guidelines for School Library Media Programs.* Chicago: American Library Association.

American Association of School Librarians. 1998. *Information Power: Building Partnerships for Learning.* Chicago: American Library Association.

American Association of School Librarians. 2002. "Promote Advocacy with AASL's New Toolkit" (Press release). Available: www.ala.org/ala/aboutala/hqops/pio/ pressreleasesbucket/promoteadvocacy.cfm (accessed November 22, 2008).

American Association of School Librarians. 2007. *Standards for the 21st-Century Learner.* Chicago: American Library Association. Available: www.ala.org/ala/mgrps/divs/ aasl/aaslproftools/learningstandards/AASL_Learning_Standards_2007.pdf (accessed October 15, 2008).

Anderson, L.W. and D.R. Krathwohl, eds. 2001. *A Taxonomy for Learning, Teaching and Assessing: A Revision of Bloom's Taxonomy of Educational Objectives.* New York: Longman.

Bloom, Benjamin S. 1956. *Taxonomy of Educational Objectives.* New York: Longmans, Green.

Dewey, John. 1903. *Studies in Logical Theory.* Chicago: University of Chicago Press.

Frye, Northrup. 1957. *Anatomy of Criticism.* Princeton, NJ: Princeton University Press.

Kennedy, X.J. and Dana Gioia. 1998. *An Introduction to Fiction,* 7th ed. New York: Longman.

Krathwohl, David R. 2002. "A Revision of Bloom's Taxonomy: An Overview." *Theory Into Practice* 41, no. 4 (November): 212–218.

Kuhlthau, Carol, Leslie K. Maniotes, and Ann K. Caspari. 2007. *Guided Inquiry: Learning in the 21st Century.* Westport, CT: Libraries Unlimited.

Moore, David, et al. 1999. *Adolescent Literacy: A Position Statement.* Newark, DE: International Reading Association. Available: www.reading.org/downloads/positions/ps1036_adolescent .pdf (accessed June 22, 2008).

National Council of Teachers of English. 1998–2008. *Standards for the English Language Arts.* Urbana, IL: National Council of Teachers of English.

Probst, Robert. 1984. *Adolescent Literature: Response and Analysis.* Columbus, OH: Charles E. Merrill Publishing.

Rabinowitz, Peter J. 1987. *Before Reading: Narrative Conventions and the Politics of Interpretation.* Columbus: Ohio State University Press.

Rosenblatt, Louise. 1978. *The Reader, the Text, the Poem: The Transactional Theory of the Literary Work.* Carbondale: Southern Illinois University.

Sendak, Maurice. 1963. *Where the Wild Things Are.* New York: Harper and Row.

Williams, Tennessee. 1945. *The Glass Menagerie.* New York: Random House.

Chapter 2

The YA, Theoretically Speaking

INTRODUCTION

In his poem "Of Necessity, Weeb Jokes About His Height," Charles Webb (1991) portrays the concerns and emotions of Weeb, who experiences many familiar traumas of adolescence in a single poem. Weeb progresses from idealistic dreams to shock, denial, truth, desperation, choices and limitations, doubts, wishes, and contempt to a revision of his hopes and dreams. He suffers imaginary bullies and the loss of drab girlfriends and settles on weightlifting, a rock-and-roll band, and becoming an intellectual. The adult poet looks back and captures his adolescence in the context of recognizable psychosocial, physical, and cognitive perspectives. Adults understand Weeb (and Charles Webb).

Those who work with young adults (YAs) find a structure for understanding human development in the adolescent years by looking to cognitive psychology (Piaget), psychosocial development (Erikson), human development (Havighurst), social cognition (Selman), and moral development (Kohlberg, Gilligan). These theoretical perspectives shape collections and programs meaningful to YA readers, and they demonstrate how the content of YA literature intersects with the theoretical teenager (Figure 2.1).

COGNITIVE PSYCHOLOGY: JEAN PIAGET

Cognitive psychology (or cognitive development) is "a field of psychology that studies memory and cognition" (Weber, 1991: 258). Its focus is analyzing the internal mental processes of thinking, including memory and language acquisition. Jean Piaget identified cognitive development as four distinct stages through which people progress in a fixed sequence and at generally predictable age ranges:

Figure 2.1. Theoretical Contexts of Adolescent Development				
Estimated Age (years)	Erikson's Psychosocial Stages*	Havighurst's Developmental Tasks	Piaget's Cognitive Stages	Selman's Social Perspective-Taking Stages
18	Teen years to 20+: Crisis: Intimacy vs. isolation	Mature relations with age-mates; masculine or feminine social role; accepting physique; emotional independence of adults; prepare for marriage and family; prepare for career; develop ethical system/ideology; socially responsive behavior	Formal operations	In-depth and societal perspective-taking
17				
16				
15				
14				
13	Age 6 to teen years: Crisis: Identity vs. identity diffusion			
12				
11		Skills for games; wholesome attitude toward self; get along with age-mates; gender role; read/write/calculate; everyday living; moral values; personal independence; attitudes toward social groups	Concrete operations	Mutual perspective-taking
10				
9				Self-reflective thinking
8				
7			Preoperational	Differentiated or subjective perspective-taking
6				
5	3 to 5 years: Crisis: Initiative vs. guilt	Walk; take solid foods; eliminate wastes; sex differences and sexual modesty; language to describe social and physical realities; getting ready to read		Egocentric undifferentiated
4				
3	18 months to 3 years: Crisis: Autonomy vs. shame, doubt			
2			Sensorimotor	
1	Birth to 18 months: Crisis: Trust vs. mistrust			
*Except stage 7, adulthood, and stage 8, mature age.				

1. In the *sensorimotor* stage, birth to 2 years, children learn by linking sensory experiences with activity and movement.

2. In the *preoperational* stage, ages 2 to 7, children use language and play to understand their environments symbolically, being egocentric and thinking from one detail to another without generalizing.

3. In the *concrete* operational stage, ages 7 to 11, children show the ability to reason logically, classifying objects, perceiving relationships, sequencing, and performing concrete operations, such as addition and subtraction.

4. In the *formal* operational stage, ages 11 to 15 and older, young people develop the ability to think abstractly without using concrete objects.

Since Piaget published his theory in the mid-twentieth century, many researchers and theorists have expressed concerns about its potential limitations and inadequacies. Among their concerns are that the research was limited to small samples of young boys in an early twentieth-century European culture, it assigned an apparently simple and orderly structure to the intricacies and complexities of children's experiences, and it did not account for the complex analytic abilities of many young children. Furthermore, Lev Vygotsky challenged Piaget's lack of attention to the effects of instruction and social interaction on human cognitive development. However, Piaget's theory of cognitive development has continued to be useful to researchers in the field of child and adolescent development and to practitioners who attempt to relate to YA developmental levels and to offer meaningful challenges that encourage them to stretch cognitively toward the next level.

Piaget's Five Cognitive Abilities of Formal Operations (Stage 4)

According to Piaget, adolescents are moving into stage 4, or the formal operational level, by middle school when they can develop an understanding of the concepts of literary criticism and abstractly apply those concepts to literature. By age 15, many adolescents function well across Piaget's *five cognitive abilities* within the formal operational stage:

1. Introspection
2. Abstract thinking
3. Combinatorial thinking
4. Logical reasoning
5. Hypothetical reasoning

Many adults never develop these *formal* stage 4 cognitive abilities. To encourage *metacognition* (thinking about one's thinking) among adolescents, an adult guide may consider teaching young people the five cognitive abilities within Piaget's stage 4 of formal operations and challenge them to apply that taxonomy to literary discussions by encouraging them to think about thought, imagine what is possible, consider all of the important details, arrive at correct conclusions, and form a hypothesis.

Summary of Piaget's Stage 4 Cognitive Abilities

1. **Introspection**—thinking about thought: How did the author use words to develop a literary work's action, protagonist, or setting in such ways that they could be imagined?

2. **Abstract thinking**—imagining what is possible: What universal truth does this work convey?

3. **Combinatorial thinking**—thinking that takes into consideration all of the important details: How do the literary elements work together to produce the effect of a literary whole?

4. **Logical reasoning**—the ability to arrive at correct conclusions, including, for example, determining cause and effect: What would have been the effect of altering a single literary element (especially, for example, point of view)?

5. **Hypothetical reasoning**—forming a hypothesis and proving or disproving with evidence: Does the literary work reflect events or experiences in the author's life? If so, what are they? (Source: Adapted from Piaget, 1953.)

Application of Piaget's Stage 4 Cognitive Abilities to Katherine Paterson's *Jacob Have I Loved*

1. Introspection

How did the author use words to develop a literary work's action, protagonist, or setting in such ways that they could be imagined?

First, introspection is engaged as readers consider how the figurative language of *Jacob Have I Loved* (Paterson, 1989) paints the island setting. For example, Paterson describes the Island Rass, "lying low as a terrapin back on the faded olive water of the Chesapeake" (p. 1) with "the steeple of the Methodist Church [leaping] . . . from the Bay, dragging up a cluster of white board houses" (p. 1). In the final pages, the adult Wheeze compares the town of Truitt, the mountain-locked valley where she lives with her husband and their twins, to Rass Island; Truitt is "more like an island than anything else I know" (p. 212).

Figurative language also shapes readers' views of the characters. Call goes on "mumbling like a little old preacher about the importance of truth" (p. 7); "Call's cuss words were taught to him by his sainted grandmother and tended to be as quaint as the clothes she made for him" (p. 11). Wheeze's father had "huge weathered hands [that] stuck out rather like the pinchers on a number one Jimmy" (p. 195). Finally, figurative language illuminates action. For example, "Nobody worked on the Sabbath. It was as bad as drinking whiskey and close to cursing and adultery" (p. 75). And, as an adult, Wheeze starts the morning out "[s]hiny as a new crab pot, all set to capture the world," having been recommended for a university scholarship (p. 202).

2. Abstract Thinking

What universal truth does this work convey?

Paterson's novel also challenges young people to imagine what is possible. After Wheeze learns that Call and Caroline will marry, the captain tells Wheeze, "You can make your own chances. But first you have to know what you're after, my dear" (p. 192). Some readers may interpret this statement as an explicit theme. It is a universal truth that, when young people know what they want, they can make their own chances. However, as readers, they imagine the possibilities for Wheeze, who responds, "I might—I want to be a doctor" (p. 193).

3. Combining Literary Elements

How do the literary elements work together to produce the effect of a literary whole?

Jacob Have I Loved has a literary unity that allows young people to take into consideration how all of the important details work together to produce the effect of a literary whole. The first person narrator takes the reader into the mind of Wheeze, who confesses, "I was proud of my sister, but that year, something began to rankle beneath the pride. Life begins to turn upside down at thirteen. I know that now. But at the time I thought the blame for my unhappiness must be fixed—on Caroline, on my grandmother, on my mother, even on myself. Soon I was able to blame the war" (p. 21). The title takes on a symbolic meaning as the reader is introduced to twins, Wheeze and Caroline, and Wheeze is able to see that only Caroline is beloved in the family. Jealousy overwhelms Wheeze, who has "a burning desire to hit" Caroline (p. 32), a longing for her parents to worry about her, a dream that she will someday play the role of Joseph whose family eventually bows before him, and the perception that her heart has been hardened by God (p. 158). Wheeze's family tensions are intensified by her role as a female who in the 1940s had few options. She works hard as a waterman, realizing:

> There are few jobs in this world more physically demanding than the work of those men who choose to follow the water. For one slightly lame man alone on a boat, the work was more than doubled. He needed a son and I would have given anything to be that son, but on Rass in those days, men's work and women's work were sharply divided, and a waterman's boat was not the place for a girl. (p. 21)

Furthermore, her isolation on the island intensifies her conflicts. Her interactions with her mother, her father, her friend Call, her scripture-quoting grandmother, her musically talented sister Caroline, and the Captain provide constant opportunities for betrayal. Like the Rass Island that washes away with every storm, Wheeze feels diminished by every conflict. She perceives that Caroline's life is always sunny. It is only after Wheeze has the courage to make her own chances that she leaves Rass and discovers that beloved infant twins may each have very different needs.

4. Logical Reasoning

What would have been the effect of altering a single literary element (especially, for example, point of view)?

Point of view in the novel is an important element that can be explored by imagining how the story would have been altered by the use of a different point of view, for example, that of Caroline. In considering what effect Caroline's point of view would have had on the perception of gender roles, the interpretations of the other characters, the theme, and the actions that made up the conflict, young people would be challenged to find many details remaining the same. YAs' exploration of the effect of an omniscient point of view could also lead them to imagining a completely different plot. Thus, the literary discussion becomes one of cause and effect.

5. Hypothetical Reasoning

Does the literary work reflect events or experiences in the author's life? If so, what are they?

Finally, young people would be thinking within the aspect of hypothetical reasoning if they formed, for example, the thesis that Katherine Paterson's own life experiences are reflected in the novel. They could consult a biographical resource, such as *Something About the Author* (Senick, 2002: 134–144), and suggest links between Paterson's life and her novel, identifying such issues as her appreciation for music, concern for feminist issues, Christian beliefs, sympathy for the downtrodden, role as the middle child of five children, her father's loss of a leg in World War I, and her childhood feelings of being a poor and foreign misfit. Details from the novel should provide supporting evidence for the hypotheses that young people develop.

PSYCHOSOCIAL DEVELOPMENT: ERIK H. ERIKSON

Psychosocial development refers to "the development of the personality, and the acquisition of social attitudes and skills, from infancy through maturity" (*Dorland's Pocket Medical Dictionary*, 1989: 171). One of the most influential psychologists in the field is Erik H. Erikson, who brought together his experiences in art, Montessori teaching, and psychoanalysis when creating his eight-stage life span theory. As his signature work, the psychosocial stage theory is not explicitly age linked but sequential. Each of Erikson's stages is marked by a distinct crisis whose severity and duration will vary for each person. Erikson (1968: 16) defines *crisis* to mean "not impending catastrophe" but "a necessary turning point, a crucial moment, when development must move one way or another, marshaling resources of growth and recovery." Ideally, the individual integrates or resolves the crisis.

Resolution of a crisis will rarely be completely negative or completely positive. Instead, a balance of the tensions within a crisis is normal. The stages are described as binary opposites (negative and positive), but Erikson emphasized that the positive is an ideal, not a goal, and that people need a ratio between the two poles (e.g., young children need a healthy amount of *mistrust* when it comes to speaking to strangers). Because personality can best be realized in one's relationship to others, social interaction is crucial at every stage. Emphasizing the interdependency of the generations within the life cycle, Erikson stressed that society should provide institutional (e.g., family, school, religion) *guardians* to serve various roles and to support and guide individuals as they progress through the stages. Success depends on nurturing environments, and more positive outcomes of mastering the environment unique to each stage will strengthen the ego. Erikson (1982: 56–57) articulates the discrete stages of his psychosocial developmental theory of binary oppositions (positive to negative) and the phase of life when each becomes important as follows:

Stage 1—Trust/mistrust (infancy)
Stage 2—Autonomy/shame or doubt (early childhood)
Stage 3—Initiative/guilt (play age)
Stage 4—Industry/inferiority (school age)
Stage 5—Identity cohesion/role confusion (adolescence)
Stage 6—Intimacy/isolation (young adulthood)
Stage 7—Generativity/stagnation (adulthood)
Stage 8—Integrity/despair (old age)

Erikson's Stage 5 Crisis

The first five psychosocial developmental stages represent approximately the first 25 years of a person's life, and Erikson devoted much attention to stage 5, which is most associated with adolescence, a time when young people face the challenges of identity and role confusion. However, Erikson came to see identity as "a movable crisis because forming an identity is a life-long crisis. Some people would like to imagine that it is a crisis you go through once and put behind you. But others welcome the idea of life as a continuing series of challenges" (Woodward, 1994: 8).

Despite his refinement of the notion of identity, Erikson (1968: 128) understood that adolescence was a potentially tumultuous period, "almost a way of life between childhood and adulthood." It is important for the teenager to come to terms with certain inevitable changes (e.g., biological and physiological). For Erikson, "Indeed, in the social jungle of human existence there is no feeling of being alive without a sense of identity" (p. 130). One way that teenagers deal with finding out who they are is to become involved in various subcultures "with what looks like a final rather than a transitory... initial identity formation" (p. 128). Young people's experimentation with different roles (e.g., dressing to fit in with certain cliques) is essential for identity development and should not necessarily be seen by adults as a negative activity, according to Erikson's theory.

Erikson (1968: 133) saw the psychosocial advantage of the peer group to teenagers' development: "Adolescents not only help one another temporarily through discomfort by forming cliques and stereotyping themselves, their ideals, and their enemies; they also insistently test each other's capacity for sustaining loyalties in the midst of inevitable conflicts of values." Seeking fervently for something to have faith in, young people may become avid believers and activists for their religion, political party, or other social causes. As young people try to integrate the new roles they have constructed for themselves, they may still face uncertainties regarding future adult roles, such as those of becoming a spouse or a parent.

Erikson emphasized the importance of the individual's active, conscious search for identity, including the need for time and freedom to explore options. Erikson (1968: 128) described the need for a "*moratorium*," or a time out for an active engagement with exploring alternatives. As a socially sanctioned period of life, a moratorium can be many things, depending on the place and time. Sometimes a moratorium can be postponing college for an interesting job or, for those who can afford it, for travel. Whatever the individual chooses to do is preferable to the consequences of *foreclosure*, or of stalling out before giving any thought to or participation in a few of life's many options.

Erikson's theory has been challenged for its potential biases toward white, middle-class males, but contemporary scholars in the field continue to refer to his framework as a starting point when presenting their own theories on psychosocial development.

The Dimensions of Erikson's Stage 5

In addition to the eight stages of life, Erikson's theory also identifies specific, interrelated, and *oppositional dimensions* that are unique to each stage. An individual in the midst of any stage deals with particular issues that Erikson labeled as oppositions, or extremes, and as in the life span stages, the positive is not a goal but an ideal. For example, adolescents may at times experience identity *diffusion*, the psychological term for a person's incomplete sense of identity. Of interest to this chapter are the interrelated dimensions of Erikson's stage 5. In the following list, each dimension of stage 5 is identified, explained, and applied as a point for discussions.

Summary of Erikson's Stage 5 Dimensions

1. **Anticipation of achievement versus work paralysis:** The crisis develops with idealistic needs for a unique kind of achievement that the adolescent's environment cannot offer, and it is ameliorated with an apprenticeship or a moratorium that provides a delay of adult commitments and lessens the potential for destructive behavior.

   Application: Is the YA character finding pride and accomplishment in an activity that he or she may translate into a career, discipline of study, or avocation? Or, is the individual lacking or failing to take advantage of such opportunities?

2. **Leadership and followership versus authority diffusion:** This crisis occurs as the adolescent begins to relate to the larger community and cannot find his or her way to participate as either leader or follower among peers because of an unrealistic view of those roles. The adolescent who can neither lead nor follow is isolated and may struggle to join a group. Isolated teens may choose a group whose nonconformity actually carries tacit rules of exaggerated conformity in such outward demonstrations as clothes, hairstyles, and ideals. The leader of such cliques (e.g., jocks, nerds, goths, or socs) may exert an extreme amount of power over other members who, emotionally ambivalent toward the family, are vulnerable to popular culture and perceived big brothers.

   Application: Within a peer group does the YA character exhibit the ability to lead and to follow? Is he or she coming to terms with authority in other social environments (e.g., family, school, and community)?

3. **Self-certainty versus self-consciousness:** The self-consciousness crisis is resolved by a revision of the child's self-identity that has ideally been fostered in the comfort of a family from which the adolescent feels compelled to separate as peers or other adult leaders assume greater influence over his or her life.

   Application: Whose recognition counts in the YA character's life?

4. **Role experimentation versus role fixation:** The characteristic of this crisis is that adolescents inevitably must experiment with roles and be aware of the limitation of accepting a single role too soon.

   Application: How is the YA character balancing experiences in different or nontraditional roles and groups with those experiences traditionally expected as adult dreams and hopes?

5. **Time perspective versus time diffusion:** This crisis is often demonstrated by an adolescent's intense sense of immediate urgency or by the opposite misperception that nothing will ever change. The crisis is successfully resolved by a realistic interpretation of time in which the identity may develop more fully.

   Application: Does the YA character have a realistic sense of time and its passage—past, present, and future?

6. **Sexual identity versus bisexual diffusion:** This crisis occurs when the adolescent consciously considers the issue of his or her sexual identity.

   Application: Does the YA character feel socially comfortable with his or her gender?

7. **Ideological commitment versus diffusion of ideals:** Erikson describes the seventh dimension as a crucial turning point at which adolescents commit to a set of values that society may view more or less positively.

   Application: Does the YA character make a free and true commitment to an ideology (religious or political creed, a belief system, a structured worldview, and/or set of personal ethics)?

Application of Erikson's Stage 5 Dimensions to Robert Cormier's *The Chocolate War*

Robert Cormier's (1975) novel *The Chocolate War* introduces two adolescents, the protagonist Jerry, a freshman, and the antagonist Archie, a senior. Each searches for a personal identity in a closed environment bereft of guardianship, and the resulting conflict is one of good versus evil, with evil having the advantage over innocence. Still popular and popularly banned, the book resonates with YAs. Erikson's theory of psychosocial development illuminates a new response from readers who focus not only on literary aspects but also on the verisimilitude of the classic *identity crisis* of adolescence.

1. Anticipation of Achievement versus Work Paralysis

Jerry finds his hopes for achievement met when he becomes a quarterback on his high school football team—a rare accomplishment for a freshman. After Jerry's best game, he enjoys a moment of "absolute bliss, absolute happiness" (Cormier, 1975: 62). The reader appreciates Jerry's emotional response especially because he has agonized about wanting to "do something, be somebody. But what?" (p. 53). Conversely, Jerry's best friend Goober becomes involved in a teacher's nervous breakdown and quits his beloved running, the football team, and the school itself, waylaying the development of his identity. Perversely, Archie hates athletics and athletes, especially football players, and engages in intricately and psychologically destructive behavior, choosing to excel in the manipulation of his schoolmates and teachers.

2. Leadership and Followership versus Authority Diffusion

After the death of his mother and with the emotional detachment of his father, Jerry loses his former perspective on the role of family authority in his life. He loves and respects his father, but Jerry can no longer rely on his dad for advice or guidance. Jerry observes his dad "sleepwalking through life" and fears that he will become a "mirror image" of him (p. 53). Furthermore, his respect for adult authority is shattered by Brother Leon's cruel and public humiliation of Greg Bailey, which renders Jerry physically ill as he silently curses his hatred for the teacher. Again, perversely, Archie, who holds all authority over the secret club of the Vigils, feels promoted by Brother Leon, who had sought out Archie's help in gaining control over Leon's irresponsibly conceived chocolate fundraiser. Leon has given Archie proof of what he always has suspected about adults: "that they were running scared" (p. 22) and were easy to deceive and control. Although Archie had never had a relationship with the adults at Trinity School, he becomes a leader and equal co-conspirator who will use Jerry to gain more power over Brother Leon.

3. Self-Certainty versus Self-Consciousness

Jerry, who must look beyond his family for recognition and inclusion, receives unexpected admiration from his coach and the team. However, this success is short-lived when Jerry gets his assignment from the Vigils. He assumes that the assignment will hold the same opportunities for success that his football playing holds, and he conforms without question and keeps silent as is the tradition of the club. Archie, the Assigner, devises a unique plan well-suited to guarantee the most shame and humiliation to each of his victims. As a diabolical leader with supreme self-certainty, Archie orchestrates a task that only he knows will harm Brother Leon and change Jerry from a winner to a loser. Without a caring adult in authority, the school is permeated by the hatred and terror of a student body frozen by Archie's supreme self-certainty. Regarding the students' identities, the students are aware only of their own silent conformity.

4. Role Experimentation versus Role Fixation

Jerry finds himself isolated as he follows through on Archie's assignment that he refuse to participate in the school's chocolate sale for ten days. Jerry fits uncomfortably into the new role that Archie has assigned him; Jerry is both a conformist (doing what Archie tells him to do) and antiauthoritarian (seeming to rebel against school administration). When Jerry experiments beyond the tenth day to report that he has still made no candy sales, he enrages both Brother Leon and Archie, who have much at stake in their evil covenant. They cannot permit an individual to stand against them. However, Jerry's brave commitment catches the attention of many students, including Brian Cochran, the secretary of the candy sale, who reflects that individuals are no less important than the group. Jerry tries to explain his own motives to himself when he thinks, *"Was it because of what Brother Leon does to people, like Bailey, the way he tortures them, tries to make fools of them in front of everybody?"* Jerry will learn that the reason is "more than that, more than that" (p. 91).

5. Time Perspective versus Time Diffusion and 6. Sexual Identity versus Bisexual Diffusion

Despite other ongoing identity issues, Jerry's attention turns to Ellen Barrett, a pretty girl he admires on the bus each day but has hesitated to approach. Jerry has overcome the embarrassment of buying girlie magazines (p. 18) and now hopes to leave behind his most urgent worry: dying before he embraces a girl who can love him. Later, when he calls Ellen, she is rude, thinking he is a boy named Danny, and accuses him of being a pervert. She is not the good-natured girl he expected her to be, and Jerry senses "his bridges [are] burning behind him, and for once in his life he ... [doesn't] care" (p. 129). The telephone call had been a miserable failure; however, Jerry takes pride in the fact that he "had made the call, taken a step" (p. 129). This pivotal moment is a good illustration that Erikson's crises are not necessarily discrete. That is, the time and gender dimensions work together in the way that Jerry perceives his choices.

7. Ideological Commitment versus Diffusion of Ideals

Early in the novel, Jerry thinks about his grieving, withdrawn dad, "Wasn't each man different? Didn't each man have a choice?" (p. 52). The answer came slowly to Jerry through trial-and-error interactions with Brother Leon, Archie, the Vigils, and Goober. The answer came from a poster that had played mysteriously on Jerry's mind. That poster portrayed a man standing alone on a beach and included the question, *"Do I dare disturb the universe?"* (p. 97), a line from T.S. Elliot's "The Love Song of J. Alfred Prufrock." At first he stands up to Brother Leon and sees the poster as one of desolation. However, after he experiences interrogation, vandalism, violence on the football field, and harassing phone calls, he asks himself, "Do I dare disturb the universe?" He makes his choice and practices the question and answer at home until he can publicly assert his firm, clear response, "Yes, I do" (p. 142). Claiming the personal ethics that he slowly and painfully comes to articulate, he faces tragedy with dignity.

HUMAN DEVELOPMENT: ROBERT HAVIGHURST

Human development (or developmental psychology) is "the field of psychology which studies the physical and psychological changes that take place throughout the lifespan" (Weber, 1991: 262). With a background as varied as experimental education, physics, and chemistry, Robert Havighurst is most relevant for his *Developmental Tasks and Education* (1972). Havighurst (1972: 2) defined a *developmental task* as one that "arises at or about a certain time in the life of an individual, successful achievement of which leads to his happiness and to success with later tasks, while failure leads to unhappiness in the individual, disapproval by the society, and difficulty with later tasks."

Havighurst's Adolescent Developmental Tasks

Havighurst (1972) identifies three sources of an individual's developmental tasks: (1) from the individual's physical maturation; (2) from his or her personal sources; and (3) from the pressures of society. Havighurst began his research on human development during the 1940s and quickly discovered that the large number of tasks for childhood and adolescent stages was too "pedagogically unmanageable" (Gay and Williams, 1997: 569) to be useful for those who work with young people. At this early point in creating his framework, Havighurst combined the larger number into "'task-lets'" of approximately eight to ten tasks for each stage (Gay and Williams, 1997: 569). Figure 2.1 includes an abbreviated list of Havighurst's tasks for children and YAs. Of most interest are his tasks for adolescents. As a set, these adolescent tasks describe YAs' interests, challenges, and sources of pride or of conflict. Literature for YAs often reveals Havighurst's adolescent tasks.

Application of Havighurst's Adolescent Developmental Tasks to YA Novels

The following annotations of YA novels demonstrate how all of Havighurst's developmental tasks for adolescents realistically define YA characters and their conflicts and how the characters appeal to YA readers.

1. The acceptance of one's physique and the ability to use one's body effectively for work and play replaces the painful self-consciousness of adolescence.

   K.L. Going. 2003. *Fat Kid Rules the World*. New York: G.P. Putnam's Sons. Grades 8–12.

   Three-hundred-pound Troy Billings had survived thus far by hiding within his interior monologues full of self-deprecations, imaginary losses, and bad predictions until Curt MacCrae, psycho-guitarist legend, shows "Big T" how to see and use his size and strength as an advantage and to encourage him to become a participant in the world of punk rock music, a love they both share.

2. The achievement of new and more mature relations with peers of both genders takes YAs into friendships that require social skills on which they will rely throughout their lives.

   Catherine Gilbert Murdock. 2007. *The Off-season*. Boston: Houghton Mifflin. Grades 7–10.

   Multi-gifted athlete D.J. Schwenk earns acceptance as a member of her high school boys' football team, gives acceptance to her best friend Amber's same-sex lover, helps her spinal-injured older brother adjust to life in a wheelchair, and learns that to deserve her, a boy must be brave and "strong enough to take on a whole herd of trouble when it comes their way" (p. 277).

3. The achievement of a masculine, feminine, or other identity requires that YAs also negotiate its meaning in the flux of cultural and societal transitions.

   Wendelin Van Draanen. 2001. *Flipped*. New York: Knopf. Grades 6–9.

   In the second grade Julie Baker, with her overwhelming personality and messy yard, flipped for Bryce Loski and his blue eyes. However, Bryce dodged her until the romance reversed in the eighth grade when he flipped for Julie with her independent spirit and devotion to family.

4. The achievement of emotional independence from parents and other adults necessitates that adolescents move beyond dependence and rebelliousness toward empathy and respect.

Harriet McBryde Johnson. 2006. *Accidents of Nature.* **New York: Holt. Grades 8–11.**

During her first time away from her parents, 17-year-old wheelchair-bound Jean attends Camp Courage. Here she meets the "arch and irritating" Sara (p. 73), who introduces Jean to the real world of "'The Crip Nation'" (p. 82). By the time her parents arrive to pick her up, Jean has replaced old assumptions about normalcy with empowering ideas about her future that include a new love and appreciation for her parents.

5. The ability to prepare for an economic career depends on adolescents' discovery of what they want in their lives.

Kashmira Sheth. 2007. *Keeping Corner.* **New York: Hyperion. Grades 8–11.**

Hindered by an entrenched caste system and ancient patriarchal traditions that make of her a powerless child-widow, 13-year-old Leela achieves independence through the help of a devoted teacher, the attention of her progressive older brother, and the *satyagrah* of Gandhi, from which she arrives at her decision to become a scholar pledged "to fight against all that is wrong and cruel" (p. 246).

6. The preparation for marriage and family life, made challenging by changing social structures, requires a positive attitude and emotional maturity.

Angela Johnson. 2003. *The First Part Last.* **New York: Simon and Schuster. Grades 7–12.**

After the death of Nia, the mother of 16-year-old Bobby's baby daughter, Bobby struggles and sacrifices to be responsible for the newborn and plans a future with her.

7. The desire for and achievement of socially responsible behavior leads YAs toward a place in society where they find meaning in their lives.

Kate Morgenroth. 2004. *Jude.* **New York: Simon and Schuster. Grades 8 and up.**

Fifteen-year-old Jude, accused of the murder of his drug-selling father, is introduced to a mother he never knew. In an attempt to protect her, Jude is tricked into pleading guilty and receiving a five-year imprisonment throughout which he is determined to prove his innocence and win her acceptance.

8. Acquiring an ethical system provides young people with meaningful values.

Alma Fullerton. 2007. *Walking on Glass.* **New York: HarperTempest. Grades 9 and up.**

An angry and guilt-ridden 16-year-old unnamed narrator takes a perilous journey into his conscience as he decides whether he should turn off the machines that are keeping his mother alive but in a vegetative state after her unsuccessful suicide attempt. He must answer several ethical questions, such as: What is life? What is murder? He arrives at the answers with a mature perspective on the complexities of the meaning(s) of life.

Professionals apply an understanding of these tasks when planning and delivering literature programs, selecting materials, providing reader guidance, relating to YAs' concerns, and working with those who serve young people.

SOCIAL COGNITION: ROBERT SELMAN

Social cognition is that form of cognition "in which people perceive, think about, interpret, categorize, and judge their own social behaviors and those of others" (VandenBos, 2007: 863). Work in social cognition began in the 1970s and eventually achieved status as a field within social psychology. Since the establishment of the multidisciplinary journal *Social Cognition* in 1982 the field has remained very active, especially with the rise of the Internet and of research in the relationship between the user and information technologies. According to Ostrom (2001: 1554), "The social cognition approach views the human mind as an information-processing system. Information is received from the stimulus world, processed through the cognitive system, and drawn upon when engaging in social behavior." Social cognition covers many topics, including customs, the self, social conventions, and role-taking (or perspective-taking).

Considered the leading authority on the subject of *perspective-taking* in children, Robert L. Selman began his studies with a look at the relationship between the ability to put oneself into another's perspective and its role in the formation of moral development. While working as an associate to Lawrence Kohlberg, Selman referred to the centerpiece of his development model as *role-taking*. As his research progressed, however, Selman realized that, in the social sciences, the term *role-taking* has multiple meanings. Selman then referred to his concept as *perspective-taking*, "a core human process underlying social thought and action" (Schultz, Barr, and Selman, 2001: 7). In order to understand another's point of view, Selman (1971: 80) believed, young people must first possess the cognitive ability to make inferences about "the capabilities, attributes, expectations, feelings and potential reactions of others."

Selman's Perspective-Taking Model

Key to Selman's (1971: 80) theory is that young people's social cognition develops through an invariant sequence of stages, "each stage being a reorganization of, rather than a mere addition to, the previous stage." Selman's *perspective-taking model* consists of the following stages (Mendelsohn and Straker, 1999: 71):

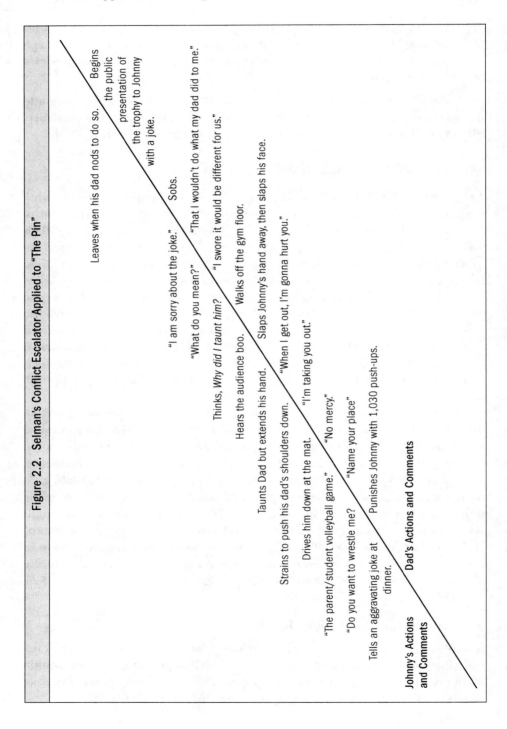

Figure 2.2.   Selman's Conflict Escalator Applied to "The Pin"

Stage 0—Egocentric viewpoint

Stage 1—Social-information perspective-taking.

Stage 2—Self-reflective perspective-taking.

Stage 3—Mutual perspective-taking (For example, in *Jacob Have I Loved*, Wheeze, from an adult perspective, experiences the epiphany that beloved twins can have different needs.)

Stage 4—Social and conventional system perspective-taking

Figure 2.2 (facing page) illustrates a conflict escalator for Chris Crutcher's (1991) short story "The Pin" with the actions and comments of the protagonist and his father as they engage in a dramatic struggle founded on the inability of each of them to take the other's perspective. The application of Selman's perspective-taking in the next section explains the conflicts that are resolved when one person begins to take the perspective of another, using the conflict escalator as a guide.

Application of Selman's Perspective-Taking to Chris Crutcher's "The Pin"

Told entirely from the first-person protagonist, Chris Crutcher's (1991) short story "The Pin" illustrates escalating conflicts between two characters' perceptions of each other. The conflict creates a significant unity in the story. Johnny Rivers discovers that his trademark sense of humor is his best weapon of self-defense against his abusive and overly controlling father, Cecil B. Rivers. Their battle has lasted as long as Johnny can remember, even working its way into his thoughts and peppering his language with violent figures of speech. His dad "applies Mike Tyson disciplinary techniques" (p. 37) and "handles his calculator like a six shooter" (p. 36). Johnny describes a friend's father as a parent who "would shove molten steel slivers beneath his fingernails before he'd lay a hand on [his] kid" (p. 37). But 17-year-old Johnny now turns his father Cecil's abuse to his own advantage: "The funny thing is, I don't hate [Dad] when he tries to push me around physically, maybe because that's how I think we're finally going to get things settled between us" (p. 45), indicating that Johnny foresees an inevitable showdown.

A former U.S. Marine and college wrestler, Cecil belittles or ignores his wife, further angering Johnny, who readily acknowledges, "Dad and I don't always see eye to eye—to the extent that at times we see eye to black eye" (p. 36). Johnny prepares for the chance "to put him in his place so maybe he'll go a little easier on Mac," Johnny's two-year-old brother (p. 40). Johnny intentionally tells more of his "sick jokes" (keenly aware what Cecil's response to them will be), but Johnny transforms Cecil's punishment push-ups into small victories for himself as each push-up builds the stamina Johnny will need to defeat his physically well-conditioned dad. Cecil interprets Johnny's wordplay as a sign of disrespect and fails to see his son's underlying motivations. In a moment of inspiration, Johnny comes up with the idea for a "Generational Wrestlemania" and issues Cecil a face-to-face show-no-mercy confrontation before a crowd of 300 students and parents.

Father and son compete in a familiar arena, but for the first time Johnny gets to fight back. They insult each other back and forth in ever-increasing volatility, the words fueling their anger and providing energy for their muscles, as each combatant strives for *the pin—the fall* that will award the winner full control over Johnny's life. When he sees Cecil's waning strength return, Johnny receives "a slide show" of painful memories, catalysts that propel him "deep inside [his] meanest part," giving him the strength to win the most important battle of his life (p. 56).

After Johnny's successful pin, Cecil twice refuses to shake his son's hand, confusing Johnny, and when Cecil slaps him in the face, Johnny falls on the mat "as if dropped by a hammer," hurt and stunned (p. 57). After achieving his revenge, Johnny does not understand why he feels sadness and defeat instead of glory. But his sympathies go out to his father, who has shamed himself before their neighbors. Johnny is enlightened when Cecil reveals an old promise (kept secret): "I swore it'd be different for you and me. . . . That I wouldn't do to you what my dad did to me" (p. 59). Facing great personal failure and loss, Cecil realizes he must let go of Johnny after never having known him, never having accepted his son's love. But Johnny wins doubly when his dad stands before the winter sports award banquet, presents Johnny his state championship trophy, and begins his talk with one of Johnny's signature stories, symbolic of a huge step for Cecil, who seems able to put things in a better perspective. Father and son begin a journey of true understanding, and both are stronger after clearing up years of misperceptions.

THEORIES OF MORAL DEVELOPMENT

Lawrence Kohlberg

Moral development is the process by which people acquire knowledge about right and wrong. Among most notable moral development theorists are Lawrence Kohlberg and his colleague, Carol Gilligan. Kohlberg was especially captivated by Piaget's view of the child as philosopher, extending Piaget's theory on moral development by analyzing the cognitive processes that gird the development of children's moral reasoning. Thus, Kohlberg ushered in the systematic empirical method that other theorists have since used as one paradigm with which to study moral development.

After his work with European refugees from the Holocaust, Kohlberg rejected any notion of a value-neutral education. By using longitudinal studies, smaller six-year studies, and a variety of cross-sectional studies, Kohlberg formulated his six-stage theory of moral development. Following Piaget, Kohlberg theorized that stages are hierarchically structured organized systems that progress (usually) without skipping any stages.

From the perspective of moral behavior, Kohlberg maintained that individuals were influenced by factors other than judgment (such as environment) and could revert to a less mature moral rationale. He believed that young people's progression to a higher developmental level could be promoted through participation in discussions of moral issues. To support these discussions, Kohlberg created scenarios that presented ethical or moral dilemmas that progressed in complexity from a lower to a higher level and were used by professionals interested in discussing moral choices with young people. Those who work with YAs may consider introducing moral development as a theory worthy of discussion and debate and a theory in support of metacognition (thinking about one's thinking) as applied to YA literature.

Kohlberg (1975: 49) described his theory as consisting of three levels with two stages for each level: level 1, pre-conventional (stages 1 and 2); level 2, conventional (stages 3 and 4); and level 3, post-conventional (stages 5 and 6). *Pre-conventional* children react at the level of reward or punishment. Stage 1 of level 1 is sometimes referred to as the "might makes right" form of thinking for its characteristic of power through punishment. Stage 2 is sometimes referred to as "tit for tat" for its characteristic of exchange of favors.

Conventional (level 2) children see certain groups (parents, teachers, policemen) in society as those who have the power to determine what is right and what is wrong. At stage 3, children value conformity and loyalty and often identify with those involved in maintaining the order of things. Stage 3 is sometimes referred to as the "good boy—nice girl" orientation for its characteristic of one's behaving to please. Stage 4 is sometimes referred to as the "law and order" orientation for its characteristic of one's maintaining and supporting fixed rules and of showing respect for authority. In his early studies, Kohlberg found that most people arrive and remain at stage 4.

At *post-conventional* (level 3), people make moral decisions with a less rigid view of right and wrong, even allowing each individual to ascertain what is right and what is wrong as a personal choice. Stage 5 emphasizes a legal point of view with the possibility of changing law based on rational thought such as the system of making and amending laws in the United States. Stage 6 is "the universal-ethical-principle orientation" (Kohlberg and Hersh, 1977: 55). As the highest stage of justice reasoning, stage 6 is characterized by decisions based on conscience or on abstract and ethical principles, such as the Golden Rule, but Kohlberg asserts that the appeal is still to logic, universality, and consistency.

Kohlberg's Levels and Stages of Moral Development

Readers may respond to literature by discussing the following questions from Kohlberg's levels and stages of moral development (adapted from Kohlberg, 1975 and 1990).

Level 1: Pre-conventional (1975)

Stage 1: *Obedience and punishment*
> Does one base a decision on the avoidance of punishment?

Stage 2: *Exchange and trade-off*
> Does one make a decision expecting a fair exchange in kind?

Level 2: Conventional (1975)

Stage 3: *Conformity and approval based on significant others*
> Does one make a decision that will conform to expectations of family and/or friends?

Stage 4: *Conformity and approval based on authority/society as final arbitrator*
> Does one make a decision based on authority/established conventions and fixed rules for their own sake?

Level 3: Post-conventional (1990)

Stage 5: *Social contract/or personal loyalty considerations*
> Does one make a decision within a social contract or act responsibly to change a law when there is a need to do so?
> With a special responsibility to family or friend, does one make a decision based on relationship-specific and context-specific factors?

Stage 6: *Principled conscience*
> Are one's decisions consistent with justice and benevolence and congruent with universal human rights?

Moral Development in a Different Voice: Carol Gilligan

Although Kohlberg's theory had been under challenge since its inception by some scholars, religious groups, and educators for various reasons, it was his colleague Carol Gilligan whose concept of moral development shaped a new paradigm, one focused not on justice but rather on care and connectedness as she explained it in *In a Different Voice: Psychological Theory and Women's Development* (1982). After noting that females scored consistently lower than males in Kohlberg's findings, Gilligan attributed the difference to his exclusion of women from his theory-building studies. Gilligan's approach used interviews and one-on-one listening sessions that revealed that females typically respond to moral dilemmas in what she calls "a distinct voice" (Gilligan, Lyons, and Hanmer, 1990: 318). Gilligan asserted that, unlike Kohlberg's model, her care and connectedness orientation has no stages (ages) or levels (Lyons, 1990: 42); furthermore, although males and females use both orientations, studies indicate that males gravitate toward justice and females toward care (Gilligan et al., 1988).

Gilligan et al. (1988: xvii) recognized that "adolescents are passionately interested in moral questions," and, as many teachers report, students "hunger" for material that makes them think about vital moral issues. Her care orientation emphasizes the importance of relationships, of a response to others in their own terms and particular situations, and of an evaluation of each decision. Her perspective of caring and connectedness guides the following questions adapted from Gilligan (1982):

Gilligan's Caring and Connectedness Perspective

1. Does one base a moral decision on
   a. the belief that being good means taking care of others and oneself,
   b. a desire to reduce tension between others and oneself, or
   c. the understanding that it is psychologically more important to maintain a satisfying relationship with a person than to do anything that might harm that person and/or the relationship?
2. Does one, recognizing the interdependence of humankind, condemn exploitation and violence while making decisions?
3. Does one approach a life-altering decision by attempting to solve a conflict in such a way that no one (including oneself) is hurt?

Application of the Moral Theories of Kohlberg and Gilligan to Mark Twain's *The Adventures of Huckleberry Finn*

After a review of the Gilligan and Kohlberg orientations, the following questions may be useful in considering application of the theories to a literary discussion.

- Using either Kohlberg's or Gilligan's orientation, how would you describe the protagonist's moral judgment? What details would support your description?
- Using either orientation, how would you describe the protagonist's moral behavior?
- How do you explain any discrepancies between judgment and behavior?

Another dimension to an introduction of moral issues in literary discussions is that many topics of moral development are value laden. Kohlberg (1975) identified a list of ten such subjects: punishment, property, roles and concerns of affection, roles and concerns of authority, law, life, liberty, distributive justice, truth, and sex. Kohlberg (1975: 673) explained, "A moral choice involves choosing between two (or more) of these values as they *conflict* in concrete situations of choice." Thus, these topics should have a high correlation to the dilemmas faced by fictional characters and could be used as abstract concepts for an introductory discussion to, for example, a critique of *Huckleberry Finn*.

In the following paragraphs, Kohlberg's stages and Gilligan's orientations are applied to Mark Twain's (1961) *The Adventures of Huckleberry Finn*. This novel is the classic example of an adolescent enmeshed in a moral dilemma. However, because Twain chose a naïve narrator, his own sophisticated wisdom presents Huck as a young person unaware of his own goodness. Huck can function beyond his developmental and social capacity because Twain's art leads the reader to envision what is right and fair. With a reliable narrator, there would be no irony, no humor, no growth—only an adventure story. Few can read this novel without thinking of Huck's upbringing, goodness, and moral alienation.

Kohlberg

Stage 1: Huck's caretakers teach him that anyone who sins will go to "the bad place" with its "everlasting fire," stressing fear and punishment to shape his behavior (*Huckleberry Finn*, Chapters 1 and 2).

Stage 2: Huck's experiences with the villagers along the Mississippi River show that people tend to help others only if they can receive something in return. When Huck encounters two armed slave hunters who question him about "the other white person" on his raft, Huck protects Jim's identity by tricking the men into thinking that his "father" (Jim) has the dreaded smallpox. Before the men flee, they give Huck $40 as fair exchange to assuage their guilty consciences for abandoning a child in need (Chapter 16).

Stage 3: After Pap Finn loses parental privileges, Huck receives his moral lessons from some of the most respected members of his village. Huck learns at home, church, and school the consistent belief that slavery is socially acceptable and that slaves are property without the same feelings as white people. Huck, Tom Sawyer, and the gang feel comfortable teasing Jim and playing pranks on him as they conform to their elders' expectations, maintaining the subservient status of the slaves while asserting their right to do so.

Stage 4: Huck expresses the traditional antebellum view that the worst person in society was "a dirty Abolitionist." To most of Southern citizens, abolitionists undermined the very foundation of the South and committed the serious crime of theft of another person's property. When Jim speaks excitedly about his plans to hire an "Ab'litionist" to steal his children out of slavery, Huck "most froze to hear such talk," reminding Huck of his own responsibility to support the slavery laws (Chapter 16). When Tom Sawyer volunteers to become an abolitionist and help free Jim, Huck finds it "outrageous" that with Tom's respectable upbringing he would "stoop to this business, and make himself a shame, and his family a shame, before everybody" (Chapter 34). Ironically, it is only in the final pages that Huck discovers Tom had known all along that Jim had been set free in Miss Watson's will. Huck correctly knew that as a respectable Southern boy, Tom would never break with his society's most important moral convention.

Gilligan

1a: Huck spends much of his childhood suffering verbal and physical abuse from his Pap Finn. When Pap kidnaps Huck and drinks himself into hallucinations and it is clear he intends to kill Huck, the child devises a clever escape to save his own life without causing any harm to Pap (*Huckleberry Finn*, Chapters 6 and 7).

1b: Huck demonstrates his desire to keep life on the raft as peaceful and tension-free as possible, as shown when the Duke and the King come aboard. Huck realizes the two con men are not royalty as they claim, but he does whatever they want in order to "keep peace in the family" and to keep Jim and himself safe from the law (Chapter 19).

1c: In several episodes, the reader sees Huck make his decisions not from an outside convention but rather from his personal sense of fairness and goodness. His decisions arise naturally from his developing sense of the importance of actively protecting others from harm. He identifies with children and orphans who are at the mercy of family feuds or who are swindled by scoundrels, and, in order to keep the innocent out of danger, he feels compelled to fix any plans arranged by adults (Chapters 17–30). For example, Huck goes to great lengths to stop two men from carrying out their plan to murder a third, but he goes to even greater lengths to preserve the lives of the murderers themselves (Chapter 13).

2: Two incidents occur that compel Huck to seriously question moral beliefs that he had been carefully taught. After Huck humiliates Jim with a practical joke, Jim chastises the boy for making a fool out of him and of breaking his heart. Jim calls Huck no better than trash and makes clear his personal code of conduct based on "do unto others," especially regarding friends. And, Jim considers Huck a true friend. In responding, Huck feels great shame and asks Jim for forgiveness, placing himself in one of the most degrading positions for an antebellum white (Chapter 15). Huck learns from an earlier prank that Jim can suffer physical pain (Chapter 10), and now he sees Jim can suffer emotional pain as well. Later, Huck hears Jim cry and blame himself for his daughter 'Lizbeth's illness (Chapter 23). Huck's picture of Jim as fully human gradually emerges and will become a forceful image for him in his climactic battle with his conscience.

3: Huck's crucible comes in Chapter 31 when he must decide once and for all what to do about Jim. He and his conscience begin a lengthy dialogue as Huck asks himself direct questions but receives the same answers that defined why a good Southern child should inform the law about a runaway slave. "The more I studied about this the more my conscience went to grinding on me, and the more wicked and low-down and ornery I got to feeling" (p. 213). He wants to follow his conscience (a set of fixed rules based on authority), but he continues to recall images of Jim as friend, caretaker, and decent human being (a picture that carries its own authority based on Huck's experiences with Jim). He reflects on his lessons that "learnt you that people that acts as I'd been acting . . . goes to everlasting fire" (p. 213). Huck's compassionate realization that he and Jim depend on each other forbids him from inflicting pain and suffering on Jim by returning him to a life of slavery. Huck's words and actions show he will sacrifice himself for Jim: He destroys his note to Miss Watson that would reveal Jim's whereabouts and accepts the consequences of his actions—social ostracism and ultimately going to "the bad place."

SUMMARY

Cognitive psychology (Piaget), psychosocial development (Erikson), human development (Havighurst), social cognition (Selman), and moral development (Kohlberg and Gilligan) illuminate theoretical YAs, their literature, and their responses to literature. It is at the discretion of those who work closely with YAs to decide if their students are prepared to consider any of the theoretical questions self-consciously as one way to respond to literature. Certainly, YAs are prepared to consider their own moral development as they test their beliefs through their own behaviors. The following annotated bibliography identifies books that can be approached from developmental perspectives and suggests ways that YAs may respond beyond a first reading to new understandings, both personal and critical.

ANNOTATED BIBLIOGRAPHY

Bingham, Kelly. 2007. *Shark Girl*. Cambridge, MA: Candlewick. Grades 6–10.

Fifteen-year-old Jane Arrowood survives a shark attack but loses her right arm and faces the challenges of adjusting to her new self. Jane is enraged at others' easy clichéd advice, angry at the loss of her career as artist, hates the pity, wishes she had died, and lives with a negative-scripted monologue that expresses her low self-esteem. This multi-genre narrative provides opportunities for readers to discuss how Jane handles her adolescent crisis made harder because her body image changes so dramatically.

Henkes, Kevin. 1996. *Lilly's Purple Plastic Purse*. New York: HarperCollins; and Shannon, David. 1998. *No, David!* New York: Scholastic. Grades pre-K–2.

These picture books introduce two likeable and exuberant characters, Lilly and David, whose childish imperfections are addressed in loving families. Lilly's beloved teacher, Mr. Stringer, chastises Lilly for not keeping her new purse inside her classroom desk, and Lilly responds with fury. David, a boisterous little boy, creates wild shenanigans (e.g., tracks dirt and topples the cookie jar) as his mother responds with "no" in a variety of disciplinary phrases. Young people can develop a graphic of Selman's conflict escalator for either picture book.

Koja, Kathe. 2007. *Kissing the Bee*. New York: Frances Foster Books, Farrar, Straus, and Giroux. Grades 7 and up.

Friends since the fifth grade, high-school seniors Dana and Avra dramatically split when Dana realizes she no longer fits her previous role as "worker bee" to high-maintenance Avra's "queen bee." The identity crisis that Dana experiences coincides with her recognition that she is in love with Emil, Avra's current steady. Readers can discuss the (developmental) issues that Dana experiences (e.g., her moral dilemma arising over her love for Emil and her loyalty to Avra, her decision about a career in science writing, and her increasing independence from her mother while seeing her in a new way as a wise woman who can listen to her).

Lisle, Janet Taylor. 2002. *Art of Keeping Cool*. New York: Simon and Schuster. Grades 5–8.

Thirteen-year-old cousins Robert and Eliot spend time together at their grandparents' home in Rhode Island during World War II. Robert and Eliot react differently to the tensions of the war and the family secrets. Young people can explore Eliot's moral conflicts by choosing two of Kohlberg's ten moral issues (punishment, property, roles and concerns of affection, roles and concerns of authority, law, life, liberty, distributive justice, truth, and sex) and discussing how the two (e.g., law and affection, law and liberty, or punishment and affection) define Eliot's moral conflicts and the varying effects on his judgment and behavior.

Muth, Jon J. 2005. *Zen Shorts*. New York: Scholastic. Grades 3 and up.

This picture storybook has three Zen stories framed within a larger story in which two brothers and a sister share their experiences with a Zen-storytelling panda. The encompassing plot demonstrates the structural effect of repetition when a story is placed within a story (or when three stories are placed within a story). Thus, the abstract themes of the Zen stories are shaped for readers who encounter them within their fictional frame, and an adult reading the picture book aloud to young people could stop the sequence of the book after the first Zen story, reading the second and third Zen stories before reading their introductions in the frame story, giving young people an opportunity for metacognitive thinking as they construct two abstract themes (Piaget's stage of formal operations) and relate them to everyday living.

Nakaya, Andrea C. 2006. *Opposing Viewpoints: Obesity*. Detroit, MI: Greenhaven. Grades 8–12.

Following the template of the series, this title looks at the social, economical, and historical aspects of a health issue of interest to young people who, according to Havighurst, have the task of realistically accepting themselves. Articles represent experts from the fields that have a stake in the issue, and the book's features include illustrations, questions, and an index. That many points of view are represented indicates that most complex topics have more than two "sides" and that coming to accept one's self can also be a complex task. As a group, young people can construct a collage from magazine advertisements (pictures and words) that depict the popular culture view of ideal body shapes.

Schrag, Ariel, ed. 2007. *Stuck in the Middle: Seventeen Comics from an Unpleasant Age.* **New York: Viking Press. Grades 7–9.**

The short stories in this anthology of diverse comic styles illustrate the major developmental issues facing middle school YAs. The 17 stories have boys and girls as main characters and tones that range from somber to light. Highlights include the huge importance of lunchtime intrigues in Tania Schrag's "Snitch" and in Aaron Renier's "Simple Machines" wherein a lonely boy, who carries his ADD tag with embarrassment, falls in with the school's self-proclaimed nerds who find his art skills important to the group's afterschool activities. Working in pairs, YAs can discuss and evaluate the stories for their realism in capturing middle school developmental issues.

Volponi, Paul. 2005. *Black and White.* **New York: Penguin Putnam. Grades 7–12.**

With their friendship as proof to the world that racism is dead, Marcus Brown (*Black*) and Eddie Russo (*White*) share success on their high school basketball team and their guilt in a robbery during which a man is accidentally shot. With moral dilemmas that involve friendship and choices, the story provides the opportunity for discussion on many questions (e.g., Is the justice system organized in such a way that not everyone is equal before the law? If not, what are the reasons for the inequity? How far should loyalty in a friendship go?).

Watson, Larry. 1993. *Montana 1948.* **New York: Simon and Schuster. Adult book for YAs.**

After discovering that his beloved Uncle Frank (a medical doctor) has committed a violent crime, 12-year-old David Hayden watches his father, Sheriff Wes Hayden, grieve over his personal and professional dilemma: to protect his brother Frank from the punishment he deserves or to honor the law he has sworn to uphold. The novel provides rich material for a discussion of Kohlberg's and Gilligan's moral dilemmas for each character.

Westerfeld, Scott. 2004. *So, Yesterday.* **New York: Penguin. Grades 7–12.**

Hunter is the trend-spotting protagonist in this fast-paced mystery set in the cutting-edge marketing environment of New York City, where he meets up with Jen, an original thinker and innovator. The two are creative and independent as they participate in a glitzy, urban fashion clique, take leadership roles, and conform with a nonconformity that is at once enticing and jaded. The episode in which the two dress in innovative and unique party clothes and crash a corporate party as they search for the missing consultant can inspire young people to create body biographies of the main characters by working from life-sized tracings of peers or from smaller paper figures.

REFERENCES AND SUGGESTIONS FOR FURTHER READING

Cormier, Robert. 1975. *The Chocolate War: A Novel.* New York: Pantheon.
Crutcher, Chris. 1991. *Athletic Shorts: Six Short Stories.* New York: Greenwillow Books.

Dorland's Pocket Medical Dictionary. 1989. Abridged. Philadelphia: W.B. Saunders.

Erikson, Erik. 1950, 1963. *Childhood and Society,* 2nd ed. New York: W.W. Norton.

Erikson, Erik. 1968. *Identity: Youth and Crisis.* New York: W.W. Norton.

Erikson, Erik. 1980. *Identity and the Life Cycle.* New York: W.W. Norton.

Erikson, Erik. 1982. *The Life Cycle Completed.* New York: W.W. Norton.

Gay, James E. and Robert B. Williams. 1997. "Identifying and Assisting School Children with Developmental Tasks." *Education* 117, no. 4 (Summer): 569–578.

Gilligan, Carol. 1982. *In a Different Voice: Psychological Theory and Women's Development.* Cambridge, MA: Harvard University Press.

Gilligan, Carol, et al., eds. 1988. *Mapping the Moral Domain: A Contribution of Women's Thinking to Psychological Theory and Education.* Cambridge, MA: Harvard University Press.

Gilligan, Carol, Nona P. Lyons, and Trudy J. Hanmer, eds. 1990. *Making Connections: The Relational Worlds of Adolescent Girls at Emma Willard School.* Cambridge, MA: Harvard University Press.

Havighurst, Robert. 1972. *Developmental Tasks and Education.* New York: D. McKay.

Kohlberg, Lawrence. 1975. "Moral Education for a Society in Moral Transition." *Educational Leadership* 33, no. 1 (October): 46–54.

Kohlberg, Lawrence. 1990. "Beyond Justice Reasoning: Moral Development and Consideration of a Seventh Stage." In *Higher Stages of Human Development,* edited by Charles N. Alexander and Ellen J. Langer, pp. 191–207. New York: Oxford University Press.

Kohlberg, Lawrence, and Richard H. Hersh. 1977. "Moral Development: A Review of the Theory." *Theory Into Practice* 16, no. 2 (April): 53–59.

Lyons, Nona P. 1990. "Listening to Voices We Have Not Heard: Emma Willard Girls' Ideas About Self, Relationships, and Morality." In *Making Connections: The Relational Worlds of Adolescent Girls at Emma Willard School,* edited by Carol Gilligan, Nona P. Lyons, and Trudy J. Hanmer, pp. 30–72. Cambridge, MA: Harvard University Press.

Mendelsohn, Michaela, and Gill Straker. 1999. "Social Perspective Taking and Use of Discounting in Children's Perceptions of Others' Helping Behavior." *Journal of Genetic Psychology* 160, no. 1 (March): 69–83.

Ostrom, T. 2001. "Social Cognition." In *The Corsini Encyclopedia of Psychology and Behavioral Sciences,* Vol. 4 of 4, edited by W. Edward Craighead and Charles B. Nemeroff, pp. 1554–1555. New York: John Wiley and Sons.

Paterson, Katherine. 1980. *Jacob Have I Loved.* New York: Crowell Publishing.

Piaget, Jean. 1953. *The Origin of Intelligence in the Child.* London, England: Routledge and Paul.

Schultz, Lynn Hickey, Dennis J. Barr, and Robert L. Selman. 2001. "The Value of a Developmental Approach to Evaluating Character Development Programmes." *Journal of Moral Education* 30, no. 1 (March): 3–27.

Selman, Robert L. 1971. "The Relation of Role-Taking to the Development of Moral Judgment in Children." *Child Development* 42, no. 1 (March): 79–91.

Selman, Robert L. 2003. *The Promotion of Social Awareness: Powerful Lessons from the Partnership of Developmental Theory and Classroom Practice.* New York: Russell Sage Foundation.

Senick, Gerald J. 2002. "Katherine Paterson." In *Something About the Author,* Vol. 133, pp. 134–144. Detroit: Gale Research.

Twain, Mark. 1961. *The Adventures of Huckleberry Finn*. New York: Holt, Rinehart and Winston.

VandenBos, Gary R., ed. 2007. *The APA Dictionary of Psychology*. Washington, DC: American Psychological Association.

Webb, Charles. 1991. "Of Necessity: Weeb Jokes About His Height." In *Preposterous: Poems of Youth*, edited by Paul B. Janeczko. New York: Orchard Books.

Weber, Ann L. 1991. *Introduction to Psychology*. New York: HarperCollins.

Woodward, Kenneth L. 1994. "Erik Erikson: Teaching Others How to See." *America* 171, no. 4 (August 13–20): 6–8.

Chapter 3

Reading Continues as Readers Respond

INTRODUCTION

The two basic roles of adults who work with young adults (YAs) and their literature are to motivate reading and to encourage reflection after the book is closed. These two roles are interwoven with the roles of YAs because the best motivation to read occurs among YAs themselves and because the best reflection is one shared among peers, one that continues imaginative, diverse, and provocative interactions with a text. Therefore, adults should motivate reading and encourage reflection among YAs to ensure that YAs themselves can also motivate reading and encourage reflection; that is, the tools and modes of literature programming become the tools and modes of YA responses to their literature. Those who work with YAs not only encourage reading by developing and presenting booktalks but also by teaching young people to develop and present booktalks. For YAs, writing the booktalk becomes the reflection, and presenting the booktalk becomes the motivation for other YAs to read. Thus, a well-designed literature program extends an adult guide's reach in the promotion of YA reading and response.

Developing a literature program rich in response requires that professionals in the field of YA literature are first able to defend the use of time and resources required for such activities as readers theatre, storytelling, and book discussion. The first step in the defense of a literature program that moves beyond the standard essay, book report, or objective test is to quell the notion that creative response and discussion for their own sakes are frivolous activities in either a school or a public library setting. In describing the environment in which reader-response approaches flourish, Robert Probst (1984) communicated the sophistication of library and classroom settings in which young people can think creatively and productively about their reading, describing them as places with the following characteristics:

1. YA ideas and comments and points of view are welcome, and YAs are emotionally secure—and, in fact, secure enough that they can risk spontaneously building on each other's ideas (pp. 24–25).

2. All ideas are tentative in that certainty is not needed before YAs express thoughts or feelings. There, YAs may speculate, offer up the draft of an idea, or reverse their positions (p. 25).

3. Rigor is demanded for both the participating adult and the responding YA so that both are willing to evaluate a hasty response, identify assumptions, and consider all points of view. Such a process is one of rigorous thinking by both and not inculcation by the adult. Probst describes the process as one that "may change the reader's awareness of the personal or even sharpen it. Developing a tolerance for ambiguity and uncertainty, coming to accept the idea that meaning and understanding are private creations, not absolutes to be discovered, [young people] . . . may be weaned from the traditional demand: 'Now that we've discussed this for an hour, tell us what it means'" (pp. 25–26).

4. Cooperation is demonstrated by young people who trust one another and realize that they will sometimes be bored, that others may digress, but that they each have a responsibility in the activity and that they may always be learning from each other (p. 26).

5. There are literary works worthy of careful reading and thoughtful reflection (p. 27).

Probst emphasized that his philosophy for guiding responses to literature was set forth earlier by Louise Rosenblatt (1968: 71), who had described her vision of an environment supportive of response:

> A situation conducive to free exchange of ideas by no means represents a passive or negative attitude on the part of the teacher. To create an atmosphere of self-confident interchange he must be ready to draw out the more timid students and to keep the more aggressive from monopolizing the conversation. He must be on the alert to show pleased interest in comments that have possibilities and to help the students clarify or elaborate their ideas. He must keep the discussion moving along consistent lines by eliciting the points of contact between different students' opinions. His own flexible command of the text and understanding of the reading skills it requires will be called into play throughout.

Guiding literary response, therefore, demands the abilities to understand knowledge as a personal invention, to manage group interactions, to know well YA literature and the emotional and cognitive development of young people, and to create a welcoming environment.

PERFORMANCE

Readers Theatre

Definition

A definition of readers theatre that supports its interpretation in this chapter is "theatre of the mind" (Coger and White, 1973) because it is ultimately a performance activity that occurs not on stage but rather in the imaginations of the audience. However, before an actual presentation, young people may be involved in reading a work, considering its structure and meaning, and finding and adapting a script. Thus, it offers many values to a YA literature program, including the following:

- YAs' presentation of readers theatre scripts (written either by a professional or by themselves) to an audience of their peers allows their direct participation in the promotion of a literary work as they read aloud. Those who step aside and involve YAs in motivating YA reading have the best possible ambassadors for their literature programs.
- YAs have positive social interactions in the teamwork required to develop and present a script.
- YAs write for a specific audience, and they have the rare opportunity to register the audience's appreciation of their writing and presentation efforts.
- In adapting a script, YAs are writing from an exemplary model, the literary work, and this use of a model is especially important for young people who are learning English as a second language or for young people who find writing difficult when they face a blank page and need a spark for their creativity.
- Presenting readers theatre scripts enables young people to read before an audience and interpret voices and moods and intentions while always performing in a group—never alone in the spotlight. Readers theatre offers the shy or self-conscious YA a protected way to gain confidence before an audience.
- Unlike drama, which requires much practice time, memorization, and elaborate stage designs and costumes, readers theatre can be delivered spontaneously with little time away from other activities and with a clear focus on literature and story.
- Readers theatre encourages young people to consider a literary work across many levels of thinking.

A good scene for introducing readers theatre is in the first chapter of Stephen Crane's *The Red Badge of Courage* (1895, 2008), a classic title in the high school canon. The format of the script (Latrobe and Laughlin, 1989: 19–22) is consistent with the approach of Leslie Coger and Melvin White, and it is a format that can be easily taught to YAs as a structure (and scaffolding) for their creative endeavors in theatre of the mind (see Figure 3.1).

Figure 3.1. A Readers Theatre Script from *The Red Badge of Courage*

Staging

The narrator stands at a lectern. The three soldiers sit on tall stools.

Henry Fleming

Wilson, the loud soldier   X   Conklin, the tall soldier

X   X

Narrator

X

Narrator: The following script is from the first chapter of Stephen Crane's *The Red Badge of Courage*, which is the psychological account of Henry Fleming's experiences in combat during the Civil War. In our presentation, Henry, an uncertain young soldier, read by _____; and two other soldiers, Jim Conklin, the tall soldier, read by _____; and Wilson, the loud soldier, read by _____, debate the question of courage in battle. I am _____, the narrator.

     Tonight Henry is giving the question of courage serious attention. He thinks about the lurking dangers of the future and fails to see himself standing stoutly in the midst of them. He recalls his earlier visions of glory; however, the panic of the moment grows in his mind. Deciding that he knows nothing about himself, he suddenly springs from his bunk just as the tall soldier and the loud soldier enter the tent arguing with each other.

Henry: (frantically) Good Lord, what's the matter with me?"

Tall Soldier: (loudly wrangling) Conklin, that's all right. You can believe me or not, jest as you like. All you got to do is sit down and wait as quiet as you can. Then pretty soon you'll find out I was right.

Loud Soldier: (grunting stubbornly) Well, you don't know everything in the world, do you?

Tall Solder: (sharply) Didn't say I knew everything in the world.

Henry: (nervously) Going to be a battle, sure, is there, Jim?

Tall Soldier: Of course there is. Of course there is. You jest wait 'til tomorrow, and you'll see one of the biggest battles ever was. You just wait.

Henry: (loudly) Thunder!

Tall Soldier: (with self-assurance) Oh, you'll see fighting this time, my boy, what'll be regular out-and-out fighting.

Loud Soldier: Huh!

Henry: Well, lie as not this story'll turn out jest like them others did.

Tall Soldier: (exasperated) Not much it won't. Didn't the cavalry all start this morning? The cavalry started this morning. They say there ain't hardly any cavalry left in camp. They're going to Richmond, or some place, while we fight all the Johnnies. It's some didge like that. The regiment's got orders, too. A feller what seen 'em go to headquarters told me a little while ago. And they're raising blazes all over the camp—anybody can see that.

Loud Soldier: Shucks!

Henry: Jim!

Tall Soldier: What?

(Cont'd.)

Figure 3.1. A Readers Theatre Script from *The Red Badge of Courage (Continued)*

Henry: How do you think the reg'ment 'ill do?

Tall Soldier: (with cold judgment) Oh, they'll fight all right, I guess, after they once get into it. There's been heaps of fun poked at 'em because they're new, of course, and all that; but they'll fight all right, I guess.

Henry: (persisting) Think any of the boys 'll run?

Tall Soldier: (in a tolerant way) Oh, there may be few of 'm run, but there them kind in every regiment, 'specially when they first goes under fire. Of course it might happen that the hull kit-and-boodle might start and run, if some big fighting came first-off, and then again they might stay and fight like fun. But, you can't bet on nothing. Of course they ain't never been under fire yet, and it ain't likely they'll lick the hull rebel army all-to-once the first time; but I think they'll fight better than some, if worse than others. That's the way I figger. They call the reg'ment 'Fresh fish' and everything; but the boys come of good stock, and most of 'em 'll fight like sin after (with emphasis) they once git shootin'.

Loud Soldier: (scornfully) Oh, you think you know—

Tall Soldier: (angrily) Why you don't know nothin' yerself.

Henry: (interrupting and laughing as if to mean a joke) Did you ever think you might run yourself, Jim?

Loud Solder: (giggles)

Tall Soldier: (profoundly) Well, I've thought it might get too hot for Jim Conklin in some of them scrimmages, and if a whole lot of boys started and run, why I s'pose I'd start and run. And if I once started to run, I'd run like the devil, and no mistake. But if everybody was a-standing and a-fighting, why, I'd stand and fight. Be Jiminey, I would. I'll bet on it.

Loud Soldier: Huh!

Narrator: The reassurance that the tall soldier gives Henry is short-lived. The army does not move out, and the waiting, the worrying, the self-doubts grow. Henry concludes that the only way to prove himself is to go into battle and to watch his legs to discover their merits and faults. To gain the answer, he needs blaze, blood, and danger. Finally, the opportunity to prove himself comes—not once, but again and again; and Henry learns not only about his cowardice and fear but also about his courage and endurance.

The End

Source: Adapted from the novel by Stephen Crane by Kathy Latrobe and Mildred Laughlin, 1989.

Suggestions for Selecting, Writing, and Presenting a Readers Theatre Script

YAs' first experiences with readers theatre should be their introduction to a fully developed script that they may present to an audience of their peers. However, young people should also learn to select scenes from literature and adapt those scenes into scripts. Ideally, their chosen responses to sharing a book or fulfilling a school assignment to report on a book would include developing and presenting readers theatre scripts. In preparing groups of young people for activities in readers theatre, it is useful to have a philosophical understanding that readers theatre is "theatre of the mind" and to share the approach to scripting demonstrated in the script for *The Red Badge of Courage*. A single approach simplifies teaching the process, building a set of unified scripts for group sharing and creating a predictable format, which allows young people to deliver scripts quickly and spontaneously. Such a prescription also reduces editing for adult guides and helps young people communicate clearly.

For YAs' first attempts at script writing, a supportive adult may plan outlines for scripts. Such outlines should identify the specific scene from a novel and include staging directions, opening narrator lines, suggestions for specific scripting techniques, and closing narrator lines. The specific scene should not be chosen until the adaptor has read the entire work. Adults can suggest the following recommendations for YAs to develop their own scripts:

1. Select a scene that
   a. occurs in the first third of a book, because an adaptor will not want to spoil the story's suspense for future readers or necessitate explaining too many events that have already occurred in the story;
   b. has dramatic appeal, such as emotional intensity (e.g., figurative language or a quarrel), and, to provide a satisfying experience, contains a sense of beginning, middle, and end;
   c. does not depend on action, because readers do not move during the presentation; and
   d. has few characters, because having too many readers to follow will confuse an audience;

2. Incorporate sound scripting techniques by
   a. eliminating unnecessary descriptions or narration;
   b. displaying and explaining the staging before the narrator begins reading;
   c. beginning the script with the narrator's opening lines, which introduce the literary work, its characters, and its setting (lines are also developed for the narrator to bridge gaps in the listeners' understanding or lapses in time and to summarize action);
   d. often addressing the characters being spoken to by name in order to help the audience follow dialogue;
   e. keeping the number of characters in one scene down to four or five by omitting unnecessary characters or by combining the lines of multiple characters so that an audience can delineate the characters and follow the story;
   f. communicating the emotions of the characters to the reader by describing the tone of voice (e.g., *angrily*) with words set aside by parentheses; and
   g. in the final lines, delivered by the narrator, linking the scene to the plot and theme of the original work.

3. Incorporate physical presentation techniques, such as changing tones of voice, changing facial expressions, and using small hand gestures, to set the scene in the listeners' imaginations.

Poetry in Two Voices

Young people can reflect on classic poetry by developing and presenting adaptations of poems that contain two voices, such as those in Paul Fleischman's (1988) *Joyful Noise.* When young people adapt a *classic* poem into two voices, they can experiment with reading and writing as they work within the original sounds and rhythm of the work. Jonathon Hunt's (2006) article "Script Novels" describes how novels that blend features of poetry, performance art, and playwriting have broken traditional genre conventions and have provided one way to introduce poetry in an accessible way. Julius Lester's (2006) *Day of Tears: A Novel in Dialogue* presents dialogues, poems, and the makings of scenes from a play (without stage directions) based on the dramatic subject of the largest one-day slave auction in U.S. history, with perspectives from slaves as youths and later old people as well as the owners', the auctioneer's, and the white buyers' disconcerting points of view.

For an introduction to poems in multiple voices, the strong rhythm and exaggerated language of Edgar Allan Poe's "The Bells" (1849, 1938) presents a good opportunity for adaptation (see Figure 3.2). Poe's familiarity with most young people puts readers at ease, his popularity has remained high, and his other poems may inspire YAs' adaptation into multiple voices.

The Bells

By Edgar Allan Poe (1849, 1938)

Hear the sledges with the bells—
Silver bells!
What a world of merriment their melody foretells!
How they tinkle, tinkle, tinkle,
In the icy air of night!
While the stars that oversprinkle
All the heavens, seem to twinkle
With a crystalline delight;
Keeping time, time, time,
In a sort of Runic rhyme,
To the tintinnabulation that so musically wells
From the bells, bells, bells, bells,
Bells, bells, bells—
From the jingling and the tinkling of the bells.

Figure 3.2. From Edgar Allan Poe's "The Bells," Adapted for Two Voices

Hear the sledges with the bells—	
Silver bells!	Silver bells!
What a world of merriment their melody	*What* a world of merriment their melody
foretells!	foretells!
How they tinkle, tinkle, tinkle,	Tinkle, tinkle, tinkle, tinkle
Tinkle, tinkle, tinkle, tinkle	How they tinkle, tinkle, tinkle,
In the icy air of night!	In the icy air of night!
Oversprinkle, oversprinkle	While the stars that oversprinkle
	All the Heavens, seem to twinkle
With a crystalline delight;	
Keeping time, time, time,	Time, time, time, time, time,
In a sort of Runic rhyme,	
	To the tintinnabulation that so musically wells
From the	
Bells,	
	Bells,
Bells,	
	Bells,
Bells, bells, bells-	Bells, bells, bells—
From the jingling and the tinkling of the bells.	Jingling, jingling, tinkling, tinkling of the bells.

With the development of genre-blending novels, readers of YA literature have more options for self-expression. Performance art may include selections from Jaime Adoff's books, such as *Jimi & Me* (2005), a novel in verse about a boy's finding comfort in the music of Jimi Hendrix, or *Names Will Never Hurt Me* (Adoff, 2004), whose monologues reveal the inner thoughts of troubled young minds.

Readers should be encouraged to browse the library's poetry collection and find works they would like to share aloud. Creative readers could combine two or more into a single reading, and song lyrics are likely to be a popular choice for them to adapt. In adapting poetry, students should be aware that regardless of the poem's layout, all the original sounds and rhythms should be retained.

Reading Aloud

Reading aloud to young people is of unquestionable value when they are lap size, but reading aloud to YAs is an uncommon classroom, library, or home experience for them. Yet, hearing stories read aloud offers many benefits to YAs as they

- learn new words and hear them pronounced correctly, thus, narrowing the reading/listening gap, especially for reluctant learners as well as English language learners;
- listen to sentence patterns, forms of language, and styles of writing;

- gain motivation for new and different reading experiences, becoming acquainted with genres and authors they might never have sampled otherwise;
- have access to stories above their reading levels;
- experience what good reading aloud sounds like;
- improve listening skills;
- increase their attention span through induced imagery;
- enjoy a story and relax within it;
- become a community engrossed in an immediate and shared literary experience; and
- absorb the enthusiastic spirit unique to each reader.

The successful reading aloud experience must include a carefully chosen work. In addition to meeting standard criteria for selection, the material must engage the audience no matter how narrow or diverse it is. Thus, a read-aloud literary experience should grab most listeners almost immediately; few listeners will tolerate overly long descriptions of time, place, and character unless the reader well prepares them for it. The work should be covered in a single listening experience or should be broken down into multiple dramatically satisfying sessions. For some, horror and humor can be more gripping than ordinary subjects addressed in ordinary ways. Importantly, as Jim Trelease (2001: 104) points out, a good read-aloud story is not always from an award-winning book.

In addition to becoming good listeners, YAs should develop reading aloud skills. Interesting, creative, and purposeful settings for reading aloud will foster these skills as well as provide opportunities for YAs to learn how to appeal to an audience based on the audience's interests and needs. Within a school, YAs may read to younger students, and they may also read to their peers as they, for example, individually contribute a factual introduction to the topics in a class research project. Read-aloud venues that can especially motivate YA readers include reading for the blind as a community service, talking into a mike, recording stories on cassettes, and reading for a video recording to be played over a community channel.

Furthermore, when YAs find and share literary passages that reflect significant philosophical or ethical issues, their peers (who have not read the work) can be engaged in identifying points of the issues, debate aspects of their concerns, and seek to read further, including the book from which the material read aloud was taken. For example, such a read-aloud passage could be a foreword or prologue to a literary work like the one in Susan Bartoletti's (2000: 7) *Hitler Youth*, which includes the following paragraphs:

> Formed officially in 1926, the Hitler Youth offered its members excitement, adventure, and new heroes to worship. It gave them hope, power, and the chance

to make their voices heard. And for some, it provided the opportunity to rebel against parents, teachers, clergy, and other authority figures.

Adolph Hitler admired the natural energy and drive that young people possess. He understood that young people could be a powerful force that could help shape Germany's future. In his quest for power, Hitler harnessed their enthusiasm and loyalty.

"I begin with the young," said Hitler. "We older ones are used up. . . . But my magnificent youngsters! Are there finer ones anywhere in the world? Look at all these men and boys! What material! With them I can make a new world."

Without having read the book, an audience can recognize and discuss issues about the nature of a hero, the perception that one's voice is seldom heard, the power of group think, antagonism toward authority figures, the exploitation of trust and innocence, the vulnerability of people when their nation has lost its way, the unquestionable acceptance of a false prophet, and the courage to stand up alone for what is right. Those interested in these issues may be motivated to read the book or pursue an issue.

Suggestions for Reading Aloud

The following suggestions will help readers young and old to have a successful read-aloud experience:

- Select a story that is personally liked and can be read with enthusiasm.
- Choose a story with an unfamiliar plot in order to maintain suspense.
- Be familiar with the story or excerpt and test it aloud.
- Have an awareness of the effects of voice on mood and meaning.
- Encourage listeners to doodle.
- Ask listeners to save questions until the end of the reading.
- Give thought to the book's introduction (e.g., provide a display or information about the author, genre, or subject).
- Start the reading slowly to gain listeners' attention.
- Move around through the audience.
- Use different voices and sound effects, if comfortable.
- Provide time for discussion.
- Delete extraneous, repetitious, or unnecessary words or passages.
- Stop the reading of a work that is obviously unsuccessful.

YAs and adults should share and alternate reading aloud so that they can experience the listening pleasure and the literary response within each role.

Storytelling

Storytelling, as the legacy of the oral tradition, is a process

. . . whereby a person (the teller), using mental imagery, narrative structure, and vocalization or signing, communicates with other humans (the audience) who also use mental imagery and, in turn, communicate back to the teller primarily via body language and facial expressions, resulting in the co-creation of a story. (Roney, 1998: 23)

Thus, storytelling is complex and enduring, and, significantly, storytelling is both a literary form and a literary response.

Storytelling offers cognitive and affective benefits to young people. Among the cognitive values for young people are storytelling's capacity to

- strengthen speaking and listening skills,
- expand vocabulary,
- emphasize the rhythms of language,
- extend the reading experience, and
- foster awareness of cultures.

Among the affective benefits for tellers and listeners are

- self-understanding and awareness,
- realization of the power and joy of story,
- creation of a shared group experience, and
- awareness of one's own value system as well as those in other cultures.

Because storytelling is a performance activity, YAs should be led into it by example. Listening to stories is an activity of pleasure and understanding for all ages—young and old alike; however, the complex tasks of storytelling require experienced readers who can make a story their own. Thus, the activity of storytelling is appropriately first introduced to young people in middle schools and high schools.

Suggestions for Storytelling

The following suggestions will help readers perfect their storytelling:

- Find stories you truly enjoy (i.e., stories that are interesting, appealing to the senses; stories with an appropriate length).
- Relax into your own storytelling style (e.g., use of voice and its tone, volume, and pace; placement of pauses; gestures; body language).
- Structure the presentations according to the steps in a progressive plot (i.e., exposition, conflict, rising action, climax, denouement, and conclusion). An awareness of plot structure ensures a dramatic whole and lessens the likelihood of memorization.
- Schedule adequate time for practice.
- Maintain eye contact, which allows for audience feedback that encourages tellers and increases their confidence.

Storytellers can find sources of folktales in library collections. Traditionally, folktales are an excellent genre for first-time storytellers because these tales have proven themselves by developing and thriving in the oral tradition. Furthermore, a tale from a collection of stories is typically a better subject than a tale told and illustrated in picture book format because the pictures will carry much of the story, leaving the teller to assume that the words alone can relate the content of an engaging picture book. YAs may enjoy earlier, unedited versions of classic folktales that have not been retold for a younger audience. Likewise urban legends fascinate and entertain listeners of all ages.

Booktalks

Designed to encourage the reading of books, especially good books, a booktalk is a brief presentation to a group of potential readers who share similar interests and needs. Booktalking has been represented in the professional literature since the 1930s, and there are as many approaches to booktalking as there are booktalkers.

Presenting booktalks to young people not only encourages their reading books but also models the ways they can deliver booktalks to their peers. Booktalking involves YAs in reading, writing, and presenting, and each phase of booktalking benefits cognitive development. For example, reading that supports booktalking leads YAs into a more thoughtful consideration of the book, encouraging awareness of details and their significance. Writing a book-talk requires synthesis to interpret the whole work for an audience while at the same time creatively preparing the presentation. Furthermore, writing a booktalk requires a YA to think out loud and to weigh the power and meaning of each word. The editing may continue even during the presentation, which should be well studied but not memorized. Each of the three phases (reading, writing, and presenting) requires critical thinking, evaluation and judgment, and knowledge of the book and the audience. Booktalking by YAs is probably their most challenging response to literature, because it is a unique and genuine product created from a reading experience and performed for an audience. Professionals who share their skills with young people create in them an affective sense of pride and confidence, ensuring YAs know that a good booktalk is worthwhile.

Creative booktalks may take unexpected forms. For example, a booktalk about Jean Fritz's (1988) *China's Long March: 6,000 Miles of Danger* could focus on the book's introductory map projected for the audience to follow as the booktalker describes the challenges and dangers that soldiers face as they march across a burning bridge, scale a pass so high that birds don't fly there, and slip over the edges of sheer cliffs. Alternatively, a booktalk about Orson Scott Card's (1985) *Ender's Game* could be one of key words arranged alphabetically.

Alphabet Booktalk for Orson Scott Card's *Ender's Game*

A	Andrew Wiggin, a child genius
B	Betrayed by his mentors
C	Chosen child at Command School, playing computer-simulated battles
D	Doubt dwells in Ender's mind
E	Ender, a new name for a new life
F	Fate of the world on his shoulders, as the best military commander in history
G	Guessing games rigged for murder
H	Humans—free—except when humanity needs them
I	Inhumane war games
J	Jumping into the eye of the Giant in Fairyland
K	The kid whom nobody takes to right away
L	Looking for peace
M	Manipulating and maneuvering brilliantly but destructively, wearing a
N	Nematic flash-suit stinking with sweat
O	Orbiting earth in the Battle School
P	Peter Wiggin, pretending to share power, a murderer at heart
Q	The Queen regretted, "If only we could have talked to you"
R	Remembering how it felt to lead his soldiers in a rapacious and bloody war
S	Soon to be Speaker for the Dead
T	Tending the new colony
	Trusting, teaching
	Transforming himself
U	Unplugging a brain for all time
V	Valentine, always faithful
W	Weightless disorientation
X	Xenocide
Y	Yielding to his best instincts
Z	Zero-sum game

Adult guides may find the following suggestions useful to themselves and to their YA booktalkers:

- Booktalk books you have read—not because the audience will think it is nifty to read what you read but so that you maintain credibility when they ask questions.
- Let the book shape and guide what you talk about.
- Maintain eye contact with the audience.
- Remain matter of fact about the set of books, focusing on the book's content rather than on your judgment.

- Emphasize through structure of delivery one of the book's memorable features (e.g., theme, issue, character, plot, or scene).
- Develop your own style, never closing off creative experiments (such as the map booktalk and the alphabet booktalk).
- Write out the booktalk.
- Practice the booktalk.

VISUAL RESPONSES AND VISUAL LITERACY

Contemporary learning theorists confirm that young people need direction in achieving *visual literacy*, or attaining the ability to understand and to recognize information and ideas communicated via visible actions or images. In addition, visual literacy includes thinking about images, interpreting images, and creating new images. In *Visual Literacy: Learn to See, See to Learn*, Lynell Burmark (2002: 3) asserts, "A lack of visual literacy is as much a handicap as the inability to read and write." In "Design Drawing," Eric Anderson (2003: 17) emphasizes, "Learning to visualize is an essential component of a student's cognitive development and an important skill activity of problem solving." Three tools for interaction with literature include graphic organizers, literary maps, and body biographies.

Graphic Organizers

A *graphic organizer* is a pictorial representation of ideas and of the patterns or relationships among those ideas. The theory behind using graphic organizers asserts that isolating an important idea makes it more easily understood, and its connection with other ideas becomes clearer with the visual representation. Research shows that constructing graphic organizers requires the use of both verbal and visual languages, which encourages active learning. Graphic organizers also make it easier to remember important ideas through colors, shapes, and imagery. Visual tools integrate prior knowledge with new knowledge and encourage focused discussions. Although there are many mass-produced templates in print and online, the ideal is for each reader to construct an original graphic organizer as a response to literature. The following annotations suggest how seven different graphic organizers can be used to visually respond to literature.

Spider

Wilhelm, Doug. 2003. *The Revealers*. New York: Farrar, Straus, and Giroux. Grades 6–8.

Witty seventh-grade narrator Russell Trainor is the personal scapegoat of Ritchie Tucker. Russ finds support and a brilliant solution to his problem when he and two other victims join forces to shed much-needed light on bullying. A spider map (with eight legs for eight story items) shows how one topic or theme is developed through story elements.

At the center is the topic of bullying. One group of legs shows the bullies and their names and traits. Another group indicates the three targets and their traits. A third shows conflict resolution through the characters' creation of their online school newspaper, *The Darkland Revealer*, a peaceful way for Parkland's targets to confront their bullies in an open forum.

Time Line/Story Map

Myers, Walter Dean. 1999. *Monster*. New York: HarperCollins. Grades 7 and up.

On trial for murder, Steve Harmon copes with the horrors of prison by night (by writing in his diary) and with his "flexible" self-concept by day during the trial (by writing his movie script), shifting back and forth (21 times). Unable to define his own character as the trial advances day by day, he waits for the verdict that will determine the ownership of his soul. Because the plot alternates between the diary and the script, two time lines can be drawn. The script contains flashbacks, while the diary entries are chronological.

Arc

Crutcher, Chris. 1995. *Ironman*. New York: Bantam. Grades 8–12.

Impulsive and hot-tempered Bo Brewster confronts himself in an enforced anger-management class where he finds more than self-control as he is changed by the group's adult mentor and the other troubled students. An arc makes a good visual tool to depict character development. Bo Brewster is clearly a teenager with a hot temper. Readers can list on the left of the arc Bo's actions and traits that cause him to be assigned to anger management. They can list in the middle the characters and conflicts that begin Bo's turnaround. On the right of the arc emerges the changed Bo.

Sociogram

Jacobson, Jennifer Richard. 2005. *Stained*. New York: Simon and Schuster. Grades 9 and up.

After living as a social misfit in a small New Hampshire town, Jocelyn meets a boy she truly loves, but events force her to recall a repressed episode of abuse connected with her childhood friend Gabe and to uncover a terrible secret shared by a group of boys. A sociogram (chart plotting the structure of relationships in a group situation) works well to depict the sets of relationships distorted by a town's many secrets.

Pyramid

Paterson, Katherine. 1991. *Lyddie*. New York: Dutton. Grades 5–9.

Forced to set out on her own in the 1840s, 14-year-old Lyddie works in an inn, labors at a textile factory in Massachusetts, and experiences firsthand the unjust system that preys on society's most vulnerable. Considering race, class, and gender, young people could create a pyramid to illustrate the novel's social power structure by placing those groups with the least power nearer the base of the pyramid.

Cause and Effect Chain

Ellis, Deborah. *I Am a Taxi.* **Toronto, Canada: Groundwood Books. Grades 5–8.**

In Bolivia, 12-year-old Diego Juarez and his best friend Mando leave their imprisoned families behind for the opportunity (or so they have been told) to make a lot of money by working for rich men who live deep in the jungle. Diego had been a "taxi"—an errand boy—while he lived with his mother and sister in San Sebastian prison, making a little money as an honest businessman, and he is angry when he learns he and Mando are working as slave laborers for a cocaine ring. Young people could create a cause and effect chain by illustrating the causes and effects in each of Diego's episodes that boil down to his eventual fight for his very life against the powerful gringo boss.

Matrix

Four groups of readers, one group for each of the following novels, could use a matrix to chart the likely elements in four *romantic gothic novels*:

1. A large dark, isolated structure (i.e., a boarding school or an estate)
2. A vulnerable female character
3. A dark, mysterious male
4. Supernatural or potentially supernatural events
5. A mysterious or dangerous mood

Bray, Libba. 2004. *A Great and Terrible Beauty.* **New York: Delacorte Press. Grades 9 and up.**

Attending a girls' boarding school in England in the late nineteenth century, 16-year-old Gemma Doyle adjusts to being an orphan and a possessor of magical powers while trying to solve the mystery of the death of a Gypsy girl.

DuMaurier, Daphne. 1938, 1994. *Rebecca.* **New York: Avon. Classic.**

An unnamed narrator describes her marriage to the dashing but moody Maxim de Winter, whose beautiful but oppressive Manderley Estate holds mysteries that shock the young bride.

Hahn, Mary Downing. 1995. *Look for Me by Moonlight.* **New York: Clarion Press. Grades 6–10.**

Choosing to spend some time with her father and stepmother in the Maine inn they operate, Cynda falls under the spell of Vincent, a guest whose charms belie his evil intentions.

Nixon, Joan Lowery. 1998. *The Haunting.* **New York: Delacorte. Grades 6–10.**

Whispering ghosts, objects that fly through the air, and a haunted mansion cast an eerie mood in this tale of 15-year-old Lia Blevins and her cousin Charlotte, whose diary holds details of a mystery to be solved.

Literary Maps

Literary maps come in two categories, those that show the names and locations of authors who live within a common state or region and those that illustrate the locale of a novel or other narrative, especially one whose protagonist's journey is the central motif. Young people easily picture the settings of the books they read, especially science fiction and fantasy whose universes entertain faithful series readers. But other genres are amenable to literary maps as well.

Contemporary mysteries are often set in colorful locales. Biographies and historical fiction are ideal for literary maps and for opportunities for YAs to research a time period. For example, Julia Alverez's (2002) historical novel set in the 1960s, *Before We Were Free*, opens with two black-and-white maps drawn by the protagonist Anita. One illustrates the compound in the Dominican Republic where she and her family first live. The other shows the second floor of the Mancinis', the neighbors who hide Anita and her mother when they are seeking refuge from the secret police. Its simple style resembles how a 12-year-old girl might draw her surroundings as a way to overcome her fears and stay courageous for her mother's sake.

Two examples from professional collections serve as models of literary maps. Mary Ellen Snodgrass' (2002) *Literary Treks: Characters on the Move* details the routes of 28 YA protagonists and provides a guide on how to use literary maps as a response to fiction. Barbara Strachey's (1992) *Journeys of Frodo* contains over 50 maps with notes and descriptions showing the protagonist's many adventures in *The Lord of the Rings*.

Constructing a literary map leads readers to interpret literature by focusing on setting and mood, often important but sometimes neglected story elements. To construct a literary map, if computer software programs are not available, readers can create even more imaginative maps the old fashioned way on paper. Readers should be alerted *before* they begin to read that they need to take note of important details of the story's locale. Suggestions to consider when guiding readers who are creating literary maps for the first time include the following:

- Identify a book in which setting and action will ensure a successful literary map.
- Gather materials (e.g., paper, rulers, pencils, pens, and markers).
- Establish a reference point for the map (e.g., protagonist's home, school, landmark, or the climactic scene of the plot).
- Refer to atlases and include important map features such as legends and standard symbols.
- Use original or symbolic "pictographs" (e.g., a dollar sign for money or a yellow circle with radiating black lines for the sun) if appropriate.
- Display all the maps.

Body Biographies

When young people reflect on the characters in the books they read, a body biography provides a flexible format in which to express a response to literature. A body biography entails creating a visual interpretation of a fictional or biographical figure. The Folger Shakespeare Library's online site offers creative ways for readers to respond to dramatic works and opens with National Council of Teachers of English standards for cognitive processes and aesthetics that YAs will experience while constructing a body biography. In this activity, according to Margolis (2002), YAs will

1. apply a wide range of strategies to comprehend, interpret, evaluate, and appreciate texts for their own purposes;
2. adjust their use of spoken, written, and visual language to communicate effectively with a variety of audiences and for different purposes; and
3. build an understanding of the many dimensions of human experience

How to Construct a Body Biography

The following sequence can be used to introduce readers to the concept of body biography:

- Assemble materials, such as paper, colored pens and pencils, glue, magazines, newspapers, clip art, and collage material.
- Select a literary character and work in pairs or small groups.
- Ask for a volunteer to lie on a long sheet of butcher block paper while another traces or outlines the figure. (A smaller figure can be hand drawn on a sheet of construction paper or poster board if space is a problem.)
- Brainstorm the strengths and weaknesses of the selected character, and keep a list of all ideas.
- Identify the colors and symbols that come to mind when thinking about the character. Does the author describe the character by using specific colors? Are there any objects that could be symbolic? Is there a symbolic meaning in the character's name or other characters' names or in the setting?
- Use sticky notes or tabs to mark passages that contain images or visual details that can be incorporated into the body biography.
- Use direct quotations, paraphrases, or summaries to explain each element added to the body biography and include page numbers.
- Determine the character's motives, goals, or needs at the beginning of the story. Did the character change? If so, how did the character change? What events and conflicts brought about the change? Who were the characters involved in the change? Is the character better or worse for his or her change?
- Choose the best placement for each visual on the appropriate part of the figure. For example, a human heart, spine, and head can symbolize many character traits such as kindness or cruelty; weakness or courage; intelligence or recklessness. The heart contains what a character loves; the head contains dreams and future plans
- Present the body biography to the group, describing the decisions that were made to complete the project.

The placement and arrangement of visuals on a body biography indicate how carefully the readers interpreted, analyzed, and evaluated their responses to the literary work. In oral presentations, a reader's description of how he or she made decisions to complete the project involves metacognitive skills.

A Written Response Based on a Body Biography for Gail Giles' Shattering Glass

Gail Giles' (2002) *Shattering Glass* is a contemporary realistic novel that provides an excellent opportunity for young people to explore the mode of body biography. The novel opens as Rob Haynes, an out-of-state transfer to Brazos Vale High School, wastes no time becoming "Big Man on Campus" (as he had schemed to do) after he steals leader-of-the-pack Lance Ansely's girlfriend. Rob quickly establishes himself as the center of attention and the most popular student, but he becomes bored with ordinary manipulation of those in his clique. When he notices the school's most well-known social outcast being taunted and humiliated, Rob decides to transform Simon Glass into a member of the in crowd. Rob's interest in Simon influences the other guys, who had bullied Simon since elementary school, to join in the "fun," an exterior makeover. The boys show Simon how to dress and how to be cool. His rise in popularity gives Simon the confidence to devise and carry out the perfect revenge against this same group of boys who had made his school life miserable.

As the only student with the courage to stand up to Rob, Simon should elicit sympathy, but in his search to find and then reveal each boy's most vulnerable and embarrassing secret, Simon becomes less simple and more complex as he executes his evil acts of revenge. With several well-developed characters from which to choose, this contemporary realistic novel elicits diverse interpretations. As a twisted version of the Pygmalion motif, it ultimately reveals the dark dynamics that are possible in high school life, with its bullying and deep-rooted system of cliques.

First-person narrator Thaddeus R. Steward IV (or, "Young," for short) immediately gives away the novel's ending: "Simon Glass was easy to hate. . . . [W]e each hated him for a different reason, but we didn't realize it until the day we killed him" (p. 1). As each chapter opens with a statement from one of many characters who comment on Simon's death and on the key players in the mystery, the reader discovers that the events occurred five years earlier. At the conclusion when he out tricks the master trickster Rob, Simon metaphorically brings the alpha male to his knees. With the boys' secrets "gleefully" exposed, Simon seems to have been the winner after all. However, Rob grabs a baseball bat and ruthlessly pounds Simon while the other boys follow their leader, as usual. Young never hits Simon but silently accepts the blame for all of those who were involved in the beating.

Simon's outward change in appearance—the "right" clothes, hair style, and weight reduction—suggests that superficial transformation can be easily achieved. For a body biography, a group can draw a before-and-after version of Simon. Before, Simon wore thick glasses, an unattractive hair style, and trousers too short. He was clumsy and unable to talk to girls. By the end, with his new appearance, Simon is the most popular boy in school. But the inner Simon leaves room for discussion. Young tells the reader that he never liked Simon, indicating he may have sensed Simon's dark side all along. To survive, Simon had found escape in computers, which he uses to get most of his information on Rob and the other boys in the clique. In what way can his previous tool of escape be converted into a tool of revenge?

How can readers illustrate a character whose anger and revenge reach cruel proportions? How can Simon's "need" for revenge, and not justice, be depicted? Because shattered glass is a prominent image, it can be included in the body biography (e.g., as pieces of a cracked mirror or broken eyeglasses).

A body biography for Rob Haynes could focus on the big difference between what he appears to be and who he really is, the son of a convicted murderer and abuser. (He lies about his last name for his school records.) Rob's good looks and charm captivate everybody, adults and young alike. He seems to possess finely tuned interpersonal skills and convinces others that he truly cares about them. But when Simon reveals Rob's secret to the others, the cool Rob changes into a vulnerable, enraged killer, just like his dad. The last image of Rob shows him with a blood-spattered baseball bat in his hand. How can the relationship between Rob and his father be depicted since his parent is still in prison and not actively involved in the plot?

The novel ends with many unanswered questions, especially about Young. Young's doctor–father insists he go to medical school, but Young wants to be a writer. He hates himself for lacking the spine to stand up for himself and caving in to parental pressure. Other characters who play key roles in the conflict are Ronna Perry, Young's girlfriend and the conscience of the story, and "Coop" Cooper, a kindhearted and gifted athlete and the only boy who tries to save Simon's life.

Included in the YALSA's list of Best Books for YAs in 2003, *Shattering Glass* has been compared to *The Chocolate War* and *Lord of the Flies* with its portrayal of young people left to their own devices to find a moral and ethical center. A group should be able to produce a set of unique body biographies after discussing this complex and in-depth study of characters.

DISCUSSION: THE READING CIRCLE

Given the high interest and popularity of book clubs, it is natural for those who work with young people to implement their own groups. Reading circles are "small, peer-led discussion groups whose members have chosen to read the same article, chapter, or book" (Daniels and Zemelman, 2004). Sometimes they are called literature circles or book clubs. Whichever name is preferred, reading circles advance cognitive and affective skills.

Louise Rosenblatt's (1978: 68) influential transactional theory calls the role of discussion "a unique mode of experience." She sees small group discussion as "a communication *among readers*" (p. 146). She writes, "As we exchange experiences, we point to those elements of the text that best illustrate or support our interpretations. . . . Sometimes we may be strengthened in our own sense of having 'done justice to' the text without denying its potentialities for other interpretations" (p. 147). The fact that readers will see for themselves the different ways their peers respond to the same text is reason enough to support book clubs. As readers learn to criticize ideas and not people, they build a foundation for a community of readers and for metacognitive thinking, or thinking about thinking. It is important to note that the structure of book circles is very flexible. "True engagement with literature within a community of learners can't possibly be prescribed—it can only be described" (Noe, 1999).

Daniels and Zemelman (2004: 209) suggest giving each reader a specific role "because each one embodies a kind of thinking that mature readers actually use. So the roles can be a 'back door' way of introducing or reinforcing good reading-as-thinking strategies." However, some groups may prefer to formulate their own roles and let the book be their guide. Typical roles and their names, according to Daniels and Zemelman (2004), are the following:

1. Connector finds connections between the text and the world (p. 207).
2. Passage Master finds memorable, interesting, puzzling quotes (p. 207).
3. Vocabulary Enricher finds words worth knowing (p. 208).
4. Illustrator draws or sketches ideas or events (p. 208).
5. Researcher digs up information the group wants or needs (p. 209).

A beginning book circle might explore humorous novels, among the most popular genres with YAs. Although YA humor has tended to be gender specific, there are many contemporary titles that appeal to both girls and boys. Within that broad appeal are the two humorous graphic novels annotated below. Figure 3.3 provides brief examples of five suggested roles from the novels and what each role could discuss.

Goscinny, Renee and Albert Uderzo. 2004. *Asterix and the Roman Agent*. London: Orion. Grades 5 and up.

Set in 50 BCE Gaul, this 30-book series features pint-sized Asterix and his good-hearted sidekick Obelix as they outwit Julius Caesar in all his attempts to control their little village. In this story, Caesar sends a spy to create disorder and suspicion among the villagers. Children like the book's visual gags, and older readers see puns and allusions to classical culture and contemporary or well-known figures. Despite its occasional humorous anachronisms, the series does present historically accurate information for those who enjoy that element.

Barry, Lynda. 2002. *One Hundred Demons.* **Seattle, WA: Sasquatch. Adult book for YAs.**

A 2003 Alex Award winner, this "autobifictionalographic" book takes its title from a Zen painting exercise that promises relief after drawing one's demons and covers such worries as dancing, boyfriends, and bad skin. When focusing on common teen worries, Barry comforts readers who see themselves in her world. But Barry's personal demons point out how painfully funny adolescence can be even when reflected on years later as she has done in this unique book.

Figure 3.3. Reading Circle Roles in Two Graphic Novels		
Roles	Asterix	One Hundred Demons
Connector	Connections to history and famous historical figures	Every topic (e.g., appearance, boyfriend/girlfriends, parents, and peers) in the book is a common concern among YAs
Passage Master	Citations of types of humor, including puns, malapropisms, and anachronisms	Quotations about the poignant and funny examples of contemporary teen life
Vocabulary Enricher	Explanations/translations of Latin phrases, words, place names, and historical events	Examples of coined words; background on the concept of the "100 demons" from a book on Zen; general use of teen slang
Illustrator	Examples of how the artwork furthers theme and plot and use of color	Emphasis on author's techniques; see the book's "Afterword" for creating an original 100 demons book
Researcher	Potential suggestion from the group: to explain Gaul in 30 BCE	Potential suggestion from the group: to explore the concept of therapy through art

REFERENCES AND SUGGESTIONS FOR FURTHER READING

Adoff, Jaime. 2004. *Names Will Never Hurt Me.* New York: Dutton's Children's Books.
Adoff, Jaime. 2005. *Jimi & Me.* New York: Jump at the Sun/Hyperion.
Alvarez, Julia. 2002. *Before We Were Free.* New York: Alfred A. Knopf.
Anderson, Eric. 2003. "Design Drawing: A Means Toward Visual Literacy and the Exploration of Ideas in the Classroom." *Technology Teacher* 63, no. 2: 15–17.
Bartoletti, Susan Campbell. 2000. *Hitler Youth: Growing Up in Hitler's Shadow.* New York: Scholastic.
Burmark, Lynell. 2002. *Visual Literacy: Learn to See, See to Learn.* Alexandria, VA: Association for Supervision and Curriculum Development.
Card, Orson Scott. 1985. *Ender's Game.* New York: T. Doherty.
Coger, Leslie Irene, and Melvin R. White. 1973. *Readers Theatre Handbook: A Dramatic Approach to Literature,* rev. ed. Glenview, IL: Scott, Foresman.

Crane, Stephen. 2008. *The Red Badge of Courage: An Authoritative Text, Background, and Sources Criticism.* New York: W.W. Norton.

Daniels, Harvey and Steven Zemelman. 2004. *Subjects Matter: Every Teacher's Guide to Content-Area Reading.* Portsmouth, NH: Heinemann.

Fleischman, Paul. 1985. *I Am Phoenix: Poems for Two Voices.* Illus. Ken Nutt. New York: Harper and Row.

Fleischman, Paul. 1988. *Joyful Noise: Poems for Two Voices.* Illus. Eric Beddows. New York: Harper and Row.

Fritz, Jean. 1988. *China's Long March: 6,000 Miles of Danger.* New York: Putnam.

Giles, Gail. 2002. *Shattering Glass.* Brookfield, CT: Roaring Brook Press.

Hunt, Jonathon. 2006. "Script Novels." *School Library Journal* 52, no. 3 (March): 52–53.

Latrobe, Kathy Howard, and Mildred Knight Laughlin. 1989. *Readers Theatre for Young Adults: Scripts and Script Development.* Englewood, CO: Teacher Ideas.

Lester, Julius. 2005. *Day of Tears: A Novel in Dialogue.* New York: Hyperion Books for Children.

Margolis, Marjorie. 2002. "Creating a Body Biography." Folger Shakespeare Library. Available at: www.folger.edu/eduLesPlanDtl.cfm?lpid=650.

Noe, Katherine L. Schlick. 1999. "Overview of Literature Circles." Literature Circle Resource Center. Available at: http://facstaff.seattleu.edu/kschlnoe/web/LitCircles/Overview.

Poe, Edgar Allan. 1849, 1938. "The Bells." In *The Complete Tales and Poems of Edgar Allan Poe,* pp. 954–957. New York: Modern Library.

Probst, Robert. 1984. *Adolescent Literature: Response and Analysis.* Columbus, OH: Charles E. Merrill Publishing.

Roney, R. Craig. 1998. "Defining Storytelling: Some Theoretical Thoughts." *Storytelling World* no. 13 (Winter–Spring): 23.

Rosenblatt, Louise. 1968. *Literature as Exploration.* New York: D. Appleton-Century.

Rosenblatt, Louise. 1978. *The Reader, the Text, the Poem: The Transactional Theory of the Literary Work.* Carbondale, IL: Southern Illinois University Press.

Snodgrass, Mary Ellen. 2002. *Literary Treks: Characters on the Move.* New York: Random House.

Strachey, Barbara. 1992. *Journeys of Frodo: An Atlas of J.R.R. Tolkien's* The Lord of the Rings. New York: HarperCollins.

Trelease, Jim. 2001. *The Read-Aloud Handbook,* 5th ed. New York: Penguin Books.

Part II

Genre

Chapter 4

Genre Criticism

INTRODUCTION TO GENRE CRITICISM

There are two aspects of genre criticism: "(1) the classification and description of literary texts and (2) the evolution or development of literary forms" (Makaryk, 1993: 79). The two are interrelated; neither is fixed. The concept of classification and description may be communicated to young people as categories, types, kinds, expectations, or assumptions; however, young people may most relate to Ludwig Wittgenstein's analogy of family resemblances, as summarized by M.H. Abrams (1999: 110): Some critics "propose that, in the loosely grouped family of works that make up a genre, there are no essential defining features, but only a set of family resemblances; each member shares some of the resemblances with some, but not all, of the other members of the genre." This analogy also illuminates the concept of evolution or development, explaining the emergence of a new genre (family) or subgenre (family members). Thus, historically, what the Greeks considered to be the complete set of genres (epic, drama, and lyric) has expanded to the nearly absurd: for example, "chick lit," a subgenre of the novel, boasts its own 15 subgenres online (Montgomery, 2003).

Introducing readers to *genre* as a literary term not engraved in stone allows them a sophisticated flexibility of criticism that will support their continued literary growth and understanding for lifelong reading. They will continue to study self-consciously and compare conventions and structures, seeing possibilities and not contradictions as the social construct that *genre is* continues to evolve. This fluid perspective is at the center of contemporary criticism in which "genre distinctions" are "useful descriptive devices but rather arbitrary ones. *Genre* boundaries have been much subject to flux and blur in recent times, and it is almost the rule that a successful work will combine *genres* in some original way" (Harmon and Holman, 2000: 231). Finally, reader response as a core concept in this work is encouraged through genre criticism as readers interact critically across texts and families of texts. In responding to literature through genre criticism, readers may consider the following questions for discussion:

1. How does a reader describe and differentiate a genre? (A short story, unlike a novel, can be read in one sitting, has a single effect, and focuses on one conflict.)

2. What is the relationship between genre and understanding? (A reader expects a work of science fiction to have a premise based on scientific fact or theory. A reader of picture books assumes that the illustrations will communicate as much as or more than the text. A reader of contemporary realistic fiction expects the story to be possible, and a reader of nonfiction expects the text to be accurate and true. How can a work of fiction, through emotional truth, seem more real to some readers than a work of nonfiction?)

3. How does a genre achieve its effects? (What conventional elements of a gothic novel establish its atmosphere?)

4. In what ways can a genre challenge its audience? (What are the additional demands on a first-time reader of the graphic novel? What is the challenge of setting for the reader—and author—of historical fiction and fantasy?)

CONTEMPORARY REALISTIC FICTION

Contemporary realistic fiction for young adults (YAs) is a category of imaginative literature that accurately portrays a young protagonist's life as it is lived now or in the recent past. The concept of the creation of an imaginative reality was expressed succinctly and memorably by Bromden, the narrator of *One Flew Over the Cuckoo's Nest*: "It's the truth even if it didn't happen" (Kesey, 1962: 21). Unfortunately, according to most critics, this definition did not apply to YA literature until the late 1960s. The literature that had often impersonated contemporary realistic fiction for YAs was described by Frank G. Jennings (1956: 531) as "pastel, gum-drop fiction." Novels that he saw as "mealy-mouthed" (p. 526) failed the wants and needs of the audience he described: "Here are young people, trembling on the threshold of adulthood. They want to know what it is like to hope and fail, to suffer, to die, to love wastefully. They want to have spelled out some of the awful consequences of going against society's grain" (p. 526). Deploring the dishonest overprotection in YA novels and their third-rate literary quality, Jennings also called for a new form of criticism for the evaluation of books for the YA. Much change followed in YA contemporary fiction in the next 50 years.

In 1965, G. Robert Carlsen (1965: 22) emphasized that YAs read for the content in three areas—their life direction, understanding society's problems and "the bizarre, the off beat, the unusual in human experience." But at the same time, Carlsen noted that the novels written specifically for YAs lacked certain other themes found in books written specifically for adults, themes such as the

1. "individual caught in the web of his own decisions" (p. 24),
2. "exploration of the boundaries within which life can be lived" (p. 24),
3. "helplessness of man against cosmic forces indifferent to his fate" (p. 24), and
4. "acceptance of life's limitations and resignation to them" (p. 25).

Perhaps Carlsen realized that authors and publishers were willing to take on the tough questions; or, more likely, such critical analysis was contributing to artistic and social change that could support the publication of the first honestly realistic YA books like S.E. Hinton's (1967) *The Outsiders*, Paul Zindel's (1968, 2005) *The Pigman*, and Robert Cormier's (1974) *The Chocolate War*.

Unfortunately, quality was not consistent. Contemporary realistic fiction at times was almost synonymous with the "problem novel," and the serious themes identified by Carlsen were rarely realized in single-issue books. However, this would change. In 1975, Al Muller reported the results of his study of a set of YA contemporary novels, seeking to identify whether then-contemporary novels that increasingly addressed more sophisticated subjects—"premarital sex, death, drugs, and street life" (p. 531)—were also becoming more artistically sophisticated. He found that the genre was moving away from plot-driven stories, linear plots, an omniscient point of view, and a generic style and moving toward a unity of action and character and the use of interior monologue, multiple points of view, sophisticated imagery, flashbacks and time shifts, *in media res*, literary allusions, and complex imagery. Muller concluded that the "junior novel" (as realistic fiction was still being called) had become sophisticated enough to prepare young people for reading more serious adult novels, apparently the primary value of reading YA novels at that time. Furthermore, he found that the genre had continued to develop both in verisimilitude and in literary sophistication.

Since the time of Muller's study, YA authors have been rewarded not only as recipients of the long-standing Newbery Award but also of more recently created YA literature awards, including the Margaret Edwards and the Michael Printz Awards. The National Book Award for Young People includes titles for teens. YA contemporary realistic fiction consistently breaks previously taboo subjects, thus becoming more inclusive (e.g., books on sexual identities), accepting of genre blends (e.g., verse novels, novels in dialogue, mixed formats), portraying characters from American minority groups and from other countries in translation, and striving for emotional realism.

Evaluating Contemporary YA Literature

1. Is the story set in the present?
2. Is the story told from the perspective of a YA protagonist?
3. Can YAs identify with the protagonist?
4. Is the protagonist a multidimensional, dynamic character?
5. Does the protagonist interact realistically with the events of the plot?
6. Does the protagonist realistically experience major developmental tasks and challenges faced by all adolescents?
7. Does the protagonist come to significant, universal human truth(s) as he or she progresses toward adulthood?

Annotated Bibliography of Contemporary Realistic Novels

Acampora, Paul. 2006. *Defining Dulcie*. New York: Dial Press. Grades 8–10.

Sixteen-year-old Dulcie's father is fatally poisoned by a freak chemical reaction that leaves Dulcie, her mother, and her grandfather coping with the loss in their own ways. Dulcie clings to the world she has known, her mother strives to start anew, and her grandfather reaches out to help an abused adolescent. Young people can explore the reality of the characters' grief by comparing their reactions to those Elisabeth Kübler-Ross (2005) identified as the stages of the grieving process—denial, anger, bargaining, depression, and acceptance.

Adoff, Jaime. 2008. *The Death of Jayson Porter*. New York: Jump at the Sun/Hyperion. Grades 9 and up.

As a 16-year-old biracial teenager who feels he does not belong anywhere, Jayson has been seriously considering suicide. When his best friend Trax dies in a methadone explosion in apartment 777, Jayson finally leaps from the seventh floor of the projects. Because he survives the seven-story jump, he can say that the old Jayson Porter is truly "dead." The mixed genre, first person novel portrays the dark, harsh life of urban poverty, depicting in nonstereotypical ways the archetypal urge to maintain family no matter how bad things may get. Readers may choose certain monologues to perform, such as "After" (pp. 3–6) or any scene during his hospitalization.

Anderson, Laurie Halse. 1997. *Speak*. New York: Farrar, Straus, and Giroux. Grades 8–12.

Melinda, raped at a popular party in the summer before the ninth grade, finds herself an outcast by calling the police and then by keeping the attack a secret. The following school year is one of increasing isolation as she fights the culture of petty conformity by withdrawing. She then finds expression in her art and comes to realize her own voice as the rapist attempts to attack her a second time when she does have the strength to fight back. An activity that would illustrate Melinda's multidimensional, dynamic character could involve a young person reweaving self-selected passages to create a one-person script that, through performance, would lead listeners into Melinda's interior monologue and be a catalyst for discussion.

Crutcher, Chris. 2001. *Whale Talk.* **New York: Greenwillow Books. Grades 8–12.**

By inviting his school's "least likeliest to succeed" to become members of the swim team he is coaching, T.J. Jones scores points for instilling pride and discipline in those who have never before experienced athletic success. With characters that young people will recognize from their own school lives, the novel realistically portrays a protagonist with whom readers can identify. Young people can compose an "I Am" poem about T.J. and compare their responses.

Frank, E.R. 2002. *America.* **New York: Atheneum. Grades 9 and up.**

Abandoned by his crack-addicted mother, betrayed by adult caretakers, and removed into a foster care system that forgot about him, America narrates his life in alternating "Then" and "Now" until the two time periods merge and the pieces of the puzzles of his childhood fall into place for his unbelievably patient psychotherapist, Dr. B. America's distinctive voice transforms from that of a child—"I'm in America and America is me!" (p. 22)—to that of a preteen—"America is a boy who gets lost easy and is not worth the trouble of finding" (p. 16)—to that of an adult. The fully developed Dr. B., a very wise physician, takes pains to convey to America that he will not give up on the boy whose suffering has left him frozen silent. Readers can discuss the book's contemporary issues (e.g., urban poverty, child abuse, foster care system).

Haddon, Mark. 2003. *The Curious Incident of the Dog in the Night-Time.* **New York: Doubleday. Adult book for YAs.**

Fifteen-year-old Christopher Boone is a mathematical genius who leaves his safe and comfortable environment to seek his long-lost mother in London. Told through the autistic Christopher's point of view, readers are introduced to the misunderstood world of autism as well as to the truth found in human emotions as the boy solves a neighborhood mystery along with the mystery of his life. Young people can create an alphabetical poem for Christopher Boone.

Lupica, Mike. 2006. *Heat.* **New York: Philomel. Grades 6–9.**

Twelve-year-old Michael, an orphan immigrant from Cuba, fears that social services will become aware of his needs and separate him from his 17-year-old brother; yet, he is a fantastic baseball pitcher and has an opportunity to play in the Little League World Series in Yankee Stadium. With energetic dialogue and realistic characters who have independent voices, this is an entertaining sports story that will allow adolescents an outsider's view of the Little League World Series. Young people can discuss the contemporary issues that glorify and cloud the sport, and they can contrast popular culture with the dreams of talented players who play for the love of the game.

McCaughrean, Geraldine. 2007. *The White Darkness.* **New York: HarperTempest. Grades 9 and up.**

The protagonist Sym faces two opponents: her human traveling companions (including her deceitful and obsessed uncle Victor) and the surreal setting of Antarctica, both deadly antagonists. Sym is led to Antarctica by the uncle and by her long interest in the brave and romantic Antarctic explorer Captain Lawrence Oates, whose diary had recorded in detail the tragedy of Captain Robert Scott's expedition to Antarctica in 1911. Sym counters the dangers of the setting with imaginary conversations with Oates and with information she remembered from reading his 1911 diary. Young people can consider how the quote from Kafka, "A book must be an ice axe to break the sea frozen inside us" (p. 371), relates to author and readers, as McCaughrean notes.

Na, An. 2006. *Wait for Me.* New York: Putnam. Grades 8–11.

Straight-A Mina, a high school senior, leads a double life: on the surface she fulfills her controlling mother's dreams of perfection but lives a lie to do so. Likewise, currents of conflict flow among all the members of Mina's family and the immigrant workers in the family's dry-cleaning business. To explore graphic organization and discussion, young people can identify the book's many moral quandaries and their implications from the section Theories of Moral Development (see Chapter 2) comparing Robert Kohlberg's and Carol Gilligan's different notions.

Nolan, Han. 1997. *Dancing on the Edge.* New York: Harcourt. Grades 7–10.

In an attempt to "disappear" herself by setting her clothes on fire, Miracle McCloy comes to live up to her name a second time by accepting the help of Dr. De Angelis whom she describes as "a doctor of scars you can't see" (p. 160). Although Miracle may seem eccentric at first, her actions reveal her to be a realistic, dynamic character. As a way to illustrate character development, young people can read the Emily Dickinson poems that Miracle reads ("I'm Nobody" in Chapter 1 and "To die—without the Dying" in Chapter 25) and discuss why she reacted so differently to each poem.

HISTORICAL FICTION

In the traditional sense, "[T]he historical novel is a fictional narrative in which there is an identifiable time, place, and historical agent, written sometime after the event or period depicted" (Dickinson, 1958: 11). In the introduction to *Waverly, Or 'Tis Sixty Years Since*, Sir Walter Scott (1814, 1972) established the convention of having a historical novel's setting precede its re-creation by 60 years. However, over time and with a consideration for YA audiences, the boundaries of the genre have softened to sometimes include works that were created as contemporary realistic fiction (e.g., Upton Sinclair's 1906 novel *The Jungle*) but endured over time as historical fiction. Classified as historical fiction, such a novel requires that young people view the genre without the social enlightenment brought by a distance of 60 or more years. Including these older but once contemporary works carries the potential confusion of requiring that young people hold in mind contemporary social constructs as well as those of the author who was a participant observer in the novel's setting and who thus may bring, for example, racism and condescension into the fiber of the novel. Regarding reader response, it is worthwhile to consider those contemporary but now classic works through the lens of historical or cultural criticism rather than genre criticism. Thus, elements of a classic novel (e.g., racism and sexism) that would be divisive in most environments become rich topics for discussion in historical or social criticism. However, Sir Walter Scott's convention of 60 years is an arbitrary span that deserves to be tempered by YAs' life views, which may include only 13 years.

Reading historical fiction enables young people to look at history repackaged into an appealing format that can creatively engage and motivate their learning—learning that can be emotionally and cognitively internalized. Young people who identify with historical characters sympathize with humans in conflict, develop understandings of personal aspirations and their social limitations, and come to realize the universal nature of humankind across eras and geographies. Thus, to readers of historical fiction, the fortunes of cultures and nations wax and wane, rendering change the only inevitable promise of any time or place. Furthermore, each experience with historical fiction leaves readers with another landmark on individually conceived time lines that exist as cognitive scaffolding for future learning.

Julius Lester's (2005: 176) take on historical fiction epitomizes what many of the genre's African-American writers feel about their work: "History is not only an accounting of what happened when and where. It includes also the emotional biographies of those on whom history imposed itself with a cruelty that we can only dimly imagine." As Lester concludes, his body of work is his attempt "to make real those who did not have the opportunity to tell their stories for themselves" (p. 176). Indeed, most of historical fiction is a mixture of "ghosts and documents" (Byatt, 2005: 1), emphasizing its factual and imaginary elements, both of which are primary in the evaluation of the genre. Each requires balancing to ensure a story that is a pleasure to read and that enriches understanding. This balancing of fact and imagination is most challenging in historical fiction, where too many descriptive facts can weigh against pleasure and too much imagination against understanding. Therefore, evaluation criteria are focused on both pleasure and understanding.

Evaluating Historical Fiction

Pleasure

1. Is the *style* engaging?
2. Does the *plot* have an easygoing pace that is not overwhelmed by long descriptive passages?
3. Can YAs identify with the *characters*?
4. Can YAs vicariously enter another *setting* (time and place)?

Understanding

Accuracy

5. Is the text historically accurate?

6. Does the author provide evidence that the work is based on research, inform readers when the story deviates from factual history (e.g., anachronisms), and include a bibliography for further reading?

Authenticity

7. Is the language of the text authentic without being distracting. That is, do the dialogue, figures of speech, idioms, and dialect create a realistic impression of the setting?

8. Do background details (costume, differences in values and points of view, family life, conventional beliefs and sensibilities, attitudes, conduct or behavior, scientific advancement, modes of work and communication, transportation, and geography and weather) create a realistic reproduction of the era?

9. Does the theme address the human condition across time and place?

Annotated Bibliography of Historical Fiction

Cushman, Karen. 2006. *The Loud Silence of Francine Green.* **New York: Clarion Books. Grades 6–9.**

The nostalgic 1950s appear less warm and cozy and more confused and frightful when seen through the eyes of a 13-year-old Catholic girl who had always lived her life by trying to stay out of trouble. When she meets rebel-with-a-cause Sophie Bowman, Fran eventually makes her first serious challenge to authority. Francine's narrative brings the fifties to life with her inclusion of dozens of historical details (e.g., names of products, radio shows, books, movie stars) and events, (e.g., Hollywood blacklisting, McCarthyism, HUAC) and with her realistic, naïve, and humorous voice. Young people can create body biographies for opposites Francine and Sophie, including items that capture the look of the fifties, Sophie's nonconformist political stances, and their shared middle school Catholic education.

Doctorow, E.L. 1975. *Ragtime.* **New York: Ballantine. Adult book for YAs.**

By weaving the lives of three fictional families into the lives of historical figures, and by presenting a wide range of details from popular culture, the unnamed narrator tells a gripping story of the social changes in the United States at the turn of the twentieth century. With no fewer than 70 allusions to historical figures and dozens of historical events as background, the novel provides young people with ideas they can illustrate in bulletin boards, collages, or music using the novel's many references to art, ragtime music, sports, journalism, big business, and politics by finding archival photographs, making original drawings, or citing memorable passages from the text.

Erdrich, Louise. 2005. *The Game of Silence.* **New York: HarperCollins. Grades 5–8.**

Young Omakayas, first introduced in *The Birchbark House* (1999), is a young Ojibwe who gives up her childhood and her home in the 1850s on a beautiful Lake Superior Island to play the game of silence not with her rowdy brother but rather in earnest against the encroaching white people as her family and tribe seek safety beyond the reach of settlers. The author has created an authentic sense of family and everyday life that has been compared to the world remembered by Laura Ingalls Wilder. Young people can construct body biographies (e.g., of her mother, brother, and other central characters) that communicate background details of Omakayas' life and culture.

Innocenti, Roberto. 1985, 1996. *Rose Blanche.* **Mankato, MN: Creative Books. Grades 5 and up.**

In picture book format, the author/illustrator tells the horrific story of a young German girl who takes food to the children in a concentration camp near her town until she is caught in the crossfire of soldiers. The drab illustrations convey authentically the somber realities of masses of soldiers, vast buildings, and a landscape without a sky—all seen through the eyes of an innocent child whose hair is bound in swastika-like red ribbons. Through a focus on the visual details, young people can explain what is never stated: the meaning of the graffiti, the daily risk that Rose takes, the ultimate fate of Rose, why the concentration camp exists so close to the town—all powerful realities communicated without words.

Kadohata, Cynthia. 2004. *Kira-Kira.* **New York: Atheneum. Grades 6–12.**

Lynn and Katie, respectively 14 and 10 years old, are sisters who grow up culturally isolated and much alone in rural Georgia during the 1950s while their Japanese mother and father work a total of three grueling shifts a day processing poultry. This dark side of the American dream is balanced by the strength of a loving family and the naïve narrator, Katie, who is able to tell more than she understands with humor (e.g., her fantasy husband is named Joe-John Abondondalarama) and honesty (e.g., the anger she feels when Lynn, dying from lymphoma, throws milk on the floor). Young people, in a book discussion, can include their perspectives on the difficulty in completing the basic tasks of adolescence (see discussion of Havighurst's tasks in Chapter 2) when coping with cultural isolation like that of the two sisters.

Lester, Julius. 2005. *Day of Tears: A Novel in Dialogue.* **New York: Jump at the Sun/Hyperion Books. Grades 6–9.**

Blending historical and fictional characters and told from several points of view, this narrative of the largest slave auction in U.S. history portrays one enslaved family's struggle to be free. Lester's nonlinear plot moves back and forth between past and present through the alternation of characters from the historical era (the book's present) and some of the same characters as elderly persons (the future), thereby advancing the plot without repetitions and contrasting the beliefs in the "virtues" of slavery in the words of owner Pierce Butler and anger and grief in the words of Emma and her parents after she has been sold away from them. Young people can search Lester's suggested Web sites, such as PBS's "The Weeping Time" (www.pbs.org/wgbh/

aia/part4/4p2918.html), for primary documents, photographs, and excerpts from abolitionist (and former wife of Pierce Butler) Fanny Kemble's book on the evils of slavery.

Lisle, Janet. 2000. *The Art of Keeping Cool*. New York: Simon and Schuster. Grades 6–8.

Cousins Robert and Elliot come of age along the Rhode Island coast during World War II in a complex novel driven by fear—fear within their town, their family, and their world at war. The integral setting includes a refugee German artist, huge naval guns overlooking the dangerous waters of the Atlantic Ocean, and moms who have their first jobs away from home. Acknowledging and facing fear dominate the novel's theme, and young people can be encouraged to discuss how authentically the layers of fear were justified in the novel.

McCaughrean, Geraldine. 2003. *Stop the Train! A Novel*. New York: HarperCollins. Grades 5–8.

In a colorful melodrama, set during the land rush of 1893 in Oklahoma Territory, a trainload of settlers populate the town of Florence, which is little more than empty prairie surrounding a small train stop. They include an unconventional teacher, a troupe of actors, a baker, a wheelwright, a newspaper man, feuding families, and a villain. Young people can dress in costume, pose for selected scenes from the novel, and, when photographed, produce illustrations for the novel and of early days on the prairie frontier.

Schmidt, Gary D. 2004. *Lizzie Bright and the Buckminster Boy*. New York: Clarion Press. Grades 7–12.

Turner Buckminster is a 13-year-old outcast, being the son of a minister and having no baseball skills. Lizzie Bright is an African American who lives on a nearby island and who, experiencing intense racism, is driven from her island home to an insane asylum where she quickly dies. The death of Lizzie is a tragedy authentic to the times, and for Turner her death is one of a series of tragedies, each revealing new dimensions of his developing character. To illuminate Turner's growth, YAs can identify pairs of words that first describe Turner's early behavior and second describe his more developed character (e.g., from *timid* to *outspoken*; from *friendless* to *beloved*; from *outcast* to *hero*).

Sturm, James. 2001. *The Golem's Mighty Swing*. Montreal: Drawn and Quarterly. Grades 6–12.

This third work in a graphic novel trilogy is set during the 1920s when minor league baseball teams like the Stars of David barnstormed the Midwest playing before small-town crowds where they faced two opponents, one on the field and another in the stands from which come a barrage of racial epithets toward the Jewish athletes. Sturm's sepia-toned cartoon style authentically portrays the uniforms, the plays, the jargon, and the difficult life on the road for minority baseball teams, such as those composed of first- or second-generation Jewish immigrants. Young people unfamiliar with this part of baseball history can search the Internet for sites devoted to teams that have been lost to history, those such as the Stars of David and others from the sandlot or minor leagues.

MYSTERIES

Mysteries, thrillers, capers, or suspense stories require the solution of a puzzle involving a crime. Thus, the genre focuses on the puzzle (a crime to solve) and the pursuit (the way to the solution). Careful readers develop better skills of deduction and observation with each story they read. Plot-centered and fast-paced, mystery stories engage impatient or reluctant readers and increase reading speed as young people rush to an exciting conclusion. Furthermore, a well-developed series or protagonist maintains the interest of readers who enjoy the intelligence, humor, and eccentricities of the detective. In YA mysteries, the detective is an adolescent, while any adults usually play secondary roles. Psychological appeal lies in young people's participating in risky but vicarious behaviors, or identifying with the criminal mind and having the subconscious "guilt" erased when the perpetrator is brought to justice. Traditional mysteries end with order restored and with a sense that good triumphs over a well-defined evil.

Evaluating Mysteries

1. Is there a crime?
2. Is the plot suspenseful, believable, and fast paced?
3. Does the plot's mystery arise directly from the protagonist's personal conflicts and situation?
4. Does the plot's conclusion not only solve a mystery but also illuminate a life?

Annotated Bibliography of Mysteries

Arnold, Tedd. 2007. *Rat Life*. New York: Dial Books. Grades 6–10.

Gifted "gross out" fiction writer 14-year-old Todd Anthony is in the middle of a true crime story that involves his new friend Rat, a Vietnam veteran whose mother enlisted the boy at age 14 and whose "'so-called father'" (p. 124) holds the answer to the murders and to Rat's life, "an unimaginable story. An unimaginable life" (p. 162). This Edgar Allan Poe Award winner fulfills all the evaluation criteria, especially the illumination of a life, as the first person narrator learns more about himself—that he can write about emotional pain without being maudlin—than he learns about the unknowable Rat whose short life involved more pain than he had ever read in any fictional story. Readers can choose one of Todd's brief stories to read aloud, written in penmanship font, especially the puppy scene (pp. 40–41) and its parallels with the dilemma that Rat faces in the novel's conclusion.

Cormier, Robert. 2001. *The Rag and Bone Shop*. New York: Random House. Grades 7 and up.

Twelve-year-old Jason, falsely accused of murder, faces the relentless questions of Trent, who is recruited by the police to extract a confession from Jason. The title, taken from a poem by Yeats ("the foul rag and bone shop of the heart") describes the territory that Trent explores as he coerces a confession from Jason, presenting a scene suitable for a readers theatre script. The fine line between guilt and innocence is explored in Jason's questioning his own sense of reality, which offers young people the discussion topic of whether Trent has revealed the heart of killer, created the heart of a killer, or destroyed a heart's innocence.

David, Peter. 2002. *SpyBoy: Undercover, Underwear.* **Milwaukie, OR: Darkhorse Comics. Grades 9–12.**

An American high school student applies his skills and technology against international assassins who have taken his partner hostage somewhere in the Middle East with plans to sell her to a white slave trader. With nods to Ian Fleming's agent 007 spy series (i.e., protagonist Alex Fleming and his father Sean; strong female spies; elaborate devices and modes of transportation), this graphic novel series places international espionage right in the suburbs of America. Readers who like their spy stories light and humorous may compare how successfully this series parodies more serious works of intrigue.

Doyle, Arthur Conan. 1901, 1959. *The Hound of the Baskervilles.* **New York: Bantam. Grades 9–12.**

An eighteenth-century superstition about a wealthy family's curse brings Holmes and Watson to a country estate after a horrifying murder seems to confirm the legend. As the definitive fictional detective, Sherlock Holmes took on a life of his own until Doyle murdered him off in 1894. The public outcry against this act is a landmark in the history of the mystery genre, with Doyle's reluctantly resurrecting Holmes in *Hound.* YAs can perform some original detection by searching print and online sources to solve the following puzzles: (1) Why did Doyle kill his most popular, money-making character? (2) What were London newspapers reporting about the "death" of Holmes? (3) What traits in Holmes (and perhaps in Watson) made him so popular that readers felt as if Holmes were real? (4) Why did Doyle bring Holmes back to life?

Halliday, John. 2003. *Shooting Monarchs.* **New York: Margaret K. McElderry Books. Grades 9–12,**

Macy and Danny start their lives under severe disadvantages, but each takes a different path that eventually brings the two together when Leah Hoffman is abducted and becomes the prey of a teenaged serial killer. By intentionally leaving the narrative with an open ending, readers will decide for themselves the fate of a convicted killer. YAs can join discussion groups on the social and moral issues raised in the story: (1) What role does childhood abuse play in creating violent behavior in teenagers? (2) What is the nature of justice? (3) Is childhood bullying taken seriously enough by adults? (4) Does society pay enough attention to the victims of crime? How does the book show the way violent crime affects family members? (5) Do people tend to value physical attraction more or less than they value kindness and compassion?

Karr, Kathleen. 2003. *The Seventh Knot.* **New York: Marshall Cavendish. Grades 6–9.**

During the Gilded Age, Chadwick Hoving Forrester III ("Wick") and his younger brother Miles begrudge their punishment for school pranks—they must accompany grumpy Uncle Eustace in his search for art bargains that old, rich European families need to sell for money. Miles and Wick move from one episodic mystery to the next, each boy's skill being put to good use—Miles' chemistry and Wick's precision—and climaxing in two getaways in an air balloon. From this Agatha Award winner, readers can re-create one of the episodes in visual form (e.g., cartoon panels, body biographies, posters, or period illustrations).

McNamee, Graham. 2003. *Acceleration.* New York: Wendy Lamb Books. Grades 8 and up.

When dreams about the drowning girl that he did not save return to haunt his nights, Duncan decides that an anonymous diary holds the answer to giving him a "second chance" (p. 59) to rescue another girl who is in danger of losing her life. Working in the lost and found office of Toronto's subway system seems like a dungeon or a morgue to Duncan, and references to death, dying, and corpses abound in this ever-accelerating mystery plot until the climax, when readers race (along with Duncan) to discover who Roach really is. Readers can examine the way that Duncan and friend Vinny choose details from the killer's diary and then apply them to the FBI's serial killer profiling techniques as they narrow their search into the madman's very neighborhood (pp. 84–91, 115–117, 122–127).

Morgenroth, Kate. 2004. *Jude.* New York: Simon and Schuster. Grades 8–12.

Fifteen-year-old Jude witnesses the murder of his father and is thus drawn into a world of deceit and treachery, sacrificing himself to years in jail to protect his mother who is running for re-election as district attorney. The character of Jude is well developed and contributes to the believability of the plot and to the development of the theme that love of family satisfies a profound human need. This book can be paired with Walter Dean Myers's *Monster* (2001, HarperCollins), presenting the opportunity for young people to compare and contrast 15-year-old Jude and 16-year-old Steve, both antiheroes.

Sebold, Alice. 2002. *The Lovely Bones.* Boston: Little, Brown. Adult book for YAs.

Fourteen-year-old Susie Salmon tells the story of her rape and murder from heaven as she watches her family and friends grieve and then recover. The novel is an extraordinary crime story in that Susie watches the earthly characters, including the murderer, for ten years, fully exploring the dimensions of the crime's psychological impact on all the characters. Sebold's *Lucky: A Memoir* (1999, Back Bay) relates her own brutal rape and also traces that crime's effect on herself, her family, and her friends. Young people can discuss the common theme of both books—the profound effects on those who are victims of violence or crime.

Werlin, Nancy. 1998. *The Killer's Cousin.* New York: Delacorte. Grades 8–12.

Two cousins, both killers, come to live under the same roof in Cambridge when David moves in with Aunt Julia and Uncle Vic and cousin Lily, who taunts David about his accidental killing of his girlfriend while hiding her role in the death of her sister. The psychological terror in this novel is sustained by its gothic elements. Young people can be challenged to identify the gothic elements in this contemporary mystery and use a tree graphic organizer to show how the effects of the gothic elements are established through the characters, the plot, and the setting.

BIOGRAPHY

A good biography is the melding of historical facts and literary storytelling. Biographer Olivia Coolidge (1974) described the facts as building blocks. She noted that she liked to have as many facts as she could to assist her in designing her book. However, for Coolidge, biography is not a collection of surplus information. If that were so, the more information that a biography contained the better it would be. Of course, that would be a disaster for young people to read. In her "struggle with the facts," Coolidge (1974: 146–151) identifies the needs to

- recognize which facts are important,
- decide which factual discrepancies deserve attention,
- sort facts from judgments,
- determine a purpose for writing,
- set reasonable limits for research,
- integrate facts and documentation with a readable style, and
- sort facts from opinions.

Thus, the challenge for authors of YA biographies is to seek, select, and integrate facts in order to meet the needs of YA readers who often lack a rounded understanding of the setting, who do not have sufficient time or depth of interest to invest in a definitive treatment of the main character, who can be engaged by storytelling shaped by a compelling theme but not by tedious explanations and extended citations, and who require accuracy and factual documentation as they develop and structure their understandings of history. Emphasizing the role of the facts in a biography or history, Russell Freedman (2002: 165) explains, "I have a pact with the reader to stick to the facts, to be as factually accurate as human frailty will allow."

However, when Freedman (2002: 165) begins a new biography, he thinks of himself "first of all as a storyteller" who gives dramatic shape to the subject that is "worth telling," and he wants "to tell it as clearly, as simply, and as forcefully" as he can. A fine example of his storytelling approach in biography is his Newbery Honor book, *Eleanor Roosevelt: A Life of Discovery* (1993). Freedman (1993, Preface) develops the multifaceted character of Eleanor Roosevelt whose life and words make explicit the theme that the "life of discovery" comes when "You gain strength, courage and confidence by every experience in which you really stop to look fear in the face. . . . You must do the thing you think you cannot do." In an engaging story supported by formal photographs and snapshots, Freedman relates chapter by chapter the non-negotiable circumstances that forced Eleanor Roosevelt to face fear, first as a plain, shy child always called "Granny" by her glamorous socialite mother and then progressively as a conventional society matron with no interests of her own, stymied by her mother-in-law and betrayed by her husband; as a first lady criticized for her liberal views and busybody, meddlesome activities; and finally as a person on her own who toward the end of her life could say, "I long ago reached the point where there is no living person whom I fear, and few challenges that I am not willing to face" (p. 168). Freedman's engaging life story is a romance in which Eleanor Roosevelt's sense of duty drives the quest and fortifies her courage.

Freedman uses other literary elements to enliven the biography. He introduces suspense, for example, by using cliffhangers, such as the ending to Chapter 5 when Eleanor Roosevelt is left holding Lucy Mercer's love letters to President Roosevelt. Freedman includes some humor, such as the comment by Eleanor's uncle, Theodore Roosevelt, upon her marriage to her fifth cousin, once removed, "Well, Franklin, there's nothing like keeping the name in the family" (p. 45). He also makes the setting integral to the development of the character and the theme with the use of photographs, among which are those of the little rich girl, the pair of elegant town homes with the pass-through that gave her mother-in-law constant access to her home and family, Eleanor wrestling on the lawn with her daughter or riding a coal car two-and-a-half miles down into an Ohio mine, and of her crowning achievement at the United Nations upon the passage of the Universal Declaration of Human Rights.

Robert Carlsen (1980) categorized biographies according to their purposes and formats:

- Fictionalized biographies include invented scenes or dialogue that probably happened. "Actually, no biography is completely free of such fictionalization" (p. 181).
- Definitive biographies present "all the known facts about a person" (p. 181).
- Interpretive biographies are based on facts selected, organized, and interpreted to support an author's theme.
- Monument biographies glorify their subjects.
- Gargoyle (debunking) biographies focus on subjects' negative qualities.
- Critical biographies reevaluate past or accepted interpretations within individual biographies.
- Collected biographies offer brief overviews of a set of individuals linked by an issue or topic
- Classic biographies, such as "the four Gospels in *The Bible*" (p. 183), are few in number.
- Autobiographies, or memoirs, may also vary in purpose and format as well as supporting research and documentation.

Evaluating Biographies

1. Does the biography have literary merit?
   a. Is the subject's character round and dynamic?
   b. Can a reader understand how the subject shaped the character's life?
   c. Is there a worthwhile theme that has evolved from research?
   d. Do setting and style add to an understanding of the subject's time and place?
   e. Will the style appeal to YA readers?
   f. Do facts and documentation interfere with the story; is background material woven unobtrusively into the story?

2. Is the subject interesting to YAs and worth reading about?
   a. Does the author communicate an interest in the subject?
   b. Does the author demonstrate a thorough understanding of the subject?
   c. Is the work within the interest and comprehension range of its intended audience?

3. Is the biography accurate?
   a. Does the author differentiate fact and opinion?
   b. Does the author use and document primary sources?
   c. Does the author avoid glorifying and debunking the subject?
   d. Do illustrations add understanding and credibility to the text?
   e. Does the author maintain a balanced presentation?

Annotated Bibliography of Biographies

Aronson, Marc. 2000. *Sir Walter Ralegh and the Quest for El Dorado.* New York: Clarion Press. Grades 9–12.

Rising from a country farm to the Elizabethan court, this complex and calculating adventurer was a social and political force that ensured England's role in the New World. Strengths of this biography include the author's intense interest in the subject; the presentation of a complex social background that supports and clarifies the varied dimensions of Ralegh's character; the author's thorough research; features such as endnotes, bibliography, and time line; and reproductions, such as maps, sonnets, and a suicide note. Young people can take an episode from Ralegh's life and produce a storyboard for an imagined graphic novel.

Engle, Margarita. 2006. *The Poet Slave of Cuba: A Biography of Juan Francisco Manzano.* Illustrated by Sean Qualls. New York: Henry Holt. Grades 7–10.

Set in the nineteenth century, this fictionalized biography in verse introduces to many readers the life of one of Cuba's greatest poets, whose first 16 years were spent in slavery to two owners, the "benevolent" elderly Dona Beatriz—who encourages Juan's skills at memorizing poetry—and then the demented Marquesa—who takes out her berserk rage against the boy in merciless beatings and emotional traumas that nearly kill him. This whole brutal picture of slavery ranges from the nuances of class based on the lightness of one's skin to unimaginable brutality that can destroy one's spirit and creativity but instead test Juan's determination and will to survive in order to write his poems. Readers can learn more about slavery in North America and Latin America in Allen, Tepper, and Stratigakis' (1998) comparison of the lives of Frederick Douglass and Juan Francisco.

Fradin, Judith Bloom, and Dennis Brendell Fradin. 2006. *Jane Addams: Champion of Democracy.* **New York: Clarion Books. Grades 6 and up.**

By balancing the story of Addams' lesser known commitment to pacifism along with her more familiar commitment to Hull House, the story of the woman called "Miss Kind Heart" (p. vii) and "The most dangerous woman in America" (p. 148) within the same decade portrays a complex historical icon. Features include an introduction, bibliography, illustrations, and an afterword that promote interest in Addams' productive life. When young people encounter some of Jane Addams' words from her letters or speeches included in this title (e.g., pp. 123, 130–131, 135, 152), they may find that her perspective on world peace seems relevant to the early years of the twenty-first century. YAs can read aloud some of the excerpts from her letters and speeches and discuss the question: Is world peace possible or just a dream?

Goldstein, Nancy. 2008. *Jackie Ormes: The First African American Woman Cartoonist.* **Ann Arbor: University of Michigan Press. Adult book for YAs.**

As a model, commercial artist, fashion designer, entrepreneur, political activist, doll designer, and cartoonist, Ormes epitomizes the successful, upper-middle-class black socialite of post–World War II urban America. That some of her cartoon characters resemble her is no accident, as Ormes challenged all the stereotypes of black women as then portrayed in the media. "Torchy Brown: From Dixie to Harlem" tells (somewhat autobiographically) about a teen who finds success in her rags-to-riches transformation to a Cotton Club dancer where black women are witty and stylish in their ritzy social settings. Patty Jo, five-year-old child pest, torments her older, fashion-plate sister Ginger with remarks that poke fun at social issues within the safety of a comic panel. The inclusion of 40 pages of annotations that help put the cartoon characters in their historical and social contexts makes this an intriguing way to study the Chicago Renaissance of African-American history.

Greenberg, Jan. 1998. *Chuck Close, Up Close.* **New York: DK. Grades 6 and up.**

The innovative artist Chuck Close, well known for enormous portraits and respected by family and friends, overcame learning disabilities as a child and physical impairments as an adult to achieve recognition for his creative interpretations and earn his place in the history of portraiture. Strengths of this biography include its visual appeal, the insights expressed in Close's own words, the reproductions of some of his artwork, and the author's respect for the subject. Young people can search the Internet to compile a virtual collection of Close's portraits.

McClafferty, Carla Killough. 2006. *Something Out of Nothing: Marie Curie and Radium.* **New York: Farrar, Straus, and Giroux. Grades 7–10.**

Overcoming poverty, class and gender discrimination, fear, depression, and grief, Marie Curie, France's most famous scientist, is portrayed from her childhood in

Russian-controlled Poland (where her native language was forbidden to be spoken or read) through her acceptance of a second Nobel Prize. The focus of the book is twofold: to show the obstacles that Marie faced with her indefatigable genius and to reveal her greatest contribution to science, the discovery of a new element, radium, and its beneficial and detrimental uses. Readers can visit the author's suggested Web site for the Curie Museum, housed in the Radium Institute in Paris.

McKissack, Patricia, and Fredrick McKissack. 1998. *Young, Black, and Determined: A Biography of Lorraine Hansberry.* **New York: Holiday House. Grades 7 and up.**

Daughter of a prosperous Chicago family that expected her to be politically engaged, Lorraine Hansberry became a civil rights activist and playwright (best known for *Raisin in the Sun*, 1959). Strengths of this biography include the McKissacks' enthusiasm for their subject and insights from their interviews with Hansberry's sister. Young people can view the play or film and relate Hansberry's life experiences to her literary work.

Partridge, Elizabeth. 2002. *This Land Was Made for You and Me: The Life and Songs of Woody Guthrie.* **New York: Viking Press. Grades 6–12.**

With personal resources and health as strained as that of any dust bowl victim, troubadour musician Woody Guthrie traveled across America, writing over 3,000 songs and assuring the displaced that they were good and there were things to love. Strengths of this biography include frank presentation of the effects of Huntington's disease on Guthrie and his mother, excerpts from lyrics as well as original drafts of lyrics, reproductions (e.g., photographs, telegram, and news clippings), and insights from the author's interviews with Pete Seeger and Guthrie's children. Young people can explore his music, especially the plight of the displaced, considering, for example, his song, "Tom Joad," about the protagonist of Steinbeck's *The Grapes of Wrath*.

Rappaport, Doreen. 2008. *Lady Liberty: A Biography.* **Illustrated by Matt Tavares. Cambridge, MA: Candlewick. Grades 3–8.**

Lady Liberty is approached as a project where stage by stage in different places by many individuals and teams the statue was created. The project managers were Henri Martin, a historian, who wanted to celebrate 100 years of American and French Independence; Auguste Bartoldi, a sculptor, who sketched and modeled Liberty; Bartoldi's assistant, Marie Simon, who enlarged the model; coppersmiths who pounded the copper onto Liberty's molds; Gustave Eiffel, a structural engineer, whose calculations keep Liberty upright; Emma Lazarus, poet of Liberty's welcome to the tired and poor; Charles P. Stone, construction supervisor, who built a foundation 65 feet tall; and Joseph Pulitzer, who raised cash to pay for Liberty's pedestal. Their individual stories are told in free verse on side panels of a large-format picture book. Young people can assume roles and read aloud parts of Liberty's remarkable story.

Reef, Catherine. 2001. *Sigmund Freud: Pioneer of the Mind.* **New York: Houghton Mifflin. Grades 9–12.**

The father of psychoanalysis proposed and revised theories to explain the subconscious mind, experienced controversy when his convictions alienated Victorian society, and laid a foundation for scientific research of the mind. Strengths of this biography include a clear presentation by the author, quotations, details of Freud's family life, explanations of his theories and their reception, glossary, bibliography, source notes, and reproductions of photographs. YAs can explore and discuss the *Newsweek* cover story (March 27, 2006) regarding Freud's contributions to modern science.

Sis, Peter. *The Wall: Growing Up Behind the Iron Curtain.* 2007. New York: Frances Foster Books, Farrar, Straus, and Giroux. All grades.

Feeling the need to show his family the cold, hard facts about his life before he settled in America, Czech-born Sis creates a stunning book that is also a tribute to his love of drawing and of music (both of which helped him keep hope alive) in Cold War Czechoslovakia. The picture book's design facilitates the integration of text (dates and events) into the work's illustrated content through black-and-white drawings with touches of red and through the use of illustrated full-color borders. Sis tells his story chronologically at the bottom of each unnumbered page and includes entries from the journals he kept when he was a child and a teenager. The dangers, fears, terrors, restraints, and censorship of that period literally overpowered every day and every part of his life at that time. Sis portrays this in his work, for example, by drawing himself as a tiny figure almost lost among hugely drawn Russian tanks, secret police, vicious dogs, and the ever-present red, pig-faced soldier spies. Readers can learn more about propaganda posters by going online and viewing a few of the thousands that were produced during the Cold War (e.g., the Soviet Poster a Day blog at http://sovietposter.blogspot .com—with advertisements—or Creative Stock Images at crestock.com, which emphasizes the posters' design and aesthetics).

NONFICTION OR INFORMATIONAL BOOKS

The most common terms for this genre are *informational books* and *nonfiction*, and the terms are used interchangeably. However, for YAs the term *nonfiction* is often favored. The Association for Library Service to Children (ALSC) succinctly defines works in this genre as "those written and illustrated to present, organize, and interpret documentable factual material" (ALSC, 2008). The ALSC also emphasizes "high quality in writing and illustration" (ALSC, 2006). To neglect the literary aspect of nonfiction is a put-down to the genre, to its authors, and to its readers because, as Milton Meltzer has noted, if only the facts count, then the telephone directory is nonfiction—"mechanically assembled . . . with no feeling behind it" (Carter and Abrahamson, 1990: 52). Yet, fact cannot be neglected, either. As Kathleen Krull (2006: 1) wrote, mixing fact and fiction "seems like cheating." Clearly, both documentable facts and literary creativity are required elements in nonfiction.

Thus, the genre's dual nature (facts melded with literary artistry) meets the demands of academic and leisure reading and benefits young people in a number of ways. As YAs peruse a range of informational books, they eventually learn that research is a process that concludes (sometimes) in a product. As YAs use the research aids that come with today's nonfiction, they have models for their own writing. They can see the variety of ways a table of contents can be formatted and examine the array of reproduced primary source materials now routinely found in nonfiction books. Using a bibliography and recommended readings, young people learn to become critical thinkers, realizing there may be many points of view on a given topic.

Marc Aronson (2006: 42), in an article in which he describes "art appreciation for nonfiction," noted that "the essence of the best nonfiction is originality" and addressed the issues of fact and art in nonfiction by adding that writers need to be "original not only in our theories but also in how we transmit them." Aronson identified five elements of nonfiction with which a work's originality can be evaluated: *conception* ("how the author thought about his or her work"), *organization, voice, research strategies,* and *design* (p. 43). By exploring these five elements, YAs can learn to evaluate works of nonfiction, whether it is works they read or works they create.

Evaluating Nonfiction

1. **Conception:** Has the author thought about the subject in a new and fresh way that represents a synthesis of his or her understanding and encourages an interest in the topic?

2. **Organization:** Has the author developed an original way to organize and present the information, or has the author mechanically assembled the facts (as they are in a telephone book) with no feeling for them? Is the organization evident? How does the organization function to enhance the narrative; that is, how does the organization flow from the author's conception?

3. **Voice:** What is the author's attitude toward the subject (e.g., biased or balanced)? What is the author's attitude toward the reader (e.g., respectful or condescending)? Does the author's style (manner of expression, such as figurative language) enhance the impact of the narrative for pleasure and understanding?

4. **Research strategies:** Did the author's research strategy (e.g., use of historical artifacts) support the conception of the book? Is the documentation sufficient to indicate that the work is accurate and to fulfill the reader's potential need for further reading? Is the presentation fair and balanced?

5. **Design:** Do the layout and the appearance (including the choice of graphics and their placement) engage and inform the reader?

Annotated Bibliography of Nonfiction

Armstrong, Jennifer. 1998. *Shipwreck at the Bottom of the World: The Extraordinary True Story of Shackleton and the Endurance.* New York: Scholastic. Grades 6 and up.

With the goal of being the first to cross the continent of Antarctica, Ernest Shackleton and 27 men depart in 1914 on a ship whose name, *Endurance,* becomes eerily ironic as the explorers survive the ship's sinking, life on moving ice floes, and near starvation before they are rescued. The author's voice is strong, employing a dramatic style, figurative language (e.g., "the fist of Antarctica" and "the face of the deep"), and vivid quotes from the survivors' journals. A character whom young people might find especially intriguing is Blackborrow, a teenage stowaway whose story is told in McKernan's (2005) *Shackleton's Stowaway*, a fine example of historical fiction, rich in research that links the two books for a potentially provocative discussion.

Colman, Penny. 1995. *Rosie the Riveter: Women Working on the Home Front in World War II.* **New York: Crown. Grades 10–12.**

Rosie the Riveter, an icon of American history, became the symbol of the social and historical milieu of World War II that motivated women to step into much-needed factory jobs. This exceptionally designed nonfiction book could inspire young people to use online resources to construct a poster created around the concept of Rosie to show the social history of the 1940s and her impact on the future. Two good Web sites are the Library of Congress's "Rosie the Riveter: Real Women Workers in World War II" (www.loc/gov/rr/program/journeys/rosie) and "Rosie the Riveter Home Front National Memorial Park" (www.rosietheriveter.org).

Fleischman, John. 2002. *Phineas Gage: A Gruesome but True Story About Brain Science.* **Boston: Houghton Mifflin. Grades 6 and up.**

Skilled and meticulous railroad foreman Phineas Gage lived to tell how a 13-pound iron rod flew 30 yards and drove through the frontal lobes of his brain. The author's research strategies involve the use of reproductions of artifacts, such as a historical photograph of Gage's skull and a drawing of the nineteenth-century pseudoscience of *phrenology* (determining the personality and character of a person by reading the bumps on the skull). Other illustrations demonstrate mid-nineteenth century understanding of how the brain worked. This story makes a riveting booktalk for YAs to prepare and present.

Freedman, Russell. 2007. *Who Was First? Discovering the Americas.* **New York: Clarion Books. Grades 5–9.**

Refuting that Columbus discovered America, this account of early North American history discusses artifacts and evidence of Viking runes, Chinese legends, Mayan stonework, and other objects yet inexplicable and mysterious. The work addresses long-held assumptions and presents history as an ever-evolving search for truth and understanding. Young people can browse the history books at their library and find statements that appear to disagree with the factual and documented evidence presented by Freedman. They can also speculate why some libraries keep works that appear out of date and other libraries discard them.

Hart, Christopher. 2001. *Manga Mania: How to Draw Japanese Comics.* **New York: Watson-Guptill. Grades 5 and up.**

For those who love to draw caricatures or cartoons, Hart introduces the basic elements of creating original art in the highly stylized format used in some Japanese comics.

Hart organizes the details of manga art by moving from the most basic shapes to sophisticated archetypal images in which a single line can define an emotion, age, or era. Young people can create their own manga by beginning at the point in the book that best suits their skill.

Janeczko, Paul B. 2004. *Top Secret: A Handbook of Codes, Ciphers, and Secret Writing.* **Illustrated by Jenna LaReau. Cambridge, MA: Candlewick Press. Grades 5–9.**

Presented in a spirit of fun and the camaraderie of two detectives (a boy and a girl in trench coats), the subject of language takes readers down a path where date shift ciphers, concealment techniques, and invisible inks rub elbows with word grille and pig Latin. The book's strength is Janeczko's playful voice, a sense of mock mystery, and the practicality of field kits to engage young people who might enjoy working in teams to solve the puzzles that Janeczko presents and solves.

Macauley, David. 2003. *Mosque.* **Boston, MA: Houghton Mifflin. Grades 5 and up.**

Inspired by the events on September 11, 2001, David Macauley undertook the building of a mosque. As in most of his works, Macauley, through design, takes readers inside, outside, upside, and downside at wide angles and narrow to the center of an architectural creation. Through discussion, young people can explore the universal human activities that the building's design serves.

Murphy, Jim. 2003. *An American Plague: The True and Terrifying Story of the Yellow Fever Epidemic of 1793.* **New York: Clarion Press. Grades 6–12.**

When yellow fever spreads to every Philadelphia neighborhood in 1793, almost everyone flees, leaving behind some freed slaves, a governmental group of 12, the poor, and the stricken. The synthesizing concept of this work is the use of individual perspectives in the chapters that reveal the dimensions of the horror, the blaming, the heroism, and the chaos. Young people can also read Anderson's (2000) *Fever 1793*, a historical novel with an eight-page appendix of historical and scientific information, and compare their emotional involvement in the novel with that in Murphy's individual chapters that present historically detailed perceptions.

Nathan, Amy. 2008. *Meet the Dancers: From Ballet, Broadway, and Beyond.* **New York: Henry Holt. Grades 5–8.**

Sixteen chapters, each devoted to a successful professional dancer, present a rounded view of childhood and teen efforts that contribute to adult careers in dance. The dancers share performance tips, recommendations for audition attire and preparation, and their schedules for practice, exercise, rehearsals, company classes, and returning home in the evening. Young people who are considering a career in dance will reflect on the different opportunities in the field and the many avenues to reach their goals and yet will understand challenges of uncertainties, including that of a relatively short career.

Nelson, Kadir. 2008. *We Are the Ship: The Story of Negro League Baseball.* **Illustrated by Kadir Nelson. New York: Hyperion. Grades 5–8.**

This beautifully illustrated book relates the history of Negro baseball in nine innings (chapters), presenting superstar players, the social context of a "rough life," a proud tradition of rivalry, and the league's economic downfall as white team owners picked one by one the best players without just compensation to owners of Negro teams. The book's title comes from a quotation by Rube Foster, "We are the Ship; all else is the sea" (n.p.). When the work is introduced to young people, they can be encouraged to discuss the metaphor from which the title was developed.

Springer, Jane. 2006. *Genocide*. Toronto, Canada: House of Anansi. Grades 7 and up.

This concise introduction to the concept of "'the most racist of crimes'" (p. 99) shows how thoughtful organization makes a work more accessible for young people. With only seven chapters, the book provides an annotated time line of genocides through history (pp. 120–125), definitions for every term (e.g., lengthy, legal definitions of *genocide, racism, ethnocentrism, bystanders, comfort women*, and *genocidaires*), a map, and further information. Although the author clearly believes that the world should deal with genocide more aggressively, she does explain the complications that make it difficult sometimes for countries to intervene in genocide. Young people can go online to Genocide Watch (www.genocidewatch.org) for more detailed information about the history and current status of the subject.

PICTURE BOOKS

Picture books are those works in which illustrations carry at least half the message. If pictures are less than half of the message, the work is an illustrated book. If pictures carry all of the message, the work is a wordless book. Traditionally, the audience of a picture book was the prereading child who sat near an adult and listened to the reading of the book while gathering meaning from the illustrations. By the 1980s, the targeted audience for picture books included young people in the upper elementary grades, but, at that time, if the picture book made its way into a high school setting, it was probably part of the art curriculum or parenting classes. English teachers were also early users of picture books from which they made concrete the abstract elements of criticism.

By the 1990s, the audience for picture books was unlimited. YAs who had grown up with picture books did not put them aside, and their parents displayed works like Graeme Base's (1987) *Animalia* at home. Furthermore, children's picture books were evolving from linear stories that lived comfortably on the page to nonlinear, postmodern tales with unexpected points of view, multiple meanings, and potential contradictions (e.g., David Macaulay's [1990] *Black and White*) that challenged the critical thinking of YAs.

In the 1990s, professionals in public and school libraries were widely promoting picture books to YAs. Bette Ammon and Gale Sherman (1996: xii), in *Worth a Thousand Words: An Annotated Guide to Picture Books for Older Readers*, listed "The Top Ten Reasons Why Teachers, Librarians, and Parents Should Provide Picture Books for Older Readers," emphasizing the broad appeal of picture book themes, art worthy of display in galleries, the importance of verbal and visual connections in learning, and the rich and succinct language of picture books. From vocabulary development and reading motivation to the introduction of complex subjects, picture books have found their way into library booktalks, high school secondary science classes, and professional workshops for librarians and teachers.

The Cooperative Children's Book Center's "Never Too Old: Picture Books to Share with Older Children and Teens" keeps an up-to-date list of picture book titles by genre (Schliesman, 2007). *Literature Lures: Using Picture Books and Novels to Motivate Middle School Readers*, by Nancy Polette and Joan Ebbesmeyer (2002), mixes picture books with YA novels by division into subjects and themes. Molly B. Pearson's (2005) *Big Ideas in Small Packages: Using Picture Books with Older Readers* encourages collaboration by organizing titles that link the books with the curriculum.

Evaluating Picture Books

To evaluate picture books for YAs or by YAs, the essence of picture book criticism lies in the integration of text and illustrations. Readers, to understand the art and meanings in picture books, benefit from knowing about the following:

- Basic media and techniques (e.g., chalk, pencil, collage, oil, pastel, watercolor, woodcuts, pen and ink, linoleum and wood cuts, tempera, cut paper, photography, scratchboard, and mixed media)
- Styles of art (e.g., cartoon, impression, expressionism, representational, realism, surrealism, pointillism, op-art, and folk art)
- The elements of art (e.g., line, texture, shape, and color)
- Basic design, including, page and book design (e.g., arrangement, framing, movement, emphases, format and size, balance, font size and type, position of text, the use of end-papers)

Consideration of these dimensions of picture book illustration can bring new insights from the seamless interworking of text and pictures, especially when focusing on the question: How are mood, perspective, culture, characterization, theme, setting, and action shaped by the work's media, artistic elements, style, and design?

Annotated Bibliography of Picture Books

Goldstein, Bobbye S., ed. 2003. *Mother Goose on the Loose: Cartoons from the* New Yorker. New York: Harry N. Abrams. Grades 6 and up.

This irreverent and witty collection of cartoons, many published in the *New Yorker*, invites YAs to take a second look at Mother Goose rhymes. These well-known classics of the nursery become twentieth and twenty-first century parodies and social commentary through pictures and text that reinterpret characters, setting, and actions.

Young people can be encouraged to produce an original cartoon after considering how three contemporary bears could use technology to find Goldilocks, how the dish might have reconsidered a marriage to the spoon, and what a cow might say to a pig as they watch a cow jump over the moon.

Hurston, Zora Neale. 2005. *Lies and Other Tall Tales*. New York: HarperCollins. Grades 6 and up.

Christopher Myers, adapter and illustrator, used paper and fabric collages to create literal interpretations of hyperbole and tall tales collected by Hurston from African-American traditions. A reader, when sharing the work with young people, can pause once after sharing the first of an episode (e.g., "The weather do make for some strange sights, I agree"), pause to let listeners imagine a comparison (e.g., "Like once, I seen it so dry, the fish came swimming up the road in dust"), invite young people to imagine what the scene would look like, and then share the collage of fish swimming in dust (p. 28). Young people can construct collage illustrations of scenes from tall tales or the figurative language and explain their use of color in light of the style and subject of the text.

Marzollo, Jean. 1993. *I Spy Mystery: A Book of Picture Riddles*. Illustrated by Walter Wick. New York: Scholastic. All grades.

Two pairs of rhyming couplets pose a riddle to be solved in each of the book's 13 double-page spreads of a photographed collection of objects. Many of the photographs use light and shadow to create a mood compatible with the collection or add information for the riddle's solution (e.g., the haze and shadows from sun spilling through a window behind a florist's cluttered workspace; long shadows that reveal side-view silhouettes of objects photographed from above; or the placement of camera and light to leave no shadow or sense of perspective). Young people can work in pairs to produce their own picture riddles, writing couplets for any of the book's photographs or for their own photographs of collections they assemble, as well as compile their own e-books for a library or classroom Web site.

Moore, Clement Clarke. 1989. *The Night Before Christmas or a Visit of St. Nicholas: An Antique Reproduction*. New York: Philomel. All grades.

The classic poem is illustrated by reproduced stone lithographs of an unknown artist who has defined the text's setting. Young people can consider this work and identify the visual details that create an integral setting, defining time, place, style, technologies, class, and portrayal of a traditional character. As an activity, young people can bring their own family editions of Moore's poem, creating a chronological display of illustrated versions that invite such comparisons as the evolution of the portrayal of St. Nicholas in popular culture.

Shea, Bob, and Lane Smith. 2008. *Big Plans*. New York: Hyperion. Grades 2 and up.

This picture storybook is about a little guy with big plans that spring from his imagination as he is obviously being kept after school for misbehavior. Marching through board rooms and the states of Missouri and Pennsylvania and on to the moon, he shouts, "I have plans. Are you in?" There is much for YAs to discover: The first double-page spread is rich in visual clues about the protagonist, presenting his self-defeating behaviors (e.g., his scheming bossiness revealed on the chalkboard), his isolation after school (3:00 displayed on the wall clock and empty seats in the classroom), and the source of his imaginative travels from wall maps and charts (e.g., phases of the moon and birds of the world). Young people can be encouraged to analyze the chaotic illustrations as a setting for an unlikable protagonist who does not know how to reach out to others, choosing to be important rather than "nice."

POETRY

Poetry, the oldest of genres, is the most difficult to define, although it does exhibit predictable traits. Poems

- probably look different on a page than a passage of prose;
- typically have rhythm or a beat;
- are expected to be compact and concise;
- may be as simple as a nursery rhyme or as abstract as a metaphysical ode;
- can express the full range of human emotions;
- take many forms (limericks, nonsense, sonnet, concrete); and
- must be experienced by a reader.

The difficulty in defining the genre is that the genre can be categorized by its shape, rhyming pattern (rhyme scheme), length, purpose (elegy), and topic. Furthermore, if prose and poetry were opposite ends of a continuum, there is no definable point that would separate poetry from prose. Traditional poetry flows into free verse, which except for line breaks may be indistinguishable from poetic prose (e.g., the King James Bible), which is a form of written language, and much of written language is often very much like ordinary spoken language. If one considers poetry's general traits, the only requirement is that it emotionally involves the reader, and that emotional involvement is based on the sounds and images within the poem. Therefore, one could define poetry as a concise and compact form of literature that utilizes sounds and images to involve the reader emotionally.

Poetry is usually the first genre a child is exposed to and can be drawn to its rhythm and rhyme and react with joy to the images in nursery rhymes. Yet, it has also been recognized as the genre that traditionally loses popularity with children as they grow up and as adolescents mature. What is all too often lost between the nursery and high school graduation is the emphasis on the pleasure that comes from the playfulness with the images and sounds of language. What often has been traded for the pleasure of the child is the formal critical analysis of poems read and not heard. However, adults who work with young people are increasingly aware that YAs who share poetry aloud recognize it as a natural form of expression that gives pleasure and understanding. Avenues for this kind of poetry sharing include self-selections of contemporary works that young people enact; presentation through multiple voices, poetry slams, open mikes, recitations, poet recordings, and monologues; and translations into artistic experiences that are musical or visual. In its simplest sense, "A poem is a composition written for performance by the human voice" (Ferguson, Salter, and Stallworthy, 1996: lxi) and that performance is poetry's connection to human emotions. Furthermore, the activities of selecting and reading poems shifts the ownership of the poem from adult to YA.

Evaluating Poetry

1. Is the work emotionally involving? (Did you like the poem? Did the poem leave you with questions? Did you enjoy rereading the poem? What personal experiences did you recall while reading the poem? What alternative title would you give the poem? Did you sense that other listeners had similar or different reactions to the poem? Did the poem suggest a universal truth? Is there someone you wish could hear the poem?)

2. If so, how do the sounds of the poem involve the reader? (What word sounds lingered in your mind after reading the poem? Are there any exact phrases or lines that you enjoy remembering? How would you describe the rhythm and rhyme of the poem? Did you hear any wordplay?)

3. How do the images of the poem involve the reader? (What images came to your mind while reading the poem? Can you imagine being what you have envisioned; can you be the fog on little cat feet? Are descriptive words startling or comforting or amusing or surprising or bewildering? Did you notice any figurative language?)

Annotated Bibliography of Poetry

Carlson, Lori M. 2005. *Hot Salsa: Bilingual Poems on Being Young and Latino in the United States.* New York: Henry Holt. Grades 7–12.

The lives of adolescents (secrets, family responsibilities, prejudice, parties, and, of course, love) are explored on every page of this book. Addressing the sounds of the collection, the author describes a typical but lively conversation in a contemporary urban setting: "a mix of languages, in a streety English hip-hop and a swoony lyricism spiked with Spanish" (p. ix). When read aloud, these poems offer young people an opportunity to compare the poetic rhythms of Spanish and English.

Eleveld, Mark, and Marc Smith. 2003. *Spoken Word Revolution: Slam, Hip Hop & the Poetry of a New Generation.* Napierville, IL: Sourcebooks. Grades 8–12.

With poems and ideas about enjoying poetry from Billy Collins, Sherman Alexie, Andre Condrescu, and Luis J. Rodriguez, this book emphasizes the musicality of poetry, and it comes with a CD. Black and white illustrations (with slices of red) add energy to the lively text. This book and *Slam,* by Cecily von Ziegesar (2000), will give students a fine introduction to poetry slams and performance art.

Engle, Margarita. 2008. *The Surrender Tree: Poems of Cuba's Struggle for Independence.* **New York: Henry Holt. Grades 9 and up.**

By presenting the history of Cuba's nineteenth-century struggle for freedom through the eyes of a legendary healer, Rosa la Bayamesa, and others, this narrative in verse portrays history as close to the earth as possible and in the present tense as if the events had just occurred. Magic realism lives around Rosa and her husband Jose, who heal anyone they encounter, including slave-hunter turned soldier Lieutenant Death, Rosa's lifelong enemy who has sworn to kill her. The Cuban struggle for independence coincided with the freeing of its slaves and ended at the Surrender Tree in Santiago, Cuba, when Spain gave the Cuban people over to the United States. Young people can discover more about the three wars (although to Rosa it seemed like one long war) by going online to such sites as the History of Cuba Web site (www.historyofcuba.com/cuba.htm, created and maintained by J.A. Sierra).

George, Kristine O'Connell. 2002. *Swimming Upstream: Middle School Poems.* **New York: Clarion Press. Grades 4–7.**

The years spent in middle school, which can be a period of major transition in a young person's life, are the setting for the speaker to record her tumultuous years' experiences. A variety of 65 poems is presented, including an acrostic poem, free verse, and haiku, all of which punctuate the collection with the progressing development of the speaker's flute expertise and, thus, her own personal growth. Young people can take photographs in their school and use them to illustrate the poetic images in the collection or to illustrate their own poems.

Grandits, John. 2004. *Technically, It's Not My Fault: Concrete Poems.* **New York: Clarion Press. Grades 6–8.**

Twenty-eight concrete poems express the gamut of interests and concerns of middle school YAs, such as sports ("The Lay-up" and "Robert's Four At-Bats"), computers ("New Game, Old Computer"), and food ("Stop Playing with Your Food!"). Each poem is an integration of visual and verbal imagery. Emphasizing the book's humor and play is the last poem, "The Little House," which explains, "Building a poem is like building a little house" and then illustrates how simple it can be for YAs to create their own concrete poems.

Nelson, Marilyn. 2005. *A Wreath for Emmett Till.* **Boston: Houghton Mifflin. Grades 6 and up.**

The tragic story of a child's senseless murder is structured in the form of a crown of sonnets, evoking the grief caused by the crime that ignited the Civil Rights movement. Nelson uses an old sonnet form, the *crown of sonnets,* defined as "a sequence of sonnets so interwoven as to form a 'crown' of formal praise for the one to whom they are addressed" (Preminger, 1974: 174). Focusing on the image of the crown as one of honor, students can understand the circular nature of the 15 poems as each one begins with the last line of the previous poem, thus making "Rosemary for remembrance, Shakespeare wrote" the first line of the first and fifteenth poems and the last line of the fourteenth poem.

Nye, Naomi Shihab. 2002. *19 Varieties of Gazelle: Poems of the Middle East.* **New York: Greenwillow Books. Grades 5 and up.**

The author's introduction to the anthology explains, "All my life I thought about the Middle East, wrote about it, wondered about it, lived in it, visited it, worried about it, loved it. We are blessed and doomed at the same time" (p. xii). Rich images create the paradox of being blessed and doomed. Young people can discuss the poetic images that communicate Nye's diverse feelings toward her subject.

Plath, Sylvia. 2004. *Ariel.* **The Restored Edition. New York: HarperPerennial. Adult book for YAs.**

Written during a harsh London winter, this emotionally involving collection reflects the imagery of a poet struggling with her successes and failures, her love for her children, and her troubled marriage. This restored edition presents Plath's original selections and their arrangement and includes some facsimile drafts. Kate Moses's (2003) *Wintering: A Novel of Sylvia Plath* uses the poems in *Ariel* for her chapter titles, including the final called "Wintering." Young people can read *Ariel*, then *Wintering*, and discuss Plath's imagery, which stuns, shocks, and engrosses.

Rosenberg, Liz, ed. 2000. *Light-Gathering Poems.* **New York: Henry Holt. Grades 7–12.**

Alphabetically arranged poems focused on one topic yields a serendipitous reading of verses from the familiar (Robert Frost) to the classic (Issa and Rumi). Young people may become especially involved in the poetry by rereading a poem after reading the poet's biographical sketch in the editor's endnotes. Alternatively, they may choose to construct a bulletin board of quotations they like, for example, "I had a lover's quarrel with the world" Robert Frost (p. 110).

Shakur, Tupac. 1999. *The Rose That Grew from Concrete.* **New York: Pocket Books. Adult book for YAs.**

Presented as reproductions of his handwritten copies, the 72 brief poems cover such topics as love, family, poverty, and life in the 'hood. Young people can compare the work's title poem ("The Rose that Grew from Concrete") with "Flower in the Crannied Wall" by Alfred Lord Tennyson (1809–1892), considering motifs (image) used by a Victorian poet and a twentieth-century rapper.

Smith, Hope Anita. 2008. *Keeping the Night Watch.* **Illustrated by E. B. Lewis. New York: Henry Holt. Grades 5–8.**

Thirty-five free verse poems chronicle the fall, winter, and spring of the return of 13-year-old C.J.'s dad into the life of his family. Family members sit stiff and awkward at their first dinner together; their conversations are too nice; their questions unanswerable. YAs who find this poetry (perhaps after hearing a booktalk) are ready for the story they expect, and they may appreciate emotional space for reflection or choose a structured response like readers theatre.

SHORT STORIES

Written in prose, the short story is a compact, fictional narrative that tends to focus on character and action, to have tightly unified literary elements, and to create a single effect or impression on the reader. Short stories have more structure than sketches or tales but less interrelated development of character and action than novels. Edgar Allan Poe (1842: 887–896), in his classic essay "The Philosophy of Composition," emphasized the short story's unity of effect (which he linked to the author's genius), its power to integrate every word and literary element toward a unique effect, and its brevity, which allows a complete reading within one sitting (or one hour). About the genre's unity, Poe explained that a skillful literary artist begins a short story with a preconceived single effect and uses every word to achieve that end.

In one sense, the short story is as old as human storytelling—a traditional and universal medium for transmitting the brief narratives that have taught and entertained people across cultures and eras. Yet, when discussing the origin of the short story, some people identify Poe, the first to clearly articulate its nature, to be its creator. First influenced by romanticism, genre writers incorporated succeeding literary theories as well. However, it was the New Critics' emphasis on the literary text and on the importance of compactness and economy that renewed for the twentieth century Poe's early appreciation of the artistic skill required by the short story. Furthermore, the multicultural experiences and visions of the twenty-first century are enriching the short story and also integrating it once again with the tales and myths of the oral tradition.

For their brevity alone, short stories have a special place in YA collections and programs. Because they can be read in one sitting, short stories are well suited to read-alouds in classroom or library settings, and they can be recommended to parents who want to read and discuss literature with their YAs. Furthermore, readers who want to sample a specific genre (e.g., fairy tale revisions or horror/supernatural) can do so easily (and without the time commitment required for a novel) with an anthology of such stories written by a variety of outstanding authors. For literature programming, a large group may share a short story that introduces a literary movement (e.g., realism or naturalism), a historical setting (e.g., the Civil War), or a genre and discuss the work's significant aspects before breaking into smaller groups for a deeper consideration of different sets of novels. Finally, collections that are not sequences can be chosen for in-depth study of a particular theme (e.g., Betsy Hearne's [2003] *Canine Connection*), topic or issue (e.g., Marion Dane Bauer's [1995] *Am I Blue?*), or culture (e.g., the stories in Jane Kurtz's [2004] *Memories of Sun*) that, through multiple lenses, create an overall effect greater than their sum.

A special consideration for short stories, as for poetry, involves ease of finding and accessing them. In addition to multiple retrospective and current printed finding aids, there is also H.W. Wilson's (2008) electronic database "Short Story Index," which provides author, title, and subject information about more than 72,000 short stories as well as how to access them, locally or via interlibrary loan. Another consideration about the use of the short story collection, again as for poetry, readers need time to browse and develop a feeling for the variety and range of anthologies and collections available, fulfilling the information-seeking strategy of berry picking, as described by Marcia Bates (1991).

Evaluating Short Stories

1. Is the plot clear, coherent, and satisfying?
2. Is the plot launched in the first line, advancing without detours to the end of the story?
3. Does the story have a simplicity of style that involves the reader on a direct and concrete level as well as a complex and symbolic level?
4. Are the characters typical (and believable) yet distinctly individual through an unobtrusive development that includes little direct description to interfere with the imaginative vision of the reader?
5. Does the narration represent the shortest possible distance between the beginning of the story and a swift conclusion?

Annotated Bibliography of Short Stories

Abrahams, Peter, et al. 2008. *Up All Night: A Short Story Collection.* **New York: Laura Geringer Books/HarperTeen. Grades 8 and up.**

Six stories by six authors share setting: all take place in that "vulnerable" hour (p. 113) between deep night and nearly morning. The stories also share protagonists who change in some quiet, but for them, powerful way. Lara and Neddy lead their mother out of her despair and into hope following the unexpected death of their father in Peter Abrahams' "Phase Two." Sarah and Phil meet for the first time and discover it is the "fear of loneliness" (p. 150) that keeps people from opening up to others in David Levithan's "The Vulnerable Hours"; the calm, cool unnamed narrator of "Orange Alert" teaches her army stepfather Ed that she is to be respected—or else. YAs will find this anthology a perfect source to use for a booktalk.

Carter, Alden R. 2006. *Love, Football, and Other Contact Sports.* **New York: Holiday House. Grades 8–11.**

The usual cliques (jocks, bullies, and nerds) who attend small-town Argyle West High School tell their upbeat stories from first person points of view. Argyle's most popular students, star football player Keith and school journalist Sarah, are one thread that connects the 14 stories; another is the theme of the community of YAs and the ways they resolve conflicts and discover for themselves the right things to do. Young people, after reading the chronologically arranged stories, can assume the point of view of one of the characters who appears in multiple stories and explain that character's point of view and motivation as they discuss familiar school-life issues that they confront, such as gender equality, dating, or bullies.

Fleischman, Paul. 1998. *Whirligig.* **New York: Holt. Grades 7 and up.**

Unknown to Brent Bishop, the whirligigs he has built in the four corners of the United States (as restitution for the accidental death of Lea Zamora) have restored the lives of strangers who observe certain qualities within each work that he has built. With the controlling focus being Brent's initiation, the book's nine nonlinear stories are told from different points of view in which the reader is more aware of the theme of renewal through redemption than Brent, who cannot perceive the outcomes of his endeavors. Young people can choose one of Brent's constructions and create their conception of it in their format of choice.

Gallo, Donald R., ed. 2004. *First Crossing: Stories About Teen Immigrants.* **Cambridge, MA: Candlewick Press. Grades 7 and up.**

YAs whose countries of origin include Romania, Palestine, and Kazakhstan find life in the United States a mix of pleasure and discomfort. Alden R. Carter's "The Swede" relates the antagonist's point of view, a boy whose hatred and revenge fuel his bullying of the teen Swede, resulting in the protagonist's emotional conflict and regret. Young people can use a graphic organizer like a branching tree to illustrate how various issues (e.g., errors in communication or jealousy) can lead to conflict and misunderstanding among cultures.

Kurtz, Jane. 2004. *Memories of Sun: Stories of Africa and America.* **New York: Amistad/ Greenwillow Books. Grades 5–10.**

In exotic settings such as Kartoum, Senegal, and Tunisia, a variety of young immigrants share common problems, such as the search for identity, as they struggle to fit in with peers and adults in their new countries. A dozen stories and three poems comprise this collection of many voices that explore "Africans in Africa," "Americans in Africa," and "Africans in America." Readers can create a large literary map of Africa and pinpoint all the locales of the stories and share their illustrations with others.

Lanagan, Margo. 2005. *Black Juice.* **New York: Eos. Grades 9–12.**

This Printz Honor Book collection provides new insights into the forces of good and evil in unfamiliar environments. Some characters reach an epiphany as they move through frightening or dystopian settings. Comparisons with classic stories will be inevitable, such as "Sing My Sister Down" with Shirley Jackson's "The Lottery." "Wooden Bride" should strike a chord with those who find the excesses of contemporary weddings an appropriate target for social satire. Young people can examine one of the ten stories for its use of inventive language, whether its approach illuminates the theme or the success or failure of its social satire.

Levithan, David. 2008. *How They Met, and Other Stories.* **New York: Alfred A. Knopf. Grades 9 and up.**

The elusive subject of love is brought down to earth in this collection of 18 vignettes told from various points of view and by characters of different ages, although most of the protagonists are teenagers. While some of the stories are poignantly realistic, many employ a humorous narrator, such as Gabriel in "Starbucks Boy," who tells how his six-year-old charge, Arabella, plays successful matchmaker for him; Damon in "The Good Witch," who escorts his friend Sally to the prom and is left speechless when he sees her in a poofy pink dress that reminds him too much of *The Wizard of Oz*'s Glinda; and James and Sally, who, in "A Romantic Inclination," consider the possibility of becoming more than friends by using the terminology of physics to arrive at their conclusion. YAs can create a visual art work that addresses any of the stories' subjects.

Myers, Walter Dean. 2000. *145th Street: Short Stories.* New York: Delacorte. Grades 6 and up.

Using a *cinema verite* style to portray all the dimensions of life in present-day Harlem, the collection remains true to the vagaries of fate as well as to the role of self-determination within a community of finely drawn individuals (e.g., "Monkeyman" presents a young artist who uses his intelligence to defeat the street's most violent gang; "Fighter" is about an unsuccessful boxer who ignores his wife's pleas to stop his career in the ring; or "The Streak," about Jamie Farrell, who has a long run of good luck). With its variety of teen and adult characters, the collection provides opportunities for graphic and illustrated responses, such as bulletin boards, body biographies, or collage art.

Oates, Joyce Carol. 2003. *Small Avalanches and Other Stories.* New York: HarperCollins. Grades 9–12.

Illustrating the deft handling of short story criteria, these dozen eerie stories share the common theme about the role that fate plays in life brings change but not necessarily for the better. Nancy, in the title story, answers a stranger's every question with, "I don't know," resulting in rescuing herself from his menacing clutches but questionably involving herself in his probable death. In "Capricorn," Melanie's Internet chat-mate shows up and transforms Melanie's self-image of "14 going on 19" into that of a confused child haunted by guilt. For discussions, young people can read short stories written from a male perspective, such as Adam Bagdasarian's (2002) *First French Kiss: And Other Traumas.*

Peck, Richard. 2004. *Past Perfect, Present Tense.* New York: Dial Press. Grades 7 and up.

Divided into four sections—"The First," "The Past," "The Supernatural," and "The Present"—the stories provide inside information on the genesis of some of Peck's most popular characters and books. Besides the 13 stories, there are two chapters on writing, "How to Write a Short Story" and "Five Helpful Hints." Young people familiar with Peck's books and interested in writing will enjoy discussing his ideas on the craft.

SPECULATIVE FICTION

The Library of Congress (www.loc.gov/acq/devpol/scific.html) Collection Policy on fantasy and science fiction states that

Fantasy includes the sub-genres of science fiction, horror and adaptations of traditional myths. The distinguished writer, Arthur C. Clarke, has stated that "any sufficiently advanced technology is undistinguishable from magic" (*Omni*, April 1980: 87). This view is borne out by the fact that the distinctions between science fiction and the various other sub-genres of fantasy are indeed blurred at times and usually artificial. In fact, many authors in the genre frequently cross these artificial barriers in mid-work or mid-career. Publishers, furthermore, often confuse these sub-genre identifications even further by failing to differentiate among them.

The Library of Congress's definition of fantasy is artistically and practically liberating. It is compatible with G. Robert Carlsen's (1980) explanation that fantasy and science fiction exist as opposite ends of a continuum where the author's imagination drifts between what a reader knows to be clearly fantasy and clearly science fiction. Furthermore, in *Literature for Today's Young Adults*, Donelson and Nilsen (1989: 187) addressed the two as imaginative literature and set criteria for it:

- A smooth, unhackneyed way of establishing the imaginative world
- An originality of concept—enough relationship to the real world so that the reader is led to look at the world in a new way or from a new viewpoint
- Something that stimulates readers to participate in that author's creative thinking and to carry the story further in their own minds
- A rigorous adherence to the "rules" of the imaginative world so that the story is internally consistent even though it may break with the physical laws of this world as they are now known

These criteria are comfortable at either end of Carlsen's (1980) continuum.

Although the most censored of genres, speculative fiction is also considered by many authors and critics to be the most moral. Its overarching value to readers is that it is encourages the extension of personal ethics to a universal perspective unlimited by the familiar or the contemporary. The genre also encourages reading because of its audience's proclivity to follow a series (e.g., *Harry Potter*), an author (e.g., Garth Nix), a topic (e.g., the left behind), or an issue in the popular culture (e.g., advancements in biotechnology). Subgenres of speculative fiction include the following:

- *Fantasy*, which extends the magical world of mythology to contemporary adolescent readers
- *Gothic*, which allows young people to consider and investigate the nature of unexplainable evil without risk
- *Science fiction*, which requires that we consider the societal and personal consequences of scientific change

Furthermore, some readers of science fiction find motivation from being part of a large and diverse fan base.

Fantasy

Fantasy is a "fictitious work in which the characters, actions, and/or setting are deliberately freed from reality. . . . There are two types of fantasy: high fantasy (which occurs in another world where physical and human laws do not exist) and low fantasy (which, though set in the real world, presents events that are magical)" (Latrobe, Brody, and White, 2002: 70–71). Either high or low, fantasy allows readers to look at themselves from a distance; however, it is high fantasy that often forces the hard questions about human assumptions, including those about good and evil. High fantasy forces these questions in a spirit of respect and seriousness, and it is high fantasy that reaches back across the millennia to its roots in the ancient mythologies that inspire wonder and define archetypal themes. However, in modern high fantasy, each story must be fresh and ingenious and especially believable, or pages will not be turned.

Evaluating Fantasy

1. Is the work original and ingenious and fresh? (How does the author creatively manage the plot?)

2. Is the work believable? (Are magical elements internally consistent and logically framed? Is the fantasy grounded in reality, buttressed by careful details, and confirmed by the beliefs and understandings of any characters? Does the story's conclusion confirm the existence of imaginary elements? How does point of view function in the development of the story's credibility?)

3. Do the author's language and attitude create a sense of wonder? (How do style [e.g., use of elegant language] and tone [e.g., portrayal of the author's genuine investment in the story] work together to encourage a reader's suspension of disbelief and participation in the author's creativity?)

4. Does the work have a significant theme? (Within the fanciful world, does an eternal verity emerge from the imaginary struggle between good and evil? How does the main character's value system overcome his or her vulnerabilities?)

Gothic Literature

One of the most popular genres with YAs, but one of the most contentious for its detractors, gothic literature includes such classics as Christopher Marlowe's (c. 1588, 2008) play *The Tragical History of Doctor Faustus*, which portrays the protagonist who sells his soul to the devil; and Horace Walpole's *The Castle of Otranto* (1764, 2001), which portrays the defining gothic setting, a dark, isolated one, suspenseful to the extent that perceptions cannot distinguish the supernatural from the natural. The popularity of gothic stories over time is remarkable. Among significant and classic gothic works are Charlotte Bronte's *Jane Eyre* (1847, 2006), Bram Stoker's *Dracula* (1897, 1993), William Faulkner's "A Rose for Emily" (1930, 1950), and Robert Cormier's *Fade* (1988), along with bestsellers by Anne Rice and Stephen King. New Zealander Juliet Marillier's novels (2000–2008), classified as fantasy but containing elements of mythology, historical saga, and romance, have been received with popular and critical success. But the biggest success in the early twenty-first century is Stephenie Meyer's "Twilight Saga" series (2005–2008), attracting readers who ordinarily do not read gothic fiction that features vampires.

Evaluating Gothic Literature

1. Do techniques of characterization reveal complex psychological figures?
2. Is the atmosphere emotionally palpable, integral, and/or symbolic?
3. Are familiar archetypes (or even stereotypes) of the genre strengthened or augmented by the author's original creation (e.g., the housewife in Levin's [1967] *Rosemary's Baby* may outwardly be a sophisticated New Yorker but also is a woman isolated in an apartment and vulnerable to the man she loves).

Science Fiction

What is science fiction?

Jules Verne: *voyages extraordinaire*
H.G. Wells: *scientific romance*
Ursula LeGuin: *thought experiment*
Robert Heinlein: *speculative fiction*
Damon Knight: *what we mean when we point at it*

Science fiction is a restless genre that defies conventions. Its fluid and often limitless nature stems perhaps from its having origins in both the arts and literature and the scientific disciplines. From the arts and literature, the genre has shifted and grown as literary elements (e.g., romance, adventure, historical fiction, and mystery) have been integrated into the genre. From the sciences, the genre has evolved with each new scientific discovery and theory. The integration of science fiction and science has been obvious to critics of the genre who argue that fiction influences science (e.g., the exploration of space and humankind's landing on the moon) and that science influences fiction (e.g., representation of the submarine in Verne's [1870, 2001] *20,000 Leagues Under the Sea*). Thus, the genre appears to be evolving from two modes of thinking—the imaginative and the scientific.

Science fiction author and critic Damon Knight was not flippant when he defined science fiction as "what we mean when we point at it" (Gunn and Candelaria, 2005: x). Definitions of the genre often reflect the intuitive individuality of the definer. Damon Knight had set out to accommodate the breadth of the genre and the readers' need for an idiosyncratic perspective. His solution was to list many definitions of science fiction, categorizing the most promising in terms of inclusion in science fiction literary works. He then applied them to award-winning works

(Knight, 1977: 63), creating a list of elements that appeared in works accepted to be science fiction. Based on the ideas of six different authorities of the genre—J.O. Bailey, Reginold Bretnor, Basil Davenport, Hugo Gernsback, Robert Heinlein, and Walter Miller—Knight (1977: 63) defines science fiction as that which contains:

1. Science (Gernsback)
2. Technology and invention (Heinlein, Miller)
3. The future and the remote past, including all the time travel stories (Bailey)
4. Extrapolation (Davenport)
5. Scientific method (Bretnor)
6. Other places—planets, dimensions, etc., including visitors from the above (Bailey)
7. Catastrophes, natural or manmade (Bailey)

Knight (1977: 64) maintains that a "story containing three or more of the elements . . . is usually perceived as science fiction; with two, it is perceived as borderline; with one or none, it is non-science fiction." For example, George Orwell's (1949) *1984* has three of the listed elements (technology, the future, and extrapolation) and is thus perceived as science fiction, whereas Lewis Carroll's (1971) *Alice in Wonderland* has only one element (other places) and therefore is not perceived as science fiction.

Although the genre has its modern roots in English romanticism, and although many critics would identify Mary Shelley's (2001) *Frankenstein* or Edgar Allan Poe's psychological short stories or Jules Verne's (1870, 2001) *20,000 Thousand Leagues Under the Sea* as the first science fiction, the genre's modern history had at least begun by 1929 when Hugo Gernsback coined the term *science fiction* in his magazine *Science Wonder Stories*. (Perhaps the term would have been used earlier if grammarians had allowed a noun to modify a noun.) The first generally acclaimed literary novel published at the beginning of the genre's modern history is Aldous Huxley's (1932) *Brave New World*, establishing one of the genre's major subjects (dystopia) for the remainder of the twentieth and into the twenty-first century.

During the 1930s, Gernsback and other editors of inexpensive pulp magazines introduced an array of new science fiction authors to the mass market. In the late 1930s the physicist, writer, and editor John W. Campbell had a significant influence on the genre; he

- raised the standard for acceptable scientific fact and theory in science fiction;
- emphasized human issues in science fiction;
- demanded rounder characters, discarding old stereotypes (e.g., the mad scientist) and emphasizing realistic characters, such as engineers; and
- discovered and promoted the best science fiction writers of his day (e.g., Heinlein, Asimov, Clark).

Perhaps unique to the genre of science fiction is its large and influential number of fans. Since the 1940s, the genre's highly energetic fans have exponentially affected what was already a fluid and seemingly limitless genre. Roger Luckhurst (2005: 17) explains the fans' influence as "one of the most distinctive anthropological elements of SF [science fiction] culture: the dedicated fan-base that has generated its own world of magazines, newssheets, *samizdat* [i.e., clandestinely printed and distributed] commentary, conventions and fan-fictions."

Critics recognize that fans contribute to the genre's literary integrity; for example, Algis Budrys (1983: 402) notes that fans consider a novel worthy of attention only if it reflects a serious attitude by the author and possesses "character development," pointing out that fans "have a considerable contempt for the mere action novel." It was also fans (members of the World Science Fiction Society) who, in 1953, established the Hugo Award, and it is still the fans today who attend the conference each year and vote for the award winners.

The science fiction novels published after World War II were "with a few exceptions, published by fan presses established for [this] purpose" (Gunn, 1983: 329). (However, Scribner's distributed Heinlein's "Future History" series, bringing to libraries reputable science fiction for YAs from 1950 to 1958 and illustrating the unique path by which science fiction developed.) Gunn also explains that few traditional publishers were interested in science fiction and that the fan presses rarely survived beyond the publishing "of a few books" (p. 329).

Finally, science fiction blockbuster films have contributed to science fiction's increasing popularity. One measure of the relationship between the genre and popular culture is the fact that science fiction is "the most fertile area of writing in the production of new words which *endured* in the English language—a position held up till the mid-thirties by poetry" (Delaney, 1983: 412).

Evaluating Science Fiction

1. Which of the list of Knight's seven elements for defining science fiction are represented in the work?
2. How do these elements demonstrate moral or ethical dilemmas for the characters?

Annotated Bibliography of Speculative Fiction

Fantasy

Almond, David. 1998. *Skellig*. New York: Delacorte. Grades 5–9.

Fighting back despair over his yet to be named infant sister's poor health, Michael takes on the care of an enigmatic winged creature that has lost all hope. Lyrically written, the novel contains allusions and motifs, including the motif of birds (Falcon Road, Mina and her bird drawings, multiple owl characters, the ominous blackbirds). Young people may be reminded of the novel's question, "'How can a bird that is born for joy / Sit in a cage and sing?' William Blake" (p. 50) and be encouraged to frame Michael's confrontation with mortality, truth versus reality, the importance of creativity, and the name "Joy" given to the baby sister.

Hoffman, Mary. 2003. *Stravaganza: City of Stars*. New York: Bloomsbury Publishing. Grades 7 and up.

Reaching the point of no return in order to get away from her abusive stepbrother's "harassment of hate" (p. 20), Georgia O'Grady creates a fantasy world "where horses had wings and she could fly away from her troubles forever" (p. 54). Second in the "Stravaganza" series, in this sixteenth-century parallel world, it is Remus who defeated Romulus, and his legacy is a hotbed of Machiavellian treacheries. Georgia learns she is one of the special Stravagantes, "a traveler between two worlds" (p. 88), and keeps her talisman always with her. YAs could create a literary map based on Georgia's descriptions of the dazzling city with its zodiac-like layout of the streets into the Twelve of Remora (Chapter 3).

Marcus, Leonard S., ed. 2006. *The Wand in the Word: Conversations with Writers of Fantasy*. Cambridge, MA: Candlewick Press. Grades 6–9.

Indicative of the respect now afforded to a once neglected genre, this anthology offers YAs a behind-the-scenes look at the composition of some of their favorite stories. Marcus interviews 13 authors (including Lloyd Alexander, Philip Pullman, Jane Yolen, and Diana Wynne Jones) and provides for each two photographs (current and as a child or YA), a sample of revised pages, and a list of popular titles. Young people are encouraged to follow up on their favorite authors online and search for fan Web sites or official Web sites.

McCaffrey, Anne. 1976. *Dragonsong*. New York: Atheneum. Grades 6 and up.

After Menolly's father prohibits her from displaying her musical talent, she runs away to the mysterious but friendly Weyr people, who respect her love of music and the "fire lizard" eggs that she has found and nurtured. This fully realized fantasy set on the planet Pern is a novel in the Harper Hall trilogy. "Thread spores," "Masterharper," "Holdmaster," and "fire lizards" are imaginative words found in the series; young people may be encouraged to brainstorm the imaginative terms they might have used for these denotations as well as other terms that arise in this trilogy or other high fantasies.

Naifeh, Ted. 2002. *Courtney Crumrin and the Night Things*. Portland, OR: Oni. Grades 8–12.

Living with her uncle Aloysius and her notorious family name, the new girl in town disables goblins, uses potions to exact justice against school bullies, and thwarts a mutant hobbit and a doppelganger. Under the tutelage of her gentle uncle, the Master Magician, Courtney's story shows how life at school and at home can sometimes be more frightening than the "night things" that lurk under a child's bed, as Naifeh points out in the introduction to this volume. In discussions, YAs could compare how Courtney, other fictional characters, and real young people deal with such common problems as confronting fears, feeling like an outcast, or lacking self-confidence.

Paolini, Christopher. 2003. *Eragon.* **New York: Knopf. Grades 7–12.**

This high fantasy, the first in the Inheritance trilogy, introduces an adolescent hero and a magical dragon whose partnership allows them to pursue evil but then results in their pursuit by evil. The integral and detailed setting is introduced on the book's endpapers as a literary map. Young people may be encouraged to illustrate specific sites on the map and in a book discussion to explain how their illustrations depict details that define the relationship of the boy and dragon characters and the plot's conflict of good and evil.

Pullman, Philip. 1998. *Clockwork—Or All Wound Up.* **Illus. Leonid Gore. New York: Scholastic. Grades 5–8.**

On a wintry evening long, long ago in Glockenheim, Fritz entertains friends around a cozy fire to tell one of his popular ghost stories, when the party is interrupted by the appearance of one of the characters he has just created, the malevolent Dr. Kalmenius. Only Karl, a clockwork apprentice, remains to hear what Kalmenius has to offer him. As in many good fantasies, the theme reveals how the power of love is greater than the power of evil. YAs can read the story aloud and comment on the contribution of illustrations in creating the tale's eerie, menacing atmosphere.

Sandell, Lisa Ann. 2007. *Song of the Sparrow.* **New York: Scholastic Press. Grades 8 and up.**

In this verse novel that relates an Arthurian tale, young Elaine of Ascolat inadvertently helps Arthur win an important battle as she takes an arrow through her heart, creating a diversion, as Saxon warriors believe she is really dead. As a child, Elaine watched as Picts terrorized and then murdered her mother; as a teenager, she performs healing arts on the knights within Arthur's encampment, feeling like a member of their family. Students may read Tennyson's *The Lady of Shalott* for a comparison of the theme of a young woman's breaking out of confinement.

Tolkien, J.R.R. 2001. *The Hobbit: An Illustrated Edition of the Fantasy Classic.* **Illustrated by David Wenzel and adapted by Charles Dixon with Sean Deming. New York: Ballantine. Grades 5–12.**

When Gandalf asks Bilbo Baggins to assist him in taking back their king's treasures from an evil dragon, the once-timid Bilbo plunges into the adventure which ends at Lonely Mountain. This acclaimed graphic novel artistically and faithfully adapts Tolkien's fantasy with panels of bright colors that augment the medieval setting. Young people may listen to a reading of Tolkien's narrative description of a setting (perhaps, for example, a passage related to one of the novel's large panel illustrations) and be challenged to consider how the illustration contributes to their more developed understanding of setting.

Gothic Novels

Allie, Scott, ed. 2004. *The Dark Horse Book of Witchcraft.* **Milwaukie, OR: Dark Horse Books. Adult book for YAs.**

Beginning with an adaptation of the scene of the three witches just prior to the arrival of "something wicked" in Shakespeare's *Macbeth*, this anthology of five graphic narratives, one interview, and one illustrated prose story presents variations on old legends and tales along with entirely new ones having to do with the stereotypes of witches. Evan Dorkin and Jill Thompson's humorous "The Unfamiliar" received the Eisner Award for Best Short Story for its slant on a world takeover attempt by cats and their goddess, Sekhmet, that is stopped by the bravery of one little orphan cat and Rex the dog. The diversity of art styles provides YAs the opportunity to discuss how a story's art illuminates theme or other story elements.

Atwater-Rhodes, Amelia. 1999. *In the Forests of the Night.* New York: Random House. Grades 7 and up.

Set in Concord, Massachusetts, during the dawn of the Age of Reason, this first person narrative of how Rachel becomes Risika the vampire captures the eerie atmosphere of New England that is reminiscent of Nathaniel Hawthorne. Risika immediately dismisses most of the myths about vampires and does so almost tongue in cheek. Although now dead over 300 years, she defies the stereotype through her independence, strength, and intelligence. YAs who like this first of Atwater-Rhodes' now ten books on vampires and shape-shifters might enjoy visiting her official Web site at Random House and read about this interesting young author.

Durant, Alan. 2004. *Vampire.* Boston, MA: Kingfisher. Grades 5–10.

This selection of 18 vampire stories includes a wide range of authors—from Bram Stoker, Saki, and Arthur Conan Doyle to Jane Yolen and Woody Allen. The stories, varied in style, include a classic excerpt from *Dracula* (Stoker, 1897, 1993). An adult could introduce these stories by reading one, for example, Woody Allen's "Count Dracula," which ends with the baker's wife's comic line, "Does this mean dinner's off tonight?"

Gaiman, Neil. 2002. *Coraline.* New York: HarperCollins. Grades 6-8.

Coraline copes with two worlds, a real one with love but busy parents and a surreal one with evil and terrifying elements capable of stealing her real parents. The surreal images are a powerful element in this haunting novel. Young people may be encouraged to develop collage illustrations suggested by the novel's eerie black and white sketches.

Gaiman, Neil. 2008. *Coraline: Graphic Novel.* New York: HarperCollins. Grades 6–8.

The graphic novel format of the above gothic novel exceeds expectations for an adaptation. As a story, the novel is enhanced by the additional artwork, which flows seamlessly with the new text. One example of the format's ability to enhance the power of storytelling is the sequencing of illustrations that become more surreal as Coraline's distance from her mother increases. YAs who compare the original novel with its graphic adaptation can compare and contrast the strengths of each, gaining new critical perspectives.

Hurley, Tonya. 2008. *Ghostgirl.* New York: Little, Brown. Grades 7 and up.

Tired of being invisible to the popular students, Charlotte Usher spends the summer making herself over to look like Petula and the cheerleaders in order to gain the attention of the boy of her dreams, Damen Dylan. However, on the first day of school, Charlotte chokes to death on a gummy bear and awakens to find herself in Dead Education with others who died as teenagers, a limbo time when she must resolve a major issue and "'learn the thing you never had a chance to learn in life'" (p. 142), which involves convincing Petula's younger sister Scarlet to let Charlotte "possess" her body in order to go to the Fall Dance with Damen. This spoof of gothic literature is a perfect title to use for reading circles. Although YAs may select the titles for their roles, suggestions from Daniels and Zemelman (2004: 207–209) include (1) The Connector (e.g., school life and popularity; cliques; making fun of teachers); (2) Passage Master (e.g., the prologue of each chapter, which dispenses common sense advice with humor); (3) Vocabulary Enricher (special words created just for this story, such as *Deadiquette*; the special names attached to the Dead Kids, such as Buzz Saw Bud and their DIEaries); (4) Illustrator (descriptions of Hawthorne Manor, the truly haunted house where the Dead Kids live; Scarlet's goth attire); and (5) Researcher (one reader may note the references to gothic, e.g., the name Usher from Poe's story and title for Chapter 13, "The Fall of the House of Usher"; the school name, Hawthorne High; the principal's name, Mr. Styx; *The Twilight Zone*, *Psycho* [movie]; Buffy the Vampire Slayer; *Night of the Living Dead*).

Macaulay, David. 1985. *Baaa*. Boston, MA: Houghton Mifflin. Grades 6 and up.

This black and white illustrated book relates in 61 pages the life of sheep that appear alone on earth after the last human has vanished. The work is distinguished through biting satire: "It was a time of great prosperity. Everything was plentiful. Gas was cheap. The population grew." Young people could sketch a black and white single page that features a dimension of the sheep's world, building on the premise that the sheep are devouring one another (e.g., as the book portrayed sheep wearing masks and hiding behind dark corners, concession sellers of baaascream, and a dinner scene featuring mint sauce).

Meyer, Stephenie. 2005. *Twilight*. New York: Little, Brown. Grades 9 and up.

In the rainiest little town in the United States, weather conditions are perfect for vampires who might want to remain off the radar, and 17-year-old Isabella Swan soon discovers why after she struggles with her attraction for Edward Cullen, whose handsome good looks and emotional distance intrigue her. In this first of the Twilight Saga, the Cullen coven exhibit the classic vampire traits (pale skin, beautiful eyes, eternally young) but have committed themselves to living a life of benevolence toward others, being labeled the "cold ones" by vampires who take the more traditional, blood-thirsty route. As of 2008 the saga has become a best-selling phenomenon. Fans of the novels could discuss their opinions about the casting of the major characters in the film version (Smith, 2008).

Noyes, Deborah. 2004. *Gothic! Ten Original Dark Tales*. Cambridge, MA: Candlewick Press. Grades 6–12.

This anthology introduces ten gothic stories by popular contemporary authors, including Vivian Vande Velde, Joan Aiken, Neil Gaiman, and Garth Nix. Its strength lies in its fine introduction to the subgenre and the tales' various tones (from campy to terrifying). An adult could introduce each story by using the author's biographical endnotes, and small groups could each read one story aloud and then discuss in a large group the various conventions of gothic literature.

Shelley, Mary. 1818, 1985. *Frankenstein or, the Modern Prometheus.* **New York: Penguin Books. Classic.**

Pursuing nature in all of its darkest hiding places, the once happy Victor falls under the spell of alchemy. The young scientist seeks the secret of life, but he produces a creature whose existence brings its creator to ruin. The elements of the novel are united in developing one of the book's themes—that humans have a responsibility for what they create. Young people may write a readers theatre script about the theme that is illuminated in Chapter 15 when the creature attempts to make friends with the blind and accepting Mr. De Lacey but encounters the violent wrath of the De Lacey family and gives up all hope.

Westerfeld, Scott. 2005. *Peeps.* **New York: Penguin. Grades 10 and up.**

This Best Books for Young Adults' top 10 book for 2005 is a contemporary vampire/romance/horror story. The protagonist, Cal Thompson, college freshman, was infected with a parasite that he then spread to his girlfriends, causing them to become vampires. As Cal searches to find the girlfriends in order to prevent further spread of the disease, he encounters urban gothic settings (e.g., a dark, dank terminal infested with rats, littered with beds of newspapers, and partitioned by broken windows) that young people could compare to classic gothic settings and analyze for their effect on the work's tone and revelation of characters.

Wooding, Chris. 2004. *The Haunting of Alaizabel Cray.* **New York: Orchard. Grades 9–12.**

Following an old family tradition of hunting down the bad guys, Thaniel Fox wends his way through Victorian London in a futile attempt to forestall the city's takeover by the archetypal villains, the Fraternity (a powerfully elite group). Strong in plot and characterization, the narrative reveals why gothic has become a popular genre for readers of all ages. YAs can create a literary map of Thaniel's journey through London's lamp-lighted streets.

Science Fiction

Anderson, M.T. 2003. *Feed.* **Cambridge, MA: Candlewick Press. Grades 9–12.**

Titus lives in a corporate-controlled world where data (shopping information, entertainment, school) feeds automatically into brain implants. The novel is a satiric and fast-paced dystopia where spring break means a trip to the moon and lack of information is a misfortune of birth. YAs may scan contemporary magazine advertisements and translate one into a satiric "feed" message for Titus and his friends.

Butler, Octavia. 1993. *Parable of the Sower.* **New York: Four Walls Eight Windows. Grades 9–12.**

This first of a trilogy introduces the main character Lauren Olamina, who escapes her decayed and savaged society to establish a community built on a new philosophy, *Earthseed*, which emphasizes the importance of nurturing communities (illustrating Carol Gilligan's theory of moral development). Lauren's dynamic character drives the plot as she gradually becomes the leader of people who lack her vision. Young people could construct a body biography of Lauren, incorporating her poems, stated beliefs, and actions into the image.

Doctorow, Cory. 2008. *Little Brother.* **New York: Tor Teen. Grades 10 and up.**

After successfully circumventing his school's security system in order to participate in an ARG (alternative reality game), 17-year-old Marcus Yallow and his friends find themselves perilously close to the site of a terrorist attack that destroys the Bay Bridge in San Francisco. Arrested by Homeland Security agents, tortured (in a place referred to as "Gitmo-by-the-Bay"), and threatened into silence, Marcus uses his cyber skills to create an underground hacker network of young people to sabotage the government's draconian surveillance systems. YAs may respond to any of the book's issues through their choice of digital format(s).

Doran, Colleen. 1997. *A Distant Soil: The Gathering.* **Fullerton, CA: Image Comics. Grades 7–12.**

Fleeing the laboratory that had imprisoned them as guinea pigs, Liana and her brother Jason assemble a select group of earthlings to return with them to wage a war for their home planet. The first of the Distant Soil graphic novel series, this work is an excellent portrayal of technology integrated into the plot. Young people could discuss why there are so many science fiction narratives in graphic format. What are the science fiction conventions and criteria that work so well in graphic novels?

Farmer, Nancy. 2004. *The House of the Scorpion.* **New York: Simon Pulse. Grades 8–12.**

Matt's world is shattered after he discovers a horrifying secret about his identity and his imminent death. Touching on current ethical debates about cloning and organ transplantation, the narrative also raises questions about what it means to be human, the issues of immigration and border control, the enslavement of powerless people, and the obsession for immortality. Individually or in groups, young people could refer to Kohlberg's and Gilligan's theories of moral development (see Chapter 2) in a discussion of contemporary moral dilemmas.

McNaughton, Janet. 2005. *The Secret Under My Skin.* **New York: Eos. Grades 6–9.**

Following a global ecological nightmare in 2368, a shadowy dictatorship, The Commission, grabs control and murders scientists and discarded children, but one lucky orphan, Blay Raytree, discovers The Weavers Guild (women) and the Masters of the Way who want to return democracy and science back to society. As one of the lowest ranking people in her society, Blay retrieves discarded materials and learns her full identity when the microchip she carries reveals the truth about her parents and herself. Young people may respond by creating a collage of the issues the book highlights (e.g., climate change, ozone, rampant consumerism).

Miller, Frank. 1986, 2002. *The Dark Knight Returns.* **New York: DC Comics. Grades 9 and up.**

In this now-classic landmark graphic novel, Bruce Wayne watches as Gotham's crime rate goes out of control, but the public has tired of his brand of vigilante justice and the new police commissioner wants to put him in jail. For the first time, readers see a fully human Batman, who bares his dark side throughout the story in one reverie after another. The demons he has envisioned originate from within him, not from without, and he acquires a new partner in Carrie Kelly. Young people can divide this edition into its four books and discuss the psychological state of Batman's mind in each.

Pearson, Mary. 2008. *The Adoration of Jenna Fox.* **New York: Henry Holt. Grades 8 and up.**

Jenna is faced with certain death after a car crash. Her father (a scientist) illegally uses state-of-the-art technology to save her life, and Jenna awakens with 10 percent of a human brain reinforced with microchips, a life expectancy of 2–200 years, and a new existence that she must both discover and invent. The truth of Jenna is captured on random gray pages in free verse poetry while the first person narrative races forward. In discovering the truth, Jenna and her boyfriend, Ethan, work out an explicit theme that YAs can explore: "The greater part of what . . . neighbors call good I believe in my soul to be bad, and if . . . [one] repents of anything . . . it is very likely to be . . . [for] good behavior" (p. 241).

Reeve, Philip. 2003. *Mortal Engines: A Novel.* **New York: HarperCollins. Grades 7–12.**

The post-nuclear Traction City of London spreads out, devouring small towns in an effort to process every scrap of technology to use for an international power struggle in which human life carries no value except as slave labor. The novel's strength is its originality of concept in which "Municipal Darwinism" (p. 159) shapes the dystopian society of two orphaned protagonists. Young readers can illustrate the mechanistic cities and the eccentric characters that the protagonists encounter. This is the first in The Hungry City Chronicles series.

Strahan, Jonathan, ed. 2008. *The Starry Rift: Tales of New Tomorrows.* **New York: Viking. Grades 9–12.**

The 16 outstanding science fiction short stories in this anthology are by well known authors, including Garth Nix, Scott Westerfeld, and Neil Gaiman, whose "Orange" has an especially original format (a set of 70 numbered responses to an investigator's written questionnaire). In "Orange," there had been an extraordinary event at Jemima Ramsey's home, where her young sister Nerys had begun misusing tanning creams and had become a pulsating, glowing orange phenomenon who floated above the floor, took control of the house, turned emergency workers into goo, and eventually boarded a space ship after aliens gave Jemima's mother the recipe for the fluorescent bubble mixture. This anthology is recommended for readers of science fiction and for those sampling the genre, and some may respond by composing their own stories in a "numbered answers" format.

Werlin, Nancy. 2004. *Double Helix: A Novel.* **New York: Dial Press. Grades 8–12.**

Eli Samuels walks through the doors of Wyatt Transgenetics with the intention of beginning his brilliant career in science, but his research leads him into territory that alters his perceptions of his society, his family, and himself. The novel addresses the issues of genetic engineering while captivating readers with a fast-paced mystery. Students can have lively debates over the novel's ethical questions. How does one decide when to have a genetic test for a fatal inherited disease? Is it ethical to select genetic characteristics (e.g., gender, intelligence, height) for the unborn? Should funding alone determine who conducts genetic research? Who owns human sperm and eggs? Who is responsible for the human conceived in a test tube?

REFERENCES AND SUGGESTIONS FOR FURTHER READING

Abrams, M.H. 1999. *A Glossary of Literature*, 7th ed. New York: Harcourt Brace.

Allen, Dick, ed. 1983. *Science Fiction: The Future*, 2nd ed. New York: Harcourt Brace Jovanovich.

Allen, Iris, Julian Tepper, and Diana Stratigakis. "North American Slavery vs. Latin American Slavery: A Comparative Look at Frederick Douglass and Juan Francisco Manzano." George Washington University (1998). Available at: www.gwu.edu/~e73afram/ia-jt-ds .html.

Alter, Robert. 1996. *The Pleasures of Reading in an Ideological Age*. New York: W.W. Norton.

Ammon, Bette and Gale Sherman. 1996. *Worth a Thousand Words: An Annotated Guide to Picture Books for Older Readers*. Littleton, CO: Libraries Unlimited.

Anderson, Laurie Halse. 2000. *Fever 1793*. Fort Worth, TX: Aladdin.

Aronson, Marc. 2006. "Originality in Nonfiction." *School Library Journal* 52, no. 1 (January): 42–43.

Association for Library Service to Children. "Sibert Medal Terms and Criteria." Chicago: American Library Association (May 2006). Available at: www.ala.org/alsc/awards.

Association for Library Service to Children. "2008 ALSC Robert F. Sibert Informational Book Medal Homepage." Available at: www.ala.org/ala/mgrps/divs/alsc/awardsgrants/ bookmedia/sibertmedal/index.cfm.

Bagdasarian, Adam. 2002. *First French Kiss: And Other Traumas*. New York: Farrar, Straus, and Giroux.

Bailey, James Osler. 1972. *Pilgrims Through Space and Time: Trends and Patterns in Scientific and Utopian Fiction*. Westport, CT: Greenwood Press.

Base, Graeme. 1987. *Animalia*. New York: Harry N. Abrams.

Bates, Marcia J. 1991. *The Berry-Picking Search*. Westport, CT: Greenwood Press.

Bauer, Marian Dane. 1995. *Am I Blue? Coming Out from the Silence*. New York: Harper Trophy.

Bretnor, Reginold, ed. 1953. *Modern Science Fiction: Its Meaning and Its Future*. New York: Coward-McCann.

Bronte, Charlotte. 1847, 2006. *Jane Eyre*. New York: Penguin Books.

Budrys, Algis. 1983. "The Many-Featured Land." In *Science Fiction: The Future*, 2nd ed., edited by Dick Allen, pp. 397–405. New York: Harcourt Brace Jovanovich.

Byatt, A.S. 2005. "Byatt Explains Compulsions of Historical Fiction." *College of William and Mary News* (June 2006). Available at: wmu.edu.

Carlsen, G. Robert. 1965. "For Everything There Is a Season." In *Readings About Adolescent Literature*, edited by Dennis Thomison, pp. 21–28. Metuchen, NJ: Scarecrow Press.

Carlsen, G. Robert. 1980. *Books and the Teenage Reader*, 2nd ed. New York: Harper and Row.

Carroll, Lewis. 1971. *Alice in Wonderland*. New York: W.W. Norton.

Carter, Betty, and Richard F. Abrahamson. 1990. *Nonfiction for Young Adults: From Delight to Wisdom*. Phoenix, AZ: Oryx.

Coolidge, Olivia. 1974. "My Struggle with Facts." *Wilson Library Journal* 49 (October): 146–151.

Cormier, Robert. 1974. *The Chocolate War*. New York: Pantheon.

Cormier, Robert. 1988. *Fade*. New York: Delacorte.

Daniels, Harvey, and Steven Zemelman. 2004. *Subjects Matter: Every Teacher's Guide to Content-Area Reading*. Portsmouth, NH: Heinemann.

Delaney, Samuel R. 1983. "Critical Methods/Science." In *Science Fiction: Future*, 2nd ed., edited by Dick Allen, pp. 406–416. New York: Harcourt Brace Jovanovich.

Dickinson, A.T., ed. 1958. *American Historical Fiction*. New York: Scarecrow Press.

Donelson, Kenneth L., and Alleen Pace Nilsen. 1989. *Literature for Today's Young Adults*, 3rd ed. Glenview, IL: Scott, Foresman.

Faulkner, William. 1930, 1950. "A Rose for Emily." In *Collected Stories of William Faulkner*, pp. 119–130. New York: Random House.

Ferguson, Margaret, Mary Jo Salter, and Jon Stallworthy, eds. 1996. *The Norton Anthology of Poetry*, 4th ed. New York: W.W. Norton.

Freedman, Russell. 1993. *Eleanor Roosevelt: A Life of Discovery*. New York: Clarion Press.

Freedman, Russell. 2002. "Russell Freedman." In *The Essential Guide to Children's Books and Their Creators*, edited by Anita Silvey, pp. 164–166. Boston: Houghton Mifflin.

"Genocide Watch: The International Campaign to End Genocide" (1998). Available at: www.genocidewatch.org.

Goldsmith, Francisca. 2002. "YA Talk." *Booklist* 98: no. 2 (February): 986.

Gunn, James. 1983. "On the Road to Science Fiction: From Heinlein to Here." In *Science Fiction: The Future*, 2nd ed., edited by Dick Allen, pp. 321–338. New York: Harcourt Brace Jovanovich.

Gunn, James and Matthew Candelaria, eds. 2005. *Speculations on Speculation*. Latham, MD: Scarecrow Press.

Harmon, William, and C. Hugh Holman. 2000. *A Handbook to Literature*, 8th ed. Upper Saddle River, NJ: Prentice Hall.

Hearne, Betsy Gould. 2003. *Canine Connection: Stories About Dogs and People*. New York: Margaret K. McElderry.

Hinton, S.E. 1967. *The Outsiders*. New York: Viking Press.

Huxley, Aldous. 1932. *Brave New World*. Garden City, NY: Doubleday, Doran.

Jennings, Frank G. 1956. "Literature for Adolescents: Pap or Protein?" *English Journal* 45: 526–531.

Kesey, Ken. 1962. *One Flew Over the Cuckoo's Nest*. New York: Viking Press.

Knight, Damon, ed. 1977. *Turning Points: Essays on the Art of Science Fiction*. New York: Harper and Row.

Krull, Kathleen. "Frequently Asked Questions" (2006). Available at: www.kathleenkrull.com.

Kübler-Ross, Elisabeth. 2005. *On Grief and Grieving: Finding the Meaning of Grief Through the Five Stages of Loss*. New York: Scribner.

Kurtz, Jane. 2004. *Memories of Sun: Stories of Africa and America*. New York: Amistad/Greenwillow Books.

Latrobe, Kathy, Carolyn S. Brody, and Maureen White. 2001. *The Children's Literature Dictionary: Definitions, Resources, and Learning Activities*. New York: Neal-Schuman.

Lester, Julius. 2005. *Day of Tears: A Novel in Dialogue*. New York: Hyperion.

Levin, Ira. 1967. *Rosemary's Baby*. New York: Random House.

Luckhurst, Roger. 2005. *Science Fiction*. Cambridge, MA: Polity.

Macaulay, David. 1990. *Black and White.* Boston: Houghton Mifflin.

Makaryk, Irena R., ed. 1993. *Encyclopedia of Contemporary Literary Theory: Approaches, Scholars, Terms.* Toronto, Canada: University of Toronto Press.

Marlowe, Christopher. c. 1599, 2008. *The Tragical History of Doctor Faustus: A Critical Edition.* Orchard Park, NY: Broadview.

McKernan, Victoria. 2005. *Shackleton's Stowaway.* New York: Knopf Books for Young Readers.

Montgomery, Rian. 2003. "Sub-Genre." ChickLitBooks. Available at: www.ChickLitBooks .com.

Moses, Kate. 2003. *Wintering: A Novel of Sylvia Plath.* New York: Anchor Books.

Muller, Al. 1975. "New Reading Material: The Junior Novel." *Journal of Reading* 11 (April): 531–534.

Orwell, George. 1949. *Nineteen Eighty-four: A Novel.* New York: Harcourt, Brace.

Pearson, Molly Blake. 2005. *Big Ideas in Small Packages: Using Picture Books with Older Readers.* Worthington, OH: Linworth.

Poe, Edgar Allan. 1842, 1967. "The Philosophy of Composition." In *The American Tradition in Literature*, Vol. 1, 3rd ed., edited by Sculley Bradley, Richmond Croom Beatty, and E. Hudson Long, pp. 887–896. New York: W. W. Norton & Company.

Polette, Nancy and Joan Ebbesmeyer. 2002. *Literature Lures: Using Picture Books and Novels to Motivate Middle School Readers.* Greenwood Village, CO: Teacher Ideas Press.

Preminger, Alex. 1974. *Princeton Encyclopedia of Poetry and Poetics.* Princeton, NJ: Princeton University Press.

Schliesman, Megan. 2007. "Never Too Old: Picture Books to Share with Older Children and Teens." Cooperative Children's Book Center. Available at: www.education.wisc .edu/ccbc/books/detailListBooks.asp?idBookLists=259.

Scott, Sir Walter. 1814, 1972. *Waverly, Or 'Tis Sixty Years Hence.* New York: Penguin Classics.

Sebold, Alice. 1999. *Lucky: A Memoir.* New York: Scribner.

Shelley, Mary. 2001. *Frankenstein.* New York: Oxford University Press.

Sinclair, Upton. 2003. *The Jungle.* Tucson, AZ: Sharp Press.

Smith, Patrick Thomas. 2008. *Twilight.* Directed by Catherine Hardwicke. Goldcrest Pictures. 121 min. DVD, March 2009.

Stoker, Bram. 1897, 1993. *Dracula.* New York: Penguin Books.

Swanson, Diane. 2001. "A Wish for a New Century." In *The Best in Children's Nonfiction: Reading, Writing, and Teaching Orbis Pictus Award Books*, edited by Myra Zarnowski, Richard M. Kerper, and Julie M. Jensen, pp. 53–56. Urbana, IL: National Council of Teachers of English.

Tennyson, Alfred. 1995. *Selected Poetry.* New York: Routledge.

Verne, Jules. 1870, 2001. *20,000 Leagues Under the Sea.* New York: Signet Classic.

Von Ziegesar, Cecily, ed. 2000. *Slam.* New York: Alloy Books.

Walpole, Horace. 1754, 2001. *The Castle of Otranto.* New York: Penguin Press.

Wilson, H.W. 2008. "Short Story Index." New York: H.W. Wilson. Available at: www.hwwilson .com/databases/storeindec.htm.

Zindel, Paul. 1968, 2005. *The Pigman.* New York: HarperTeen.

Part III

Critical Theories

Chapter 5

New Criticism/ Formal Criticism

INTRODUCTION TO NEW CRITICISM

The focus of formal criticism, or New Criticism, is the literary work itself, and the fundamental concern of formalism is that of literary unity. Thus, *New Criticism*, or *formalism* (the terms are interchangeable), analyzes and evaluates a literary work by considering its elements (e.g., plot, character, tone, style) and weighing how they work together to create meaning. Certainly the formalist critic knows that a literary creation has an author who shaped the work based on personal philosophies, motivations for writing, and past experiences; knows that a literary work exists in a universe that contains the subject, determines its attributes, and defines what is expected, acceptable, or realistic; and knows that each reader has a unique creation of the work as it exists in his or her imagination. However, the formalist critic, rather than analyzing the author, potential readers, or an interpretation of the real world, carefully explores the literary work itself, reading closely to study the interdependent effects of the literary elements as they work together to create a meaningful, harmonious, and unified literary experience.

Emphasizing the text, or the printed page, New Criticism does not include scholarship or research that addresses the reader, the milieu, or the author. Abrams (1993: 246–247) describes the general tenets of New Criticism as follows:

1. A poem [literary work], it is held, should be treated as such—"primarily as poetry and not another thing"—and should therefore be regarded as an independent self-sufficient verbal object.

2. The distinctive procedure of a New Critic is explication, or *close reading*: the detailed and subtle analysis of the complex interrelations and *ambiguities* (multiple meanings) of the components within a work.

3. The principles of the New Criticism are basically verbal. That is, literature is conceived to be a special kind of language, whose attributes are defined

by systematic opposition to the language of science and of practical and logical discourse.

4. The distinction between literary genres, although recognized and used, does not play an essential role in the New Criticism.

In the United States the theory took its name from a work by John Crowe Ransom (1941), *The New Criticism*. In England the approach is called *practical criticism*, after the title of I.A. Richards' (1929) groundbreaking *Practical Criticism* that initiated the importance of *close reading*, the signature feature of New Criticism. Ransom and other Southern writers and critics, such as Allan Tate and Robert Penn Warren, asserted that literature was a special form of knowledge that deserved its own special reading approach. Cleanth Brooks and Robert Penn Warren (1938) supplied such an approach in their *Understanding Poetry: An Anthology for College Students*. Reacting against theories that relied on extrinsic sources for the interpretation of a work, Brooks and Warren prefaced their textbook with a "Letter to the Teacher" explaining why they had eliminated the usual "substitutes" for studying poems, including biographical, historical, and impressionistic sources. Brooks and Warren analyzed several poems through close reading, thereby illustrating for teachers and their students which elements to identify and how to interpret a text with the unity of all the elements in mind as final evaluation of any single poem's success.

Some of the most influential names in twentieth-century literary criticism have been associated with New Criticism—Northrup Frye, R.P. Blackmur, John Crow Ransom, Yvor Winters—although some would not have labeled themselves as New Critics. Northrup Frye's (1957) *Anatomy of Criticism* is often cited as a landmark work of New Criticism, but it also is considered by others as a landmark work of archetypal criticism. As with any other literary theory, however, few of its practitioners are "really 'pure' formalists, perhaps for the reason that the poem 'in itself' supplies no base for a theory of value" (Keesey, 1987: 78). Generally speaking the New Critics helped to form (or to continue with) the male-dominated canon, and they favored analyzing poetry over fiction, except for novellas and short stories.

The hegemony of the New Critics spanned the decades from the 1930s through the 1960s until attacks from other theorists were aimed at the text-only approach. New Criticism still holds the distinction of being the pivotal position against which subsequent twentieth-century and twenty-first century theories have had to define themselves. As the point of departure for sociological, feminist, and reader response, New Criticism would seem to be dead. However, as James R. Bennett (1992: 678) pointed out, the theory "remains a dominant mode for critical writing in the public schools and colleges, despite declarations of its demise." Hans Bertens (2001: 26) agreed with that evaluation, calling the theory "still a force to reckon with."

NEW CRITICISM REVIVED

Long after the widespread influence of New Criticism had waned, writers began to comment on its staying power. In "The Restless Ghost of the New Criticism," Anthony G. Medici (1997: 760) contends that the theory "has often been treated as a scapegoat in modern critical discourses." Medici also reminds critics of the theory's long history, of its struggle that "was not uncontested, that the critical voice was not univocal, that the movement was not monolithic, and that the boundaries of discourse have never been quite fixed" (p. 769). Another scholar points out that New Critics "present such easy targets" (Friedberg, 2005: 31) that they continue to be the scapegoat of new theories. In *Praising It New: The Best of New Criticism*, Garrick Davis (2008) suggests that it remains one of the most important sources for groundbreaking criticism and continues to be a controversial approach to reading literature.

Close Reading

One of the legacies attributed to New Criticism is its technique of *close reading*. Richard Ohmann (1995: 79) defines *close reading* by using such phrases as

- exactness,
- sensitivity to shades of meaning,
- the need to see pattern and order,
- the effort to shut out from consciousness one's own life situation while reading the poem [work], and
- the need to pry the words loose from their social origin.

In their anthology *Close Reading: The Reader*, Lentricchia and Dubois (2003: ix) bring together essays written by the original New Critics (e.g., Ransom and Brooks) and essays and analyses of works written by other theorists who are committed "to close attention to literary texture"—Stanley Fish, reader response; Catherine Gallagher and Stephen Greenblatt, new historicism; and Gilbert and Gubar, feminist psychology. In "Paradigms of Reading" John Phillips (2004: 140) calls close reading "a peculiarly American" tradition that is still much admired. Scholars in developmental education presented a four-part series on "Critical Thinking and the Art of Close Reading" that approached some of the specific skills that can be shared with readers (Paul and Elder, 2003, 2004a,b; Elder and Paul, 2004). Christopher Clausen (1997) addresses "Reading Closely Again," wherein he explains the legacy of the New Critics, who, as college teachers, had originally been motivated by their observations of their students. These teachers had bemoaned the fact that too many of their students were "inexperienced or careless readers [who] had tended to equate poems with their messages" (p. 55). Clausen admonishes most of the subsequent theories for their "turning the practice of criticism into a weapon of assault against such extramural targets as American foreign policy, capitalism, imperialism, and patriarchy" (p. 56), thereby targeting socialist, postcolonial, and feminist theories.

Elaine Showalter (2003: 98) explains that in the classroom she teaches young adults close reading "as a deliberate attempt to detach [them] from the magical power of story-telling and pay attention to language, imagery, allusion, intertextuality, syntax, and form." Close reading also helps readers to break old "habitual and casual reading practices. It forces [them] to be active rather than passive consumers of the text" (p. 98). Showalter prefers to use meaningful excerpts from selected novels or stories for close reading instead of an entire novel, to her an unacceptably burdensome activity. Finally, one contemporary defender of the theory, Mark Bauerlein (2007: B7), concludes in *The Chronicle of Higher Education* that "schools of thought come and go" and that the New Critics "were the first professional theorists, the first humanists, to make theory into a recognized disciplinary activity... [with] devised principles of interpretation that were both ingenious and convertible into disciplinary standards." Significantly, it is both New Criticism and reader-response criticism that have been developed with YAs in mind and that have been the most often employed in consideration of YA literature.

The Elements of Fiction and Suggested Questions for a Close Reading

Applying New Criticism to reading and responding to literature involves identifying each literary element and analyzing it as it relates to the work's theme. The author's creative management of the basic literary elements defines the evaluative criteria for this theory. The eight elements of fiction are presented in this section with suggested questions for a close reading or discussion. Not all questions may apply to a given work, nor should they be presented in the given order. The individual work and its formal analysis should govern responses—written or discussed.

The Eight Elements of Fiction for a Close Reading

Plot

1. How does the author arrange the events in the story?
   a. Episodic (loosely structured episodes, incidents, or short stories)
   b. Progressive (rising action, climax or crisis, resolution)
   c. Nonlinear (structure that may be shaped by shifts in points of view, time, format, etc.)
2. What is the conflict?
   a. Person against person
   b. Person against nature
   c. Person against society
   d. Person against self

3. How does the author apply any special techniques to the development of the plot?
   a. *In media res* (starting in the middle of the action)
   b. Flashback
   c. Story within a story
   d. Foreshadowing (and its possible counter to coincidence)
   e. Narrative hook
   f. Suspense
   g. Cliff-hanger
   h. Open or closed ending

4. How does the plot flow from and contribute to other literary elements?

Character

1. Are the protagonist and antagonist multidimensional (round as opposed to flat) characters?

2. Is the main character dynamic (fundamentally changed)?

3. How are characters revealed?
   a. Dialogue
   b. Appearance
   c. Interior thoughts
   d. Actions

4. How do characters interact with other elements (especially plot) to create literary unity?

Setting (time, place, atmosphere)

1. Is the setting merely a backdrop (superficial, indeterminable, generalized), or is it integral (operating as a symbol, reflecting tone, influencing the mood, becoming the antagonist, explaining the conflict)?

2. Beyond defining time, place, and atmosphere, what roles does the setting have?

Tone

1. What is the author's attitude (e.g., comic, sympathetic, angry, attacking, melancholy, skeptical, hostile, playful, or neutral) toward the following?
   a. Reader
   b. Characters/subject
   c. Genre
   d. Work itself

2. How does the author's attitude shape the reader's interpretation of the work?

Style

1. What is unique or personal about how the author writes? For example, how does the author's creativity employ
   a. Diction (e.g., choice of words, such as connotation/denotation, sentence structure and length)
   b. Imagery and figurative language (frequency and complexity)
   c. Dialogue
   d. Description
   e. Structure/format (e.g., the appearance and ordering of the story's parts)
2. How does the author's style shape literary unity?

Point of View

1. What is/are the narrative vantage point(s) or perspective(s)?
   a. First person
   b. Second person
   c. Third person
2. What does the narrator know?
   a. Omniscient (the narrator has access to all the thoughts of all characters)
   b. Limited omniscient (the narrator has access to the thoughts of one or a few characters)
   c. Objective (the narrator does not have access to the thoughts of any characters)
3. What characterizes the narrator(s)?
   a. Reliable or unreliable (naïve)
   b. Atypical
   c. Authoritative and intrusive
   d. Interior monologue
   e. Introspective
4. What is the pattern of narration (e.g., alternating chapter by chapter or varying by format)?
5. If there are multiple narrators, how does this technique affect reliability?
6. How does the narrator's control of information affect the readers' understanding of the characters and their actions?

Theme

1. What is a theme of the book (a statement of a universal truth expressed in a single sentence)?
2. Is that theme explicit (stated in the book)?
3. Or, is that theme implicit (derived by the reader from the work's title, repetitions, symbols, etc.)?
4. How does the theme develop from other elements to create literary unity?

Mode

1. What is the book's mode (as described by Northrop Frye [1957])?
   a. Romance (tells of wishes and quests fulfilled and the triumph of good over evil and presents a main character who moves toward understanding and experience)
   b. Tragedy (presents a protagonist who, neither all good nor all evil, moves from happiness to disaster but does not lose human dignity; or presents a protagonist who possesses a fatal flaw that inevitably leads to disaster)
   c. Irony/satire (features an average or below average individual as the main character who struggles only with ordinary, everyday issues and thus suggests the need for individual or social change)
   d. Comedy (tells of hope and renewal, moving from chaos to order)
2. How is mode linked to other literary elements (especially to the development of the main character, the plot's crisis and resolution, and the theme) to create literary unity?

APPLICATION OF NEW CRITICISM TO WALTER DEAN MYERS' *MONSTER*

Monster (Myers, 1999) centers on the internal struggles of 16-year-old Steve Harmon. Living in New York City, he has admired the young urban toughs on the street and longed to be identified with them and to be held in their esteem. When invited to serve as a lookout at a neighborhood store robbery, he passively accepts, knowing that he will need to do nothing if everything is clear for the robbery to proceed. The day of the robbery, the toughs wait outside the drugstore, and when Steve exits to the sidewalk without saying anything, they accept his sign of silence and enter the store, robbing and murdering the owner. Steve has not considered he could suffer any consequences because he did not *do* anything. Therefore, he had not considered the possibility of being arrested, imprisoned, and tried. Neither had he considered the possibility of having to face himself as a murderer, a monster. The novel's crisis passes when the jury decides that he is innocent of the felony murder charges. However, Steve is not at peace. Although he rationalizes that he did nothing, he cannot escape the reflection of guilt he sees in his attorney's eyes, his father's eyes, and his own mirror. Thus, he is unable to frame the question of what is truth; or, more specifically, he cannot face the truth that he owed respect to the neighborhood shopkeeper and now holds responsibility for his death. The ending is open, leaving the reader to ponder whether Steve will ever accept responsibility for his actions, whether omitted or committed.

The progressive plot, however, is not chronological. It opens with a powerful narrative hook *in media res*: "The best time to cry is at night, when the lights are out and someone is being beaten up and screaming for help" (Myers, 1999: 1).

That the novel begins in the middle of the action is emphasized in the first chapter: "Sometimes I feel like I have walked into the middle of a movie" (p. 3). By the end of the first brief, hand-printed chapter, the reader knows that the narrator is telling his own story from prison, that prison is terrifying, that he cannot recognize himself in the cell's mirror, and that the prosecutor has given him a name: Monster. Shifts in point of view, setting, and style or format advance the nonlinear plot to explain Steve Harmon's uncertainties and anxieties. It is the author's control of these three elements that draws the reader into Steve's world and creates suspense from events of the rising action to the crisis (the jury's decision) and the denouement. Thus, in the first chapter, these elements establish the plot's scope: Why is Steve in jail? Is he guilty? Will the jury find him guilty? Will he ever be able to face himself?

A synopsis of the plot of *Monster* inevitably loses all aspects of the author's style, and it is *how* Myers tells the story that shapes and unites all other literary elements. The novel's most obvious stylistic device is the pair of alternating chapter formats, the journal and the movie script. The movie script is introduced in Chapter 2, and thus style itself continues the analogy that Steve's circumstance is like a movie to him. However, Myers makes remarkable use of an array of other stylistic devices: the mirror's reflection, unrecognized by Steve as a symbol of a lost identity; framing the story with placement of the mirror at the novel's beginning and the end (p. 280); figurative language (e.g., the fear of being raped was "like a little ball in the pit of my stomach" [p. 139]; the use of grainy black and white photographs that indistinctly show the main character as an isolated figure; the directions for camera shots in the script to emphasize characters' actions and reactions; the inclusion of prison language (e.g., a "calendar" is a "year"); and the use of substandard English to set the prisoners apart. Finally, there are the chilling images of prison horror and of the protagonist whose head is down early in the novel but who by the end of the novel is not intimidated by a look.

Stylistically, the alternating excerpts of script and diary not only advance the plot but also contrast Steve's wavering self-perception by providing him a dual point of view, that of first person in the diary and objective in the script. The script format takes the reader into Steve's mind by relating what he hears and sees in court as well as his previous conversations with other characters. However, neither point of view is reliable. Also, the script itself relates the conflicting testimony in which Steve denies his participation but others implicate him. Furthermore, at the end of the movie script, the jury determines that Steve is not guilty, and Steve turns, arms outstretched, to hug his attorney who turns away. Thus, Steve, as scriptwriter, enforces both his innocence and his guilt. Steve cannot even face himself in his personal diary. Steve is the captive of his own creative but unreliable constructions. However, the reader understands Steve's guilt and perceives his lack of taking responsibility and his remorse.

Another important element of the novel, the setting, shapes the action, clarifies the protagonist, and creates its mood. Multiple aspects of New York City are integral to the story: the crime scene allows the protagonist to move easily between roles of observer and perpetrator; long nights in the cell create fear that overwhelms Steve with sounds of verbal and physical abuse echoing down the hallways; the courtroom forces his future into the dichotomy of guilt or innocence; the school illuminates Steve's capacity for artistic creation; the neighborhood tempts the unreflective teenager into the role of accomplice to murder through the possibility of a more exciting persona; and his home, warm and nurturing, contrasts the privilege he once enjoyed with the ultimate loss of family relationships. Together, such details shape plot and character in a complex urban environment where those who cannot define themselves will be defined by circumstance.

The novel's dominant literary element is the main character, Steve, a multi-dimensional but static protagonist who is revealed by dialogue, appearance, thoughts, and actions. In the opening chapters he focuses on one word from the prosecutor's statements, "monster" (p. 5), and he scrawls *"Monster"* in his diary and across his script notes. In the courtroom the defense attorney crosses out "Monster" on the script and is determined to convince the jury Steve is innocent. Thus, the dual nature of the courtroom enters the character of Steve. Confused and bitter after being labeled a monster, Steve convinces himself he looks just like the other jailed accused men. In response to state prosecutor Petrocelli's use of older thugs as witnesses against him, Steve protests how she manipulates the jury to see that he and the others look the same. More devastating yet is Steve's reaction after a visit from his father: "It's like a man looking down to see his son and seeing a monster instead" (p. 116). Petrocelli, performing her job with the vigor of a true believer and relying on name-calling, provides Steve with a new, destructive image of himself, so deeply ingrained that he feels as if the word *monster* were tattooed on his forehead. However, internally, Steve holds no image of himself. Gazing into the symbolic mirror that is engraved with the names of prisoners who had come before, he thinks, "I see a face looking back at me but I don't recognize it" (p. 1). The old Steve is no where to be found.

Unlike the script, Steve's memoir does not introduce the issue of his guilt or innocence until nearly halfway through the novel (p. 140). He does this by asking a series of questions, some unanswered, that with their repetition suggest he is struggling with his conscience. Sometimes his answers say that he is innocent. Later, his (rhetorical) questions become more specific to the crime. Conveniently omitted is the unasked, unanswered question: Was Steve the lookout, as Petrocelli maintains, or did he chicken out at the last minute and just go through the motions of his part of the crime, thereby rationalizing and relinquishing his moral responsibility for "doing" anything?

Of course, Steve is too young and too intelligent to hold back the floodwater of truth. During one frightening prison situation, Steve remembers that he had wanted to be tough like the other boys. This motive of trying to change his neighborhood image of being "just a lame looking for a name" (p. 81) had only been hinted in the script but surfaces as he wrestles with his inner conflict. Steve begins to listen to the other prisoners as they make excuses for their crimes, including one who says since the robbery went awry, and he really did not have a gun, only his hand in his pocket to look like a gun, he reasons he did not actually "do" anything wrong. Interestingly, Steve thinks to himself it is obvious the man is guilty and trying to convince himself of being innocent. Only in the quiet of the night long after his mother's poignant visit does Steve reflect, "I knew she felt that I didn't do anything wrong. It was me who wasn't sure. It was me who lay on the cot wondering if I was fooling myself" (p. 148). As Steve begins to think he might be culpable, the reader sees there might be hope for him, maybe even redemption that is found within the pages of the Bible his mother brings him.

But the closer Steve moves toward facing the truth of his involvement, the more emotionally and physically damaged he becomes. The guilt seems to be crushing his chest. The dialogue between the script and the journal gains momentum as the novel reaches the concluding arguments. When the prosecutor Petrocelli delivers her closing, she clarifies his behavior, her words echoing his earlier fears: "I can imagine him trying to distance himself from the event... that he has successfully walked the moral tightrope that relieves him of responsibility" (p. 261). Steve's testy response reveals his tone of hostility toward himself, his antagonist: "What decisions did I make? What decisions didn't I make?" (p. 270). His journal responses even begin to sound like a petulant child's. He prefers to get back to his mind movies complete with a soundtrack of cellos and violas, a description whose connotations suggest his hostility with the prosecutor's uncanny ability to see through his façade. His self-delusion has worked. Now a dehumanized monster, Steve sees truth in whatever form he wishes.

Steve's script eventually illustrates the emotional damage he has suffered for his failure to face the consequences of his actions. For example, after the state rests its case Steve introduces an animated segment into his movie script featuring a small, clownish man. Where did this fantasy come from? His movie had presented entirely realistic characters and techniques until this abrupt change. Another dramatic change occurs when Steve awaits the jury's verdict. The script suddenly ceases all dialogue. Neither codefendant James's nor Steve's verdict is spoken. Instead, the stage directions indicate their obvious verdicts, James King being led away in handcuffs, Steve reaching to embrace defense attorney O'Brien but left to face the camera alone while his image distorts into a

Rorschach that looks, of course, like a monster, and the script ends on this frozen image.

The author's tone toward Steve is not ambivalent; he has little tolerance for Steve's lack of repentance and seems to hold little hope that Steve will look deeper than Miss O'Brien's expression toward him or the myriad of poses that he records with a camera. However, his attitude for readers is quite different. Never didactic or patronizing, Myers respects the readers, offering them a complex perspective through which to experience Steve's fear, envy, indecision, dishonesty, and loss. The result of the two differing tones is that readers are sympathetic to Steve's overwhelming fear of prison but repelled by his lack of remorse and inability to accept responsibility.

Set in the ironic mode, Steve Harmon's story is that of an ordinary teenager who errs in his daily activities when he is presented with the opportunity to play the role of a neighborhood tough in a real crime. Suddenly he faces the cold, unforgiving, and complex world of experience, an urban world of guns, street crime, concrete, iron bars, and a courtroom that delivers justice bluntly. Before the verdict, the reader wishes someone would confront the self-focused and immature protagonist with the truth yet realizes that the truth will plunge him further into the horrors of prison. However, the reader also knows that he is equally lost in a world of freedom and privilege where the sense of responsibility to protect others, face guilt, accept remorse, and attempt restitution cannot be found in a mirror image or in his visual recordings. The novel holds an equal sense of hopelessness toward an imperfect justice system that leaves little potential for a developing identity to mature and that supports the social construct of incarceration that is indifferent to violence, intimidation, rape, bets on verdicts, and witnesses less perfect than those they testified against. Furthermore, the structure of the novel itself is ironic. Steve knows that he does not have the freedom to explore truth when he writes, "Before she left Miss O'Brien warned me not to write anything in my notebook that I did not want the prosecutor to see" (p. 137). Although he is freed from prison, he remains locked in his self-deceptions. Thus, Myers melds style, point of view, setting, plot, and character within an ironic mode.

Among the themes readers may discover in the novel is one implicit in the biblical passage Steve's mother marked (Psalm 28) and asks him to read: "The Lord is my strength and my shield; my heart trusted in him, and I am helped: therefore my heart greatly rejoiceth; and with my song will I praise him" (p. 146). The psalmist's plea that he "not be dragged away with the wicked" expresses the theme that, like Steve and the psalmist, humankind struggles not to be dragged away with the wicked. This theme is related to the open ending, which leads to the question of Steve's future, and it represents his worst fear and greatest longing. The psalmist honestly reflects on his actions, takes responsibility, and asks for help. Steve cannot.

ANNOTATED BIBLIOGRAPHY

Character

Rylant, Cynthia. 2006. *Ludie's Life*. Orlando, FL: Harcourt. Grades 9 and up.

Born in Alabama in 1910, starved as a child by her stepmother and married at 15, Ludie raised her six children in the West Virginia coal fields, kept a spotless house, raised some of her grandchildren, liked JFK, and did not like pets. Choice of a third person (anonymous) narrator to tell Ludie's story keeps readers a little distant from the remarkable but at the same time ordinary woman who learned how to live a long, good life where many could not even survive. What makes this novel in verse unique is the way Rylant turns Ludie's outwardly mundane life events into an inner drama known only to Ludie. YAs can create a layered or concentric body biography of Ludie that encompasses her life, first as a child unloved and in poverty, then an energetic young wife and mother, and finally an old woman whose only problem is loneliness.

Mode (Comedy)

Vande Velde, Vivienne. 1999. *Never Trust a Dead Man*. San Diego, CA: Harcourt Brace. Grades 6–9.

Condemned to die for a murder he did not commit, 17-year-old Selwyn bargains with a witch to resurrect a murder victim who comes to life in the form of a bat and partners with Selwyn to solve the mystery. This humorous mix of genres (supernatural and mystery) exemplifies the mode of comedy in that Selwyn, condemned to death, moves from a chaotic beginning to a just and orderly conclusion. Young people can investigate the mode of comedy by developing and presenting a readers theatre script from the scene in which the witch appears to Selwyn after he has been entombed in a dark cave strewn with bones.

Plot

Anderson, M.T. 2006. *The Astonishing Life of Octavian Nothing, Traitor to the Nation: 1. The Pox Party*. Cambridge, MA: Candlewick Press. Grades 9 and up.

The Novanglian College of Lucidity is home to Octavian and his beautiful mother, said to be of royal African lineage, where he gradually learns who he really is and what freedom really means. This amazing story about slavery and freedom, set in the early days of the American Revolutionary War, narrates its plot using first person (Octavian), letters, invitations, and notices and chronicles and makes parallel the lives of American independence to the increasingly enslaved life of Octavian. Young people may chart the plot in the graphic format of their choice, especially in Part III, "Liberty and Property," told in letters written to his sister "Shun" (Fruition) by Pvt. Goring, who keeps track of a slave he calls Prince as well as the progress of the Patriot troops.

Point of View

Hornschemeier, Paul. 2003. *Mother, Come Home*. Milwaukie, OR: Dark Horse Books. Adult book for YAs.

This graphic novel is presented from the point of view of seven-year-old Thomas Aquinas, or "T.A.," who does everything in his power to understand the death of his mother Sarah and the unrelenting grief of his father David, a professor of logic. The father and son are locked together within a sense of loss that cannot be put into words, but the color palette and positioning of T.A. amidst the adults show how powerless the child really is. YAs can review the novel and discuss specifically how the creator captures in the different styles of illustration the pathos of the tenderhearted little boy who only wants to help and to protect his father, whose deep depression is not explained until the very end; for example, T.A.'s lion mask represents his childhood; anthropomorphized chapters stress his aunt and uncle's clueless attempts to cheer up the boy ("The Grounds and the Groundskeeper").

Setting

Ihimaera, Witi. 1987. *The Whale Rider*. New York: Harcourt. Grades 5–8.

As small preteen Maori girl, Kahu will do anything to please her great-grandfather Koro, but his entrenched beliefs about women based on the Ancient's ways will not permit him to accept her as an equal with the boys. The integral setting takes place off the East Coast of New Zealand on Whangara, thought to be a whale-shaped island (p. 40), whose villagers are closely tied to their sacred rituals, legends, and ceremonies. Young people can read the book and then watch the award-winning movie version (Caro, 2002) to discuss the many differences between the novel and the film (e.g., in the book, her Uncle Rawiri gives the first person point of view and Nanny Flowers exhibits a very cantankerous personality and a matriarchal royal lineage).

Style

Moore, Alan, and Kevin O'Neill. 2000. *The League of Extraordinary Gentlemen*, Vol. 1. La Jolla, CA: America's Best Comics. Adult book for YAs.

Enlisted by the shadowy "Mr. M" to rescue Victorian England from imminent destruction, well-known fictional characters combat apes, warlords, and pirates aboard flying warships, aerial cannons, and the *Nautilus*. Stylistically emphasizing the figurative use of allusion, this graphic novel brings together different authors' characters (Captain Nemo, Dr. Jekyll and Mr. Hyde, Allan Quartermain, The Invisible Man, and Mina Murray) to create a new ensemble of sleuths. Authentic historical and cultural allusions from nineteenth-century Europe are abundant. Pairs of students can role-play as detectives in a timed, competitive library scavenger hunt to research these characters before reading this fast-paced science fiction mystery.

Theme

Vecchione, Patrice, ed. 2004. *Revenge and Forgiveness: An Anthology of Poems*. New York: Holt. Grades 7 and up.

Inspired by the tragedy of September 11, this gathering of 57 poems addresses the emotions of anger, blame, and revenge. Illuminated is the theme that, paradoxically, across time and culture, humankind has longed for revenge and forgiveness. In response to this anthology, young people can identify a poem they would have included, list a set of poems that address a theme of their choice, or create a collage (like that on the cover of *Revenge and Forgiveness*) to illustrate the theme of another anthology that they have appreciated.

Tone

Adoff, Jaime. 2004. *Names Will Never Hurt Me*. New York: Penguin Putnam. Grades 8 and up.

Presenting contemporary student tensions regarding the ever-present possibility for violence in high school, this multigenre novel establishes a painfully honest tone from the opening pages that introduce main characters Kurt, Ryan, Tisha, and Floater. The tone varies with each character but reveals Adoff's compassionate attitude toward even those who are easily dismissed as stereotypes, such as Ryan the jock and Kurt the depressed loner. Floater's interior monologues are chillingly disturbing. Young people can select any of the characters' interior monologues or dialogues for a short performance that highlights tone.

REFERENCES AND SUGGESTIONS FOR FURTHER READING

Abrams, M.H. 1993. *A Glossary of Literary Terms*, 6th ed. New York: Harcourt Brace Jovanovich.

Bauerlein, Mark. 2007. "What We Owe the New Critics." *The Chronicle Review of The Chronicle of Higher Education*, 54, no. 17 (December 21): B6–8.

Bennett, James. R. 1992. "After and Beyond 'New Criticism'."*Style* 26, no. 4 (Winter): 678–686.

Bertens, Hans. 2001. *Literary Theory: The Basics*. New York: Routledge

Brooks, Cleanth, and Robert Penn Warren. 1938. *Understanding Poetry*. New York: Henry Holt.

Brooks, Cleanth, and Robert Penn Warren. 1943. *Understanding Fiction*. New York: S.F. Crofts.

Caro, Nikki. 2002. *The Whale Rider*. Produced by John Barnet. New Market Films. DVD, 105 min.

Clausen, Christopher. 1997. "Reading Closely Again." *Commentary* 103, no. 2 (February): 54–57.

Davis, Garrick, ed. 2008. *Praising It New: The Best of the New Criticism*. Athens: Swallow Press/Ohio University Press.

Elder, Linda, and Richard Paul. 2004. "Critical Thinking and the Art of Close Reading. Part IV." *Journal of Developmental Education* 28, no. 1 (Fall): 36–37.

Friedberg, Harris. 2005. "Prose and Poetry." *Poetics Today* 26, no. 1 (Spring): 1–37.

Frye, Northrup. 1957. *Anatomy of Criticism*. Princeton, NJ: Princeton University.

Keesey, Donald. 1987. *Contexts for Criticism*. Mountain View, CA: Mayfield.

Lentricchia, Frank, and Andrew Dubois, eds. 2003. *Close Reading: The Reader*. Durham, NC: Duke University Press.

Medici, Anthony G. 1997. "The Restless Ghost of the New Criticism." *Style* 31, no. 4 (Winter): 760–773.

Myers, Walter Dean. 1999. *Monster.* New York: HarperCollins.

Ohmann, Richard. 1995. "Teaching and Studying Literature at the End of Ideology." In *The New Criticism and Contemporary Theory,* edited by William J. Spurlin and Michael Fischer, pp. 75–100. New York: Garland.

Paul, Richard, and Linda Elder. 2003. "Critical Thinking and the Art of Close Reading: Part I." *Journal of Developmental Education* 27, no. 2 (Winter): 36–37.

Paul, Richard, and Linda Elder. 2004a. "Critical Thinking and the Art of Close Reading: Part II." *Journal of Developmental Education* 27, no. 3 (Spring): 36–37.

Paul, Richard, and Linda Elder. 2004b. "Critical Thinking and the Art of Close Reading: Part III. *Journal of Developmental Education* 28, no. 2 (Winter): 36–37.

Phillips, John. 2004. "Paradigms of Reading." *European Journal of English Studies* 8, no. 1 (April): 138–144.

Ransom, John Crowe. 1941. *The New Criticism.* Norfolk, CT: New Directions.

Richards, I.A. 1929. *Practical Criticism: A Study of Literary Judgment.* New York: Harcourt, Brace and World.

Showalter, Elaine. 2003. *Teaching Literature.* Malden, MA: Blackwell.

Spurlin, William J., and Michael Fischer, eds. 1995. *The New Criticism and Contemporary Theory.* New York: Garland.

Chapter 6

Psychological Criticism

INTRODUCTION TO PSYCHOLOGICAL CRITICISM

Psychological-psychoanalytical criticism is an approach to literature based to some degree on the works of Sigmund Freud. Changing along with the subsequent psychological theories that challenged Freud, this form of criticism follows a number of theories that address the human mind and its literary expressions and that attempt to answer some of the following questions:

- What is the nature of the creative process, and from where does it originate?
- What can be discerned from an author's life that sheds light on his or her *psyche*, or state of mind, and literary work?
- How do the thoughts, motivations, actions, and conflicts of characters reflect their psyches?
- Do the structure and content of a literary work suggest psychological themes or issues?
- What is the nature of a reader's response to literature?

Freud's controversial *psychosexual theory* has been used, abused, revised, and renounced since his works were first published in the early years of the twentieth century. As one of the twentieth century's greatest figures, Freud theorized that human behavior could be understood only by analyzing people's childhoods wherein he believed the personality is formed. Freud also believed that all human behavior is motivated by biological (sexual) instinct or drive, termed the *libido*, or the psychic energy associated with sexual urge. Freud considered his concept of the Oedipus complex, wherein a boy is unconsciously at odds with his father for his mother's love, to be the foundation of his entire theory. Freud wrote extensively on the Oedipus complex and believed that Sophocles' great tragedy, *Oedipus the King*, proved the accuracy of his thesis.

Freud (1933) also offered a structural theory of the personality of which he cautioned his students from thinking in terms of sharp dividing lines. Freud advised that any personality theory that is presented along linear lines "cannot do justice" to the mind's complexities; rather, it is better to see the personality more like a modern painting, where "the areas of colour [shade] off into one another. . . . Do not judge too harshly of a first attempt [his structural personality theory] at picturing a thing so elusive as the human mind" (p. 110). Freud's three components of the personality are the following:

1. The *id*, residing in the unconscious, is pleasure seeking, morally neutral, and irrational. The id works under the *pleasure principle*, or the demand to take care of one's needs immediately. An infant, therefore, is essentially all id because its very survival depends on the instant gratification of all of its needs.

2. The *ego* consciously tries to present itself as organized, healthy, and in control. The ego works under the *reality principle*, or primary governing principle, acting as a moderating influence over the id's strong pleasure principle. The ego's work lies in dealing with the conflicts arising between the two opposites represented by the id and the superego.

3. The *superego* represses the impulses of the id. It is partly conscious and can be thought of as the mind's law and order, judge and jury, trying to abide by society's rules, maintaining an acceptable moral attitude, and often producing guilt. In the extreme, the superego can be punitive, harsh, and unforgiving.

British therapist Don D. Bannister (1966: 21) captures—as he interprets it—the psychic activity of a typical person as seen through the eyes of a Freudian: "Psychoanalytic theories seem to suggest that man is basically a battlefield. He is a dark-cellar in which a well-bred spinster lady (the superego) and a sex-crazed monkey (the id) are forever engaged in mortal combat, the struggle being refereed by a rather nervous bank clerk (the ego)."

Another of Freud's contributions to psychology is his work on the nature of dreams and how to analyze them. Freud's (1913) *The Interpretation of Dreams* presented new concepts about dreams, calling their contents *wish fulfillment*, or attempts by the unconscious to grant a desire. He and others believe that literature and dreams resemble each other: both originate in the unconscious and are creative and symbolic. Through therapy, the patient and doctor work together to arrive at the meaning of a dream, thereby confronting the hidden message from the unconscious and bringing it into the conscious mind.

HUMANISTIC PSYCHOLOGY

Those who reacted against, revised, or denounced Freud's psychosexual theory moved in many directions. Perhaps the approach most in opposition to Freud's is what is sometimes called *humanistic psychology*, which concentrates on people's positive biological, instinctual inclinations toward growth and emotional health. To its detractors, Freud's biologically determined theory was too pessimistic, stressed pathology and human limitations, and was biased against women. As humanistic psychologist Abraham Maslow wrote, "Freud supplied to us the sick half of psychology and we must now fill it out with the healthy half" (cited in Goble, 1970: 17). Humanistic psychologists also stress the here and now rather than the past and its unresolved childhood urges. Few psychologists completely reject Freud, but those who disagreed with Freud while he was still alive were no longer welcomed into his prestigious inner circle.

German-American psychoanalyst Karen Horney (pronounced HORN-eye) began her career as a classical Freudian in the 1920s. After she moved to the United States, Horney came to see that Freud's conclusions about feminine psychology were erroneous, in part, because they failed to take cultural factors into account. In addition, she disagreed with Freud's concept of the libido as the source of all compulsive instinctual drives, most of which to him were destructive. Horney (1945: 19) wrote, "Freud's pessimism as regards neuroses and their treatment arose from the depths of his disbelief in human goodness and human growth. Man, he postulated, is doomed to suffer or to destroy." Horney (1950: 368) arrived at her own definition of neurosis, "*a disturbance in one's relation to self and to others*," thereby balancing the role of environment in forming personality.

Horney recognized the importance of childhood experiences in the forming of personality. For those fortunate enough to be reared by warm, loving parents their potential for a healthy personality was good. However, for those whose childhoods were marked by any number of unfavorable environments, their potential was misdirected by their attempts to cope with bad parenting. In their desire to regain their feeling of safety and to end their isolation, children will try many defense strategies in order to (often futilely) work their way back into their parents' hearts, according to Horney.

KAREN HORNEY'S PERSONALITY TRENDS

In constructing her theory of psychological *defense mechanisms*, or the characteristic ways of defending oneself against anxiety, Horney referred to the mechanisms interchangeably as *trends, solutions, defense strategies*, or *attitudes*. Whatever term is used, the concept of her personality theory is the same: People veer in the direction of one trend over the others as a response to *basic anxiety*, or "feeling isolated and helpless toward a world potentially hostile" (Horney, 1945: 12–13). Horney (1950) found three *trends* that all people use (emotionally healthy or not) to cope and to adopt as they struggle with life's conflicts:

Summary of Horney's Three Personality Trends

I. Moving *toward* people (compliant personalities)

II. Moving *against* people (aggressive personalities)
   A. Narcissistic personalities
   B. Perfectionistic personalities
   C. Arrogant-vindictive personalities

III. Moving *away* from people (detached personalities)

Children who experience a bad environment may come to prefer one of the trends over the others for different reasons, including an unconscious desire for attaining some kind of unity or integration of the psyche. Horney (1950: 21) pictures the conflicted person as "no longer, so to speak, the driver, but is driven." Everything the neurotic person does is oriented toward the fulfillment of the demands made by the (unconsciously) chosen defense strategy, or trend.

Horney found a sort of internal logic within each of the trends, indicating their compelling nature to control one's inner conflicts (*intrapsychic*) and in relations with others (*interpersonal*). Horney (1950: 17) identified what she termed the *real self* as the "central inner force, common to all human beings and yet unique in each, which is the deep source of growth." The real self tends to get lost in the chaotic turmoil of striving for the *idealized self* that each trend encourages as it races toward goals not in agreement with the real self. Wary of the dangers of typologies in psychology, Horney kept her theory intentionally broad and did not see people as types. Healthy people freely choose (unconsciously) from any of the trends depending on the circumstances: *toward*, *against*, or *away* from others. It is only when an individual prefers one trend to the exclusion of the others that conflicts arise, as the other trends remain repressed in the unconscious.

Horney (1950) discovered that the difference between healthy and unhealthy personalities was in the quality, not the quantity, of their trends. In healthy individuals, the three trends are not mutually exclusive. A person who is relatively free of anxiety and neurosis may choose the course of action that best suits the situation: Sometimes a person wants to give affection or to give in (to be compliant). Sometimes a person needs to fight (to be aggressive). Sometimes a person wants time alone to rest or to reflect (to be detached). The three trends are normally complementary capacities necessary for dealing with one's interpersonal relationships in constructive ways without the conflict that arises from adhering tenaciously to only one solution or trend (Horney, 1950: 19), thereby stirring up personal crises. While under life's crises and uncertainties, literary characters can be thought of as "imagined human beings" whose behavior can be understood and analyzed by applying psychological models of the personality to the fiction (Paris, 1997).

HORNEY'S PERSONALITY TRENDS IN LITERARY CHARACTERS

There are scholars who have found Karen Horney's theory of inner and outer conflicts useful in responding to literary characters from a psychological perspective. In *Imagined Human Beings: A Psychological Approach to Character and Conflict in Literature*, Bernard J. Paris (1997) presents a case for considering Horney's model as a way to understand the anxieties that drive realistically portrayed characters' thoughts, motivations, and behaviors. In *Third Force Psychology and the Study of Literature*, edited by Paris (1986), scholars analyze many novels relying on the Horneyan model, including characters from Charles Dickens, William Faulkner, and William Styron. Paris has become an expert on Horney's theory as applied to literature and stresses that the Horney model works best when the characters are realistic. Even science fiction or fantasy novels can be analyzed with this theory if the characters are portrayed realistically and think and behave much like real people.

Paris does not address young adult (YA) literature in his works, but Horney's psychological theory provides an accessible way to approach YA literature. In the remainder of this section, Horney's (1950) three trends are described; the descriptions are followed by brief examples from literature or film and descriptions of traits and characteristics that Horney observed in her many years of clinical practice. (The descriptions are meant be *suggestive* of each trend and not a rigid typology).

I. Moving Toward People (Compliant Personalities)

CLASSIC AND CONTEMPORARY MEDIA EXAMPLES

Stanley Yelnats in Sachar's (1998) *Holes* feels inferior to others because of his weight and his terrible luck. Teen author Kelly McWilliams' (2004) *Doormat* portrays Jaime as the classic compliant girl who transforms herself as she tries to nurture her best friend. In the movie *The Waitress* (Shelley, 2007), young wife Jenna bakes pies to express her anger toward her physically and emotionally abusive husband, but, by the end, Jenna puts her doormat compliancy behind her and forges a better life for herself. Homeschooled Cady Heron in the film *Mean Girls* (Waters, 2004) is eager to please her new Goth friends by infiltrating "the Plastics," or socials.

CHILDHOODS

Compliant people may have grown up under the shadow of a favorite or dominating sibling or of a kind but overpowering parent. Compliant children's original coping strategy is to adopt within themselves the qualities they think will make it easier for others to accept and to love them.

INTRAPSYCHIC TRAITS

Compliant people feel helpless and weak before others, especially aggressive people. They take it for granted that everybody is better than they are and tend to underrate their own talents and abilities. Their self-esteem rises and falls with the approval of others.

INTERPERSONAL TRAITS

Compliant people find it difficult, if not impossible, to say no to any request. They feel lost if they are alone. (In their minds, being alone proves that they are not liked by everybody.) Because they trust and like everybody, they may misjudge others and be easily taken advantage of. They do not like games or competitions and are not good fighters. They may be attracted to their opposite—aggressive individuals—living vicariously through the partner's (mis)perceived strengths.

VALUES AND BELIEFS

Their values "lie in the direction of goodness, sympathy, love, generosity, and humility" (Horney, 1945: 54). However, they may *not* genuinely hold these values but are compelled to take them to extremes. They think that they must like everybody and be self-sacrificing if others are to love them.

II. Moving Against People (Aggressive Personalities)

There are three subcategories of aggressive individuals. The aggressive person may move in and out of any of the three subcategories of this trend—*narcissist, perfectionist,* or *arrogant-vindictive*—or favor one.

A. Narcissistic Personalities

CLASSIC AND CONTEMPORARY MEDIA EXAMPLES

Biff Loman in Arthur Miller's (1949) *Death of a Salesman* is the archetypal narcissist, as he tries to accept what his adoring father Willie believes Biff to be—charming and an "Adonis" athlete—until the truth of the painful illusion breaks through at the play's tragic climax. In the extreme, narcissistic characters may be some of the most violent or manipulative characters in film, and there are not as many of them in "G" rated films as in higher rated ones. However, the protagonist and main characters in *The Talented Mr. Ripley* (Minghella, 1999) are narcissists, as is Bill "the Butcher" Cutting whose sense of unlimited power over others brings mayhem in *Gangs of New York* (Scorsese, 2002).

CHILDHOODS

Narcissists may have been the favorite child in their families and believed to be precociously gifted or talented, easily winning early distinction in sports, academics, or other skills. They may, then, peak early in their lives and become bitter when they learn that success demands a lot of effort.

INTRAPSYCHIC TRAITS

Narcissists have no doubts about what they can do and maintain an unquestioned belief in their own greatness and uniqueness. They tend to overlook their own flaws or turn them into virtues. Narcissists do not seem to mind breaking promises, being unfaithful, or running up debts. They feel entitled to every privilege life can offer.

INTERPERSONAL

To other people (who may envy them), narcissists seem very charming and self-confident. They must impress others, especially new people who come into their lives. They appear full of life and forever youthful and seem to like people (although they feel superior to them). They may speak endlessly of themselves, their successes, and their perfect families. They make good fighters. They use flattery to charm others with the intention of eventually getting something back from them.

VALUES AND BELIEFS

Narcissists believe they should succeed with very little effort. They expect others to love them unconditionally. They believe their preferences always come first, thus disregarding the wishes of the important people in their lives.

B. Perfectionistic Personalities

CLASSIC AND CONTEMPORARY MEDIA EXAMPLES

Lisa Yee's (2003: 1) *Millicent Min, Girl Genius* proclaims her personality trend in the novel's opening sentence, "I have been accused of being anal retentive, an over-achiever, and a compulsive perfectionist, like those are bad things." Leonardo DiCaprio plays perfectionist Howard Hughes in the biopic *The Aviator* (Scorsese, 2004).

CHILDHOODS

Perfectionists may have grown up under a rigid, strict parental rule that made them feel inferior for not measuring up to unreasonable standards or demands. To gain acceptance, they cope by adopting the perfectionist values of their parents.

INTRAPSYCHIC

They identify themselves with their own high standards (moral, intellectual, or disciplinary). They believe that other people are not as intelligent, as moral, or as disciplined as they are.

INTERPERSONAL

Perfectionists may exhibit a convincing friendliness to others because they believe that they *should*, but they actually look down on others. They expect respect from everybody. They may demand perfection in those with whom they deal. In their careers they tend to be meticulous and possess exacting standards, leaving them easily overworked and exhausted (Horney, 1950: 315).

VALUES AND BELIEFS

They see their own success, prosperity, or good health as proof of their perfection, not something to be happy about or to be thankful for.

C. Arrogant-Vindictive Personalities

CLASSIC AND CONTEMPORARY EXAMPLES

Archie Costello in *The Chocolate War* (Cormier, 1974) is the archetypal character of this trend, as he relishes humiliating and intimidating others. In *Gangs of New York* (Scorsese, 2002), Amsterdam Vallon relentlessly seeks vindication for the murder of his father by Bill "the Butcher" Cutting.

CHILDHOODS

Arrogant-vindictive personalities experienced a childhood that was particularly bad in some way. They may have been brutalized, humiliated, or neglected, or observed others treated badly. Under such a harsh upbringing, in order to survive, they may have gone through a hardening process (Horney, 1950: 202). They choked off all tender needs and eventually gave up trying to please others.

INTRAPSYCHIC TRAITS

Arrogant-vindictive people identify with their pride in their intellectual power, in their vigilance, in their outwitting everybody, and in their foresight and planning (Horney, 1950: 204). They believe they will become great in some way, and then their success will show how wronged or misjudged they were. Vindictive revenge and triumph determine the course of their lives. Regarding others, they think, "It is out of the question that they should love me; they hate me anyhow, so they should at least be afraid of me" (Horney, 1950: 211).

INTERPERSONAL TRAITS

Arrogant-vindictive people need to intimidate others. They are extremely competitive and are very poor losers. They are openly arrogant, rude, and offensive. They humiliate others and exploit them without giving it a thought. They interact with others exclusively on the basis of serving their needs for triumph. In their careers they use others as stepping stones to their own success. In their sexuality they tend to conquer and subdue. Horney (1950: 315) notes of arrogant-vindictive people that of all the trends they are the "most prodigious" workers as they strive to satisfy their relentless ambition.

VALUES AND BELIEFS

They believe that everybody is bad and crooked and that friendly gestures (by themselves or from others) are hypocritical. They distrust everybody. They believe that nobody can hurt them and they have a right to punish anybody they deem an enemy.

III. Moving Away from People (Detached Personalities)

CLASSIC AND CONTEMPORARY MEDIA EXAMPLES

Sir Arthur Conan Doyle's Sherlock Holmes is the archetypal detached fictional character. The role of Dr. Gregory House in the TV series *House* boasts of his emotional distance from others (Shore and Singer, 2004–2008). Temperance Brennan, the main character in *Bones* (Hanson, 2005)—a television series about a forensic anthropologist based on Kathy Reich's mystery novels (1997–2008)— exhibits the traits of a detached personality to a fault, and the difference between her and her partner, FBI agent Seeley Booth, centers on his advising Temperance about the finer points of the interpersonal relationships that she lacks. Temperance, or "Bones," prefers intelligence over emotion and self-reliance over dependence on others.

CHILDHOODS

Detached people may have experienced a wide range of possible childhoods. Some may have had confining or restricting parents who made it difficult or impossible for them to openly rebel, a necessity for healthy development. The emotional atmosphere may have been so tightly controlled that the child could not develop a healthy sense of individuality.

INTRAPSYCHIC TRAITS

According to Horney (1950: 260), there are fewer patterns and greater variations within the detached trend than in the other trends. Detached persons seem to be "onlookers" of themselves and of their own lives, as they often put distance between themselves and others, thereby suppressing their emotions. Things are tested or judged from the standpoint of any possible loss of their freedom, inde- pendence, and self-sufficiency. They can suffer from claustrophobia (dislike feeling restricted or closed in).

INTERPERSONAL TRAITS

Detached people do not become emotionally involved with others, avoid social gatherings, and appear aloof, but they superficially get along well with others. They resent any illness—it forces them to be dependent on others. They prefer to get their knowledge firsthand (no group work) and keep their personal lives shrouded in secrecy. They do not want to be influenced by or feel obligated to others. They avoid long-term relationships but may seek a partner with an aggressive personality.

VALUES AND BELIEFS

Detached people believe the most important thing in life is their freedom and independence. They value their nonconformity, believing conformists live and think like robots. They may disregard rules and regulations as being too conventional and restrictive. They prize intelligence over emotion. If they possess any inherent talent, detached people can be creative or can exhibit original thinking. They do not like competition, are not good fighters, nor do they value prestige or success.

HORNEY'S PERSONALITY TRENDS IN YA LITERATURE

Considering that much YA literature features protagonists who are in the midst of loss, trauma, conflict, turmoil, or crisis, applying Horney's model can provide readers with an accessible way to discuss stories from a psychological perspective. YAs live in a fluid psychological state, experimenting with roles and trying on new hats. However, some YA characters do clearly exhibit Horney's trends and often move in and out of certain trends within the course of the narrative.

The following questions for discussion may not apply to every novel, nor are the questions intended to be used in the given order:

1. If the story relates the protagonist's childhood, how would a reader describe that childhood in Horneyan terms? What might be the expected personality trend to emerge from such a childhood?

2. From whose point of view is the story told? Does the narrator give indications of the protagonist's intrapsychic beliefs or conflicts? If so, does the protagonist seem to move toward one trend in his or her thinking?

3. Does the protagonist seem to prefer one trend in his or her interpersonal relationships? Does this trend seem to work well for the protagonist?

4. Other characters: Which trends do the other important characters seem to prefer? Does the protagonist have an antagonist with an opposing trend?

5. What are the occasions in which the protagonist moves from one trend to another, and how smoothly does he or she make these moves?

6. Does the protagonist have a close friend, a romantic interest, or a lover? Does this character show a similar or an opposite personality trend?

7. What episode(s) shows the protagonist in a dramatic use of one or more of the trends?

Application of Horney's Personality Trends to Robert Cormier's *Heroes*

In *Heroes* (Cormier, 1998), 18-year-old Francis Joseph Cassavant has returned to his hometown following an extended hospitalization for severe facial injuries incurred during World War II. Francis received a Silver Star for heroism, having fallen on a grenade and saved the lives of his comrades. His injuries are so severe that in public he covers his head and face with a silk scarf and a hat. For a while, no one recognizes him. He rents the attic room in an old boarding house, registering under an alias. The novel is actually a mystery. Francis tells the reader he plans to shoot Larry LaSalle. Using familiar military terminology, Francis calls his desire to kill his "mission." The questions at this point are, who is Larry LaSalle and why does Francis want to kill him? Why does Francis focus more on Larry than on his own devastating war wounds?

Childhood

Francis' mother died when he was 6, and his father died when he was 13, leaving the boy to live with his bachelor uncle Louis. As an orphaned teenager, Francis appreciated his uncle for giving him a home during the Depression. Francis also talks about his years in Catholic schools and the punishment meted out by his teachers. The memories of parochial school are mixed, however, as Francis and another former student discuss Sister Martha almost fondly despite her relentless commitment to strict punishment by using her infamous large ruler. The nuns' discipline encouraged young people to obey (become compliant), and Francis falls into line, becoming a faithful Catholic, a moral compass in his life.

Trying to cope without parental love or acceptance, Francis becomes very shy, although he is not a detached person. Being completely dependent on his uncle, Francis is a compliant boy, eager to please the nuns and to make a friend. An avid reader of such manly authors as Ernest Hemingway and F. Scott Fitzgerald, Francis shows a precocious intellect and wins writing contests at school. Despite the hardships of his childhood, Francis seems to have coped as well as could be expected.

Point of View

Francis narrates his story, revealing (gradually) details of why he has come to the point in his young life that he is hopeless and lives only for revenge. It is evident that traumatic events caused him to change dramatically from a balanced person who moved easily between detached and compliant trends into an aggressive, vindictive person. At present he feels that he has become transformed in some way, "When I study myself in the mirror, I don't see me anymore but a stranger slowly taking shape" (p. 84). It is not the war wounds that have changed him but his trend toward committing the ultimate revenge against another human. He even prays for LaSalle, the man he plans to kill, creating additional anxiety because his mission clearly goes against his religious and moral beliefs. Francis fills in the puzzle pieces of his life, alternating between the past and the present, but he always comes back to the point of his story: killing Larry LaSalle.

His intrapsychic trend is without question one of revenge. However, at times his behavior reflects the detachment that one would expect from a veteran who suffers from severe facial wounds that he knows takes strangers by surprise and horrifies little children. He still feels the need to move toward others, however, dropping by the local bar where other veterans gather, but he knows his secret revenge alienates him from the camaraderie of those who share his war experiences. He may no longer be in the army, but he has a mission that he plans to carry out, including "the proper method of disposal," the injured veterans' euphemism for suicide (p. 85), indicating that his mission may include his own suicide.

Other Characters

At the core of Francis' psychic wound lies his meeting Larry LaSalle, who became the director of the "Wreck Center" (recreation center) when Francis was about 13. Francis remembers how all the children were drawn to LaSalle, who seemed to lighten the dark Depression era for them. Larry was handsome with a charming smile and a good physique. He was a man of many talents, an athlete and a dancer. He seemed to like everybody and impressed everyone he met, children and adults. However, Francis notes that nobody knew much about Larry, his family, or where he came from, and Larry "discouraged questions" (p. 44). In fact, despite his popularity, Larry was still so intimidating that few ever dared to ask him any personal questions about the rumors going around about him. The children, "dazzled by his talents and his energy," liked the "air of mystery" that surrounded Larry (p. 45), suggesting certain detached traits.

The Wreck Center children were escaping lonely tenement lives and found Larry to be a happy diversion. Larry tells Francis before one big weekend activity that, even though he is not supposed to show favorites, he considers Francis and Nicole more special than the others, indicating his skill in charming and emotionally manipulating young people. Larry LaSalle fits the classic narcissistic personality trend.

Larry discerns what each child needs and suggests activities for boys like Francis who are not good at sports. It is Larry's idea that Francis take up table tennis. What boy (too short, uncoordinated, and too timid) would not fall under the spell of a hero who listens as if Francis' words "were the most important he had ever heard" (p. 112)? In the big championship table tennis tournament, Francis wins first place, but the narcissistic Larry takes away Francis' moment of triumph by challenging him to a final game. Partway through the match, Francis realizes that Larry is letting him win. The insight that Francis sees about Larry comes not from his past, but from the present and from his more mature understanding *now*.

Romantic Interest

When Francis first sees Nicole Renard in the seventh grade, he is smitten for life, but it takes the absence of Larry (in World Ward II) to cement their relationship. They both like to read and spend time in the library. Finally he gets up the courage to invite her to a movie, and they attend every Saturday matinee, holding hands and kissing. They always have a lot to talk about. Being more self-confident and independent, Nicole coaxes Francis out of his shyness. She asks about his interests and tells him he should think about becoming a writer, a talent he fails to acknowledge in himself (a compliant trait). They are both naïve and vulnerable to adult attention, but Nicole seems to move more easily from one trend to another.

When Larry LaSalle returns to town on furlough, everyone turns out to greet the Silver Star hero, including Nicole and Francis. Larry invites his favorites to attend a surprise party at the Wreck Center. He provides sodas and snacks, and they all dance. Later, when it is only Larry and Nicole and Francis, Larry tells Francis to go home. Nicole whispers twice to Francis for him to stay, but Francis recalls, "We always did what Larry LaSalle told us to do" (p. 94). The narcissistic Larry charmed the children and manipulated them to do whatever he told them. He chose those whose lives were the loneliest, like Nicole and Francis. By giving special attention to the most vulnerable young people, Larry could be assured of the adoration and affection that, as a narcissist, he always craved, although surely did not deserve.

Francis does not leave as ordered but hides in the foyer. Naïve in the ways of intimacy and vaguely aware that something wrong is going on between Nicole and Larry in the darkened Wreck Center, Francis panics and cannot think straight. He does nothing and remains hidden long enough to see Nicole stumble into the hallway, obviously having been assaulted. Francis sees in Nicole's face his "betrayal of her in her eyes" (p. 97). Worst of all, Francis thinks (p. 97), "It's amazing that the heart makes no noise when it cracks," an ambiguous reference that can apply to either Nicole or Francis.

Francis's epiphany—that his hero and his single lifeline to self-confidence was a lecherous traitor—leaves the boy shattered, shamed, and with guilt. Francis had failed to act, failed to show Nicole that she was more important to him than Larry. However, Larry had handpicked Francis because of the boy's willing-to-please and never-say-no personality. Depressed, Francis wanders aimlessly for days and tries to apologize to Nicole. After many sleepless nights, he climbs the stairs of the church's tallest steeple, intent on suicide. However, he cannot commit the act, "the worse sin of all: despair" (p. 104). He also could not disgrace his family's name. He had not been the hero that Nicole needed him to be, so at 15 years of age Francis alters his birth certificate and enlists in the army, hoping that he would die a hero in battle.

Climactic Episode

The awaited for confrontation occurs when Francis discovers that Larry has also returned. Francis carries his gun "like a tumor" on his thigh (p. 108), surprising himself with his calm. The formerly tanned and handsome Larry now looks pale and fragile. When Francis states his name, Larry of course flashes him a big smile, "the old enthusiasm back in his voice" (p. 110). Larry, surprised to learn that Francis knows about Nicole, and without any hint of remorse, tells Francis he is too hard on himself. "'You didn't do anything you should feel guilty about. . . . You couldn't have stopped me, anyway, Francis, you were just a child'" (p. 114), speaking to Francis as if they were back in the past and Francis were a boy again.

Francis pulls out his gun and aims it at Larry, but his hand begins to shake. He suddenly realizes what he is about to do and is overwhelmed by it, but Larry is completely without shame. Now emotionally locked in the past, Francis tells Larry what a hero he had been to everyone even before the war. Larry says, "'Does that one sin of mine wipe away all the good things?'" (p. 115). However, the only thing on Francis' mind is to put a bullet in Larry's heart as he had once shattered his and Nicole's hearts. He tells Larry how he has rehearsed the words many times before this moment: "'Say your prayers'" (p. 116), a moment of irony that Francis cannot see. But Larry has his own gun, indicating that Francis has fulfilled his mission except that Larry will finish the mission himself.

As Francis turns to leave, Larry wants to tell Francis one more thing, "'You would have fallen on that grenade anyway. All your instincts would have made you sacrifice yourself for your comrades'" (p. 118). Larry's remarks for once could be the truth, or they could be part of Larry's lying ways. Francis thinks, "Still trying to make me better than I am" (p. 118), a reflection of the boy's still having little self-knowledge or recognition of his positive traits.

In the end, Francis still carries his gun in his duffel bag. However, there are also signs of hope for Francis, as he reconsiders Nicole's encouragement to get serious about his writing, an army buddy's advice about going to college on the GI Bill, and Dr. Abram's offer of cosmetic surgery.

ANNOTATED BIBLIOGRAPHY

Anderson, Laurie Halse. 2007. *Twisted.* New York: Viking Press. Grades 9 and up.

After going through high school as a nobody, Tyler commences his senior year in unexpected bad-boy fame for a graffiti spree that placed him on summer community service, working out everyday and building a handsome new physique. His father has an aggressive personality and becomes emotionally detached from the family, spending every evening alone in "his lair" (p. 86), headphones in place. The ever-compliant mother, Gumby-like in her ability to twist herself into whatever excuse she comes up with for father's bad conduct, stays in denial. Tyler becomes more and more lost to himself until he finally gains his father's attention by resorting to violence and rage. Tyler Miller's story makes a good subject for a bio-poem.

Corrigan, Eireann. 2004. *Splintering.* New York: Scholastic. Grades 9 and up.

Surviving a terrifying home invasion, the Holt family maintains a wall of silence about the events of that night, each person dealing with the fear and horror in his or her own way. With the events and the aftermath narrated in free verse and from the point of view of 15-year-old Paulie and her 17-year-old brother Jeremy, the story shows how a shattered family puts the pieces of their lives back together after emotional isolation does not work for them. Young people could apply Horney's three trends to each character (e.g., Mimi moves *away*; Paulie moves *against*; Jeremy moves *toward*), showing how they eventually arrive at a healthier family.

Crutcher, Chris. 2007. *Deadline.* **New York: HarperCollins. Grades 9 and up.**

What should Ben Wolf do when he discovers he has a rare blood disease that gives him only one year to live? Ben has been a nurturing person, listening to and caring for his bipolar mother. He accepts his individuality, selectively detaching (keeping his illness a secret) while moving toward characters. He decides to cram one whole lifetime into his one last year of life and takes on more aggressive traits through difficult personal challenges (playing football) and through a romantic involvement with the girl of his dreams. YAs can read Crutcher's (2003) *King of the Mild Frontier: An Ill-advised Autobiography* and search for autobiographical elements of his life in *Deadline.*

Doyle, Malachy. 2001. *Georgie.* **New York: Bloomsbury. Grades 6 and up.**

For half of his 14 years, Georgie Bayliss has been mute, uncontrollable, and full of rage until he moves to a new school where a new teacher unlocks the secret of the child's painful past. Georgie represents the most extreme form of a detached personality whose rage has almost split him in half: he often refers to himself in the third person. YAs can create a body biography of the two Georgies, illustrating his life before and after he begins to heal.

Koje, Katha. 2004. *The Blue Mirror.* **New York: Farrar, Straus, and Giroux. Grades 9–12.**

High school senior Maggy Klass sits in a coffee shop and sketches street people, isolating herself from those in her school who seem "so foreign" and less real than the people she draws (p. 69). Maggy nurtures her alcoholic, unemployed mother and finds the best way to cope at school is to become detached: "My life is so far removed from theirs I might as well be on another planet" (p. 14). She falls under the spell of the dark, mysterious Cole, who is not what he appears to be, and then comes to see him for the charming, manipulative narcissist that he is. Young people can go online to find and compare the works of two of Maggy's favorite artists, Hieronymus Bosch and Frieda Kahlo. (Although they have different styles, both artists paint psychologically unsettling subjects.)

Myers, Walter Dean. 2008. *Sunrise Over Fallujah.* **New York: Scholastic. Grades 8 and up.**

The protagonist, Private Robin Perry ("Birdy"), arrives as a new high school graduate to serve in an Army detachment in Iraq. His feelings are revealed in a dozen letters to and from home in Harlem and from random events shocking and boring and scary:

> A dream. I was riding along some highway in the back of a truck. Then it stopped being a truck and was an ambulance. Suddenly the ambulance/ truck stopped and I got out to see what was going on. . . . Looking up . . . I saw a group of soldiers. They had lifted their guns and were pointing at me.

Somehow it seemed that I would be all right if I didn't move. I tried to stay as still as possible, but then I moved and could see the fire from the muzzles of the gun. I was hit and panicked. No matter which way I turned I couldn't get away. (p. 105)

YAs can discuss the aftereffects of war. Birdy cannot reach out or pull back. He is in a psychological dead end that he faces in his last letter before leaving Iraq. He, like his uncle before him, determines that he will not talk about what he saw or what he did in war.

Oates, Joyce Carol. 2002. *Big Mouth and Ugly Girl*. New York: HarperCollins. Grades 8 and up.

Known for his lively sense of humor and popularity, Matt Donaghy becomes a social pariah after two anonymous students accuse him of making a bomb threat, and only well-known loner Ursula Riggs steps forward to be his witness. Ursula, tall and athletic, learned long ago, "When you like people you can be hurt" (p. 10). She hates being touched, and is even claustrophobic, signs of a classic detached person. Matt, however, has always been outgoing until his friends desert him, even after he is cleared of all false charges. He moves into detachment as he resigns from class office, stops writing, and thinks that if he turns "into stone no one can hurt" him (p. 144). Both characters show development and can be the subjects of body biographies.

Porter, Pamela. 2005. *The Crazy Man*. Toronto, Canada: Groundwood Books. Grades 5–8.

After seventh-grader Emmy Bitterman survives a freak tractor accident (but with a shortened leg), her father abandons her and their farm forever, leaving her mother Clarice with no other choice than to take in a helper from the nearby mental institution. Orange-haired Angus, mentally compromised following his mother's severe physical abuse, becomes essential to Emmy and Clarice's livelihood but a pariah to neighbor Harry Records, whose intolerance nearly results in Angus's death. The increasing prejudice against Angus makes Emmy wonder what it is that makes *some* people crazy, because the gentle and kind Angus is definitely sane. Young people can create a conflict escalator that follows how Angus changes people's attitude about him from an object of ridicule to a hero.

Tashjian, Janet. 1999. *Multiple Choice*. New York: Holt. Grades 5–9.

With a worsening obsessive streak making her life more miserable, Monica Devon devises a way to decrease her decision anxiety by reducing the number of answers to four for every problem she may have. The 14-year-old perfectionist finally sees that her new word game is not working for her but not before she has done damage to herself and others. *Monica Devon* is a good name for a bio-poem that plays off some of the girl's anagrams and word games.

Winspear, Jacqueline. 2003. *Maisie Dobbs: Novel*. New York: Soho. Adult book for YAs.

Winner of the Alex (2004) and the Agatha (2004) awards, this debut novel of a mystery series reveals how a precocious 13-year-old girl rises from poverty to become a woman whose nameplate reveals her unique profession, "*Psychologist and Investigator*" (p. 292), and whose philosophy is based on the concept of "the forensic science of the whole person" (p. 49). The novel spans 1910–1929, and during this time Maisie moves from compliance as servant girl for the wealthy Compton family through detachment as a detective whose cases reveal as much about herself as the mysteries she solves.

REFERENCES AND SUGGESTIONS FOR FURTHER READING

Bannister, Don D. 1966. "Psychology as an Exercise in Paradox." *Bulletin of the British Psychological Society* 19, no. 1 (September): 21–26.

Cormier, Robert. 1974. *The Chocolate War: A Novel.* New York: Pantheon.

Cormier, Robert. 1998. *Heroes.* New York: Random House.

Crutcher, Chris. 2003. *King of the Mild Frontier: An Ill-advised Autobiography.* New York: Greenwillow Books.

Freud, Sigmund. 1913. *The Interpretation of Dreams.* London: G. Allen.

Freud, Sigmund. 1933. "The Anatomy of the Mental Personality." In *New Introductory Lectures on Psycho-Analysis,* translated by W.J.H. Sprott, pp. 82–110. New York: W.W. Norton.

Goble, Frank. 1970. *The Third Force: The Psychology of Abraham Maslow.* New York: Grossman.

Hanson, Hart. 2005. *Bones.* Produced by Kathy Reichs. Fox Network. Videocassette and DVD.

Horney, Karen. 1945. *Our Inner Conflicts.* New York: W.W. Norton.

Horney, Karen. 1950. *Neurosis and Human Growth: The Struggle Toward Self-Realization.* New York: W.W. Norton.

McWilliams, Kelly. 2004. *Dormat: A Novel.* New York: Delacorte Press.

Miller, Arthur. 1949. *Death of a Salesman.* New York: Viking Press.

Minghella, Anthony. 1999. *The Talented Mr. Ripley.* Produced by Tom Sternberg. 139 min. Paramount Pictures.

Paris, Bernard J., ed. 1986. *Third Force Psychology and the Study of Literature.* Rutherford, NJ: Fairleigh Dickinson University Press.

Paris, Bernard J. 1997. *Imagined Human Beings: A Psychological Approach to Character and Conflict in Literature.* New York: New York University Press.

Sachar, Louis. 1998. *Holes.* New York: Farrar, Straus, and Giroux.

Scorsese, Martin. 2002. *Gangs of New York.* Produced by Alberto Grimaldi. 167 min. Miramax Films. Videocassette and DVD.

Scorsese, Martin. 2004. *The Aviator.* Produced by Sandy Kliman. 170 min. Warner Brothers.

Shelley, Adrienne. 2007. *The Waitress.* Produced by Michael Roiff. 108 min. Fox Searchlight Pictures. Videocassette or DVD.

Shore, David, and Bryan Singer. 2004–2008. *House.* 20th Century Fox.

Waters, Mark. 2004. *Mean Girls.* Produced by Lorne Michaels. 97 min. 20th Century Fox. Videocassette and DVD.

Yee, Lisa. 2003. *Millicent Min, Girl Genius.* New York: Arthur A. Levine Books.

Chapter 7

Sociological Criticism

INTRODUCTION TO SOCIOLOGICAL CRITICISM

Sociological criticism "examines literature in the cultural, economic, and political context in which it is written or received" (Kennedy and Gioia, 1998: 719). Socio-literary critics identify and discuss the significance of one or more of the following in a work of literature (Laurenson and Swingewood, 1972: 91):

- Type and economic level of society in which writers are working
- Social classes and groups to which writers belong or with which they relate directly or indirectly
- The character of the writers' audiences, sponsorships, patronages
- The literary tradition in which writers work

Literary critic David Daiches (1956: 364) refers to the sociological approach as "a handmaid of criticism." In its broadest sense, sociological criticism is an approach, not a single theory, although contemporary theories (e.g., feminist, reader response, historical) may touch on sociological issues and methods in their interpretations and evaluations of literature. No matter how diverse the theories may be, however, the goal of the critic is to identify the social contexts of literature. As practiced, sociological criticism is an open and dynamic process, not fixed and static. "The sociology of literature perpetually questions the concepts on which it relies: 'the writer,' 'the public,' 'genre,' 'literature' are notions redefined by the context in which they occur" (Clark, 1982: 118). Leo Lowenthal (1961: xvi), scholar of literature and sociology, defines his work as the "endeavor to treat the documents of artistic literature as primary sources for the interpretation of the imagery of self and society as a means of rounding out our understanding of social norms and values in times past." For students of American literature, sociological criticism begins in earnest with Socialist and Marxist critics in the early years of the twentieth century, with feminist critics of the 1970s, and with its influence in postcolonial criticism.

In "Why Teach Marxist Theory Now?" Deborah Appleman (2000: 59) considers the place of Marxist and feminist theories in secondary education. Appleman points out the similarities in Marxist and feminist theories: "Both are political, both interrogate textual features with considerations of power and oppression, both invite us to consider the kinds of prevailing ideologies that help construct the social realities in which we participate" (p. 58). However, the two approaches are different enough to warrant separate discussions (p. 58). Viewed pragmatically, social criticism seems more ideologically directed than most critical approaches to literature, although the idea that all theories are political to some degree is still debated. With this notion in mind, this chapter considers wider views on sociological criticism; gender and feminist criticism is discussed in Chapter 9. The important issues that young adults (YAs) face every day—identity, gender role expectations, and family—are often found in novels whose realism provides an accessible way for discussion using textual readings based, in part, on social criticism. Written in 1885, "Foreign Children" (see next section) serves as a model for approaching literature through a social lens.

CHANGING MEANING THROUGH SOCIAL CONTEXTS: APPLICATION OF SOCIAL CRITICISM TO ROBERT LOUIS STEVENSON'S "FOREIGN CHILDREN"

Foreign Children

By Robert Louis Stevenson (1885)

Little Indian, Sioux, or Crow,
Little frosty Eskimo,
Little Turk or Japanee,
Oh! don't you wish that you were me?

You have seen the scarlet trees
And the lions over seas;
You have eaten ostrich eggs,
And turned the turtle off their legs.

Such a life is very fine,
But it's not so nice as mine:
You must often as you trod,
Have wearied NOT to be abroad.

You have curious things to eat,
I am fed on proper meat;
You must dwell upon the foam,
But I am safe and live at home.

Little Indian, Sioux or Crow,
Little frosty Eskimo,
Little Turk or Japanee,
Oh! don't you wish that you were me?

In "Foreign Children" (Stevenson, 1998) how does social context shape the values, interpersonal relationships, and social institutions of the author, the author's intended reader, and the text? What is going on here; why does it matter? Figure 7.1 offers some answers.

Figure 7.1. Sociological View of "Foreign Children"			
Social Contexts	Intended Reader	Author	Text
Values	Victorian children have a sense of "good" and "proper."	He valued patriarchal status.	To be privileged is to be civilized (to eat "proper [not curious] food."
Interpersonal relationships	Like the character, the reader is the first-person child-speaker, who is isolated from the distant children he perceives as envious of him and disdains the unrealistic and disconnected aspects of ostrich eggs, Eskimos, American Indians, lions, and scarlet trees, divided into the classic "us" and "them."	He had a painful relationship with his father, rebelling against bourgeois hypocrisies and experiencing multiple estrangements; he eventually married an American divorcee and later reconciled with his father.	The privileged child has the only voice, and there is no one to answer the rhetorical "Don't you wish that you were me?"
Social institutions	The social institutions of the child's home and homeland are nicer and safer and are to be valued over other homes and other homelands.	Stevenson was born into the privileged class of a colonial society. Traveling widely for his health, he spent much of his life in France, England, Switzerland, the United States, and the South Seas. He traveled in the Great Plains before the publication of *Child's Garden of Verses*, and he surely had seen Crow and Sioux Indians.	Colonialism provides the allure of the exotic and a distaste for what is "other," the unknown.

The poem, published in 1885, is a fixed text that shocks the sensibilities of today's reader. The shock is quite predictable; today's reader is not the author's intended reader. Understanding the sociological context of a text's creation and of its author becomes the overarching issue for the contemporary reader. Regarding the author, Robert Louis Stevenson is neither an advocate for nor an attacker of Britain's colonial empire. He is a reflection and recorder of it as a social ideal, creating the character and satisfying the intended reader. Stevenson accomplished what Lawrence R. Sipe (1999: 123) has called "rendering the ideology invisible." He is at once the beloved author who envisions the child speaker's place in the world as unquestioned and upholds the intended reader's comfortable presumptions without providing details about the fare or the homeland of the addressed "you." Today's reader can neither neutrally accept nor actively embrace the social context and may resist it on multiple levels, questioning the lack of differentiation of the foreign children and their environments or challenging the speaker's egocentrism. Thus, today's reader needs a theoretical perspective for viewing the work, and sociological criticism provides one avenue.

Discussion of Literature Through a Sociological Lens

A. **Social Content** (Are the story's elements—e.g., plot and character—true to the story's setting, that is, to the story's time and place?)
  1. Who has power; who wants power; who makes the decisions in interpersonal relationships and in the social institutions?
  2. Is there a focus on any societal issues (e.g., social, economic, political, or cultural)?
  3. What values (e.g., conformity) are celebrated, denigrated?

B. **Reader** (e.g., matter of fact, shock, anger, pity, joy, etc.)
  4. Is the reader aware of the issues in the story?

C. **Author**
  5. What are important details about the author's life?
  6. What is the author's social stance (Sutherland, 1986: 145) regarding the work's subject?
      a. Assent (reflects and reinforces societal norms)
      b. Advocacy (seeks to support sociocultural practices)
      c. Attack (denounces sociocultural practices)
  7. What are the potential audiences (readers, reviewers, marketers) that the author may have considered?

D. **Text** (including graphics/illustrations)
  8. Are there any symbols, signs, and rituals of power at work in the story?
  9. Is the work purposive or even explicitly propagandistic?
  10. Are characters multidimensional, not stereotypes?
  11. Do the author's characterization, tone, and style contribute to a social theme?

APPLICATION OF SOCIOLOGICAL CRITICISM TO GENE LUEN YANG'S *AMERICAN BORN CHINESE*

When the Chinese first began to write about their immigrant experiences in America, they most often chose autobiography as their preferred genre. What makes this a relevant fact is that "autobiography is not a Chinese form" (Chin,

1991: 11). Although *American Born Chinese* sits comfortably within an Asian-American genre, Gene Luen Yang (2006) presents his story, based in part on his own life, in graphic novel format. In the following discussion, the questions referred to are those given in the earlier section "Discussion of Literature Through a Sociological Lens."

Social Content

Question 1: Third-grade protagonist Jin Wang has little power over his life. As one of three Asian Americans in his school, Jin feels powerless to fight play-ground bullies, to correct his uninformed teachers, or to speak honestly to his strict parents. He did not choose to move from his familiar San Francisco neigh-borhood with plenty of Chinese-American friends into a Midwestern town full of strangers. Jin's interpersonal relationships do not exist until a boy from Taiwan, Wei-Chen Sun, arrives in the fifth grade, and they become fast friends. By the seventh grade, Jin discovers girls and struggles to overcome his shyness enough to speak to Amelia Harris. When he inexplicably kisses Wei-Chen's girl friend Suzy Nakamura in an impulsive moment, Jin loses his best friend and thinks the answer to his troubles is to become as white as he possibly can, denying everything Chinese in the process of attempting to transform himself.

The social institution of school is not well adapted for America's "perpetual foreigner," one of the oldest and most inaccurate of the stereotypes directed at Asian Americans. Teachers at Mayflower Elementary School do not take the time to learn how to pronounce Jin's or Wei-Chen's names and incorrectly assume that the boys have arrived immediately from China (Jin was born in America, Wei-Chen in Taiwan). When Timmy blurts out, "'My momma says Chinese people eat dogs'" (p. 31), Mrs. Greeder makes no correction and seems to hold this belief herself.

The families of both boys hold them to very strict standards regarding academics and dating. Jin has been told he cannot date until he receives his master's degree. Perhaps to emphasize how much more important his peers are to Jin than are his parents, Mr. and Mrs. Wang are not fully illustrated until the end of the novel, when they are needed as a plot device to ascertain that neither parent can claim to be related to the annually visiting cousin from China.

Culturally, one of the book's three story arcs tells of the origins of Monkey King, one of "the staples of Asian childhood from Korea to Japan, to China, Viet-nam, Thailand, and Cambodia" (Chin, 1991: 40). By beginning his book with this iconic tale, Yang announces the importance of traditional stories within the Chinese-American family. When characters sometimes speak in Chinese, the dia-logue is enclosed within "< >." Sometimes it is more appropriate for characters to speak in Mandarin, such as in the episode when Jin and his mother visit the local herbalist's wife, a very old woman who speaks little English. Although Jin can speak Chinese, he cannot read it, as we discover at the end of the story when he is unable to order from the menu of an authentic Chinese restaurant. Some cultural differences seem trivial to adults but are more serious to a teenager. At the time Jin's parents were growing up in China, people did not routinely use deodorant, and they did not purchase it for Jin. Jin learns from his older cousin Charlie how to make do while on a date: He uses the soap dispenser in the public men's room and quickly applies it to his underarms; it seems that it worked for him.

Question 2: The sociopolitical focus in the story is racism and minority status in a country established by and privileged for Euro-Americans, creating a stumbling block for young people whose search for identity is complicated enough as it is. Racism is exacerbated by the fact that Asian Americans remain such a small minority group. According to the Annie E. Casey Foundation's analysis of the 2000 U.S. Census, "over 30 percent of American children are minorities" and of those only 3.4 percent identify themselves as Asian (Agosto, Hughes-Hassell, and Gilmore-Clough, 2003: 259). There is not much exposure to anything authentically Chinese in the suburbs of America, or on television screens, or in films. Stereotypes abound. It is little wonder that the students unquestioningly believe that Chinese people eat "cat gizzards" (p. 114), arrange their offsprings' marriages when they are only 13, and have buck teeth. Jin, Wei-Chen, and Suzy are referred to at various times as *chink*, *gook*, *nippy*, and *F.O.B.* (fresh off the boat). They contend with whispers and gestures behind their backs. There are references to SARS virus within their earshot.

One story arc centers on Chin-Kee, whose name and behavior are the epitome of almost every stereotyped image of a Chinese man. He is illustrated with very yellow skin and his eyes as very slanted slits. He wears a queue (a braided pig tail) and reverses his *l*'s and *r*'s whenever he speaks. He dresses in gaudy colors and performs martial arts. Chin-Kee knows the answer to every question in class, thereby exhibiting the Asian stereotype of a model student.

Question 3: The students' mistreatment of *anyone* different is denigrated in this novel. Other marginalized characters suffer under the same microscopic lens of perceived social "differences" that the Asian-American characters do. Outsider Peter Garbinsky, oversized and underintelligent, is referred as "Peter the Eater" (p. 34). The stereotypical dumb jock, Steve, tells Jin about the first (and only) time he was bullied because of his weight. Conformity occupies its usual place on the playground when only one person steps up to defend Jin against the other boys' taunts. As the anointed best-looking boy in class, Greg, tells the others, "'Hey, be cool, man'" (p. 32), but the boys call Greg "'a little pansy-boy'" (p. 33). The more socially powerful Greg puts the boys in their place when he growls back, "'What did you call me?'" (p. 33). The students' social hierarchy, well established in elementary school, continues with little change through high school.

Reader

Question 4: By developing his plot through the thoughts and actions exclusively of young people, Yang's presumed audience may find many familiar school life episodes represented. The reader may feel sympathetic to the main characters during one especially uncomfortable episode. After school a group of boys make puns on Chinese epithets and then they laugh riotously, while Jin, Wei-Chen, and Suzy remain frozen in their places, feeling embarrassed and powerless to defend themselves. In another scene, Suzy pours out her heart to Jin about being called, yet again, a *Chink*. This time, however, she says she realizes, "Deep down inside, I kind of feel like that *all the time*" (p. 187). To maintain balance in his story, Yang portrays most of the students as mainly ignorant of, or unaware of, the pain the Asian-American students go through. Again, they are a very small minority, and their powerlessness to defend themselves sometimes nearly overwhelms them. What has previously been invisible in real life is made poignant within the pages of Yang's graphic novel, which illuminates the teenagers blindly entrapped within their majority (white) culture.

Author

Question 5: Like his protagonist, Yang was born in San Francisco of Chinese parents. He moved to a suburban school where he was one of only a few Asian Americans. Yang has said that, although his story is not strictly autobiographical, his characters are true to life from either his or his Asian-American friends' experiences. The incidents are similarly true to life. The author has seemingly come to terms with his dual heritage. He is married with one child and teaches at a Catholic high school. Yang adapts the Buddhist Monkey King folktale by incorporating some Christian ideas that more closely reflect his chosen religion. He has received many literary accolades for this book, including a National Book Award and the Michael Printz Award.

Question 6: The author attacks America's societal norms that permit children to bully and tease with impunity any vulnerable young people. He attacks America's reluctance to crawl out of its ethnocentricity long enough to learn about other peoples and countries of the world in a meaningful way. The real harm of racism is portrayed through the unnecessary pain that Jin goes through as he struggles to deal with his dual heritage.

Question 7: The character most likely to draw reader resistance is Chin-Kee, whose in-your-face depiction and behavior could be offensive to those who are opposed to any caricatured minority figure. Yang (2007) has responded to complaints about Chin-Kee in this way: "Thank you. You're supposed to be offended. That was the desired response." In fact, Chin-Kee plays an essential role in the story's plot development. It is through Chin-Kee that the Monkey King visits Jin, confronts him, and forces the boy to face the Chinese part of his heritage in order to develop a healthy identity for himself. Jin does not necessarily have to choose to be Chinese or American. Instead, by the end, he begins to recognize that he integrates both heritages.

Text

Question 8: Yang adapts the Monkey King (whose archetype includes the trickster) as the important catalyst for characterization and in the development of one of the main themes. In Chinese lore, Monkey King has the ability to transform and change his size and shape. The symbol for part of his powers resides with his hair, which he can transform into anything or anyone he wishes. (Hair figures in the other arcs as the main feature the protagonist chooses to mark his physical transformation—Jin curls and styles his, Danny bleaches his.) Monkey King is lively, smart, quick tempered, and expressive. He thinks very highly of himself, and at times his self-esteem is built on his outward achievements instead of his inner strengths. Monkey King carries the symbolic weapon of power, a magic spear, and he does not hesitate to use it to defend himself against opponents. He acquires his impressive martial arts skills through discipline and practice. All of the other gods, goddesses, and spirits come to fear Monkey King's tenacious powers. Yang weaves Monkey King into each of the story arcs, but in a slightly different way. The reader does not know until the story's end the importance of Monkey King's role in the protagonist's struggles to achieve a positive, emotionally strong self-identity after his increasingly futile attempts at transformations through outward appearance and denial of his Chinese roots.

Another symbol (Jin's favorite toy, a robot that transforms into a truck) appears in the opening pages of the second story arc. The theme of change, or of the possibility of transforming oneself, thus holds a prominent place in symbolic form. It is Wei-Chen's similar toy, a robot that transforms into a monkey, that catches Jin's eye when the boys first meet and that brings the two outcasts together as friends. Jin's attraction to technology, as represented in the robots, stands in opposition to the herbalist's wife, the old woman who continues to use and to prefer an ancient Chinese machine, the abacus. The herbalist's wife advises ten-year-old Jin that he most certainly *can* transform himself: "It's easy to become anything you wish, so long as you're willing to forfeit your soul" (p. 29). Her words ring in his memory at the climactic moment he decides to reject all ties to anyone and anything Chinese and to pass himself off on the outside as being a blond who now calls himself Danny, who believes that as white he will be entitled to participate in the rituals of school power.

Question 9: The book avoids propaganda by limiting the number of episodes that show young people as targets of outright racism. Most of the turmoil and angst occur in the protagonist's mind, as Jin suppresses his anger over many years to the point of suspecting his best friend Wei-Chen of wanting Amelia for himself, a fear that is entirely unfounded. As Jin thinks about Amelia, "It made me nervous that someone could have so much power over me without even knowing it" (p. 88). Jin's attraction for Amelia gradually cuts through the tough exterior he has built around himself. Wei-Chen even calls Jin "a cowardly turtle" (p. 92) for hesitating to take a chance and to approach Amelia. After Jin and Amelia begin to date, Greg asks him to "'do me a favor'" and to "'not ask Amelia out again'" because "'I just don't know if you're right for her'" (p. 180). The manipulative Greg knows that Jin will go along with his "friendly request," leaving the way open for Greg to go after Amelia himself. Later Jin replays the episode in his mind, and each subsequent panel shows Jin to be more and more assertive in his imagined "No" to Greg's preposterous request (p. 182).

Question 10: None of the major characters is stereotypical, with the exception of Chin-Kee, whose role in relation to the theme requires that he be as obnoxious as possible, personifying all of the prejudices directed at Asian Americans. When Danny decapitates Chin-Kee during their violent fight, the teen experiences a catharsis by roundly killing the stereotype. It takes the intervention of an archetypal character, Monkey King, to complete the protagonist's transformation. Wei-Chen reveals to Jin that he is one of Monkey King's sons and an emissary who chooses to serve humanity and to be a virtuous person. By choosing to become the blond (white) Danny (rejecting his Chinese heritage), Jin threw away his best friend and his own self-respect.

Question 11: In a graphic novel, an artist can create a story without using narrative prose. Word balloons are dialogue, *not* narration. Thus, the novel is laid out in sequential panels, relying on the conventions of cartoon art, producing a tight, concise story line. Yang maintains unity by consistently using a large white frame to surround his large panels-within-a-panel, thereby smoothly linking the diverse story arcs. Yang chooses the same color palette for all three arcs, selecting earth tones and lots of red (a traditional Chinese color). The result is a muted tone during Jin's and Danny's arcs. The Monkey King arc shows a darker background and more physically violent panels, suggesting its folktale origins with familiar Chinese imagery (e.g., peaches, rocks, the Jade Emperor). In the Chin-Kee episodes, Yang draws a laugh track along the bottom of the panels to indicate the irony between what seems to be taking place in the panel with the humiliation taking place inside Danny's head.

By the end of the novel, Yang has combined the three arcs into one, with Danny's family "comedy" ending in riotous combat (pp. 201–211) and dropping the laugh track, politely getting rid of Danny and placing Jin appropriately into his junior year of high school, waiting a month for a chance to apologize to Wei-Chen. The realistic open ending suggests possibilities for atonement and for hope of renewed friendship for two American-born Chinese young people.

WHEN SUBJECT DEFINES A LITERARY EFFORT: APPLICATION OF SOCIOLOGICAL CRITICISM TO LINDA DE HAAN AND STERN NIJLAND'S *KING AND KING* AND JUSTIN RICHARDSON AND PETER PARNELL'S *AND TANGO MAKES THREE*

A work's subject, if it is a significant social issue, can in some times and places and for some audiences overshadow all factors, even literary quality, in determining the work's place (or lack thereof) in a collection of materials. For example, a pair of picture books has been defined almost entirely by the subject of homosexuality (Library of Congress subject heading: "Homosexuality— Fiction"). These two books are

- *King and King* (de Haan and Nijland, 2002), with the Library of Congress summary: "When the queen insists that the prince get married and take over as king, the search for a suitable mate does not turn out as expected"; and
- *And Tango Makes Three* (Richardson and Parnell, 2005), with the Library of Congress summary: "At New York City's Central Park Zoo, two male penguins fall in love and start a family by taking turns sitting on an abandoned egg until it hatches."

Demonstrating *King and King*'s acceptance, a network of 1,200+ independent booksellers, as a "voice against censorship," recommended *King and King* in the fall 2004 *Book Sense* one-page brochure, "Banned Books"; and, demonstrating the book's rejection, the American Library Association (ALA) cited *King and King* as one of the ten most frequently challenged books in 2004. The ALA also cited *And Tango Makes Three* as the most frequently challenged book in 2006. Major professional journals, including *Horn Book Magazine, School Library Journal, Booklist,* and *Publishers Weekly,* reviewed both books.

In the following discussion, the questions referred to are those given in the earlier section "Discussion of Literature Through a Sociological Lens."

Social Content

Question 1: A primary source of power in each work is based within the characters' interpersonal relationships, which permit homosexual partnerships that foster a family capable of nurturing an adoption. In the literary fairy tale *King and King* (henceforth referred to as *King*), the prince, who is a stereotypical mama's boy (as indicated by a family portrait on the dining room wall), has a rude awakening early one morning by the queen, who has "had enough." She wants a king and queen to assume her responsibilities for the monarchy. By evening the prince, "dizzy" and too worn to eat, agrees, "Very well, Mother. I'll marry. I must say, though, I've never cared much for princesses." The crown kitty, who has been sitting under the table and accepting food treats from the prince, is then attracted to the downward spiral of the family portrait, which is now near the floor and within the kitty's reach. In the end the queen royally gathers and dismisses all princesses, and she sanctions the marriage of prince and prince. In *And Tango Makes Three* (henceforth, *Tango*), the interpersonal relationship of Roy and Silo, a pair of male penguins, is also powerful enough to move the plot toward their successful adoption of a penguin egg. The zookeeper interprets their warm relationship as love, and he envisions that they will be successful parents.

Question 2: In both books, a social institution shapes the ultimate outcome. In *King*, the monarchy is the institution that allows power to be transferred from the queen to the prince, and in *Tango* the social structure of the zoo and its keeper facilitates the establishment of the family for which Roy and Silo have longed. In *King*, the intense and hostile encounter between the prince and the queen is first resolved by the prince's giving in to the queen's demands and only later by her acceptance of a king and a king. Roy and Silo are more fortunate in that their desire for a penguin baby is compatible with the zookeeper's role as protector of penguins.

Question 3: Both plots place value on personal choice and happiness. In *Tango*, all becomes well for Roy, Silo, and Tango. In *King*, prince and prince, page and princess, and the retired queen mother, who in a sequel becomes the grandmother of the kings' adopted daughter all achieve happiness. Thus, the works' interpersonal relationships and social institutions challenge the traditional roles and values of marriage and family.

Reader

Question 4: The primary factor regarding the readers' awareness of the social issues is their age. Professional reviewers of the two books describe the ages of their juvenile audiences to vary between four and ten years old. However, parents, reviewers, marketers, booksellers, and politicians approach the book with full awareness of the social (as well as economic, political, and cultural) issues and their own personal values. Thus, although young people may have questions, adults are likely to hold firmly to either positive or negative views. For YAs, social criticism offers good opportunities for discussion and analysis of the works.

Author

Question 5: The authors of both books (Linda de Haan and Stern Nijland for *King* and Justin Richardson and Peter Parnell for *Tango*) are outspoken advocates for same-sex marriage.

Question 6: The authors have sought to change sociocultural practices—Haan and Nijland from the Netherlands and Richardson and Parnell from the United States.

Question 7: Specifically, to school librarians through a *School Library Journal* blog, Richardson and Parnell explained to interviewer Amy Bowllan (2007) their dismay regarding the controversy around the book: "The idea of trying to make the book less available to children, or trying to ban it completely, is angering and disheartening to hear. . . . We've received many thanks from same-sex couples with kids, from single moms and dads."

Text

Question 8: There are symbols of ritual and power in both stories. For *King*, the institution of the monarchy is a symbol of power as are the queen's demands and the fairy tale genre's expectation of a "happily ever after" ending. For *Tango*, the thinking and managerial human holds power and uses that power for the penguin egg and for Roy and Silo.

Question 9: The works meet the authors' expressed stance on the promotion of a cause, that is, for a wider acceptance of same-sex marriage. The purposive nature of the works contributes to their bifurcated acceptance or rejection in the popular culture. Whatever view an adult reader takes on the social issue determines the work to be either enlightened or alien to traditional values. Furthermore, this adult point of view (positive or negative) extends beyond the conceptual grasp of a K–2 audience, although it is well within the grasp of a YA audience.

Question 10: None of the characters is multidimensional. The works are plot driven to a purposive conclusion. Furthermore, readers of fairy tales do not expect multidimensional characters, and readers understand a romantic but flat portrayal of Roy and Silo through which their great desire for a penguin child is happily fulfilled.

Question 11: Although they are quite different in each book, the symbols, characterization, tone, and style presented through the texts and illustrations advocate the creators' purposive stance on the subject of homosexuality. In the mode of satire, *King*'s style is bold, nonsentimental, and challenges the traditions of a fairy tale life:

- The queen is dour, tired, and impatient, rudely demanding a marriage throughout a long day.
- The prince, at first bored and finally exhausted, consents.
- When the prince says, "I've never cared much for princesses," the court page gives him a sly wink; things are not as simple as they may seem.
- True to a fairy tale, the monarch (though not a king) calls all of the princesses "near and far."
- Departing from the traditional fairy tale, not one princess wins the heart of the prince; however, the court page and the most beautiful princess fall in love and marry as do her brother and the prince.

- The closing double-page spread, the scene for which tradition demands "lived happily ever after," depicts the characters playing a game of lawn chess, reminiscent of *Peter Pan* and *Alice's Adventures in Wonderland.*
- The illustrations, a bold and somewhat messy patchwork of collage, paint, and scratchboard, defy logic, gravity, and perspective and combine with the text to produce a fairy tale parody.
- The book's irony/satire mode differs from that typical of the K–2 picture storybook audience.

In *Tango*, the elements of symbols, characterization, tone, and style shape a romance, a quest for a loving family. The picture book's softly drawn shapes, expanses of white space, and watercolor illustrations render soft images, not the sharp, bold, busy images in *King*. The romance of *Tango* is stereotypically depicted through anthropomorphized penguins, Roy and Silo, whose quest is to be part of a family. (This use of anthropomorphism is reminiscent of that cited by Charlotte Huck [1976: 526], who challenged Colette Portal's portrayal of the queen bee in her picture book, *The Life of a Queen* [1964, n.p.]: "High above the earth the young queen picks her mate. With him she disappears into the blazing sunset, leaving the others behind. This is the shining moment of her life." Just as Portal's anthropomorphism distorts nonfiction, the use of anthropomorphism in relating the set of true events within the Central Park Zoo distorts Roy and Silo's story.) Of the zoo penguins, only Roy and Silo "snuggle," causing the zookeeper to comment, "They must be in love." The only penguin family drawn snuggled comfortably together under a golden sky is that of Roy, Silo, and Tango (on the work's last double-page spread). Although based on a true story, the main characters are more animated and more affectionate than the background penguin characters. They are exceedingly alive and rewarded and happy; they support a social cause.

ANNOTATED BIBLIOGRAPHY

Alexie, Sherman. 2007. *The Absolutely True Diary of a Part-time Indian.* Art by Ellen Forney. New York: Little, Brown. Grades 7–10.

Fed up with attending eight years of Indian reservation schools with their run-down buildings and their lack of adequate supplies, Arnold Spirit ("Junior") was eager to begin high school geometry. But when he spotted his mother's "*maiden* name" (p. 31) written inside his geometry book, he exploded in anger and threw the book at his teacher. He was going to have to study math in a book that was "at least thirty years older than [he] was" (p. 31). With support from his parents, Junior transfers to the all-white Reardon High School (whose mascot is an Indian!) where he lives in two worlds and conquers them both with his intelligence, wit, and "you can do it" belief, "the four hugest words in the world" (p. 189). The book's success lies in its combination of humor and realism. Readers could select some of the humorous passages and discuss the role that Junior's wit plays in his survival.

Carvell, Marlene. 2002. *Who Will Tell My Brother?* New York: Hyperion. Grades 7–10.

Seventeen-year-old Evan Hill, child of Mohawk parents, spends his senior year as a one-man Indian activist in an attempt to convince the school board to drop his school's mascot (an Indian not indigenous to the area). Attending every school board meeting the entire year to protest the mascot, Evan receives a colder and colder response from the adults and taunts and threats from the students who feel pride in their mascot. Young people can go online to find out more about the different perspectives of the ethics regarding the use of Indians as mascots (e.g., Lisa Mitten's 2008 document "The Mascot Issue" at www.nativeculturelinks.com/mascots.html and links therein).

Hautman, Pete. 2006. *Rash*. New York: Simon and Schuster. Grades 8 and up.

True believer Bo Marsten views his life within the United Safer States of America as normal until he lands in a juvenile prison where gifted inmates are allowed to participate in illegal football games without wearing mandated protective devices. The world of 2076 looks different from today but only in degree, according to Hautman's dystopian novel. YAs can discuss some of the novel's issues, such as contemporary notions of safety over freedom, the ever-growing prison population, and medicating teenagers to control their behavior.

Hesse, Karen. 1997. *Out of the Dust*. New York: Scholastic. Grades 6–8.

Fifteen-year-old Billie Joe narrates the dramatic occurrences of her personal life and of rural life in Oklahoma during the Depression. Arranged chronologically (from January 1934 to December 1935), the verse narrative gives an unusual YA perspective on the strength required to survive with one's self-esteem intact during two of the worst economic years of the twentieth-century. The strong imagery provides inspiration for visual responses, such as collages, posters, or illustrations.

Holub, Josef. 2005. *An Innocent Soldier*. Translated by Michael Hofmann. New York: Arthur A. Levine Books. Grades 6 and up.

Orphaned and betrayed by the farmer for whom he toiled, naïve 16-year-old Adam falls in line as one of the millions conscripted to fight under Napoleon against the Russians in 1811–1812, ending in a scorched earth policy and the deaths of millions. This historical novel is all about power—those who have it and those who do not—and, being a peasant, narrator Adam represents the lowest social class and their point of view. His destiny is completely controlled first by his cruel Sgt. Krauter and then successively by his kind "Well-born Lt. Konrad Klara," who selects Adam to be his personal servant; all military ranks above that; King Karl of the Confederation of the Rhine; and Napoleon. Young people can discuss how war can necessitate the breaking down of the walls of power and class as Adam and Konrad inevitably become brothers, starving together, fighting together, and sharing the same beliefs about war.

Levine, Ellen. 2007. *Up Close: Rachel Carson*. New York: Viking. Grades 7 and up.

The life history of biologist Rachel Carson is thematically powerful, depicting a woman of modest means who advanced through the studies she most wanted, cared for multiple generations of her family, struggled financially, yet met her obligations and published science for scientists and science for the masses. It was her work *Silent Spring* that made environmental issues a concern among nonscientists, and it is her legacy to future generations. Young people will be engaged with the social/environmental issues; however, some may be motivated to compare and contrast life for female scientists in 1940 to that of contemporary female scientists.

Marrin, Albert. 2008. *Theodore Roosevelt: The Great Adventure and the Rise of Modern America*. New York: Dutton. Grades 7 and up.

Theodore Roosevelt's life is a dramatic story of courage and action, a story captured in one of his quotations: "It is impossible to win the great prizes of life without running risks. . . . But life is a great adventure, and the worst part of all fears is the fear of living" (n.p.). Young people can apply sociological criticism by analyzing Roosevelt as a character in the context of the early twentieth century. For example, they could site the challenges that Roosevelt as president faced, relating them to his bold actions: "Could overcrowded cities be made livable? . . . . How can Americans fight political corruption, the power of money to influence government in favor of the wealthy? How can we keep our natural resources from being plundered for profit?" (p. 9). Young people can also compare the social similarities and differences in the United States in 1908 with those of today.

McCarthy, Cormac. 2006. *The Road*. New York: Random House. Adult book for YAs.

An unnamed father and son walk toward the sea in a postapocalyptic world where the sun never shines, the rain never stops, and the hunger never disappears. The heart of the story is about primal love—the love a parent can have for a child and how the adult sacrifices everything to keep the child alive and safe. This powerful narrative provides many social, philosophical, and environmental questions for young people to consider: What happens to human interactions when society totally collapses? What happens to language when everyday objects and ideas no longer exist to pass along (meaning) to the young? Should citizens of the twenty-first century be concerned about global climate change?

Nye, Naomi Shihab. 2008. *Honeybee: Poems and Short Prose*. New York: Greenwillow. Grades 7 and up.

With mass media drawn to the honeybee's colony collapse disorder in the spring of 2007, the author created 82 poems and paragraphs that celebrate the honeybee's characteristics (navigators, communicators, pollen makers, hive ventilators, dancers ["like a bee doing its waggle dance in front of the hive," p. 51]), contrasting honeybees with humans, who amid smugness, closed libraries, and war are reminded that "Not everything is lost" (p. 164). Young people may consider how social, economic, and cultural realities relate to Nye's collection:

Never keeping up or catching up
With what we miss.
Feeling remiss. (p. 22)

Sturm, James, and Rich Tommaso. 2008. *Satchel Paige: Striking Out Jim Crow.* **New York: Hyperion. Grades 6 and up.**

This graphic novel, set in the first half of the twentieth century, presents the story of an 18-year-old black man who leaves his crops, wife, and baby to seek his fortune as a baseball player in the Negro League, playing several games before he faces the famed pitcher, Satchel Paige. The man becomes severely injured that afternoon when he makes a furious run to home plate, so he returns home to his wife, and son, and share-cropping for overbearing landlords. When his son is old enough, he takes his son to see Satchel Paige pitch and later in the day gives the boy the baseball that Satchel had given him when he played in the Negro League. The work closes with 13 illustrated panels that could support multiple small-group discussions of the story's social contexts, including, for example, the explanations of wages, the railroad, lynching, and the role of the church.

Swindells, Robert. 1985, 2000. *Brother in the Land.* **New York: Penguin. Grades 6–9.**

Danny must take care of his younger brother Ben following a nuclear war that only a few people survive. After criticism that his book was too pessimistic for young people, Swindells revised his novel's ending in a subsequent edition by providing Danny and girlfriend Kim with a small farm on an agricultural commune. Young people can discuss how they feel about the pressures that are put on authors to make major changes (e.g., censorship) in a novel targeted to young readers.

Westerfeld, Scott. 2005. *Uglies.* **New York: Simon Pulse. Grades 7 and up.**

Fifteen-year-old Tally Youngblood, inveterate prankster, eagerly awaits her next birth-day when she will be eligible for plastic surgery that will transform her into one of the Pretties. The society in this futuristic world believes that it is utopian in that they rid their young people of unnecessary competition that might arise from their appear-ance. Young people will find provocative questions in this first of a series: (1) What issues in real life do you see played out in this narrative? Possible response: More teenagers are receiving plastic surgery for birthday presents or for graduation gifts. (2) Where do young people get their images of ideal physical attractiveness?

REFERENCES AND SUGGESTIONS FOR FURTHER READING

Agosto, Denise E., Sandra Hughes-Hassell, and Catherine Gilmore-Clough. 2003. "The All-White World of Middle-School Genre Fiction: Surveying the Field for Multicultural Protagonists." *Children's Literature in Education* 34, no. 4 (December): 257–275.

Appleman, Deborah. 2000. *Critical Encounters in High School English: Teaching Literary Theory to Adolescents.* New York: Teachers College Press.

Barricelli, Jean-Pierre, and Joseph Gibaldi, eds. 1982. *Interrelations of Literature.* New York: Modern Language Association.

Bowllan, Amy. 2007. "Bowllan Blog." *School Library Journal.* Available at: www.schoollibrary journal.com/blog.

Chan, Jeffrey Paul, et al., eds. 1991. *The Big Aiiieeeee! An Anthology of Chinese American and Japanese American Literature.* New York: Penguin.

Chin, Frank. 1991. "Come All Ye Asian American Writers of the Real and the Fake." In *The Big Aiiieeeeee! An Anthology of Chinese American and Japanese American Literature*, edited by Jeffrey Paul Chan et al., pp. 1–92. New York: Penguin.

Clark, Priscilla B.P. 1982. "Literature and Sociology." In *Interrelations of Literature*, edited by Jean-Pierre Barricelli and Joseph Gibaldi, pp. 107–122. New York: Modern Language Association.

Daiches, David. 1956. *Critical Approaches to Literature*. New York: W.W. Norton.

De Haan, Linda and Stern Nijland. 2002. *King and King*. Berkeley, CA: Tricycle Press.

Huck, Charlotte S. 1976. *Children's Literature in the Elementary School*, 3rd ed. New York: Holt, Rinehart and Winston.

Kennedy, X.J. and Dana Gioia. 1998. *Literature: An Introduction to Fiction, Poetry, and Drama*, 7th ed. New York: Longman.

Laurenson, Diana T., and Alan Swingewood. 1972. *The Sociology of Literature*. New York: Schocken.

Lowenthal, Leo. 1961. *Literature, Popular Culture, and Society*. Englewood Cliffs, NJ: Prentice Hall.

Moon, Brian. 1999. *Literary Terms: A Practical Glossary*. Urbana, IL: National Council of Teachers of English.

Portal, Colette. 1964. *The Life of a Queen*, translated by Marcia Nardi. New York: Braziller.

Richardson, Justin, and Peter Parnell. 2005. *And Tango Makes Three*. Illustrated by Henry Cole. New York: Simon and Shuster Books for Young Readers.

Sipe, Lawrence R. 1999. "Children's Response to Literature: Author, Text, Reader, Context." *Theory Into Practice* 38, no. 3 (Summer): 120–129.

Stevenson, Robert Louis. 1998. *Selected Poems*. New York: Penguin Classics.

Sutherland, Zena. 1986. *Children and Books*, 7th ed. Glenview, IL: Scott, Foresman.

Yang, Gene Luen. 2006. *American Born Chinese*. New York: First Second.

Yang, Gene Luen. 2007. "News." Available at: www.humblecomics.com/about.

Chapter 8

Historical Criticism

Literature is the "noise of the wheels of history."

—John Paul Russo (1994: 385)

Readers who understand themselves as contextually bound and who under-stand the historical context of what they read have a different understanding of a text than those who are isolated from such information.

—Roberta Seelinger Trites (2000: 147)

INTRODUCTION TO HISTORICAL CRITICISM

Historical criticism illuminates the basics of text, author, reader, and context. It is in many ways a criticism as foundational as reader-response criticism and does, as Trites (2000) suggests, define the reader. Traditionally, historical criticism held that there was an objective history, one that allows the re-creation of circumstances under which a work was composed. This application of historical criticism was selective, establishing and studying the literary canon and focusing on the zeitgeist (the spirit that characterizes an era or a time, as in the Romantic Era). However, in the late 1970s and early 1980s, critics conceptualized a more fluid, borderless, multidisciplinary approach to historical criticism. Thus, there is a wide acceptance of a *new historical criticism,* described as "skeptical, wary, demystifying, critical, and even adversarial" (Gallagher and Greenblatt, 2000: 9). Moving beyond political and sociological paradigms, the new historicists seek an unvarnished truth.

A similar search for an unvarnished truth leads readers into a deeper under-standing of literature. Those who study the new historicism will find an approach that welcomes invention, creativity, and playfulness in reader responses—even to the widest inclusion of library archives. Furthermore, researching a literary work for its historical contexts requires critical consideration of the inherent problem that any scientist, teacher, or lawyer approaches with caution: the problem of making assumptions. For new historical criticism, specific assumptions that should be challenged include that

171

- traditional print comprises the most important sources,
- whatever is in print is correct,
- authors' statements must be correct,
- writing reflects an unchanging and sensible past,
- generalizations about an era can apply to any work composed at that time, and
- readers can definitely come to know an author's intent.

Understanding the processes of new historical criticism will not only ensure that readers have deeper literary understandings but also ensure they will better evaluate the authority of all sources.

Historical criticism is defined as the theory that considers a literary work in terms of its historical and social contexts during the time it was produced, including relevant biographical information about the author. Historical criticism has a long history, with its origins in Europe before the sixteenth century. However, Hippolyte Taine (1965) is considered the first critic to have devised a systematic historical approach to literature in his 1863–1867 multivolume *The History of English Literature*. Composing his historical criticism as a narrative, Taine used three criteria to classify and analyze literature—milieu, national character, and race. (By *race* Taine meant an author's country of origin.) Taine's energetic narratives reveal him to have been a scholar who loved and respected literature. He began by noting that "behind every document there was a man. It is a mistake to study the document as if it were isolated" (Taine, 1970: 501). Taine's milieu included such "well-defined provinces" as "religion, art, philosophy, the state, the family, the industries" (p. 505). He also thought an era's music, architecture, and theology should be considered when examining a work, thereby defining historical criticism in the broadest way.

Contemporary Historical Criticism

In American colleges and universities, historical criticism took command during the twentieth century in courses organized by chronological survey, by the great figures of an era, or by genres. Periodization remains in most English departments to some extent today, as it is the quickest way to acquaint students with the vast background of world literature. However, in the late 1930s as the New Critics began to gain the attention of scholars and critics, "The value of the historical approach in fictional studies got temporarily lost in the formalist shuffle" (Beasley, 1985: 338). The mid-twentieth-century New Critics offered a radical new idea—to study one work at a time in close reading, analyzing its formal elements. The New Critics believed that, under historical criticism, a literary work was being lost in a barrage of data, subsumed by mostly irrelevant (to them) details. After publication of *Understanding Poetry* (Brooks and Warren, 1938) and *Understanding Fiction* (Brooks and Warren, 1943), the New Critics had their landmark textbooks and soon dominated the critical field in America. However, it was not very long before historical criticism appeared in a new guise.

New Historicism

New historicism is defined not as a theory but as "the accepted name for a mode of literary study that its proponents oppose to the formalism they attribute to both the New Criticism and to the critical deconstruction that followed it" (Abrams, 1993: 248). New historicism emerged in the 1970s, but it was not until 1982 in the introduction to a selection of essays that Stephen Greenblatt (1989: 1) used the term "new historicism" to describe the work he and others had written that did not seem to fit any other literary approach.

New historicism was developed by scholars from many disciplines besides literary criticism, such as anthropology, theology, art history, political science, and psychology. In the winter of 1983 the new historicists established their own journal, *Representations*, so named because it seemed to them that most of their arguments and discussions—no matter the discipline—boiled down to ideas about literature and its representation. For new historicists, literature is a social and cultural product that originates in a specific time and place, but they deny such notions as zeitgeist. Although new historicists recognize that "major works of art remain centrally important, they are jostled now by an array of other texts and images" (Gallagher and Greenblatt, 2000: 9). As Ann Rigney (2004: 363) points out, "Recent literary practice has forced us to rethink the limits of fiction and the limits of history and to find new ways of talking about the relationship between the two." Works considered noncanonical or from popular culture are valued by new historicists as possibilities for discovery.

Whether old or new, historicism has remained active in the academy and in secondary and college classrooms in one form or another. Those who read and interpret literature from a historical perspective defend their stance as forcefully as critics from other, newer theories defend theirs. "Historical criticism is the necessary and unavoidable counterpart of all critical procedures and while it too is subject to change and capable of progress and improvement, the supposition that it can be dispensed with is a delusion" (Jackson, 1989: 3). As Morris Dickstein (2003: B10) writes, "[T]he great justification for a historical approach to literature and criticism is that we must know everything—the life, the times, the intricate internal argument, the shape of the language. When a subject truly engages us, every detail is precious, every shred of evidence is worth considering," reinforcing both traditional and new historical stances.

YOUNG ADULT LITERATURE AND HISTORICAL CRITICISM

When introducing historical criticism to young adults (YAs), teachers can use the following questions to explore the work, its context and milieu, its author, and its readers. However, as an analytic tool, for any one work or any set of works, not all the questions will apply, and for those that do apply, responsive readers should shape their emphasis and order, following logic and purpose. The questions are offered to provide practical and broad considerations for those learning about historical criticism as an avenue of response.

Questions for Historical Criticism

I. The Work

1. When was the work written; when was it published?

2. How does the time period in which the work was created shape reader understanding of the text's literary elements? That is, for example, does the time period illuminate the work's
   a. Characterization
   b. Style (e.g., figurative language and slang)
   c. Language (e.g., connotations and associations readers would have made of certain images and characters)
   d. Content
   e. Genre
   f. Mode and theme

3. What is the reception history of this work?

II. The Content and Milieu

4. What is the setting; what are principle characteristics of time/place/circumstances?

5. What historical aspects (e.g., political, social, cultural, economic) does the work portray?

6. Verisimilitude: In considering elements of the work's context, did the author take liberties (e.g., omitting the impact of significant historical events)? If so, why might the author have taken such liberties?

III. The Author

7. What biographical (historical) details of the author's life seem to be reflected in the work; how might those details affect a reader's understanding and interpretation of the work?

8. What significant historical events were happening at the point of composition?

9. How might the events in the author's life have shaped his or her attitudes toward the work's setting, especially the values held?

IV. The Reader/Audience

10. Describe the original audience for this work, considering, for example, social class, interests, gender, and values.

11. How has the work's audiences changed over the years?

APPLICATION OF HISTORICAL CRITICISM TO MAUREEN DALY'S *SEVENTEENTH SUMMER*

I. The Work

When was the work written; when was it published? Maureen Daly says that she began to write her book after her own seventeenth summer so that she could capture the memory of her experiences immediately in order not to lose them. That means that she began to write in the fall of 1938. She continued to write off and on through college and finished the manuscript during her Christmas break in December 1941. The book was first published in April 1942.

How does the time period in which the work was created shape the reader's understanding of the text's literary elements? Being able to set the precise date of the book's composition helps in the historical research. Some critics have erroneously identified the book as a World War II novel. However, *Seventeenth Summer* depicts a small window of time in American history, the end of the Depression and the months preceding the beginning of World War II, a time when a young person could forget the larger world just long enough to fall in love.

Genre: One convention of romance stories dictates a happy ending for the couple. In Daly's novel, Angie wants to go to college while Jack feels a deep sense of responsibility toward his family and decides to postpone college while he works to save the family bakery. They must separate at the end of the summer. As a young couple in love during the Depression, Jack and Angie believe that their respective family expectations take precedence over anything else. Daly's book is more accurately classified as a contemporary realistic novel, not as a romance. In addition, in 2002 the Library of Congress gave the novel a new subject heading, adding "20th c. fiction," moving the book nearer to the category of historical fiction.

Characterization: Angie begins her story by pleading with the reader to take her seriously. As a YA of her time, Angie would have seen motion picture portrayals of teenage girls as goofy or boy crazy. She insists to her readers that her story is not silly and it definitely is not about "puppy love" (p. 1). Angie is a girl of her times, but that does not necessarily mean that she agrees with how her genera-tion—the first real generation of teenagers—is being condescendingly portrayed in films or on the radio.

At first, Angie is understandably shy and unsure of herself when she talks to Jack. After all, she attended the local parochial school and did not socialize very much with boys. She is also a serious student, and her family takes it for granted that she, like her older sister Lorraine, will attend college. Her oldest sister Margaret has chosen to work full time and is engaged to Art. No mention is made of any wedding date, indicating that the couple is typical of the Depression, having to wait until they have the money to set up their own household. Little sister Kitty is about ten years old and serves as a reminder to Angie about her own disappearing childhood. Sometimes Angie wistfully looks at Kitty and thinks how she misses the freedom from all the worries that girls must go through as they grow up.

Although she often wishes she were more like the "smooth" girls, Angie never tries to behave like them. She is the only girl in the crowd who chooses not to smoke or to drink, and this does not seem to bother the others. After one episode, she and Jack do not speak for several days, and Angie gets depressed and thinks that she does not feel like a girl anymore, having realized that a relationship with a boy has changed her somehow. Throughout her narrative, Angie expresses the feelings that she is probably too quiet and boring. What she does not understand (but the reader sees) is that being a good listener makes her attractive to boys who appreciate being the center of attention.

Angie is unaware that she is an attractive girl. First Jack, then Tony, asks her for a date, and Jack even tells her that some of his friends wished that they had asked her out first. But none of this seems to sink in to Angie. For one thing, her sister Lorraine serves as a foil of what can happen to a girl who goes "boy crazy" (p. 53). Angie loves Lorraine and sometimes remembers how much fun they had had as little girls. But Lorraine's attitude about men is not healthy, and Angie can see this. Lorraine seems to do everything deemed wrong for a young woman of her time to do: she chases after her only date, Martin Keefe; she telephones him; she goes out with him at the last minute; she comes in very late; she begins to smoke; she ignores her family. Lorraine senses that the entire family does not approve of her dating Martin, but she cannot seem to help herself. Disillusioned and hurt, she cuts her summer short and returns early to college.

Angie does develop as a character. She gradually becomes more and more confident about herself with Jack and others. After experiencing the positive feelings of being in love (along with the confusing, even scary ones), Angie reaches an epiphany and wants to share her knowledge with Jack. She has discovered that her fears about being more sophisticated had caused her to doubt herself. Now she will stop comparing herself to other girls, and she will feel more at ease. However, Jack does not even listen to her. This is an important discovery to Angie: her identity is not tied to Jack. She does not have to return his "I love you" once she realizes that love is a very big word, not to be thrown around. No matter how sad or dejected Angie might have felt at times, she was no crybaby. But after Jack proposes to her, she realizes the full implications of their love and of their inevitable separation. Angie cries, not so much for herself, but for Jack in his desperate effort to keep her with him.

After summer ends, she says good-bye to Jack and sees him standing on the platform, his hands jammed into his pockets, the familiar sign that he would be unhappy and angry for only a little while. By writing her story of the summer of her first love, she will be able to recapture those feelings and experiences forever.

Dialogue. There are a few slang words. The dialogue may sound old-fashioned when Angie refers to boys as "fellows" and when her grammar is nearly perfect. Jack and Swede, on the other hand, speak colloquially, their poor grammar an indication of their socioeconomic class.

Language/style. Michael Cart (1996: 19) finds some of Daly's writing as "bogging down in so many lengthy passages describing the fauna of Fond du Lac . . . that it seems more like a botany textbook than a novel." Indeed, Cart's observation catches a historical fact about Daly's childhood, as Daly (1986: 72) recalls her family's spending many happy days in Wisconsin's beautiful outdoors, "always bringing with us the household copies of *Burgess' Book of Birds* and *Burgess' Book of Flowers.*" The family gradually came to know most of the species of plants and flowers and birds, "as if we had them tagged and numbered" (Daly, 1986: 72).

Angie does depict several scenes of nature, but she makes a direct connection between nature and her emotional life, capturing her feelings of the moment in the familiar, lush green of a Wisconsin summer. Before the country club dance, like a medieval maiden, Angie chooses a garden flower for her hair instead of a more sophisticated ornament. Alone on the country club golf course with Jack, Angie notices that the noise of the crickets sets the pace for the beating of her heart. She also reflects how the weather seems to change and fit with her moods.

Other figurative language. On a walk with Kitty to the creek, Angie shows her little sister a meadowlark's nest with four eggs in it while the mother bird attempts to divert their attention from the nest, "singing desperately, her high breast feathers throbbing with song" (p. 60). The metaphor reminds the reader of the four Morrow daughters and their protective mother, who always refers to them as *children* who need her protection.

Motif. The moon as a motif follows Angie and serves to highlight her feelings during dramatic moments. When things are going well, the moon is "cushioned in clouds" (p. 13) or "thin like a piece of sheer yellow silk" (p. 18). After her first kiss, the moon is a "thin yellow arc" (p. 51). On the boat, the moon is "full and lush with that overripe look" (p. 160). A planned sailing is cancelled because of angry winds, and, of course, "There was no moon" (p. 233). Associations of the moon motif with love reinforce the narrative's romantic mood.

II. The Context and Milieu

What is the setting? The novel is set during the summer in small-town Fond du Lac, Wisconsin, during the late 1930s.

What are the principle characteristics of time, place, and circumstances? The late 1930s was an important transition time in American history. The Great Depression, lessening somewhat, was still affecting family life. Small-town America was patriotic. Everybody turned out to participate in or watch the Fourth of July parade, where the men were attired in suits, ties, and hats, standard wear for adult men of the time. Families lived austere lives. Leisure activities centered on the family, with Sunday drives, listening to the radio, and attending movies.

Verisimilitude: In considering elements of the work's context, did the author take liberties with history? Why might the author have taken such liberties? Daly does not mention the war in Europe or fears about the United States entering the war, both of which well-read high school students like Daly would have been keenly aware, especially from reading *Scholastic* magazine, which covered the war in Europe in detail prior to December 1941. Daly's novel focuses on one girl's story before the protagonist leaves to begin her college education. The adult, political world seems to just melt away when two young people fall in love.

Angie describes Fond du Lac as "not such a small town—we have at least eight churches, three theaters, and a YMCA" (p. 51). A check of an online 1932 telephone directory for Fond Du Lac confirms that she is correct about the movie theaters and the YMCA. However, an online search of the churches of Fond du Lac for 1938 reveals there were 6 Roman Catholic Churches and 22 other denominations. Angie (Daly) mistakes the total number of churches in her town in part because her small world revolved around her Catholic school, weekly church attendance, and being with her friends. Even in a small town, the universe of a teenager can easily become narrowly focused.

III. The Author

What biographical (historical) details of the author's life seem to be reflected in the work? Like the protagonist Angie Morrow, Maureen Daly

- lived in Fond du Lac, Wisconsin;
- attended a parochial girl's academy in high school;
- had a stay-at-home mom, three sisters, and a father who was a traveling salesman;
- read a lot and had been adamant about attending college;
- believed that a girl's appearance could help her attain popularity;
- participated in middle-class entertainments of the thirties: listening to the radio and to records, attending movies, dancing, and dating;
- understood that there was a "double standard" in dating; and
- felt optimistic about the future, not dispirited (despite the economic depression).

Unlike Angie, Maureen Daly

- had to work her way through high school and college and had no summers off from work;
- struggled to survive during the Depression; and
- was an immigrant from Ireland.

Maureen Daly was a gifted teenage writer who won two prizes for her short stories in *Scholastic* magazine competitions. She also received a prize of $1,000 for her outline of *Seventeenth Summer* as the first Intercollegiate Novel Award from Dodd, Mead.

What historical, political, economic, and social events were happening at/around the point of composition?

- The Great Depression preceded and ended the book's composition.
- Residents from the Dust Bowl moved from their homes in search of work.
- High school attendance was at an all time high, with teenagers cut out of full-time job opportunities.
- *Scholastic* magazine became an influential source of information geared specifically to high school students and a relatively inexpensive resource for money-strapped high schools.
- Marriage and birth rates were at an all-time low, as men and women postponed marriage until they had enough money to set up a separate household.
- Hollywood movies became more and more romantic as fears of censorship cut back on realistic stories.
- The New Deal programs had been in place since 1933.
- The United States entered the war in the Pacific in December 1941.

IV. The Reader/Audience

Describe the original audience for this work, considering for example social class, interests, gender, and values. Originally written for a general adult audience, the novel was well received by major magazines and journals. As general fiction, its main audience was middle class, white, and female. However, its 1948 edition appeared with watercolor illustrations by Jay Robinson. Clearly, the book was repackaged for the YA reader. All illustrations depict both Angie and Jack engaged in their romance, except for a pensive Angie portrayed waiting by the phone with a caption, "Each day it became more evident that he did not mean to call" (page preceding 119) and one illustration of Kitty (page preceding 87), who, intent on making a fortune, creates jewelry out of crayons.

What is the book's reception history? *Book Review Digest* for 1942 shows that the book received 12 reviews from 11 sources. Daly wrote her book for adults, but that young people received the book as their own is a matter of fact. Margaret Edwards (1965: 158) remembers how she held a Book Week in her Baltimore library in the 1940s "when *Seventeenth Summer* revolutionized teenage reading," and many students came to hear Daly speak and to get an autographed copy of the book. G. Robert Carlsen (1971: 44) tells about visiting a school library following the book's publication and had one librarian tell him that the library owned 70 copies and still did not have enough to meet demands. Imitation is perhaps the highest compliment a colleague can pay to a writer, and it is not surprising that several books attempted to copy *Seventeenth Summer*'s success: Betty Cavanna's (1946) *Going on Sixteen*; Rosamond Du Jardin's *Practically Seventeen* (1949) and *Showboat Summer* (1955); Beverly Cleary's (1956) *Fifteen*; and Virginia Oakey's (1955) *Thirteenth Summer*.

During the 1960s the conception of her novel began to change. First, the notion that Daly wrote *Seventeenth Summer* with a teenage audience in mind became an accepted myth. As one critic put it, "Maureen Daly's *Seventeenth Summer* presents greater depth of understanding of young first love, even though written for adolescents" (Hanna and McAllister, 1960: 9). By the 1970s, although the critics still liked the book, they began to recommend it for a younger and younger audience and to consider it a good book for reluctant readers. During the 1980s and 1990s the book received some of its first serious negative criticism. In 1985, Nilsen and Donelson reported, "Some critics, librarians, and English teachers are deeply, personally offended by Angie's innocence. They maintain that she could never have been that innocent, that naive, gullible, and unsuspecting" (p. 587), indicating perhaps the influence of feminist criticism. The book celebrated its 50th anniversary in 1992, and in 1995 *Seventeenth Summer* was named one of *Booklist*'s "Groundbreakers: Twenty-five Books that Span the Decades."

In From *Romance to Realism*, Michael Cart (1996) gave a balanced evaluation of *Seventeenth Summer* and its place in the history of YA fiction. Cart (1996: 18) surmised that the book's popularity was due to Daly's choice of first person narrator and to Daly's skill in speaking to the "life experience" of young people. Cart stressed context and noted, "For its time the book was also fairly bold" with its portrayal of teenagers "unrepentantly smoking and drinking" (p. 19). He criticized the story (from the reader's twentieth-century perspective) as being "hopelessly naïve," speaking a language that "now sounds quaintly old-fashioned," and having a plot whose pace is "glacially slow" (p. 19). However, in "Re-reading the Romance of *Seventeenth Summer*" (1996), Virginia Schaefer Carroll devised a "rubric for analyzing feminist fiction," investigating "how Maureen Daly's *Seventeenth Summer* is about female education, female identity formation, female voice, and female choice" (Trites, 2000: 151), giving new life to the novel and coming full circle in feminist criticism from its negative reception during the 1970s to its contemporary importance as historical fiction. Simon and Schuster issued a sixtieth-anniversary hardback edition of *Seventeenth Summer* in 2002, surely a testament to its sticking power and to its permanent place in the YA canon.

ANNOTATED BIBLIOGRAPHY

Bagdasarian, Adam. 2000. *Forgotten Fire*. New York: Dell. Grades 8–12.

In the spring of 1915 in Bitlis, Turkey, the life of Vahan Kendarian changed instantly on the day the police murdered his father and brothers, dispatching the 12-year-old and the rest of his family into a crowded room and leaving them to die at the hands of armed guards. Based on the true story of the author's great-uncle's tape-recorded account of the Ottoman Turks' destruction of their Armenian countrymen, the book opens with the epigraph, "Who does now remember the Armenians? Adolph Hitler, 1939, in support of his argument that the world would soon forget the extermination of a people." YAs can trace the attempt by Armenians—at different times during the twentieth and twenty-first centuries—to persuade Turkey to acknowledge the Armenian genocide, an action that Turkey has yet to admit, and discuss the pros and cons of the debate.

Dubosarsky, Ursula. 2006. *The Red Shoe.* **New Milford, CT: Roaring Book. Grades 5–8.**

In 1954, three sisters lived in Australia with their mother and father, and all of them coped independently with the father's post-traumatic stress of World War II. The context of the novel is communicated quietly in the sisters' daily routines and matter-of-factly by the interspersed Australian newspaper clippings that include reports of the defection of a Russian spy, an audience of 100,000 at a rugby game, the H-bomb, and rebels cutting trenches in French Indo-China. Using online archives, young people can locate 1954 headlines from U.S. papers and compare them with those in the novel.

Gaines, Ernest. 1994. *A Lesson Before Dying.* **New York: Knopf. Adult book for YAs.**

Feeling angry and powerless, narrator and school teacher Grant Wiggins struggles with honoring his aunt's request to teach a friend's godson, Jefferson, to recover his humanity as he awaits execution on death row. The book is set in post–World War II Louisiana under Jim Crow laws. Gaines (2005) explains in detail in the *Southern Review* how he wrote *A Lesson Before Dying.* If YAs have access to an online database in the library, they could read the article and decide for themselves if Gaines' stated intents were successful.

Giovanni, Nikki. 2007. *On My Journey Now: Looking at African-American History Through the Spirituals.* **Cambridge, MA: Candlewick Press. Grades 5–7.**

This information book presents a history of the spirituals, tracing their origins to Africa, interlacing fact with emotion, and capturing the power of literature to sustain life and create hope and a better tomorrow. Young people will enjoy sharing the book's spiritual lyrics through choral reading or singing. When the brief chapters are read aloud, they offer remarkable stories that epitomize the new historical criticism.

Kubert, Pete. 1996. *Fax from Sarajevo: A Story of Survival.* **Milwaukie, OR: Dark Horse Comics. Grades 8–12.**

In this graphic novel, Erven Rustemagic and his family fight and survive hunger, cold, bombings, homelessness, futile escape attempts, illness, lack of medicine, unsafe streets, and loss of their house and all belongings during the Bosnian war in 1992–1993. The family's only hope resides in an intermittently functioning fax machine, providing Erven news from his friends around the world who try to help them escape. New historicists would view the faxes to and from the besieged family and the outside world as testaments to history and valuable documents for interpretation. YAs can compose text-messages or other digital or electronic messages based on a current event and discuss the benefits and difficulties of each medium as a form of communication.

Peet, Mal. 2007. *Tamar*. Cambridge, MA: Candlewick Press. Grades 10 and up.

This complex novel spans six decades, three generations, and two countries, interweaving the historic deprivation, horror, and betrayal that existed at close personal levels for two British operatives near the end of the Nazi occupation of Holland in 1944. The story features three well-developed characters, the undercover agents of 1944, and a granddaughter who unravels a family mystery in 2005. The novel presents the stark realities of World War II and its affects on the human heart and mind, and young people with an interest in the era can identify some of its known realities (e.g., the use of terror, the methods and training of undercover agents, the sanctioned use of Benzedrine and its resulting nightmares, and the unrelenting stress and trauma of war) for discussion or research.

Taylor, Theodore. 1969. *The Cay*. Topeka, KS: Tandem. Grades 6–9.

Set in the West Indies at the beginning of World War II, the novel's central character is 11-year-old Phillip, who is blinded and nearly killed when a German torpedo sinks his ship, separates him from his mother, and leaves him in the care of Timothy, an old African ship hand, who saves him and whose goodwill challenges Phillip's prejudices. Winning the Jane Addams Award (1970), the novel had a strong early reception that turned bitter when discussions about the novel's handling of racism became a national debate that caused the Jane Addams Award to be rescinded. The controversy reflected the social conflict of its time and offers an opportunity for young people to explore how the novel's reception history affected its readership then and later and its author's future work, *Timothy of the Cay: A Prequel.*

Wells, Rosemary. 2007. *Red Moon at Sharpsburg*. New York: Viking Penguin. Grades 7–9.

India Moody is 12 years old in 1861 and lives in the Shenandoah Valley where "farmers are so prosperous, people say, the soil . . . so rich, that you can throw a handful of seeds in the air and have corn on the cob the next day" (p. 7). However, when the powerful Union and Confederate armies collide at the Battle of Sharpsburg, India is surrounded by terrifying events, which the author depicts in painful and brutal detail. The author's endnote states, "It was my purpose to write about Virginia at war in the 1860s without prettifying it, mindful that our history is, to paraphrase Barbara Tuchman, a lantern shining on the stern of our ship to show us where we have been" (n.p.). The endnote can suggest research questions for YAs: Do historical facts support the author's purposeful writing? Can a work of historical fiction "show us where we have been"?

White, Ruth. 2008. *Little Audrey*. New York: Farrar, Straus, and Giroux. Grades 5–7.

Set in a coal mining town of southwestern Virginia in the 1940s, this novel tells the bittersweet story of 11-year-old Audrey, who struggles to gain weight as she recovers from scarlet fever, watches her binge-drinking dad waste the family's grocery money, tolerates her young sisters she has named the three little pigs, and waits for her mom who drifts in and out of grief and painful realities. Feeling great pity, Audrey thinks, "Oh, Daddy, I'm so sorry you have to work in that place, in the dark, in the cold. I wisht I could go to you and hug your neck, and tell you how much I love you" (p. 99). Young people may be encouraged to speculate or discuss how Audrey accepts the conflicting emotions that she holds for her family.

Wolf, Allan. 2004. *New Found Land: Lewis and Clark's Voyage of Discovery.* **Cambridge, MA: Candlewick Press. Grades 7–12.**

Fourteen distinct voices in different formats narrate the building of a fort, hunting buffalo, shooting grizzlies, exploring, mapping, trading, translating, naming species, running the gauntlet, and carving their names into a celebration tree, as well as surviving frostbite, frozen rivers, starvation, near-drowning, and serious infections. New historicists posit that there are *many* histories, and this fictional account of 12 of the historical members of the Lewis and Clark expedition illustrates this notion with its narrators, each an individual whose life is changed by the journey. For a Native American perspective on the expedition, YAs can log on to National Geographic Xpedition (1996) or Teaching Tolerance's (2006) "Discovering Lewis and Clark," which asks of the bicentennial, "Is this a celebration for Native Americans?"

REFERENCES AND SUGGESTIONS FOR FURTHER READING

Abrams, M.H. 1993. *A Glossary of Literary Terms*, 6th ed. New York: Cornell University Press.
Bate, Walter Jackson, ed. 1970. *Criticism: The Major Texts*, enlarged edition. New York: Harcourt Brace Jovanovich.
Beasley, Jerry C. 1985. "Early English Criticism." *Studies in the Novel* 17, no. 4 (Winter): 334–354.
Brooks, Cleanth, and Robert Penn Warren. 1938. *Understanding Poetry.* New York: Henry Holt.
Brooks, Cleanth, and Robert Penn Warren. 1943. *Understanding Fiction.* New York: F.S. Crofts.
Carlsen, G. Robert. 1971. *Books and the Teen-age Reader.* New York: Harper and Row.
Carroll, Virginia Schaefer. 1996. "Re-reading the Romance of *Seventeenth Summer*." *Children's Literature Association Quarterly* 21, no.1 (Spring): 12–19.
Cart, Michael. 1996. *From Romance to Realism: Fifty Years of Growth and Change in Young Adult Fiction.* New York: HarperCollins.
Cart, Michael. 2002. "After Many a Summer." *Booklist* 100, no 2. (September 15): 223.
Cavanna, Betty. 1946. *Going on Sixteen.* Philadelphia, PA: Westminster.
Cleary, Beverly. 1956. *Fifteen.* New York: Morrow.
Coplan, Kate, and Edwin Costagna, eds. 1965. *The Library Reaches Out.* Dobbs Ferry, NY: Oceana.
Daly, Maureen. 1942, 1948. *Seventeenth Summer.* Illustrated by Jay Robinson. New York: Dodd, Mead.
Daly, Maureen. 1986. "Maureen Daly." In *Something About the Author Autobiography Series*, vol. 1, edited by Adele Sarkissian, pp. 69–87. Detroit, MI: Gale Research.
Daly, Maureen. 2002. *Seventeenth Summer.* New York: Simon and Schuster.
Dickstein, Morris. 2003. "Literary Theory and Historical Understanding." *Chronicle of Higher Education* 49, no. 37 (May 23): B7–10.

"Discovering Lewis and Clark." 2006. "Teaching Tolerance." Available at: www.tolerance .org/teach/magazine/features.jsp?cid=648.

Donelson, Kenneth L., and Alleen Pace Nilsen. 1989. *Literature for Today's Young Adults,* 3rd ed. New York: Harper Collins.

Du Jardin, Rosamond. 1949. *Practically Seventeen.* Illustrated by Joe and Beth Krush. Philadelphia: J.B. Lippincott.

Du Jardin, Rosamond. 1955. *Showboat Summer.* Philadelphia: Lippincott.

Edwards, Margaret. 1965. "A Long Way to Tipperary." In *The Library Reaches Out,* edited by Kate Coplan and Edwin Castagna, pp. 135–161. Dobbs Ferry, NY: Oceana.

Gaines, Ernest. 2005. "Writing *A Lesson Before Dying.*" *Southern Review* 41, no. 4 (Autumn): 770–777.

Gallagher, Catherine, and Stephen Greenblatt. 2000. *Practicing New Historicism.* Chicago: University of Chicago Press.

Greenblatt, Stephen. 1989. "Towards a Poetics of Culture." In *The New Historicism,* edited by Harold Aran Veeser, pp. 1–14. New York: Routledge.

"Groundbreakers: 25 Books that Span the Decades." 1995. *Booklist* 91, no. 19/20 (June 1): 1760.

Hanna, Geneva R., and Mariana K. McAllister. 1960. *Books, Young People, and Reading Guidance.* New York: Harper and Brothers.

Jackson, J. R. de J. 1989. *Historical Criticism and the Meaning of Texts.* New York: Routledge.

National Geographic Xpedition. "Lewis and Clark." 1996. National Geographic. Available at: www.nationalgeographic.com/lewisandclark.

Nilsen, Alleen Pace, and Kenneth L. Donelson. 1985. *Literature for Today's Young Adults,* 2nd ed. Glenview, IL: Scott, Foresman.

Oakey, Virginia. 1955. *Thirteenth Summer.* New York: A.A. Wynn.

Payne, Michael, ed. 2005. *The Greenblatt Reader.* Malden, MA: Blackwell.

Rigney, Ann. 2004. "Possible Monuments: Literature, Cultural Memory, and the Case of Jeanie Deans." *Poetics Today* 25, no. 2 (Summer): 361–396.

Russo, John Paul. 1994. "Historical Theory and Criticism." In *The Johns Hopkins Guide to Literary Theory and Criticism,* edited by Michael Groden and Martin Kreiswirth, pp. 382–388. Baltimore, MD: Johns Hopkins University Press.

Taine, Hippolyte. 1965. *History of English Literature.* Translated by H. Van Laun. New York. F. Ungar.

Taine, Hippolyte. 1970. "From the *Introduction to the History of English Literature.*" In *Criticism: The Major Texts,* enlarged edition, edited by Walter Jackson Bate, pp. 500–507. New York: Harcourt Brace Jovanovich.

Taylor, Theodore. 1993. *Timothy of the Cay.* San Diego, CA: Harcourt Brace.

Trites, Roberta Seelinger. 2000. *Disturbing the Universe: Power and Repression in Adolescent Literature.* Iowa City: University of Iowa Press.

Chapter 9

Gender Criticism

Math class is tough!
—Words spoken by the first Teen Talk Barbie doll in 1992

HISTORY OF GENDER CRITICISM

It may seem unfair that the Barbie doll, beloved by millions of little girls and once the archetype of American femininity, has evolved into a symbol (for some) of the once stereotypical female—passive, materialistic, unintelligent, and appearance obsessed. The toy continues to be collected and makes Mattel millions of dollars, but in subsequent generations some parents have not pushed or encouraged their children to choose Barbie dolls, seeing them as just one more image of femininity that promotes the wrong ideas about what it means to be a woman, to be feminine. Issues of femininity and masculinity turn out to be more complicated and to involve more than the notions of simple role models, media influence, or different brain wiring. Many of the questions surrounding the "battle of the sexes" had never been seriously challenged until the women's movement and the development of feminist criticism.

Feminist criticism is a way to read, interpret, and evaluate literature from the perspective of women and their experiences. However, both women and men approach literature from a feminist perspective. Feminist literary criticism is composed of different theories, each following its prescribed tenets (e.g., sociological, psychological, archetypal, historical). From the beginning of women's rights as an issue, women have had to deal with a rain of negative connotations associated with the word *feminist*. English novelist Rebecca West put her own twist on the term when she said, "'I only know that other people call me a feminist whenever I express sentiments that differentiate me from a doormat or a prostitute'" (Davidson and Wagner-Martin, 1995: 309).

First and Second Wave Feminism

A historical review of feminist criticism can be divided into three phases, sometimes referred to as *waves*. The first wave refers to the period marked by the women's suffrage movement from about 1850 through the passage of the Nineteenth Amendment in 1920, giving women the right to vote in federal elections. The second wave began in the late 1960s and early 1970s with the publication of several influential and groundbreaking works, including titles of literary criticism. During the second wave, feminist critics focused on specific areas that had long needed attention (Spencer, 1983: 10):

- Identification of women's works that were out of print, neglected, or misunderstood
- Analyses of the image of woman as she appears in the existing literature
- Examination and reinterpretation of the existing criticism of women writers' books, especially considering the canon.

The Second Wave: Identifying Women's Literature

With their serious entrance into the male-dominated academy and its canon, feminist critics quickly achieved a revolution in literature. Within a couple of decades, they had rewritten "the cultural history of nineteenth and twentieth century Britain and America, putting gender, not just women, in where it had been left out by an older liberal tradition of cultural history and criticism" (Kaplon, 1991: 755). Combing through archives, used book stores, and university libraries worldwide, feminist scholars reclaimed (and continue to reclaim) works by women writers. The extent of the retrieved titles and authors of lost, forgotten, or neglected works goes beyond the scope of this brief history, but a look at one feminist work indicates the contribution that second wave scholars have made to literary history.

In *Mothers of the Novel: 100 Good Women Writers Before Jane Austen*, Dale Spender (1986) located about *600 novels* written during the seventeenth and eighteenth centuries that had been completely ignored by scholars. In the introduction to her book, Spender tells of her surprise when she discovered that women had been writing novels more than 150 years before Jane Austen began her career. Spender's bigger shock was to discover that "during the 18th century the majority of novels were written—by women!" (p. 4), a fact that seriously challenged the literary history of the novel.

Traditionally, courses in the academy on the rise of the modern novel had attributed the genre's beginnings to Cervantes in Spain and/or to such giants of English literature as Daniel Defoe, Henry Fielding, Lawrence Sterne, and Samuel Richardson. Spender indicates that the men of the eighteenth century "were not amused" by the success of women writers and that for a while the men used female pseudonyms "to try and find a favoured way into print" (p. 4). It was not until the 1840s that the situation was reversed, women were returned to their place, and "women writers were adopting male pseudonyms in order to find a publisher" (p. 4). Ironically, it was women's success in writing that brought about their publishing demise.

Representations of Women in Literature

Another goal of second wave critics was to examine the image of women as they had been portrayed in literature. Because the first feminist critics had been trained in *New Criticism* (the predominant approach in the academy that interpreted works of literature by close reading of the text alone and ignoring contexts), many had to learn how to read from a new perspective, and the challenge of reading through gendered eyes revealed new interpretations and evaluations of literature both classic and contemporary.

Feminist critics scoured literature, art history, and the media for representations of women. Articles and books were written about women portrayed in stereotypical ways (e.g., as femme fatale or goddess archetypes). Naomi Wolf's (1991) *The Beauty Myth: How Images of Beauty Are Used Against Women* became a bestseller and provided a historical perspective of the cult of beauty as practiced in the West. Examination of the representations of women (and now men) in contemporary media remains ongoing, and the extent and degree of the *direct* influence that these images might have on the minds of young adults (YAs) remain debated. However, it is important that YAs be taught critical thinking skills in order to analyze gendered representations in literature and in the media. Young people are not passive receptacles of everything they see or hear, and they appreciate that adults recognize their abilities. By giving YAs the language to critique print advertisements for stereotypes of both genders, for instance, they come away with a more skeptical, questioning view of media and marketing efforts to target (and manipulate) youth as a powerful consumer group.

Third Wave Feminism

According to Baumgardner and Richards (2000: 17), "For anyone born after the early 1960s, the presence of feminism in our lives is taken for granted. For our generation, feminism is like fluoride. We scarcely notice that we have it—it's simply in the water." With these words, third wave feminists formally distinguished themselves from second wave feminists mainly by virtue of generation. There is no precise date to mark the arrival of third wave feminism, except that the term perhaps first appeared in print in *Ms.* magazine in Rebecca Walker's (1992) "Doing the Third Wave." Generally speaking, third wave feminists embrace literature, popular culture, women's global human rights, the environment, the Internet, transgender issues, and women's sports. They are even more multidisciplinary than their predecessors in the second wave in that they reach far into the popular culture for sources to analyze or to find connections with their own experiences. They review graphic novels as a serious literary form, especially works created by women (e.g., Lynda Barry, Trina Robbins, and Marjane Satrapi's autobiographical series beginning with *Persepolis*). Film studies, which had gained huge strides during the second wave, have become a force in the academy and constitute an important area of third wave criticism.

In music, contemporary sounds energize third-wavers through the rise of women's (girls') bands, whose raucous audiences and raunchy lyrics shocked some when they first appeared on the scene in the early 1990s. The music is playful and aggressive and at first was called Riot Grrrl, the name for their punk rock subgenre. "Girl power" is a phrase associated with the third wave, and, unfortunately, the media soon called the third wave movement "'lipstick feminism, consumer feminism, feminism lite'. . . . [or] 'babe feminism'" (Heywood, 2007: xix). Third wave feminists feel that they do a better job in promoting the voices of multiracial women than the second wave did. Third-wavers have been vocal in their interest in and concern for preteen and teenage girls and the social issues they face, including eating disorders, sexuality, and sexual orientation with its ramifications in life and literature.

What makes third wave feminists *philosophically* different from second wave feminists? For one thing, third wave feminists almost unanimously believe that no single person should or could "attempt to speak in the name of other women" (Henry, 2005: 83). They see a distinction between academic feminism and real-life feminism as it is played out on the streets and in the schools. Third wave feminists point out certain weaknesses in the second wave. According to Enns and Sinacore (2001: 479–480), some of their complaints about second wave feminism are that it

- is inflexible, dogmatic, too concerned with political correctness;
- promotes unspoken "rules" about what one must believe and do to be a "real feminist";
- has not made better progress in all women's social problems; and
- promotes stereotypes that portray feminists as hating men or refusing to shave one's legs.

Third wave feminists prefer their activism to be local, without leadership, to take on one specific problem or issue at a time, and (especially) to have a presence on the Internet.

During the late 1990s, women's studies evolved into programs that were more inclusive of global gender issues, and their new names reflect the changes: Yale's program is "Women's, Gender and Sexuality Studies"; University of Nebraska, "Women's and Gender Studies"; and MIT, "Program in Women's and Gender Studies." Whatever it chooses to call itself, women's studies/gender studies has definitely broadened its interests and added more disciplines to its explorations of the human experience.

Sexual Orientation and GLBTQ: Problem or Potentiality?

In discussing the role of adults in the lives of young people, Nicholas J. Pace (2007: 366–367) writes that professionals "must view gay and lesbian students as people, not as problems to be ignored, feared, or fixed. They need to focus on the humanity and potentiality of gay and lesbian students rather than on alleged differences." Since the 1970s, most research about adolescent sexual orientation has dealt with gay, lesbian, or bisexual *problems*. Heterosexuality has been viewed as the norm, and any other sexual orientation has been viewed as being associated to a higher degree with risk factors (e.g., substance abuse and suicide). In *The New Gay Teenager*, Ritch C. Savin-Williams (2005) posits that twenty-first century adolescents "minimize the significance of sexuality in their identity" (p. 6) and that "same-sex attracted young people are more diverse than they are similar and more resilient than suicidal" (p. 3). The demographic Savin-Williams identifies as the new gay teenager is represented by those who have become YAs during the twenty-first century and who feel little connection with their elders who participated in the Gay Pride movement beginning in 1969 (a similar generational difference as seen by third wave feminists).

Whether individuals seek or shun a sexual orientation label, they still need to see themselves in the books that they read. A review of the literature reveals that those who work with YAs consider it a responsibility to provide appropriate resources for GLBTQ young people (Alexander and Miselis, 2007; Patrick, 2007; Rochman, 2006; Blackburn and Buckley, 2006; Cart, 2005; Swartz, 2003). With a philosophy based on egalitarianism regarding all topics, adult guides include students of all sexual orientations in discussions about sex and gender. "GLBTQ teens have urgent information needs and the library is a primary source in their search for information" (Alexander and Miselis, 2007: 43), and this includes Internet access. The fact that GLBTQ YAs have been underserved in the past is beginning to change. The many articles calling for change, such as "Out and Ignored" (Whelan, 2006: 46), have had an impact on those who select books and materials for YAs. Some topics to cover when considering GLBTQ materials include the following.

Understanding the Terminology

Although some people may resist being labeled according to their sexual orientation, others do identify themselves by using certain terms.

- *Gay* refers to homosexual males, although it is used informally to refer broadly to the gay community as a whole.
- *GLBTQ* (or *LGBTQ*) stands for gay, lesbian, bisexual, transgender, and queer or questioning.

- *Transgender* describes a person whose gender identity differs from his or her biological sex. Transgender children feel they are one gender in their minds and another gender in their bodies.
- *Queer* is still a controversial word. Originally, queer was a disparaging term. During the Gay Pride movement, activists took back the word that had been a derogatory term and used it as an umbrella term to unite the gay community, or, as used in the academy, as a neutral term. In the 1990s Queer Studies began as a multidisciplinary field that addresses cultural issues and sexual orientation.
- *Questioning* applies to a person who is still exploring his or her gender and sexual identity.
- *Homophobia* is the irrational fear or hatred of homosexuals or homosexuality.

Fighting Stereotypes

Originally, most YA novels with gay-themed characters focused on the protagonists' problems or punishments. Invariably, the character was what Christine Jenkins (1998: 300) calls, "the generic gay person . . . urban, middle-class, white, educated male involved in the arts and likely to encounter hardships directly related to anti-gay prejudice." Jenkins points out the need for more stories whose protagonists are lesbians, and of color, and who are not isolated but live and interact with others in their own communities. However, Michael Cart (2005: 1356) writes that recent YA GLBTQ fiction "has moved from its former status as ghetto genre to the mainstream of YA fiction." It is important for those who work with YAs to remember the role that the library can play in the lives of those who live on the social margins of secondary school life. The alienation that some GLBTQ young people experience can be partially assuaged with the selection of the best fiction and nonfiction titles and with classrooms and libraries establishing themselves categorically as a safe haven for everyone.

Philip Charles Crawford (2007: 473), a school library director, writes in *Horn Book*, "Being a sissy has never been easy." Crawford notes the important role that reading played for him as a YA, especially when he discovered Jo and Laurie, in Alcott's *Little Women*, who "were everything society told me I shouldn't be" (p. 473). Crawford adds, "For boys like me, the book was a godsend, a world where sissy boys could not only be themselves but where they thrived and were nurtured" (p. 473). Fortunately in the early years of the twenty-first century, there are many books of literary quality that feature GLBTQ protagonists.

Fighting Homophobia

Regarding homophobia, secondary schools have been characterized as being "'virtual cauldrons' of homophobic discrimination and anger" (Kaplan, 2003: 8), having a "near-toxic environment" of intolerance (Pace, 2007: 344), and, at the very least, ignoring "a passive form of homophobia embedded in culture" (Vare and Norton, 2004: 190). One scholar goes so far as to call secondary schools "the most homophobic institution in American society" (Unks, 1995: 5). Some young people aim derogatory words at certain individuals and use those terms with ease in hallways, locker rooms, and lunchrooms.

Those who work with YAs realize that *all readers* benefit from books that tell realistic stories expressive of diverse experiences, desires, and points of view. As YA novelist James Howe writes, "Whether or not a child is gay, all children live in a world among gay people and they need to overcome their discomfort and the bigotry they've been taught in order to be accepting of themselves and others" (cited in Pavao, 2003: 25), speaking for one logical reason to support previously muted voices in YA literature.

FEMINISM, GENDER, AND YA LITERATURE

Until gender criticism arose as a broader field of studies within the academy, feminist criticism was received by some scholars as biased or too "ideological." Often with a Marxist, psychological, or sociological bent, feminist criticism asked some of the following questions:

- What is the gender of the author? What influence does the historical context(s) have in interpreting or analyzing the work?
- How are women or girls depicted in the work?
- Are there any stereotyped characters whose role in the story is not just functional (e.g., in a nineteenth-century novel, the nosey, unmarried aunt, or in a war novel, the self-sacrificing nurse)?
- Are the important women characters three dimensional, or round, not stereotypes?
- What is the novel's point of view? How well is a woman's point of view represented in the narrative?
- In the novel's historical context, how does patriarchy function in the society of the novel's setting? Are there discernible biased points of view regarding women's role in society?
- Does the author seem sympathetic or condescending toward women?

Taking an ideological stance when writing about literature is one approach to use when responding to a work. However, the trend is moving in the direction of gender studies wherein critics believe that society shares some of the responsibility for the communication problems that arise between men and women. People are products of both their biology (nature) and their environment (nurture). At this point, no one knows for sure if nature or nurture is more influential in forming adolescent gender identity. Many see, however, that contemporary Western society often places unnecessary limits and unrealistic expectations onto each generation of its young people. Readers may find that focusing on common issues (parents, dating, appearance, peer acceptance) provides more realistic contexts for discussions while at the same time encouraging more diverse points of view. Emphasizing oppositions, binaries, and differences sometimes shuts down discussion as people take sides for or against, for example, "feminists," a term whose meaning has a very long, complex history. As sociologist Michael Kimmel (2004: 15) writes, thinking in terms of opposite sexes is not as productive as thinking in terms of "neighboring sexes" to better engage readers in lively dialogues.

Discussing Gender in YA Literature

The following questions are suggested for thinking and talking about gender in YA literature. They may be considered in any order, and some questions may not apply to every work.

Evaluating Gender in Literature

- Do societal gender expectations and stereotypes cause conflict or limit the character's range of options?
- Does the character think critically to reconcile real experiences with gender expectations?
- Does the character demonstrate independence (from gender expectations) in making decisions? If so, does the character pay the social price?
- Does the character achieve acceptance from other characters and self?

Application of Gender Criticism to Brad Land's *Goat: A Memoir*

Brad Land's (2004) *Goat: A Memoir* is a first-person account of a young man who has had two violent, traumatic encounters in under two years—one random and illegal, the other sanctioned. After giving two strangers a ride home following a party, Brad is viciously beaten and left for dead. He manages to get to safety but lives with serious physical and emotional scars. In an attempt to repair his life, Brad decides to attend Clemson University with his younger brother, Brett, and to join his brother's fraternity. Rather than cure his problems, the fraternity experience accentuates Brad's nightmares, fears, and insecurities. Land's true story shows how young men who live through events that shatter their identity are left alone to deal with the fallout of those events. More often than not, there are no societal nets in place for those men who experience severe trauma. They are expected to bear up and deal with it themselves in the stereotypically manly fashion.

Expectations and Stereotypes

As a Southern boy in the late 1990s, Brad feels he is expected to be physically strong and "manly." He weighs only 132 pounds, plays the guitar, likes to read, and wears glasses. He compares himself to his younger brother Brett, who clearly fits the stereotype of Southern masculinity, being tall and broad-shouldered. The athletic Brett also receives a college scholarship for his performance in sports, a symbol of the ultimate in masculine success. Brett genuinely admires and respects his older brother Brad's different strengths, such as his intelligence and creativity, but Brad dismisses his own talents. As the older brother, Brad understands the oddness of their almost reverse role, since most people think Brett (larger and stronger) is the older brother.

Conflicts from Gender Expectations and Stereotypes

Brad is reserved and becomes nervous, even shaky, fairly easily in interactions with girls or with strangers. The night that two strangers ask him for a ride, Brad acknowledges (to himself) his inability to tell anybody "no" and rejects his better instincts, which are that he should turn and go. As Brad drives the men further and further out of town, his fear grows. He never asks their names and refers to them (to himself) as *the breath* and *the smile* throughout his narrative. His imagination races to get himself out of this potentially dangerous situation. Knowing he has made a terrible mistake, Brad speeds recklessly, hoping to attract the attention of a highway patrolman. He looks for a deer, hoping to hit it and cause an automobile accident. When the two men engage him in conversation, Brad cannot hide his fear as his hand shakes and as he talks too much.

When he stops the car under their orders, the attack begins. The breath grabs Brad from behind and wrenches his neck, and, as Brad fights back, the arm does not move from around his neck until he blacks out. Once outside the car, they begin to punch and pummel his face. They take his wallet and anything of value and empty his trunk of his books. Brad begins to cry, bringing on more punches from the men who enjoy tormenting him. He resists so much that after several punches, the smile tells him to just go to sleep. After they throw Brad onto the ground, the kicking and stomping begin. The smile seems to be the leader, and each time he hits Brad, he smiles and smiles, an image that will remain with Brad in his conscious mind and in his nightmares for many months to come. They kick and smash his face into the pavement, breaking his nose. His mouth fills with blood.

The two then put Brad in the trunk and drive away. Inside the trunk he regains consciousness and thinks of possible (but not very likely) ways to escape. He finds an ink pen and imagines it as his perfect weapon. In a stream of consciousness passage, Brad uses the pen like a knife and attacks the men's throats, jamming it deeply into their necks. Brad sees their fingers oozing red and blue. The reader acknowledges that the pen really is Brad's only weapon and that he will be able to use it in the future when he eventually writes his story.

The breath and the smile stop the car and remove Brad from the trunk. They only want his car, but they continue to let him know that they are going to kill him.

He begs for his life, saying that he will never tell, but they drag him to the front of the car, an action that Brad interprets as their intention to run over his body. Once again they press his face and body into the pavement. To his surprise, a calm suddenly comes over him. He awaits either a bullet to the head or the car rolling over his body. Instead, the car suddenly backs up and roars away. Brad then gets up on shaky legs, listening constantly for the sound of the retuning car. He knows that the best way out is to take the paved road, but of course he will not go near it.

Brad eventually locates a house and telephones his father for help. This begins Brad's second ordeal as he faces the scrutiny of the police, his family, and his peers. From the first interview with the police, their questions imply that Brad is somehow not a completely innocent victim. For one, they ask him why such a good-looking boy would pick up two strangers and give them such a long ride. The subtext of their questions may escape Brad but not the reader. When the police ask him to pick out the men from some mug shots, he cannot focus on the faces clearly enough to identify anyone. It seems that, to the authorities, once Brad's wounds have been tended to, he should be able to detachedly identify his attackers.

Later, the police interrogate Brad in a room with a two-way mirror, telling him (lying to him) that one of the perpetrators is looking at him and that the police believe the whole episode is a drug deal gone awry. They continue to grill him along this completely false theory of the crime even as he answers their questions truthfully. When given an opportunity to write everything that happened that night, Brad starts to write and cannot stop, but his images and other phrases and experiences seem to make little sense even though, as he thinks, every word is true. The police do not know how to deal with a (male) victim who has trouble explaining the crime in a simple, straightforward way. Brad's experience in fact was so traumatic that, at this point, he cannot make sense on paper that which does not make sense in his mind.

As a typically socialized male, Brad lacks the language to express such normal emotions as horror, humiliation, and guilt. While anger would be an entirely appropriate reaction, Brad turns his anger inward instead of outward, account-ing for his depression. The authorities want a blow-by-blow account of the event; Brad mainly recalls his pain, fear, and shame. He cannot describe the perpetrators beyond their threatening qualities, smile and breath. They are only shadows to him, and he repeats that no one can catch them.

The police eventually track down the breath, and the criminal receives a jail sentence of 75 years, but the smile is never found. Although such justice is sup-posed to bring relief to victims, Brad's trauma has only begun. By never wanting to remember their actual names and referring to them only as the smile and the breath, Brad dehumanizes his tormenters, who have made of him an object of irrational hostility during their torture by moonlight. Because he failed to overpower two men all by himself, Brad becomes the recipient of names and insults that question his masculinity from the peer group with whom he once comfortably interacted.

Brad experiences some delayed physical injuries, such as a broken eardrum and infections. He is in pain most of the time and depends on Leah for his emotional support, but she does not love him and they part ways. As time passes, the attack is euphemistically referred to as "your thing," " your abduction," "the incident," "the kidnapping," "the choking," and "the trunk-thing" (p. 56). Brad realizes that he is not ready for school, and he remains at home while Brett returns to Clemson, his family's alma mater. Both their father and grandfather attended the university, and to Brad it symbolizes an important link, "this place we are supposed to be together" (p. 58), the tradition passed down through generations of his family's men. To fail to attend Clemson is to fail as a man.

In Part II, Brad narrates his life at Clemson and faces his second major conflict. In a way that is reminiscent of his rejection of his better instincts preceding the kidnapping, Brad thinks that he should go ahead to college and pledge the fraternity, even though he feels uneasy about his decision. Brad's reason for putting himself through the intensity of pledging is his equally intense desire to feel normal again. Fraternity life means acceptance, brotherhood, and safety from the outside world. Certainly Brad is ill-prepared for the reality of fraternity hazing, the details of which all members have sworn to keep secret so that no one outside the elite group can ever know the whole awful truth.

At Clemson, Brad soon observes the expected and accepted behaviors of masculine display, the script of manhood as practiced in a large university fraternity. Manly actions include eager participation in drinking games, drinking and driving, drinking during classes (pour out half the soda and add the whiskey), honoring violent acts perpetrated on others, bragging about sexual conquests, referring to girls using sexist language, and encouraging girls to get drunk. The fraternity has a strict dress code for the pledges, and Brad has switched from wearing glasses to wearing contact lenses. He also switches his major from art to English. Brad does not explain the reasons for these changes, but his actions suggest his desire to conform to the appearance of the fraternity brothers and that includes not looking too serious or too artsy.

Initiation day begins with the pledges running a gauntlet of the brothers, who push, punch, and trip the boys as they make their way down a long hall. They are ordered to scream certain words and phrases and then are punched for doing so. When asked a question, the answer will inevitably be wrong, and the pledges receive a blow to the head or stomach. The six-foot five-inch pledge master directs the major events with his threatening presence. Next the boys are taken into a darkened room and ordered to bob up and down and baa like goats. The pledges are ordered around using the same demeaning language and tone of voice that one hears from drill instructors in war movies, and most of the boys are intimidated. They are called names, especially "faggot," the preferred insult for the reason that those who use it believe that the word embodies the worst thing a "real" man could be called.

The pledges are spit on, slapped on the back of the head, and their hair filled with various solutions. Through this first phase of the initiation, Brad can hear cries and whimpers from the pledges nearby, but he will not permit himself to cry. On the way out of the room, one of the brothers whispers words of encouragement into Brad's ear, like some professional torturer who momentarily eases off in order to plant false hope into his victim's mind.

While he is narrating his own experiences, Brad includes other pledges whose experiences parallel his own. Will Fitch is one fellow pledge who may be even more nervous than Brad, but he tells Brad that there is simply no option for him to quit. Will's skewed perspective of the fraternity places their members in the realm of the myth of the American Dream with the fraternity brothers representing supermen. Brad observes Will closely, sees how his hands tremble, and watches as he becomes more frustrated.

During one typical pledge day in the dorms, a fraternity brother orders Will to somehow get himself inside the three-by-five-foot enclosed top of a tall wardrobe. The boys laugh at Will, who looks completely folded over, his head between his legs, and seven feet off the ground. The desire to belong to a socially elite group is so strong that Will believes his only choice is to place himself in degrading situations, knowing that the status he will gain is worth more than any humiliation he suffers. In fact, Brad learns later that Will had become singled out for more than the usual amount of unpleasant activities, in part because it was so apparent that Will wanted to be accepted more than anybody else did.

Reconciliation and Social Price

It does not come as a surprise when Brad resorts to some violence of his own. Angry when he finds a pledge from another fraternity passed out in his room, Brad steps hard (twice) on the boy's hand. He enlists the help of Mark (a hulk) to throw the boy out. Later he and Mark laugh it up, but for Brad, it is a "sad laugh because I know the shadows I dream about, the smile and the breath, the brothers, they're filling me up" (p. 152). To realize that he is becoming the very thing he abhors gives Brad the incentive to reconsider his decision about pledging the fraternity.

The day after the final votes are cast for the pledges, Brad learns that Will Fitch has died of a sudden and unexplained heart attack in his dorm room. Three of the "brothers" had rejected Will Fitch as a member, a rare occurrence. Both Brett and Brad are infuriated by this news and blame the brothers. Has Will paid the ultimate social price for his relentless dedication to getting into the fraternity?

Brad's anger becomes channeled into making certain that his fellow pledge and friend will not be forgotten.

But there are no memorials for Will at Clemson, and his obituary is perfunctory. The brothers who blackballed Will attend his funeral but utter no words of tribute. As he grieves with Brett by his side, Brad wants to single out the brothers who were responsible for Will's death, those whose actions had "choked this dead boy's heart" (p. 199). Brad later visits Will's grave site alone, committed to keeping Will's memory alive and the boy's useless death visible.

Acceptance

Brad Land's memoir shows the destructive results that young people sometimes experience when they focus on their peers for acceptance and validation. The book also challenges the assumption of there being only one form or concept of masculinity. Perhaps, more accurately, there are *masculinities* (Connell, 1995). One form that masculinity can take is the tough, heartless, unemotional initiation of senseless violence (the smile and the breath). Another form of masculinity rewards bragging, drinking, bullying, and humiliating others (unsupervised fraternities). Another rewards intelligence, creativity, and friendship (the ideal that Brad will seek).

The book's two epigraphs (p. 1) signal the themes that emerge from the narrative. The first epigraph comes from Cormac McCarthy's (1985) *Blood Meridian* and is a line spoken by the Judge, one of the most violent, bloody, and irrationally evil characters in all of American literature. The second epigraph is an excerpt from Brigit Pegeen Kelly's (1995) "Song," a haunting poem that tells about a little girl whose pet goat disappears one night and is not found until the next day, its head cut off and its skull tied with a rope to the school yard tree. The adults locate the boys who had done the deed, something that they ascribe as a prank or a joke, recalling the cliché "Boys will be boys!"

Like the boys in Kelly's poem, the young men in the fraternity involved in sanctioned violence believe they can have their fun and be done with it. However, they leave a trail of shattered lives behind them and must contain the memories of the acts of cruelty they committed on more vulnerable others. The irrational, violent hostility (scapegoating) that tries to pass itself off as brotherhood may be sanctioned by certain segments of society, but Brad's decision to reject this form of brotherhood puts him on the side of the good.

Brad will not let Will become anybody's scapegoat. For Brad, Will was a strong, good person who deserves to be remembered, but the boy's memory will not be visible at Clemson. Only Brad's memoir will keep Will Fitch alive, removing his scapegoat status forever. Kelly's poem suggests that the boys themselves will have paid a high price for their pranks. To mindlessly kill or destroy will lead to no good, and for those who participate in it, they can never be the same again.

Application of Gender Criticism to Stephanie Hemphill's
Your Own, Sylvia: A Verse Portrait of Sylvia Plath

The Printz Honor Book (2008) and ALA Best Books for Young Adults Top 10 (2008) *Your Own, Sylvia: A Verse Portrait of Sylvia Plath*, by Stephanie Hemphill (2007), chronicles Sylvia Plath's life through Hemphill's original poems written from the perspectives of Plath's family, friends, and detractors. Drawing on the poet's journals, letters, and prose and poetry, Stephanie Hemphill intended a YA audience by emphasizing Plath's coming of age during the 1950s. Plath led a complex, fascinating life, and her appeal to YAs, especially young women, has not abated since her tragic death in 1963.

The book's attractive format includes the addition of concise, biographical facts, or footnotes, printed in a different font and in a contrasting shade of pale gray, a technique that unobtrusively signals the reader about pertinent facts that relate to the poems above. Of the 153 original poems, Hemphill wrote 17 as "Imagining Sylvia" wherein she adopts Plath's original poem (e.g., sonnet or villanelle), keeps the same topic, and incorporates Sylvia's imagery whenever appropriate (p. 251). However, the poems are impressionist and not in imitation of Plath's poems. Hemphill draws a realistic picture of a talented young girl trapped in a time and place whose mores did not fit with her dreams of becoming a great writer. To be considered a real woman during the 1950s, Plath would have had to adopt traditional feminine roles (wife, mother, and daughter) while trying to balance her "masculine" role as writer.

Conflict or Limitations

Plath's journals are full of her anger about the double standard and about the expectations that pressured young women into accepting the belief that getting married was their most important calling. In "Put Your Studies to Good Use," speaker Senator Adlai Stevenson tells Plath's 1955 Smith graduating class that it was now the time to pursue their most important career—being a wife—a speech whose words (at the time) few people questioned. Plath yearned for role models of women writers whose lives could show her that it was possible for her to become a writer and that a career as a poet was a real option for her. Indeed, it was a cold fact of life that "there were few women publishing poetry in the States—or in England—early in the 1960s" (Wagner-Martin, 1999: 136). Hemphill's biography illustrates the conflicts that Plath was attempting to resolve in order for her to become simultaneously a successful woman and a successful writer, roles that unfortunately seemed nearly impossible to integrate.

Hemphill writes 18 poems from the point of view of Plath's boyfriends, many with whom she kept a long correspondence. Some of Plath's boyfriends refer to her in stereotypical colloquialisms that imply that girls are nothing more than objects for boys' desires. Plath's most passionate, short-termed affair is with

Richard Sassoon (related to English poet Siegfried Sassoon), who speaks of her in terms that reflect the (then) male assumption that a female is an object whose beauty reflects positively on the male who is able to capture her.

After the death of Plath's father, her mother became dedicated to giving her daughter the finest education possible. However, the family economic shortfall necessitated her applying for scholarships and prizes in order to remain in school. After she is accepted by *Mademoiselle* for a summer internship, Plath's exacting supervisor, chief editor Cyrilly Abels, selects Plath for the top guest editorship, knowing that Plath is superior to the average candidate in every respect. Hemphill's tribute to Sylvia in "Why She Writes" (p. 20) illustrates Plath's strengths and fears. Written in a villanelle—using alternating and repeating three-line stanzas—the speaker indicates that Sylvia understands how much her education costs her and her family. It also clearly indicates that Plath was keenly aware of the conflicts between her inner ambitions and her social limits and constraints.

The face that Sylvia presents to the world projects self-confidence. However, her intense work ethic, her bursts of energy and writing, and the pressures of high expectations from herself and others eventually lead her to a physical and emotional breakdown. Hemphill describes the events in a series of 15 poems. After she returns from her New York City stint, Plath falls into a deep depression, goes missing for three days, attempts suicide, and, with headlines reporting that a Smith girl goes missing, she is found barely alive. The psychiatric care she receives, considered to be excellent in 1953, sounds primitive today and far from curative. She receives different diagnoses, one psychiatrist ominously declaring that she has a (vague) form of adolescent nerves instead of the more unacceptable "mental illness," indicative of the stigma of the disease even within the profession. Even though Plath had had electroshock therapy as an outpatient *prior* to her August 1953 suicide attempt, all of the doctors agreed that she should continue with the therapy, a procedure that can obliterate memory and leave one's emotions flattened. The treatments are so traumatic that they leave Plath unable to write in her journals for over a year, the only extended time in her life without nightly writing.

Reconciliation and Gender Expectations

Plath began her prolific journal when a child, and even in junior high school she knew her boyfriends would be useful in her writings someday. Her friend Ruth thinks that Plath's experiences with boys will help her write good stories someday. Plath indicates how her relationships with boys have *already* given her plenty to write about.

One of the most difficult things Plath had to do was to reconcile her drive for perfection with physical and emotional realities that even the strongest person cannot ignore. She was already a prolific writer by the time she was chosen by Wilbury Crokett to be in his elite, but demanding, high school English class taught like a college seminar. Other relatives and characters commented about her tremendous output of writing. There are no summers off for Plath, as she must work for tuition as a field hand, nanny, or waitress. Valedictorian of her high school class, Plath demands perfection from herself in her appearance and in academics. Her intellectual energy leaves her high school principal exhausted. Her first college roommate perceives Sylvia as almost driven by an unseen force to succeed. For most of her life, Sylvia does reconcile her high expectations of herself but does so at the high price of her peace of mind.

One part of Plath's life that consciously and surprisingly filled her with satisfaction was her role as a mother. Her husband, Ted Hughes, was amazed at her capacity to deal with the children and her writing at the same time. To firstborn Frieda Rebecca, born in the spring of 1960, Plath dedicates a poem that indicates, as a mother, Plath cannot expect love but must earn it. Plath wants Frieda not to have a demanding mother, as contrast to Plath's own life. Indeed, Plath's role as mother becomes an important muse when composing her final, and considered by some, best poems.

Acceptance

Plath relies on her girlfriends for support through all the vagaries of her adolescence. Hemphill writes 34 poems from the perspectives of important girls and women in Plath's life. During one traumatic incident, Nancy Hunter helps Sylvia survive a near-assault by a rogue named Edwin. Nancy remarks that they both look out for each other, signifying the importance of friendship during the years when a girl's body matures and seems like another mystery to be dealt with.

One of Plath's most important prizes is her *Mademoiselle* guest editorship in June 1953. As one of only 20 of the top women college students selected, Plath first must interview with and be judged by Marybeth Little, who tells her how pleased they are with her and how she embodies the ideal of the *Mademoiselle* girl. Also implicit in the interview, however, is the warning that she should feel honored by the recognition and that she must not do anything to ruin her chances. It seems that as she accumulated more achievements (to her, acceptance), Sylvia paid a higher emotional price in the form of additional pressures to succeed even more.

Despite her work ethic and creative output, Plath sometimes reached a point where she could not deal with rejection. When she was not accepted into Frank O'Connor's summer fiction course in 1953, her anguish over the rejection began her slide into depression and the suicide attempt. In this state of mind, Plath cannot see or accept herself realistically. With an ongoing internal monologue berating and belittling herself despite her many accomplishments, Plath sees herself a failure, and failure (though misperceived) is not acceptable.

Independence and Social Price

Sylvia learns that she must never let up on the defense of her right to become—what would be referred to today as—empowered. Some of the boys chastise Sylvia for not dating them exclusively. Plath fights to maintain her good reputation, but even dating more than one boy at a time pushes the boundaries of acceptable behavior for a 1950s girl. Richard (Dick) Norton is perhaps her most serious, long-term relationship (before her marriage) in part because he is such a fine catch for her: Dick is tall, handsome, and a pre-medical student. But they frequently argue over Sylvia's resistance to marrying him. Dick expresses the assumptions typical of the times: there are separate spheres, one for men and one for women, and a woman is not thinking properly if she considers a life outside the home. Dick puts down her career goals as silly and pretentious. Instead, he thinks she should stick to the etiquette books on how to be a good doctor's wife. Plath's social price for her perfectly healthy desire for independence comes in the form of her defense of her right to be considered an equal.

After Sylvia arrives in Cambridge on her Fulbright in the fall of 1955, she gains independence. In February 1956 she meets poet Ted Hughes, and they marry after only five months of dating. Because of Plath's belief that Hughes is the better poet, she becomes his agent, sending his work to magazines and publishing houses, resulting in publication of two of Hughes' acclaimed books. Trying to find time for her own writing kicks her into overdrive, and she relies on Hughes for guidance and inspiration, a dependency she had never needed before.

When Smith College friend Elinor Klein visits Plath in England, she sees a woman very much in love but who has changed and is willing to play a secondary role to Ted's celebrity. Comfortable and happy in her new role as homemaker, Plath welcomes another friend, Marty Brown, who admires her hard work on their tiny flat, reflective of Sylvia's channeling her energy into creating a snug home rather than into writing a book. The couple purchase a house with two acres in Devon where new neighbors marvel at her ability to run such a large house all alone. Hughes' friend writer A. Alvarez is surprised when he discovers that Mrs. Ted Hughes was, in fact, the poet he had known (only by her poems) as Sylvia Plath. Striving for independence as a wife in a new country and with a new set of friends, Plath works as seriously in the new role as she had worked in her former role as writer.

Events of 1962 and early 1963 heighten the full range of emotions in the Hughes' marriage. Plath undergoes a miscarriage followed quickly by an appendectomy prior to second child Nick's birth. Each event brings her serious depressions, yet she is able to write, a reality that is amazing to Ted. After Ted becomes a celebrated poet in England and the United States, Sylvia eagerly awaits news of her own work. In the summer of 1962 her first book of published poetry receives poor reviews and does not sell well. She works on the second book through this tumultuous time and feels it to be her finest work. Her fictional autobiography, *The Bell Jar*, is rejected by American publishers and is marketed under the pseudonym Victoria Lucas in England. She receives more rejection notices in the mail. Then in July Sylvia learns that Ted and Assia Weevil are having an affair, and the dramatic way that she discovers the news accentuates the pain and sense of betrayal that she feels.

Friends and family record Plath's emotional decline in a series of 30 poems, giving the reader a sense from many perspectives of the intensity of Plath's feelings of rejection and failure. She felt she failed as a wife, the role that had given her the first real independence of her life. Friend Elizabeth Compton remembers Plath's description of the central betrayal of her life, "When you give someone your whole heart and he doesn't want it, you cannot take it back. It's gone forever" (cited in Alexander, 2003: 284). Hemphill does not attempt to explain or offer reasons for Plath's suicide on February 11, 1963. Plath prepared a breakfast of milk and sandwiches for her children, secured their room, and asphyxiated herself in her gas oven.

To claim that Sylvia Plath paid the ultimate social price for the conflicts arising over gender issues is of course an error. However, it is clear from her journals and from her work that she was aware of the injustices that creative women had faced when they sought to be serious professionals. The legacy of Plath's poems is what inspired Stephanie Hemphill to write the biography. To Hemphill, Plath's poetry, short stories, and fictional autobiography *The Bell Jar* are her legacy. It is likely they will remain a part of America's literary canon.

ANNOTATED BIBLIOGRAPHY

Bechard, Margaret. 2002. *Hanging on to Max*. Brookfield, CT: Roaring Brook Press. Grades 8 and up.

Attending an alternative high school that offered parenting classes and in-house day care, Sam Pettigrew begins his senior year as a single father, trying to live up to his responsibilities to himself and to little Max. As the only single father in his school's parenting community, Sam feels that his performance as a father is being judged by different standards from those of the teen mothers. The story's nonlinear narrative moves between the past and present (and, eventually, the future), as the account of how he becomes custodial parent is revealed. Young people can discuss the novel's ending: Should Sam give up Max for adoption?

Ellis, Deborah. 2000. *The Breadwinner.* **Toronto: Douglas and McIntyre. Grades 5–8.**

Dressed as a boy to disguise her gender and to move freely, 11-year-old Parvana battles the dangerous streets of Kabul, Afghanistan, in order to keep her family alive after the Taliban takeover in the mid-1990s. Parvana cringes as she dresses in her dead brother Hossain's clothes, which she must wear at all times due to severe restrictions on Muslim women. The novel (the first of the "Breadwinner" trilogy) shows the strength of women whose work together creates a resourceful community, providing emotional and physical support. YAs can participate in an informed discussion of the differences in the way women are regarded and the reasons for it in countries that severely restrict women's rights.

Flake, Sharon. 2004. *Who Am I Without Him? Short Stories About Girls and the Boys in Their Lives.* **New York: Jump at the Sun/Hyperion Books for Children. Grades 6–12.**

Nine stories set in poor, urban American cities revolve around the lives of adolescents whose main concerns involve dealing with the awkwardness of the early stages in their sexual relationships. One story well-suited for discussion is "Jacobs's Rules," which shows how one teacher involves the students in his "Boy Stuff" elective class. In the major project, referred to as "an arrangement," Mr. Jacobs pairs one boy with one girl role-playing as an engaged couple with a third student to act as recorder to evaluate the communication between the couple. Young people can discuss the pros and cons of participating in such a project.

Gerstein, Mordecai. 1998. *Victor: A Novel Based on the Life of Victor, the Savage of Aveyron.* **New York: Farrar, Straus, and Giroux. Grades 7 and up. AND** *The Wild Boy.* **1998. New York: Farrar, Straus, and Giroux. All grades.**

After a feral child is captured in the forests of southern France, he is taken in by Dr. Jean Marc Gaspard Itard, who names him Victor and works for years to teach him to speak but ultimately fails. Victor's story provides a literary example of the nature versus nurture debate. Historically, most feral children have been boys, but the film *Secret of the Wild Child* (Garmon, 1994) features the controversial true story about the case of "Genie," a 13-year-old girl who was discovered in 1970 and became the object of scientific experimentation. YAs may read Victor's story, view the film, and debate the issue of nature–nurture and how humans learn language.

Homer. 1997. *The Iliad.* **Translated by Stanley Lombardo. Indianapolis, IN: Hackett. Classic.**

This Song of Troy and of the conflict that occurred on its plain thousands of years ago remains the epic paean to war. One archetype of masculinity resides in the warrior, perhaps the most ancient figure of sanctioned violence. Although time may not allow reading the entire *Iliad*, certain passages provide a rare glimpse into the reality of war described by one who surely must have been there. In what might be called "the longest day," Books 11–18 describe one 24-hour period of the Trojan War. Young people can construct body biographies of Trojan or Greek soldiers, using Homer's realistic descriptions of soldiers as their guide.

McCormick, Patricia. 2006. *Sold.* **New York: Hyperion. Grades 9 and up.**

Leaving her remote village in the Himalayas of Nepal in the belief she will be supporting her family as a well-paid nanny in the big city, 13-year-old Lakshmi soon learns she has become a slave and is expected to work off her "debt." Told in first person free verse, Lakshmi narrates her journey from the safety of home to the violence of a Calcutta brothel. Young people can search the Internet for up-to-date statistics and information about child trafficking. McCormick recommends the Web site of International Justice Mission (1997).

Ryan, Sara. 2001. *Empress of the World.* **New York: Viking Press. Grades 9 and up.**

Writing in her archeological fieldnotes during a summer program for gifted teens, 15-year-old Nicola Lancaster discovers the love of her life with another girl, the beautiful Battle Davies. The warm and fun-loving group of friends that are quickly drawn together by the extroverted, eccentric character Katrina puts this story into a realistic and mostly positive environment for the same-sex attraction relationship of Nic and Battle. As a questioning girl, Nic does not object to the idea of assigning labels for her typology assignment in archeology, but she definitely rejects the notion of her sexual orientation being put into someone else's convenient slot. Groups can create a comic strip of an episode from the novel, such as the enforced hike on which Nic falls and becomes injured (p. 33–42).

Sanchez, Alex. 2003. *Rainbow High.* **New York: Simon and Schuster. Grades 9 and up.**

Falling in love, selecting the right college, and handling confused parents, three gay high school seniors encounter typical adolescent experiences with the additional pressure of possibly coming out. Introduced in Sanchez's (2001) *Rainbow Boys*, Nelson, Kyle, and Jason forge new friendships as they give and receive support from understanding adults, especially Jason's basketball coach. Young people can discuss how they have handled important decisions in their lives and how they took into consideration the feelings of others (as well as themselves) in arriving at their final decision.

Takahashi, Rumiko. 2003. *Ranma 1/2: Volume 1: Action Edition.* **San Francisco, CA: Viz. Grades 9 and up.**

Ranma Saotome and Akane Tendo (both exceptional martial artists) are forced into an arranged engagement by their parents and quarrel their way through this first set of adventures (of the manga series), which includes the revelation that (after receiving a curse), Ranma can transform into a girl. Much of the humor comes from the manner in which Ranma is transformed from one gender to the other: when cold water comes in contact with his body, he becomes a girl; hot water, a boy (p. 51). YAs can evaluate the unique problems that gender causes Ranma as he switches from one gender to the next, often quickly without time to think, in one of the many episodes when the transformation occurs.

Wolf, Allan. 2007. *Zane's Trace.* **Cambridge, MA: Candlewick Press. Grades 9–12.**

After his short lifetime of dealing with family deaths, diseases, and other dysfunctions, 17-year-old Zane decides to steal his brother's classic car, drive 300 miles, and commit suicide on his mother's grave. Zane's male adolescent crisis story is part traditional picaresque road trip and part verse novel that is full of eccentric but endearing characters and featuring Zane's creative penchant for writing and illustrating on any flat surface. Young people can create their own dust jackets for the book, substituting their names for the title and containing examples of "traces" from their own lives.

REFERENCES AND SUGGESTIONS FOR FURTHER READING

Alexander, Linda B., and Sarah D. Miselis. 2007. "Barriers to GLBTQ Collection Development and Strategies for Overcoming Them." *YALS* 5, no. 3 (Spring): 43–49.

Alexander, Paul. 2003. *Rough Magic.* New York: De Capo Press.

"American Memory—Women's History." Library of Congress (2000). Available at: http://memory.loc/gov/ammem.

Baumgardner, Jennifer, and Amy Richards. 2000. *Manifesta: Young Women, Feminism, and the Future.* New York: Farrar, Straus, and Giroux.

Blackburn, Mollie V., and J.F. Buckley. 2006. "Teaching Queer-Inclusive English Language Arts." *Journal of Adolescent and Adult Literacy* 49, no. 3 (November): 202–212.

Cart, Michael. 2005. "Gay and Lesbian Literature Comes of Age." *Booklist* 101, no. 17 (April 1): 1356.

Connell, R.W. 1995. *Masculinities.* Berkeley: University of California Press.

Crawford, Philip Charles. 2007. "Of Sissies, Invalids, and the Mysterious Boy in the Window." *Horn Book* 83, no. 5 (September–October): 473–477.

Davidson, Cathy N., and Linda Wagner-Martin. 1995. *The Oxford Companion to Women's Writing in the United States.* New York: Oxford University Press.

Dicker, Rory, and Alison Piepmeier. 2003. *Catching a Wave: Reclaiming Feminism for the 21st Century.* Boston: Northeastern University Press.

Edwards, Tim. 2006. *Cultures of Masculinity.* New York: Routledge.

Enns, Carolyn Zerbe, and Ada Sinacore. 2001. "Feminist Theories." In *Encyclopedia of Women and Gender,* vol. 1 of 2, edited by Judith Worel, pp. 469–480. San Diego, CA: Academic Press.

Garmon, Linda. *Nova: Secret of the Wild Child.* Produced by Linda Garmon. 60 min. PBS, 1994. Videocassette.

Hemphill, Stephanie. 2007. *Your Own, Sylvia: A Verse Portrait of Sylvia Plath.* New York: Alfred A. Knopf.

Henry, Astrid. 2005. "Solitary Sisterhood: Individualism Meets Collectivity in Feminisms' Third Wave." In *Different Wavelengths: Studies in Contemporary Women's Studies,* edited by Jo Reger, pp. 81–96. New York: Routledge.

Heywood, Leslie L., ed. 2007. "Introduction." In *The Women's Movement Today: An Encyclopedia of Third-Wave Feminism,* vol. 1 of 2, pp. xv–xxii. Westport, CT: Greenwood Press.

International Justice Mission. 1997. "For Students—Youth." Available at: www.ijm.org.

Jenkins, Christine. 1998. "From Queer to Gay and Back Again: Young Adult Novels with Gay/Lesbian/Queer Content, 1969–1997." *Library Quarterly* 68, no. 3 (July): 298–334.

Kaplan, Jeffrey S. 2003. "New Perspectives in Young Adult Literature." *ALAN* 31, no. 1 (Fall): 6–12.

Kaplon, Cora. 1991. "Feminist Literary Criticism." In *Encyclopedia of Literature and Criticism*, edited by Martin Coyle et al., pp. 750–763. Detroit, MI: Gale Research.

Kelly, Brigit Pegeen. 1995. *Song.* Rochester, NY: BOA Editions.

Kimmel, Michael S. 2004. *The Gendered Society*, 2nd ed. New York: Oxford University Press.

Land, Brad. 2004. *Goat: A Memoir.* New York: Random House

McCarthy, Cormac. 1985. *Blood Meridian, or, The Evening Redness in the West.* New York: Random House.

Pace, Nicholas J. 2007. "I've Completely Changed: The Transforming Impact of the Matthew Shepard Scholarship." *Journal of Advanced Academics* 18, no. 3 (Spring): 344–371.

Patrick, Paul. 2007. "Lesbian, Gay, Bisexual and Trans Issues in Schools." In *Genderwatch: Still Watching*, edited by Kate Myers and Hazel Taylor, pp. 89–92. Sterling, VA: Trentham.

Pavao, Kate. 2003. "Out of the Closet." *Publishers Weekly* 250, no. 48 (December 1): 23–25.

Plath, Sylvia. 1965, 1998. *The Bell Jar.* New York: Alfred A. Knopf.

Reger, Jo, ed. 2005. *Different Wavelengths: Studies of the Contemporary Women's Movement.* New York: Routledge.

Rochman, Hazel. 2006. "GLBTQ-YA." *Booklist* 103, no. 1 (September 1): 128.

Rockefeller, Elsworth. 2007. "The Genre of Gender: The Emerging Canon of Transgender-Inclusive Young Adult Literature." *Horn Book* 83, no. 5 (September–October): 519–526.

Sanchez, Alex. 2001. *Rainbow Boys.* New York: Simon and Schuster.

Satrapi, Marjane. 2003. *Persepolis.* New York: Pantheon.

Savin-Williams, Ritch C. 2005. *The New Gay Teenager.* Cambridge, MA: Harvard University Press.

Spencer, Sharon. 1983. "Feminist Criticism and Literature." *Helicon Nine* 9, no. 9: 8–17.

Spender, Dale. 1986. *Mothers of the Novel: 100 Good Novelists Before Jane Austen.* New York: Pandora Press.

Swartz, Patti Capel. 2003. "Bringing Sexual Orientation into the Children's and Young Adult Literature Classrooms." *Radical Teacher* no. 66 (Spring): 11–16.

Unks, Gerald, ed. 1995. *The Gay Teen: Educational Practice and Theory for Lesbian, Gay, and Bisexual Adolescents.* New York: Routledge.

Vare, Jonathan W., and Terry L. Norton. 2004. "Bibliotherapy for Gay and Lesbian Youth: Overcoming the Structure of Silence." *Clearing House* 77, no. 5 (May–June): 190–194.

Wagner-Martin, Linda. 1999. *Sylvia Plath: A Literary Life.* New York: St. Martin's.

Walker, Rebecca. 1992. "Doing the Third Wave." *Ms* 3, no. 2 (September): 87.

Whelan, Debra Lau. 2006. "Out and Ignored." *School Library Journal* 52, no. 1 (January): 46–50.

Wolf, Naomi. 1991. *The Beauty Myth: How Images of Beauty Are Used Against Women.* New York: W. Morrow.

Worel, Judith, ed. 2001. *Encyclopedia of Women and Gender.* San Diego, CA: Academic Press.

Chapter 10

Archetypal/Mythological Criticism

INTRODUCTION TO ARCHETYPAL/MYTHOLOGICAL CRITICISM

Archetypal criticism is an approach to literature based on the theories of Swiss psychologist Carl G. Jung, who broke from his longtime colleague Sigmund Freud, in part over their differences regarding the nature of the unconscious and the nature of archetypes. Jung hypothesized that archetypes reside in the *collective unconscious,* or common memory, of all people. Furthermore, archetypes remain unknown and unformed in the unconscious until they become *archetypal images,* that is, representations of the archetypes in dreams, world mythology, and literature. Thus, archetypes are not fixed or static. According to Jung, archetypes are inborn, infinite in number, and most evident during dreams, times of crisis, or major life transitions, such as adolescence. Archetypes overlap and interconnect with other archetypes and may be binary opposites, such as light and dark, youth and old age.

For literary critics, an archetype is "the expression of various universal, instinctual motifs or patterns of human behavior and belief that come charged with primary emotional force" (Slote, 1963: v). Psychoanalyst Marie-Louise von Franz calls the emotional component of an archetype its "affective tone" or "feeling tone" and is the most important way to distinguish the archetypes, which together act as "a unifying dynamic, relating all conscious activity to the process of individuation" (Gray, 1996: 19). (*Individuation* means the process or movement of each person toward self-identity and independence.) Archetypal images appear as characters, events, settings, situations, themes, symbols, and rituals of common human experiences (such as marriage, birth, war, and death) in, for example, children's fairy tales and folktales.

Sometimes *archetypal criticism* is used synonymously with *mythological criticism.* (In this chapter, the two are treated as essentially one.) Strictly speaking, the two literary responses do differ. The mythological critic may or may not refer to archetypes and often prefers to interpret a story based on its mythological connections rather than on its potential unconscious manifestations and unconscious origins. As a psychiatrist, Jung did not formulate a template for the analysis of literature using archetypes. Instead, the archetypes can be approached from different angles, as today's critics incorporate Jungian ideas with other critical approaches, such as gender. Closely aligned with mythological criticism is traditional literature, the first literature for most young people in the form of nursery rhymes, fairy tales, and legends.

Archetypes and Fairy Tales

For young people the most familiar archetypes probably appear in fairy tales. Although scholars have long written and discussed traditional literature, the study of fairy tales as a serious field began in nineteenth-century Europe with Jacob and Wilhelm Grimm, Joseph Jacobs, Frederich Max Muller, and Andrew Lang, to name a few. The Finnish School, led by Julius Krohn, had been active since the early nineteenth century but is best known for Antti Aarne's historical/geographical method of collecting, analyzing, and classifying all of the variants of folktales. When Aarne died before completing his work, Krohn asked the American folklorist Stith Thompson to finish the index, which was published as *The Types of the Folktale: A Classification and Bibliography* (Aarne, 1928). Thompson (1958) realized the weaknesses within the massive work and published *The Motif-Index of Folk Literature*, composed of about 40,000 distinct motifs taken from legends, myths, tall tales, and fairy tales from European oral literature.

Other scholars in folk literature include Vladimir Propp (1958), whose *Morphology of the Folktale* identified over 30 *functions*, or narrative moves, and is considered a seminal work of structural, formalist analysis of European (mostly Russian) fairy tales. Inspired by Propp's theories, Claude Levi-Strauss devised a structural theory of fairy tales positing that the myth-making of so-called "primitive" cultures actually entails complex and abstract thinking, putting to rest the notion of the "evolution" of cultures. Novelist and folklorist J.R.R. Tolkien's (1964: 38–39) notion about "fairy stories" focused on rules that should be adhered to in the realm he called "Fairy," wherein the best stories contain fantasy, recovery, escape, and consolation, or "*eucatastrophe*, the moment of joy at deliverance from evil."

Folklore and Psychology

From the beginning, scholars in psychology showed a strong interest in folklore (fairy tales, folktales, and legends). Both Freud and Jung recognized the importance of fairy tales for their deeper, psychological meanings and published articles analyzing them. In *The Uses of Enchantment: The Meaning and Importance of Fairy Tales*, another psychoanalytic work that applied the archetypes to the criticism of fairy tales, Bruno Bettleheim (1976) theorized that the reading of fairy tales to children promotes in them a healthier psychological life. (The authenticity of Bettleheim's findings has been questioned, but his book continues to be included in historical surveys of the subject.)

Marie-Louise von Franz (1997) analyzed folk and fairy tales through archetypes in her many scholarly works, such as *Archetypal Patterns in Fairy Tales*. Alan Dundes, folklorist and Freudian analyst, compiled casebooks for several archetypal characters and figures, such as *Cinderella* (1988) and *Little Red Riding Hood* (1989). Jungian Max Luthi (1984) considers the fairy tale to be the first true form of literature, as he states in *The Fairy Tales as Art Form and Portrait of Man*. Post-Jungian Bettina L. Knapp's (2003) *French Fairy Tales: A Jungian Approach* chronicles 14 stories from the oral and literary traditions of France. Some readers may be surprised to learn that folktales and fairy tales have been taken seriously for many years, and, as they reread their favorite tales, they may see the stories in an entirely different light.

Recent scholars have tried to correct the absence of psychological functions in European motif indexes. Hasan El-Shamy's work with Arab and Middle-Eastern tales includes new motifs with psychological elements. Noting how Stith Thompson "eschewed treating psychological factors" (2004: 263), El-Shamy has added two new motifs, "Maturity (growing up, independence, 'individuation') gained by leaving home" (2004: 264) and "Girl Wins against Boy in a Contest of Worth" (2004: 269). Calling these additional motifs *functions of individuation*, El-Shamy brings folklore studies into the twenty-first century, stressing "the crucial role in the development of the self" as portrayed in literature (p. 269). El-Shamy cites Mark Twain's ending of *The Adventures of Tom Sawyer* as the archetypal narrative of individuation: "So endeth this chronicle. It being strictly a history of a boy, it must stop here; the story could not go much further without becoming the history of a man" (p. 270).

Contemporary Fairy Tales

They may be adapted, retold, or revised, but in every version, the traditional tales from childhood have a brand new look and keep readers coming back for more. The tales range from dark, grim short stories (e.g., Francesca Lia Block's [2000] *The Rose and the Beast: Fairy Tales Retold*) to the romantic (e.g., Margaret Haddix's [1999] *Just Ella*) to the unique point of view (e.g., Gregory Maguire's [1995] *Wicked: The Life and Times of the Wicked Witch of the West*, Elphaba Thropp's version of the Oz story, which was eventually adapted into a smash Broadway musical). Maguire (2005) completes his "Wicked" series with *Son of a Witch*, wherein a boy, Liir, rumored to be Elphaba's son, attempts to set things right in the chaotic city of Oz. The variations seem limitless, such as Philip Pullman's (2000) *I Was a Rat! Or The Scarlet Slippers*, in which Cinderella's little coachman's life is brought up to date.

Although not as numerous as in prose, poetry retellings of fairy tales include Anne Sexton's (1971) now classic *Transformations*, a fairy tale collection with a decidedly dark, revisionist, and feminist twist, and Roald Dahl's (2002) humorous *Roald Dahl's Revolting Rhymes*. Francesca Lia Block (2006) revises the myth in *Psyche in a Dress* as a novel in verse.

A popular format for contemporary fairy tales is the short story collection or anthology. Examples include Louise Hawe's (2008) collection *Black Pearls: A Faerie Strand*, whose seven tales are set in the past but whose tone and perspectives are postmodern; and Margo Lanagan's (2007) collection *Red Spikes*, which presents unique fantasy worlds that ask readers to find their bearings as to time and locale, so to speak. Francesca Lia Block's (2008) *Blood Roses* tells stories of transformation and is meant for older readers (grades 10 and up).

Most adaptations, retellings, and revisions are stand-alone titles. In Melissa Kantor's (2005) *If I Have a Wicked Stepmother, Where's My Prince*, the protagonist's living conditions parallel Cinderella's (she lives alone in the skimpy basement) and must decide which of two boys will be her prince to the prom. Alex Finn's (2007) *Beastly* retells the beauty and the beast story from the beast's point of view (a popular high school student) as he learns a hard lesson about just what kind of beast he really is. In Gail Carson Levine's (2006) *Fairest*, the protagonist comes to terms with her appearance, which is unlike the "norm" of the society in which she lives. Janet Elizabeth McNaughton's (2004) *An Earthly Knight*, set in twelfth-century Scotland, retells the legend of Tam Lin. In *Spindle's End*, by Robin McKinley (2000), Rose confronts the wicked fairy who put a spell on her. Neal Schusterman's (2005) *Dread Locks* melds the Greek myths of Medusa and Gorgon into contemporary high school characters. Gary D. Schmidt's (2001) *Straw Into Gold* considers a what-might-have been version of the Rumpelstiltskin story. Sometimes retellings are humorous, as is Jean Ferris's (2002) *Once Upon a Marigold*, with a male protagonist and a romance.

Several fiction series are devoted to retelling traditional stories. Simon Pulse publishes "Once Upon a Time" (2002–2008) with 13 titles to date. Other popular series include Gail Carson Levine's "The Princess Tales" (1999–2002) and Michael Buckley's "Sisters Grimm" (2005–2008) for middle schoolers.

Fairy tales are also treated in some graphic novels, including Bill Willingham's "Fables" series of eleven titles (2001–2006) that feature the familiar fairy tale and folktale characters now exiled and fighting the Adversary in Fabletown in upstate New York. For more mature readers, Willingham and Matthew Sturges's series "Jack of Fables" (2007–2008) features a most unconventional

Jack and the Golden Boughs Retirement Community of old fairy tale characters who are held by forces that want to dispense with the whole idea of magic. Frank Cammuso's "Max Hamm Fairy Tale Detective" series (2002–2006) melds noir with fairy tales for a parody with caricatures that tell an unexpectedly sophisticated and hilarious story. Art Spiegelman and Francoise Mouly's "Little Lit" series (2000–2006) parodies all of the traditional tales in graphic novel or comic formats created by the best writers and illustrators in contemporary comics. In the manga series, the world-famous Rumiko Takahashi's (2003) *Inu-yasha: A Feudal Fairy Tale* features time travel along with the usual other conventions.

FAIRY TALES AS ARCHETYPE OF INDIVIDUATION: CINDERELLA

One fairy tale that chronicles a girl's individuation (growing up) is Cinderella, first studied seriously in Marian Cox's (1893, 1903) *Cinderella: Three Hundred and Forty-five Variants*. However, the number of variants of the Cinderella fairy tale worldwide is said to be at least 700 (Dundes, 1988) and still increasing. Some different names for Cinderella include Asenath (biblical wife of Joseph), Cendrillon (France), Aschenputtel (Germany), Vasilisa (Russia), and Soot-Face (Native American). Rhodopis, a short Cinderella story thought to be one of the oldest known variants, concerns a Greek slave whose beauty catches the eye of an Egyptian royal (Reiff, 1993). China's Yeh-sen dates from the ninth century (Louie, 1982), and fairy tales about Cinderella were written in the seventeenth century in Italy and in France, with Perrault's (1993) tale probably being the most familiar to young adults (YAs). Cinderella has been called "the best known fairy story in the world" (Opie and Opie, 1974:117) and is also claimed to be the most parodied of all the tales when considering the story in all of its formats.

Invariably, the Cinderella version most familiar to young people is Disney's, which emphasizes the role of the hero prince who rescues Cinderella and makes her happy by marrying her. However, contemporary versions see a different story, one with a strong girl who knows her fall from favor is unjust and works to correct her situation, such as the protagonist in Napoli's (2004) *Bound*. Besides Cinderella, other familiar characters have been transformed into stronger (or different) types than the traditional rescued archetype, as in editors Ellen Datlow and Terri Windling's anthologies, *The Faery Reel: Tales from the Twilight Realm* (2006) and *Swan Sister: Fairy Tales Retold* (2003).

Framework for the Cinderella Archetype

Graham Anderson (2000: 24–25) cites "the basic framework" for the Cinderella stories by abridging the Aarne–Thompson description.

Anderson's Five-Step Framework

1. **The persecuted heroine** is abused by her stepmother and stepsisters. She stays on the hearth and in ashes and dresses in rough clothing.

2. **Magic help** occurs when she is acting as servant (at home or among strangers). She is advised, provided for, or fed by her dead mother, or a tree on the mother's grave, or by a supernatural being, or by an animal. When the helpful animal is killed, a magic tree springs up from the remains.

3. **She meets the prince** after she has been dressed in beautiful clothing. She attends the dance several times, and the prince seeks in vain to keep her.

4. **Proof of identity** comes when she is discovered through the slipper test or through a ring that she throws into the prince's drink or bakes in his bread.

5. **She marries the prince**.

Application of Anderson's Cinderella Framework to Donna Jo Napoli's *Bound*

Napoli's (2004) retelling of the Chinese Cinderella story remains true to the plot and characters of the ninth-century original "Yeh-sen." However, the novel includes no elements of true magic, a convention of most fairy tales. In place of the usual magic, Napoli creates a protagonist whose *spiritual* (supernatural) life is as real and as important to her as is her physical life. By emphasizing Xing-Xing's commitment to her parents' spirits, Napoli shows that "magic" comes to those who remain patient because such gifts "could never be rushed. They had to come of their own accord, on their own schedule" (p. 4) and, more importantly, after an inner transformation had first occurred.

1. The Persecuted Heroine

After her mother dies, Xing-Xing is left to be reared by Stepmother, whose daughter Wei Ping is a year older but suffering severely from having her feet bound, an act forbidden by their father Wu, whose recent death gives Stepmother the opportunity to do what she has always wanted—prepare her daughter for a traditional marriage based on the importance of small feet.

Xing-Xing receives cruel and malicious treatment from her stepfamily, including being forced to hunt animals for food, an action that clearly disturbs her. Xing-Xing tries to be understanding, aware of Wei Ping's pain from oozing wounds, but she cannot deny that what Wei Ping says to her does "cut deep" (p. 6). In addition, Xing-Xing has other worries besides hard labor. She fears Stepmother will sell her off because money is short. With this knowledge in mind, Xing-Xing eagerly goes on her first solo journey under Stepmother's orders to find the area medicine man, Yao Wang, and to return home with him to heal Wei Ping. In her quest, Xing-Xing travels roads filled with dangerous strangers, confronts her worst fears, learns to trust her instincts, and stands up for the healer, Yao Wang, when he is threatened by the authorities. As in any heroic quest, Xing-Xing transforms from a child into a young woman. She makes important decisions based on her experiences, on her mother's spirit, and on her father's teachings. For her the most important part is telling Yao Wang "the whole truth," for it "made her feel energized and strong, ready for anything" (p. 93). Living with Stepmother's deceit, lies, denial, and cruelty had made her almost forget the healing power of an honest life.

2. Magic (Supernatural) Help

Xing-Xing relies on her mother's spirit (to whom she often speaks) and on her father's words (which she often recalls) to guide her and to keep her stronger than her tormentors. Her spiritual life keeps her physical abuse from destroying her. She visits her father's grave each day and takes care of it as she had vowed to do. Xing-Xing's honorable position toward religion angers Stepmother, who consistently tells her that her religion boils down to superficial rites and prayers performed only when she really needs something. Xing-Xing keeps her mother's spirit alive in the form of a beautiful white fish, which becomes her only friend and through which she feels her mother speak.

3a. Preparation for Meeting the Prince

When the ruler of the new empire announces a feast, Stepmother and Wei Ping make elaborate plans and put their hopes and dreams in finding an eligible husband in the large gathering. (In the Chinese version, there is only one feast, an annual event, understandable because the number three is not a magical number as it is in the West.) But first, suspecting that Stepmother had killed her beloved fish—an "unspeakable idea" (p. 136)—Xing-Xing pursues the truth, eventually retrieving the fish's bones from the dung heap, carefully washing them, and making them into a shrine for her mother. She has transformed Stepmother's evil act into a sacred ritual. After her hours of mourning and grief over the loss of her fish, Xing-Xing emerges from the forest with true understanding. "Xing-Xing understood—her *qi* had helped her understand—that her beautiful fish mother was dead" (p. 145).

Almost like magic, Xing-Xing's hiding of the bones lead her to discover a letter written to her from her mother along with her heirlooms: Xing-Xing will wear her mother's green silk dress, kingfisher-feathered cloak, and gold shoes to the King's feast (p. 153), though forbidden to go. The sights, sounds, and smells of the feast make Xing-Xing feel alive, and she imagines the possibility of travel and of a new life for herself. But she observes a wife being sold, and the "exchange of a person for coins" disgusts her (p. 161). She notices that all the women with men were treated poorly, and she becomes so sad that she flees the feast into the deep, dark forest where she loses one slipper and where "fear was the enemy" (p. 164). In the forest Xing-Xing realizes that her enemy had always been fear, not Stepmother, and she has the courage to be her own woman, not necessarily playing by the old rules.

3b. Meeting the Prince

In the Chinese version of Cinderella, the prince does not attend the feast but hears of the mysterious young woman's beauty. The day arrives when the old woman Xiu Mei, who arranges marriages, comes to announce that the prince will be coming to select a wife—the young woman who had been seen in the forest and who had lost one golden slipper. The prince had heard that the woman is "a rare beauty" and "touted to be the most beautiful woman in the empire" (p. 168), and of course he had to see her for himself. He intends to find the woman whose foot will fit the golden slipper. So desperate is Stepmother that she will try on the slipper herself if it does not fit Wei Ping, and she makes elaborate preparations (including prayers and offerings) for them.

4. Proof of Identity

Xing-Xing had become weary of all the shams she had seen, from her Stepmother's hypocritical religious practices to the buying and selling of persons, and of this "wickedly unkind" way for the prince to select the woman "who pleased him most," making a spectacle out of the whole thing (p. 176). She even understands how much power she now has in possessing the other golden slipper.

When the prince does arrive, she examines his appearance critically and concludes he is "nothing special" (p. 178). When the shoe does not fit any other woman in the kingdom, it occurs to Xing-Xing that perhaps the prince does see something unique in her mother's golden slipper. After a few moments of flirting, the prince wants Xing-Xing to produce the clothes she wore to the feast. Stepmother calls Xing-Xing a lunatic and forbids her to speak to the prince. But Xing-Xing disobeys and she retrieves the festival clothing, the slipper fits, and the prince proposes marriage. However, Xing-Xing "couldn't yield herself quite yet" (p. 183), but, with his promises to meet her requirements, she "put out her hand, with full understanding, and the prince took it" (p. 184).

5. Marrying the Prince

Although there are no descriptions of a wedding ceremony, the story concludes with a pun on the book's title. "[L]ife does what it does. . . . And it's bound to be better with a companion who knows how to be tender, a companion you may grow to cherish" (p. 184). Napoli's version of the story presents a strong, courageous, intelligent, and tenderhearted protagonist who will never be subservient again.

ARCHETYPAL PLOTS: SITUATIONS

Christopher Booker (2004) offers what he calls *The Seven Basic Plots: Why We Tell Stories* in which he analyzes classic novels, plays, myths, and motion pictures. Although he does not address YA literature, Booker's approach provides young people with a possible way to respond to fiction by examining archetypal plot patterns. Booker actually identifies *eight* plot patterns, but sees "Rebellion against the Other" as a new archetype—dystopian literature—that began in the middle of the twentieth century and continues into the twenty-first.

Each of the self-explanatory archetypal patterns in the next section consists of stages or phases. In the annotated bibliography section following, one YA book is annotated to illustrate each pattern.

Booker's Plot Patterns

A. **Overcoming the Monster** (p. 48). This archetypal pattern is familiar in many world myths, legends, and fairy tales, such as Jack and the Beanstalk. This archetypal plot consists of
   1. the call (p. 48),
   2. initial success (p. 48),
   3. confrontation and serious setback(s) (p. 48),
   4. final ordeal (p. 48), and
   5. miraculous escape and death of the monster (p. 49).

B. **Rags to Riches** (p. 65). The story of Horatio Alger and Cinderella are two of the more familiar of this pattern, which consists of
   1. initial wretchedness at home (p. 65),
   2. out into the world (p. 66),
   3. central crisis (p. 66),
   4. independence (p. 66), and
   5. completion, fulfillment, and union (p. 66).

C. **The Quest** (p. 83). This familiar archetype is often referred to as the hero quest, such as Harry Potter's stories, or as the male coming-of-age story. It consists of
   1. the call (p. 83),
   2. the journey (p. 83),
   3. arrival and frustration (p. 83),
   4. final ordeals (p. 83), and
   5. the goal achieved (p. 83).

D. **The Voyage and Return** (p. 105). Many adventure tales rely on this pattern, such as Christopher Paolini's "Inheritance Cycle" (*Eragon* and *Eldest*). It consists of
1. anticipation and an abrupt "fall" into the other world (p. 105),
2. initial fascination of the puzzling new world (p. 105),
3. frustration as the adventure changes to mood of oppression or alarm (p. 106),
4. nightmare (p. 106), and
5. thrilling escape and return home (p. 106).

E. **Comedy** (p. 150). This pattern has a less structured plot and somewhat follows Frye's (1957) comedy mode. It consists of
1. a little world in which people have passed under a shadow of confusion, uncertainty, and frustration and are shut off from one another (p. 150),
2. worsening confusion until the pressure becomes acute and everyone is in a tangle (p. 150), and
3. chaos to order (p. 150).

F. **Tragedy** (p. 156). This pattern is perhaps one of the oldest archetypes and follows the traditional steps so familiar in ancient Greek plays and in Shakespeare's tragedies. It consists of
1. moment of temptation or focus (p. 106),
2. dream stage (p. 106),
3. frustration stage (p. 106),
4. nightmare stage (p. 106), and
5. destruction or death wish stage (p. 106).

G. **Rebirth** (p. 204). This pattern has been identified as the coming-of-age narrative for girls but is not limited to a female protagonist:
1. The protagonist falls under the shadow of a dark power (p. 204).
2. The threat recedes (p. 204).
3. The threat returns (p. 204).
4. The dark power triumphs (p. 204).
5. Miraculous redemption occurs, and the protagonist resumes life, as if reborn, transformed, or changed (p. 204).

H. **Rebellion Against the "One"** (p. 495). Booker considers this pattern new to the middle of the twentieth century. It has become popular in YA fantasies and science fiction:
1. A dark power has taken control of society (p. 495).
2. A solitary figure is drawn into a state of resentful, mystified opposition to the controlling power or group (p. 496).
3. As an Everyman, the protagonist takes action against the dark power and achieves some initial success (p. 500).
4. The main conflict usually centers on the protagonist's loss of identity and/or the laws prohibiting citizens from having lasting relationships with others (p. 503).
5. In a final test or ordeal, the protagonist is (usually) destroyed (p. 500).

Annotated Bibliography for Booker's Archetypal Plots

A. Overcoming the Monster (Booker, p. 48)

Myers, Walter Dean. 2003. *The Beast.* New York: Scholastic. Grades 8 and up.

Spoon, a senior at an elite prep school, encounters two beasts: a subculture of drug addiction in his Harlem neighborhood and racism in a prestigious and nearly all-white school. Spoon is a complex, intelligent, reflective character whose development is forced by confronting both beasts.

1. *The call*: Spoon, one of the few black students in his school, anticipates racial problems.
2. *Initial success*: His identity is strong enough to endure a negative social environment at school.
3. *Confrontation and serious setbacks*: At winter break, Spoon returns to Harlem to discover that his beloved and gifted girlfriend, Gabi, is addicted to heroin.
4. *Final ordeal*: At the plot's climax (in "the labyrinth" chapter), Spoon rescues Gabi from a needle-strewn drug den, only to be stunned as Gabi chooses the addiction "beast" and turns her back on him.
5. *Miraculous escape and death of the monster*: Struggling with racism and the drug culture, Spoon's encounters with the two beasts lead to his profound emotional change after he faces harsh realities.

B. Rags to Riches (Booker, p. 65)

Karr, Kathleen. 2000. *The Boxer.* New York: Farrar, Straus, and Giroux. Grades 7 and up.

Wanting the American Dream for himself and his family living in New York City's poverty-stricken Lower East Side, 15-year-old Johnny Woods becomes the archetypal Rocky Balboa as he fights his way from amateur bare-fisted to professional prize fights during the rise of the sport in the late nineteenth century.

1. *Initial wretchedness*: John Aloysius Xavier Woods lived in a one-room crowded tenement apartment and worked in a sweatshop where he suffered severe burns to his hands earning slave wages to support his family after his father had deserted them. Following his arrest for participating in illegal boxing, Johnny served six months in The Tombs, where he learned the manly art of self-defense from former professional boxer Perfesser Michael O'Shaunnessey. When Johnny returns home, there are only patronage jobs for those who had connections in the city's corrupt government. He is desperate.
2. *Out in the world—initial success*: When the Perfesser contacts Johnny about exhibition fights held by the New York City Athletic Club, Johnny "the Chopper" takes on all opponents. His part-time job at the Athletic Club and his return to high school make it possible for Johnny to save some money each week, with the goal of buying a house so his siblings can grow up in a safe, healthy environment.

3. *Central crisis*: Johnny's unbeaten record at Brodie's Saloon provides incentive for Brodie to offer the boy more money by losing on purpose. Johnny must consider the offer seriously, and at first he agrees. But after he beats his opponent and is thrown out of Brodie's for good, he thinks, "Something had happened to me in that ring tonight. I'd made a decision" not to take the easy way out, a way that he considers, "[t]aking a fall into hell" (p. 80).

4. *Independence*: With a perfect record behind him, Johnny "the Chopper" confronts the lightweight champion of Australia, Sam "the Blinker" Matthews, in a prize fight organized by the Perfesser and a prominent city editor. Matthews is a dirty fighter and the referee does nothing to stop him, but Johnny's uppercut gives him a win. He goes home with a broken nose, broken ankle, a gouged eye, and the prize money.

5. *Completion*: With his defeat over the Aussie, Johnny plans to take his family to Brooklyn to buy a house and to finish his education in a profession where his potential will be put to good use.

C. The Quest (Booker, p. 83)

Park, Linda Sue. 2001. *A Single Shard*. New York: Clarion Press. Grades 5–8.

Thirteen-year-old Tree-ear, an orphan in medieval Korea, admires the art of Min (a master potter), works as his errand boy, earns an apprentice relationship, undertakes a dangerous and arduous journey, and changes his world with a single shard. This coming-of-age story is set apart by its well-developed and dynamic characters and its setting into which the details of everyday life and culture are integrated.

1. *The call*: Tree-ear is drawn to the beautiful celadon pottery of Min, the master potter.

2. *The journey*: Tree-ear works long, hard days for Min, without the promise of fulfilling his dream to become a master potter.

3. *Central crisis*: Min cannot transport his celadon pottery the long distance to Songdo to win a commission from the royal court.

4. *Independence (final ordeal)*: Tree-ear undertakes the treacherous journey to Songdo with Min's pottery. He is attacked by thieves, yet pushes ahead to Songdo with only a single shard of Min's pottery.

5. *Completion, fulfillment, and union*: Tree-ear returns to Min, delivering the commission to him, learns that his beloved caregiver has died, understands that he will learn the art and craft of pottery, and accepts a new name and a place in Min's household.

D. Voyage and Return

Carroll, Lewis. 1971. *Alice in Wonderland*, edited by Donald J. Gray. New York: W.W. Norton. Classic.

In the first of the adventure books, Alice enters Wonderland with a mixture of timidity and courage.

1. *Anticipation stage and fall into the other world*: A hot, quiet afternoon in May abruptly changes as Alice, feeling a bit sleepy, sees a White Rabbit, and, "burning with curiosity," runs after it, falling very slowly until a sudden thump ends her fall (p. 8).
2. *Initial fascination or dream stage*: Alice cannot keep her curiosity in check, and, despite her proper upbringing, she chooses to toss aside lessons of caution and eats mushrooms that alter her size as needed, swims in her own tears with a mouse, gets advice from a caterpillar, tries to rescue an abused baby (i.e., a pig), attends a tea party that never ends, and plays croquet using all-live pieces.
3. *Frustration stage*: At first, each time Alice encounters a problem (e.g., being too short to reach the three-legged table), she begins to cry. The creatures order her around, say puzzling things to her, and take her remarks to them much too personally.
4. *Nightmare stage*: To each strange creature and encounter, Alice responds politely and timidly, but some creatures, like the Duchess and the Queen of Hearts, frighten her. During "The Lobster-Quadrille," she wonders "if anything would *ever* happen in a natural way again" (p. 83).
5. *Thrilling escape and return home*: During the trial against the Knave, Alice is called as a witness and stands defiantly against the "stuff and nonsense" of the court proceedings. She says, "'Who cares for *you*? You're nothing but a pack of cards!'" (p. 97). She is immediately attacked from all sides and courageously fights them off. Suddenly, she awakens in the lap of her older sister.

E. Comedy (Booker, p. 150)

Korman, Gordon. 2000. *No More Dead Dogs*. New York: Hyperion. Grades 5–8.

Forced to serve detention in drama club practice, eighth-grade football hero Wallace Wallace uses improv to transform a boring play into an energetic and witty performance. Through multiple voices—teen and adult—the narrative skips along, providing one-liners, malapropisms, and mystery.

1. *A little world in which people have passed under a shadow of confusion, uncertainty, and frustration and are shut off from one another*: Mr. Fogelman's well-behaved drama club loses all sense of order when Wallace's honest evaluations begin to transform *Old Shep, My Pal* from scripted to ad-lib.
2. *Worsening confusion until the pressure becomes acute and everyone is in a tangle*: Coach Wrigley and the student body work to have Wallace back on the football team, causing Mr. Fogelman to become more and more frustrated, especially after someone sabotages the scenery and the props.

3. *Chaos to order.* Although Wallace's ideas for creating a lively play seem doomed, the surprising saboteur is revealed, and Wallace goes from most hated to most popular.

F. Tragedy (Booker, p. 156)

Spillebeen, Geert. 2005. *Kipling's Choice*. Boston: Houghton Mifflin. Grades 5–8.

Wanting desperately to be a hero to please his world-famous father Rudyard, 18-year-old John Kipling receives mortal injuries on his first day of battle in World War I. By alternating between scenes of frontline horrors and home-front illusions, the narrative achieves a heightened dramatic irony.

1. *Temptation stage.* Urged on by the news of more friends enlisting in military service and by his father's well-publicized war poem, John waits impatiently for his "glory moment" (p. 4).
2. *Dream stage.* Like most of his peers, John thinks of this war as "the Great Picnic" (p. 29), his only fear being that the war might end before he gets his marching orders. Rudyard Kipling's patriotic coverage of the war instills in John notions "of heroism in the starring role of his life" (p. 120), promising to showcase the younger Kipling beyond the shadow of his celebrated father.
3. *Frustration stage.* Each time John tries to enlist, his poor eyesight and frail health block his entry into the army. Through Rudyard's influence, however, John is accepted to be a lieutenant for a group of the Irish Guard.
4. *Nightmare stage.* After John is hit by shrapnel, he lies conscious on the battlefield, overhearing English and German voices that presume he is already dead. In horrible pain, John prays to die, yet describes himself lying "on his back like a fallen saint" (p. 128), a tribute to the sticking power of the war hero illusion. In England, Rudyard receives a telegram that his only child is missing in action, and the father "roars and rages like a wounded tiger" (p. 129).
5. *Destruction or death wish stage.* Lt. John Kipling's body was never officially found. Rudyard Kipling, whose "pen dried up," served on a commission that erected a memorial for all soldiers whose remains never returned home.

G. Rebirth (Booker, p. 204)

Rosenberg, Liz. 2002. *Seventeen: A Novel in Prose Poems*. Chicago: Cricket. Grades 9–12.

The ever-shy Stephanie begins her senior year with few expectations until she meets Denny Pistil, the most popular boy in the class, and they immediately fall in love. Feminist critics suggest that the archetypal pattern for a girl's coming of age is *rebirth*, not the *quest* as seen in stories with a male protagonist. Stephanie's narrative shows its Greek parallels with the myth of Persephone (Stephanie) and Demeter.

1. *The protagonist falls under the threat of a dark power.* With their first kiss, Stephanie "falls into a trance" (p. 27). Denny is described as "a tall, gaunt figure, larger

than life, dressed in black" (p. 5), like a modern-day Hades. As she and Denny become closer, Stephanie moves emotionally further away from her mother, with whom she has always shared a warm, loving relationship.

2. *The threat recedes*: Stephanie is happy about "her little power" over Denny, although she does not understand it. She also enjoys how she and Denny, "in the kingdom of their high school" are "now royalty" (p. 77). At this point, Stephanie exercises the power in their relationship.

3. *The threat returns*: After the couple makes love, things change. Denny becomes very serious; his father buys them engagement rings. They begin to argue. Stephanie loses her appetite as she senses her control slipping away.

4. *The dark power returns (and the protagonist seems imprisoned in a state of living death)*: Stephanie (like her mother) goes into a deep depression. In a chapter called "Underground," Stephanie muses, "It is delicious, this sleep of the dead," her metaphor for her depression (p. 123). There are images of imprisonment and burial through this section of the story.

5. *Miraculous redemption occurs and the protagonist the resumes life, feeling as if reborn, transformed, or changed*: In the spring, Stephanie comes back to life. From her experience, the once-shy Stephanie has gained insight: Life is composed of much more than trying to feel safe. A young woman must leave the security of her mother's arms to the exhilaration of an independent (emotional) life with others.

H. Rebellion Against the "One" (Booker, p. 495)

Lowry, Lois. 1993. *The Giver*. Boston, MA: Houghton Mifflin. Grades 6–9.

When Jonas is 12 years old, he participates in a community ceremony in which he is assigned his lifetime career: the receiver of memories. As such, he is destined to discover the truth of his family's and neighbors' frightening social environment.

1. *Dark power has taken control of society*: Jonas lives in a safe and perfect social order, controlled so that everyone lives a life without conflict, poverty, or injustice but also a life without the pain of sacrifice, the need for courage, or the joy of compassion and beauty.

2. *A solitary figure opposes the controlling power or group*: As Jonas experiences a deeper understanding, he questions the community's institutionalized values and beliefs.

3. *As an Everyman, the protagonist takes action and achieves some initial success*: Jonas flees, taking with him the physically imperfect baby, Gabriel, whom he loves.

4. *The main conflict centers on the protagonist's loss of identify and/or the laws prohibiting citizens from having lasting relationships with others*: Jonas realizes that he cannot have a lasting relationship with his family or any individual who is bound by the fixed and controlled values and beliefs of his community.

5. *In a final test or ordeal, the protagonist is destroyed*: The novel has an open ending. Jonas, with Gabriel, races on a sled down a snowy hill toward colored lights twinkling on trees behind windows where families are gathered, leaving the reader to puzzle through the explanation: Was his twinkling vision a learned memory or a joyful reality?

ARCHETYPAL PATTERNS: CHARACTERS

Psychologist and critic Carol Pearson has addressed archetypal characters for over 25 years. In *The Female Hero in American and British Literature*, Carol Pearson and Katherine Pope (1981) suggest that the heroic pattern of women protagonists in several nineteenth and twentieth century novels differs from the heroic pattern found in novels featuring men. In *The Hero Within*, Pearson (1986, 1989) focuses on archetypal characters, who, regardless of gender, embark on a hero's quest, or "a journey of individuation" (p. xxvi), echoing Jung and Marie-Louise von Franz. By choosing to name the archetypes using ordinary words, Pearson indicates that "archetypes need not seem so foreign and threatening" (p. xxvii).

In literature as in life, Pearson writes, "Individuals chart their own unique courses through these stages and there are predictable differences in the way people encounter them" (p. 6). Pearson sees the stages that a person moves through not as linear but as a spiral, in three dimensions moving forward "but frequently circling back" (p. 13), as heroes re-encounter situations that take them back to prior stages. "We learn and relearn lessons at new levels of intellectual and emotional complexity and subtlety" (p. 130).

In her later study on archetypes, *Awakening the Heroes Within*, Pearson (1991: 10–11) identifies 12 archetypes that can be applied to literature. Pearson uses *dragons* metaphorically to stand for life's problems or challenges, alluding to ancient mythic images of monsters to be slain. Any of Pearson's 12 archetypes can be expressed as a shadow side, in such figures as deniers (Innocent), victims (Orphans), and villains (Warriors). Pearson stresses the uniqueness of each archetypal image. "Not all Warriors, for example, are alike. Some are primitive and ruthless, driven by a drive for conquest. Some are competitive game players. Some engage in crusades for the good of humanity" (p. 20).

Pearson's archetypal characters provide an accessible approach to YA literature, as they avoid the technical Jungian terminology by being described in more familiar language. For comparison, the archetypes are described using the same four elements—*goal, fear, problem,* and *gift.* Young people can identify various archetypes in literature by referring to Figure 10.1. One example from YA literature for each of the 12 archetypes is annotated in the following annotated bibliography section.

Figure 10.1. Pearson's Archetypal Characters				
Archetype	**Goal**	**Fear**	**Dragon/Problem**	**Gift/Virtue**
1. Innocent	Remain in safety	Abandonment	Deny it or seek rescue	Trust, optimism
2. Orphan	Regain safety	Exploitation	Is victimized by it	Interdependence, realism
3. Warrior	Win	Weakness	Slay/confront it	Courage, discipline
4. Caregiver	Help others	Selfishness	Take care of it or those it harms	Compassion, generosity
5. Seeker	Search for better life	Conformity	Flee from it	Autonomy, ambition
6. Lover	Bliss	Loss of love	Love it	Passion, commitment
7. Destroyer	Metamorphosis	Annihilation	Allow dragon to slay it	Humility
8. Creator	Creation of a life, work, new reality	Inauthenticity	Claim it as part of the self	Individuality, vocation
9. Ruler	Order	Chaos	Find its constructive uses	Responsibility, control
10. Magician	Transformation	Evil sorcery	Transform it	Personal power
11. Sage	Truth	Deception	Transcend it	Wisdom, nonattachment
12. Fool	Enjoyment	Non-aliveness	Play tricks on it	Joy, freedom
Source: Adapted from Pearson, 1991: 10–11.				

Annotated Bibliography of Pearson's Archetypal Characters

1. Innocent (Pearson, 1991: 10–11)

Almond, David. 2000. *Heaven Eyes*. New York: Random House. Grades 5–8.

When Erin, January, and Mouse escape from their orphanage on a handmade raft, they encounter an ethereal and pure innocent named Heaven Eyes, whose mysterious past the trio soon discover.

1. *Goal*: Erin is taken aback by her first sight of Heaven: "There were webs stretched between her fingers. Her face was moon-pale. Her eyes were moon-round, watery blue. Her voice was high and light and yearning" (p. 53), the archetypal Innocent. Heaven Eyes belongs to her Grampa, who she says saved her from the Black Middens (bog) when she was just a baby. She believes he will always take care of her and he would never hurt her or the children who she now calls her sister and brothers.

2. *Fear.* At one point Heaven fears that Erin is going to leave her and go back on the river. Heaven begs the children to stay, although they fear for their lives as Grampa's behavior begins to frighten them.

3. *Problem:* When January discovers a photograph that shows Heaven as a baby with her family, he is certain Grampa is a murderer. Heaven will not leave him and does not believe that he would ever murder anybody.

4. *Gift:* In the end Grampa dies and asks the children to take good care of Heaven. Her trust in people being confirmed, Heaven agrees to live with the children—now definitely her family—at the orphanage, where she inspires others to see the world through her prism of innocence.

2. *Orphan (Pearson, 1991: 10–11)*

Rapp, Adam. 1999. *The Copper Elephant.* Asheville, NC: Front Street. Grades 9–12.

Living with a loosely organized band of survivors in a dystopian society, two damaged orphans, 12-year-old Whensday (barely literate) and 19-year-old Honeycut (reminiscent of Steinbeck's character Lenny in *Of Mice and Men*), survive by pooling their talents and learning true empathy.

1. *Goal:* Tick Burrowman saves Whensday's life by hiding her in one of his caskets—called "Bodyboxes" (p. 20)—and seems to be taking good care of her. However, when she realizes Tick is going to sell her to a woman who Whensday does not trust, Whensday flees in the night.

2. *Fear.* Fearing that the woman with the "clown makeup" would surely exploit her, Whensday runs to the only place she knows, the river and the Bone Trees. For a time she is all alone, starving, without shelter, and afraid of every sound she hears. It is illegal for anyone to be living in the Bone Trees, and Whensday meets every stranger with fear and mistrust.

3. *Problem:* Honeycut comes upon Whensday after she has been assaulted by a soldier, Second Staff Brown. The powerfully strong Honeycut tracks the soldier and kills him, showing the body to Whensday to make her feel safer. Whensday must flee again when more soldiers come looking for the missing Brown.

4. *Gift:* After a few months of deprivation, Whensday gives up and collapses. But a gentle woman in a dark-hooded robe finds her and tells Whensday that the girl is pregnant and she will now be safe. Blue nurtures and protects Whensday and her unborn child in a secret refuge for women and girls, the "Babymakers" (p. 276). Whensday has learned to accept the worst of realities with some optimism for her future.

3. *Warrior (Pearson, 1991: 10–11)*

Zusak, Markus. 2000. *Fighting Ruben Wolfe.* New York: Scholastic. Grades 7 and up.

When agent Perry Cole sees Ruben and Cameron Wolfe boxing, he offers to hire them both at $50 each per night, but they must keep the jobs secret from their unemployed, proud father.

1. *Goal:* Ruben Wolfe is a born winner. He is fearless, tough, and complex. Although the family is in the midst of hard times, Ruben will not give up. He and Cameron dream up schemes to make money.

2. *Fear:* Mrs. Wolfe volunteers Ruben and Cam to walk their neighbor's dog, Prissy, a fluffy Pomeranian, and the boys always wait until dark and wear hoods in case anyone should see them. The dog is "a dead-set embarrassment to walk.... There's only so much guys like us can get away with" (p. 24).

3. *Problem:* Ruben and Cameron listen to their parents talk each night about their increasing money problems. The boys would willingly get part-time jobs, but their father will not permit it. Ruben is tired of standing by and doing nothing as the family gets deeper and deeper in debt. He can contribute to the family's livelihood through his boxing, and his sense of family gives him reason to win every single match.

4. *Gift:* Although Ruben is a naturally talented athlete, he takes his job seriously. He prepares as if boxing were his profession. The smaller Cameron's nickname in the ring is Underdog, and he receives tips from the crowd even though he usually loses. After they give their parents the $800 they have earned boxing, the boys explain why they felt they must do their part for the family, and the parents accept the gift graciously.

4. Caregiver (Pearson, 1991: 10–11)

Johnson, Angela. 2003. *The First Part Last*. New York: Simon and Schuster. Grades 6–12.

Alternating between "Now" and "Then" chapters, first-person narrator Bobby builds suspense as the reader finally discovers why he is the single-parent caretaker of his baby daughter, Feather.

1. *Goal:* Bobby, reluctantly at first, supports the pregnant Nia. After the baby is born, Bobby has some assistance from his divorced parents, but he is entirely responsible for Feather. At the end (pp. 120–124), readers become aware of Nia's difficult delivery followed by a persistent vegetative state, leaving Bobby as the only person who wants to take care of Feather.

2. *Fear:* Bobby's initial reaction to the pregnancy is to shift all of the decision making to Nia: "I don't say it's not up to me.... What Nia wants is what it's all about. No pressure" (p. 41). When they eventually decide to put the baby up for adoption, Bobby thinks, "It's the right thing. Everybody says so.... I want to believe it's unselfish. I want to believe none of this is supposed to be about me" (p. 99).

3. *Problem:* Once he takes charge of the baby, Bobby pushes himself almost to the point of physical collapse. After one foolish act, Bobby takes full responsibility for his actions and rushes home to hold his baby daughter.

4. *Gift:* By deciding to keep the baby despite opposition from all quarters, Bobby realizes, "I know I'm being a man, not just some kid who's upset and wants it

his way" (p. 126). His final decision is to move to a small town in Ohio to be near his brother and his family and to have a better environment for Feather and himself.

5. Seeker (Pearson, 1991: 10–11)

Hinton, S.E. 1969. *The Outsiders*. New York: Viking Press. Grades 6–9.

Life is tough for a gang of high school students who live in suburban Tulsa, Oklahoma, during the 1960s.

1. *Goal*: Although he and his brothers are orphans, Ponyboy Curtis is kept in line by his older brother Darry, who expects Ponyboy to do well in school and to stay out of trouble.
2. *Fear*: To feel he belongs, Ponyboy adheres to the strict code of honor of the greasers, who live on the poorer east side of town. Another clique, the Socs (Socials), is composed of rich kids who live on the west side. Each group uses stereotypes and labels to form their expectations of the other. Ponyboy is surprised when he meets Cherry, a Soc, who shares his interest in poetry.
3. *Problem*: After Ponyboy and Johnny kill one of the Socs in an act of self-defense, they escape with a gun and some money and hide in an abandoned church for several days.
4. *Gift*: The turning point in Ponyboy's life occurs when he reads a letter Johnny writes shortly before he dies. Johnny encourages Ponyboy to "stay gold" and to make something of his life. This epiphany gives Ponyboy a purpose in life—to complete his education and to help others see young people as individuals, not as stereotypes.

6. Lover (Pearson, 1991: 10–11)

Blume, Judy. 1975. *Forever*. New York: Pocket Books. Grades 9–12.

After level-headed Katherine ("Kat") meets Michael, she realizes that she has fallen in love forever, as indicated by the locket he gives her with that definitive word engraved on it.

1. *Goal*: After meeting briefly at a party, Michael asks Kat for a date. At first, she denies to her mother that she is in love with Michael. Kat's best friend Erica calls her "a romantic" because Kat sees sex not as a physical thing but "as a way of expressing love" (p. 37). Kat strives for a mature relationship, telling Michael she needs to be "mentally ready" before she becomes intimate with him (p. 57).
2. *Fear*: When it becomes time to consider colleges, Kat and Michael will do almost anything to be near each other. Kat rushes into her counselor's office with an emergency, last-minute application to two of the colleges Michael is considering.

3. *Problem:* Kat stays in control of the relationship, especially as it nears its point of intimacy. However, after she meets an older boy at summer camp to whom she is attracted, Kat decides she and Michael should date others. It is Michael who breaks off their relationship, unable to "share" her with anyone else (p. 216).
4. *Gift:* In retrospect, Kat believes, "I'm not ready for forever" (p. 220), indicating her growth and understanding about the true nature of committed love.

7. Destroyer (Pearson, 1991: 10-11)

Green, John. *Looking for Alaska.* **2005. New York: Dutton. Grades 9–12.**

In a plot divided (like a labyrinth) into "Before" and "After," 16-year-old Miles narrates how his life was changed forever by the presence and absence, the life and death, of one charismatic friend. The novel could be read as an archetypal Greek myth, with the hero as Theseus (Miles) and his lover as Ariadne (Alaska), who supplies the thread for the hero to find his way out of the labyrinth, the central metaphor of the story.

1. *Goal:* Devoted to memorizing the dying last words of famous people, Miles has entertained an interest in death but only superficially. He likes philosophy and spends time reflecting on the meaning of his life.
2. *Fear:* The unexpected death of one member of a close-knit group of friends brings each character face to face with the Destroyer.
3. *Problem:* By devoting himself to finding out exactly how his friend died, Miles becomes depressed, confused, and angry. However, in the end, he has learned how to "navigate through life in spite of the uncontestable fact of suffering" (p. 215).
4. *Gift:* After facing the reality of death without finding answers to his specific question about how his friend died, Miles realizes that "some mysteries aren't meant to be solved" (p. 212).

8. Creator (Pearson, 1991: 10–11)

Thomas, Rob. 1996. *Rats Saw God.* **New York: Aladdin. Grades 9 and up.**

During his senior year in a new school, Steve York is truant and flunking most of his classes, but a savvy counselor sees the boy's potential and suggests he earn his much-needed English credit by composing a 100-page autobiography. The narrative moves between the present (in Houston) and his past (in California).

1. *Goal:* As his first person narrative clearly shows, Steve possesses the gift of writing witty, sardonic prose. Until his senior year, Steve had been an excellent student. But after his girlfriend Wanda's ("Dub's") betrayal, he falls apart and moves to Houston to live with his dad.
2. *Fear:* In the autobiography sections (introduced in bold penmanship with the date and his grade level), Steve begins high school by making friends with people who share his skepticism. They form an avant-garde art club, "Grace Order of Dadaists," or "GOD" (pp. 27, 30). Eventually, Steve comes to see that

the club "stands" for nothing really, just a symbolic gesture of poking fun at all high school clubs.

3. *Problem*: When confronted with the harsh possibility of his ruining his own life, Steve begrudgingly begins his autobiography. He recalls his junior year in California when he took his first creative writing class conducted by a young, friendly teacher called Sky. Through writing his autobiography, Steve is able to confront his anger over his mentor's betrayal and to see his life from a new perspective.

4. *Gift*: In writing his autobiography, Steve finds much balance and truth about his family, especially forgiveness of his father. Steve begins college at the University of Washington, feeling "safe and sound" (p. 202) and that, in all probability, he will become a writer.

9. *Ruler* and 10. *Magician (Pearson, 1991: 10–11)*

Yolen, Jane. 2003. *The Sword of the Rightful King*. San Diego, CA: Harcourt. Grades 6–9.

Fearing he is running out of time, Merlinnus must convince all of Britain to rally around Arthur as true High King through a public display of his power—pulling a sword out of a stone.

9. RULER—ARTHUR

1. *Goal*: Arthur finds the day-to-day duties of being a king boring but admits he has learned that a king is "'three parts ear to one part mouth'" (p. 59) and understands he must be "'careful with everyone. It is part of what a High King is all about, being careful'" (p. 45).

2. *Fear*: The chief creator of disorder in the realm is Morgause, whose black magic is fueled by her hatred for Arthur. She casts spells of enchantment on her sons and believes Gawaine should be on the throne by birthright. But Gawaine is a very reluctant candidate, preferring to serve Arthur.

3. *Problem*: Called "Hard Hands" by those who have felt his brutality, the hotheaded Agravaine threatens to kill Arthur's own stepbrother, Sir Kay. Arthur melts the young man's cold fury when he restrains him with a show of physical power tempered with respect. Arthur's words to Agravaine reflect his vision for Britain: "'If my kingdom is about anything it is: We who are strong are to be the caretakers of the weak'" (p. 155).

4. *Gift*: The time for all to pull the sword arrives on the Solstice, or during Midsummer madness. Men from throughout Britain arrive with the intent to pull the sword from the stone. The narrator notes, "Arthur did not like ritual, but he knew how to command a crowd's attention" (p. 321).

10. MAGICIAN—MERLINNUS

1. *Goal*: The aged Merlinnus must "find a way to bind the people—all the people—to Arthur. And soon" (p. 52). There is a sword in the stone that every man in the kingdom will have an equal chance to pull.

2. *Fear.* Merlinnus's opponent is Morgause, whose knowledge is untouched "by any morality, fed by anger, slyness, and hate; black magic instead of white" (p. 52).

3. *Problem:* Upon the arrival of Morgause at Cadbury, Merlinnus promises to turn potential disaster into success for Arthur. She is only a witch; he, a mage: "'I will soften this blow . . . Strengthen the stone . . . Put steel into Arthur's purpose'" (p. 265).

4. *Gift:* Without the wizard's being aware of it, "by his very presence, he changed what was ordinary into something else" (p. 49).

11. Sage (Pearson, 1991: 10–11)

Hesse, Hermann. 1951. *Siddhartha.* New York: New Directions. Classic.

The promising son of a Brahmin rejects his father's dream and takes his own journey in search of the meaning of life. Although the early events of the novel follow the traditional life story of Gotama Buddha (who is also sometimes called Siddhartha), this third-person narrative tells the story of a fictional protagonist who spends many years experiencing a life of extremes.

1. *Goal:* Siddhartha, an intelligent young man, feels "the seeds of discontent" (p. 5) in his education and sets out to join a small band of samanas, or ascetics, whose goal is "to experience pure thought" (p. 15) through extreme self-denial.

2. *Fear.* From the samanas Siddhartha learns "to think, wait, and fast" (p. 60), but when he meets the new Illustrious One, Gotama, the boy learns, "'Nobody finds salvation through teachings'" (p. 34). Gotama also warns Siddhartha, "'Be on your guard against too much cleverness'" (p. 35).

3. *Problem:* Siddhartha's next challenge occurs when he becomes a wealthy businessman immersed in possessions and debauchery, "playing a game without end" (p. 84). Feeling "horror and death in his heart" (p. 82), Siddhartha walks away from this life and attempts to commit suicide near a river. At his lowest point, the middle-aged Siddhartha hears the holy Om of his soul and knows, "Now I am beginning again like a child" (p. 95).

4. *Gift:* By listening to the river's many voices and by living the simple life of a ferryman, Siddhartha learns many things—that "wisdom is not communicable" (p. 142); that "in every truth the opposite is equally true" (p. 143); that "the potential Buddha already exists in the sinner" (p. 143); and that "everything that exists is good—death as well as life" (p. 144).

12. Fool (Pearson, 1991: 10–11)

Rennison, Louise. 2000. *Angus, Thongs, and Full-Frontal Snogging: The Confessions of Georgia Nicolson.* New York: HarperCollins. Grades 7 and up.

Georgia Nicolson makes her debut in the first of several novels written as diaries depicting her life and loves as a British high school student. Georgia is the archetypal comic Fool, who never has a quiet moment, romps through one misadventure after another, and prefers to discuss makeup and kissing over any other topics. She is self-absorbed, blurts out politically incorrect statements, and seems to consider no topic sacred, yet she remains loved by family, friends, and readers.

1. *Goal:* Although she wishes she were prettier, nothing stops Georgia from having fun, including attending a party dressed as a stuffed olive, reluctantly taking a part in *Macbeth*, and helping her friends plan their Viking wedding.
2. *Fear:* Georgia thinks that her parents are prudish, an indication of her viewpoint of adults in general. Her diaries and the glossaries with her witty and hilarious definitions that end each book indicate Georgia is never *not alive*.
3. *Problem:* Most of Georgia's thoughts center on boys and on how she can capture her current, elusive boyfriend SG (Sex God), or the half-Italian singer Masimo, or Dave-the-Laugh.
4. *Gift:* In each book, Georgia remains the trickster and does not develop as other teen protagonists are expected to do. Because she is the Fool, she will remain in this blessed state of self-declared freedom and joy.

REFERENCES AND SUGGESTIONS FOR FURTHER READING

Aarne, Antti. 1928. *The Types of the Folktale: A Classification and Bibliography.* Translated and enlarged by Stith Thompson. Helsinki: Academia.

Anderson, Graham. 2000. *Fairytale in the Ancient World.* New York: Routledge.

Bettleheim, Bruno. 1976. *The Uses of Enchantment: The Meaning and Importance of Fairy Tales.* New York: Knopf.

Block, Francesca Lia. 2000. *The Rose and the Beast: Fairy Tales Retold.* New York: Harper-Collins.

Block, Francesca Lia. 2006. *Psyche in a Dress.* New York: Joanna Colter Books.

Block, Francesca Lia. 2008. *Blood Roses.* New York: Joanna Colter Books.

Booker, Christopher. 2004. *Seven Basic Plots: Why We Tell Stories.* London: Continuum.

Buckley, Michael. 2005. *The Fairy-Tale Detectives.* New York: Amulet Books.

Cammuso, Frank. 2002. *Max Hamm: Fairy Tale Detective.* Syracuse, NY: Nite Owl Comix.

Cox, Marian. 1893, 1903. *Cinderella: Three Hundred and Forty-five Variants.* London: The Folk Society.

Dahl, Roald. 2002. *Roald Dahl's Revolting Rhymes.* Illustrated by Quentin Blake. New York: Knopf.

Datlow, Ellen, and Terri Windling, eds. 2003. *Swan Sister: Fairy Tales Retold.* New York: Simon and Schuster Books for Young Readers.

Datlow, Ellen, and Terri Windling, eds. 2006. *The Faery Reel: Tales from the Twilight Realm.* New York: Firebird.

Dundes, Alan, ed. 1988. *Cinderella: A Folklore Case Book.* Madison: University of Wisconsin Press.

Dundes, Alan. 1989. *Little Red Riding Hood.* Madison: University of Wisconsin Press.

El-Shamy, Hasan M. 2004. *Types of the Folktale in the Arab World: A Demographically Oriented Tale-type Index.* Bloomington: Indiana University Press.

Ferris, Jean. 2002. *Once Upon a Marigold*. San Diego, CA: Harcourt.

Flinn, Alex. 2007. *Beastly*. New York: HarperTeen.

Frye, Northrup. 1957. *Anatomy of Criticism*. Princeton, NJ: Princeton University Press.

Gray, Richard M. 1996. *Archetypal Explorations: An Integrative Approach to Human Behavior*. New York: Routledge.

Haddix, Margaret. 1999. *Just Ella*. New York: Simon and Schuster Books for Young Readers.

Hawes, Louise. 2008. *Black Pearls: A Faerie Strand*. Illustrated by Rebecca Guay. Boston: Houghton Mifflin.

Kantor, Melissa. 2005. *If I Have a Wicked Stepmother, Where's My Prince?* New York: Hyperion.

Knapp, Bettina L. 2003. *French Fairy Tales: A Jungian Approach*. Albany: State University of New York Press.

Lanagan, Margo. 2007. *Red Spikes*. New York: Alfred A. Knopf.

Levine, Gail Carson. 1999. *Princess Sonora and the Long Sleep*. Illustrated by Mark Elliott. New York: HarperCollins.

Levine, Gail Carson. 2006. *Fairest*. New York: HarperCollins.

Louie, Ai-Ling. 1982. *Yeh-Shen: A Cinderella Story from China*. Illustrated by Ed Young. New York: Philomel Books.

Luthi, Max. 1984. *The Fairy Tale as Art Form and Portrait of Man*. Translated by Jon Erickson. Bloomington: Indiana University Press.

Maguire, Gregory. 1995. *Wicked: The Life and Times of the Wicked Witch of the West*. Illustrated by Douglas Smith. New York: Regan Books.

Maguire, Gregory. 2005. *Son of a Witch*. New York: Harper Collins.

McKinley, Robin. 2000. *Spindle's End*. New York: Putnam's Sons.

McNaughton, Janet Elizabeth. 2004. *An Earthly Knight*. New York: HarperCollins.

Napoli, Donna Jo. 2004. *Bound*. New York: Atheneum Books for Young Readers.

Opie, Iona, and Peter Opie, eds. 1974. *The Classic Fairy Tales*. New York: Oxford University Press.

Pearson, Carol S. 1986, 1989. *The Hero Within: Six Archetypes We Live By*. Expanded edition. San Francisco, CA: Harper and Row.

Pearson, Carol S. 1991. *Awakening the Heroes Within*. New York: Harper Collins.

Pearson, Carol, and Katherine Pope. 1981. *The Female Hero in British and American Literature*. New York: Bowker.

Perrault, Charles. 1993. *The Complete Fairy Tales of Charles Perrault*. Illustrated by Sally Holmes. Translated by Neil Philip and Nicoletta Simborowski. New York: Clarion Books.

Propp, Vladimir. 1958. *Morphology of the Folktale*. Translated by Laurence Scott. Bloomington: Indiana University Press.

Pullman, Philip. 2000. *I Was a Rat! Or The Scarlet Slippers*. Illustrated by Kevin Hawkes. New York: Knopf.

Reiff, Tana. 1993. *Love Stories Retold by Tana Reiff*. Illustrated by Cheri Bladholm. Syracuse, NY: New Readers Press.

Schmidt, Gary D. 2001. *Straw Into Gold*. New York: Clarion Books.

Schusterman, Neal. 2005. *Dread Locks*. New York: Dutton Children's Books.

Sexton, Anne. 1971. *Transformations*. Illustrated by Barbara Swan. Boston: Houghton Mifflin.

Slote, Bernice, ed. 1963. *Myth and Symbol: Critical Approaches and Applications*. Lincoln: University of Nebraska Press.

Spiegelman, Art, and Francoise Mouly, eds. 2000. *Little Lit: Folklore and Fairy Tale Funnies.* New York: Raw Junior Book with Joanna Cotler Books/HarperCollins.

Steinbeck, John. 1937, 1993. *Of Mice and Men.* New York: Penguin.

Takahashi, Rumiko. 2003. *Inu-Yasha: A Feudal Fairy Tale.* San Francisco, CA: VIZ Media LLC.

Thompson, Stith. 1958. *The Motif-Index of Folk Literature: A Classification of Narrative Elements in Folktales, Ballads, Myths, Fables, Medieval Romances, Exempla, Fabliaux, Jest Books, and Local Legends,* revised and enlarged edition. Bloomington: Indiana University Press.

Tolkien, J.R.R. 1964. *Tree and Leaf.* London: Allen and Unwin.

Von Franz, Marie-Louise. 1997. *Archetypal Patterns in Fairy Tales.* Toronto: Inner City Books.

Willingham, Bill. 2002. *Fables: Legends in Exile.* New York: DC Comics.

Willingham, Bill and Matthew Sturges. 2007. *Jack of Fables.* New York: Vertigo/DC Comics.

Chapter 11

Popular Culture and Literacy

INTRODUCTION TO POPULAR CULTURE

Popular culture is a term that defies definition even by those who routinely use it. Is it bestsellers, blockbusters, and the Super Bowl? Is it the commercially driven mass media controlled by a handful of global businessmen whose only interest is the bottom line? Is it the mass production of a way of life that creates little monsters out of our children? Who owns popular culture? Do the consumers control the *products* (the material expressions of culture) that will be successful? Or are people's choices limited from the get-go by the deciders of corporate America? Young people who want to discuss issues in popular culture will inevitably encounter some of these questions. For the purposes of this chapter, *popular culture* means (the study of) mass media communication messages whose content is designed to entertain their respective audiences. The commercial products of expression include television shows, movies, music, and comics.

The first attempt to have popular culture taken seriously by academics was the founding of the Popular Culture Association (PCA) in 1970 by a small group of scholars. In 1971 the association started the *Journal of Popular Culture* devoted to a more holistic approach to the study of American culture. Topics in popular culture range widely and are almost limitless (e.g., television and movies, toys, music, fads, family life, religion, automobiles, media created rituals, and heroes). The disciplines from which popular culture draws include history, literature, anthropology, communications, geography, sociology, philosophy, architecture, political science, psychology, and the law. Although its detractors are becoming fewer and less disapproving, popular culture has remained in an ongoing fight for recognition from academics over the issue of "highbrow" versus "lowbrow" tastes (if it is popular, that means it cannot be any good). Contemporary and historical issues, especially those that show continuity throughout society but whose content changes with the times, such as family life, coming of age, and values, are frequent subjects of popular culture.

A study of popular culture affords young people opportunities to practice their visual literacy skills. *Visual literacy* means the acquisition of skills for reading *and* creating visible messages. The visually literate young adult (YA) learns to make sense of visual images and objects and to understand and appreciate the visual messages of others (Brill, Kim, and Branch, 2000). Twenty-first-century technology has changed the ways people communicate and has motivated the debate about how best to assist young people achieve full literacy.

In consideration of the fluid nature of popular culture and of the width and depth of its many parts, this chapter examines three popular culture media that rely on *visual literacy*—television, movies, and graphic novels—that YAs are most familiar with. Although the Internet is a vital part of YA lives, a discussion of the Internet is beyond the scope of this chapter's focus on visual literacy.

Popular Culture and YAs

For YAs, popular culture is more or less *their lives.* They text-message one another; watch videos on YouTube; keep their cell phones charged; listen to their favorite songs on their iPods; play video games; create Web sites at school; select television shows from hundreds of choices offered on cable, satellite, or the Internet; interact by voting for their favorite contestant on *American Idol;* go to movies; rent movies; rent movies on demand from their cable television; listen to audiobooks; browse the Internet; create their own profile Web page on Facebook; chat online; compose their schoolwork on their favorite brand of computer with a variety of software programs to enrich their work; use full-color printer/scanners; listen to radio stations from around the world; attend outdoor concerts; and use conventional e-mail and telephones. The phenomenon of the immersion of YAs in all of these modes of discourse—aural, visual, digital—has been called "the youth genre" (Alvermann and Hagood, 2000: 196). By looking at popular culture through a cultural lens, the "emphasis on how youth subcultures form around particular icons, texts, and artifacts in popular culture" is inevitable (Alvermann and Hagood, 2000: 195). Because popular culture comprises much of their daily lives, young people need to understand critical *media literacy.*

Media Literacy

Elizabeth Thoman (1999: 50) defines *media literacy* as the ability to achieve "personal meaning from the verbal and visual symbols that we take in every day through television, radio, computers, newspapers and magazines, and, of course advertising. It is the ability to choose and select, the ability to challenge and question, the ability to be conscious about what's going on around us." Most scholars do not believe that the media is a monolith that dispenses ideologies that young people passively absorb. Instead, scholars in popular culture tend to believe that each person reads cultural texts differently depending on personal traits. Even if members of the same audience interpret messages similarly, the texts are negotiated in relation to individual perception and all its possible variables and contexts.

Douglas Kellner and Jeff Share (2005) stress *critical* media literacy. They teach young people to exercise their analytical skills by examining the conventions of a medium, its stereotypes and values, and its potential for multiple meanings, explicit or implicit. Kellner and Share (2005: 369) believe that, in the contemporary technical and digital age, it is important to "develop robust forms of media literacy." The critical media literacy approach shows young people how to decode media texts in a similar fashion to the way they read and analyze literature. Kellner and Share (2005) put forth five core concepts of critical media literacy:

1. All media messages are "constructed." (p. 374)
2. Media messages are constructed using a creative language with its own rules. (p. 374)
3. Different people experience the same media message differently. (p. 375)
4. Media have embedded values and points of view. (p. 376)
5. Media are organized to gain profit and/or power. (p. 376)

Each concept of critical media literacy is a topic for YAs to debate and to revisit as they study popular culture through a critical prism.

POPULAR CULTURE AND TELEVISION

It is tempting to ask young people to critique their favorite television shows with the idea that they will be more interested in examining shows that they like and therefore more easily able to gain a better (i.e., *adult*) perspective after critical analysis. However, it seems wiser to remain an objective facilitator and give YAs the lead during discussion and evaluation of television viewing. For example, it would be interesting for young people to critique a television show that they already do not like or have never watched. By examining one episode of a series and giving it a close reading as if it were a text, some viewers might discover a new genre or think twice before rejecting a show because it sounds boring.

There are as many ways to critique television as there are ways to critique literature. Television shows can be read as a text from any viewpoint (e.g., gender, psychological, sociological, archetypal). Considering that television creates global viewing communities whose members often chat online about their favorite actors and shows, one way to approach criticism is from a cultural perspective.

The following questions elicit discussion from a cultural point of view. They do not need to be discussed in any particular order or to always be included in every discussion.

Discussion of a Television Series Through Popular Culture

1. **Socioeconomics:** What are the socioeconomic statuses of the main characters? How do their positions in society influence their values, beliefs, and behavior? What does the setting indicate about the socioeconomic status of the community and the main characters?

2. **Main characters:** What traits do the main characters possess? What does their physical appearance suggest about them?

3. **Secondary characters:** What are the roles, functions, and characteristics of the secondary characters? Are there stereotypes, caricatures, and stock characters in the series?

4. **Cultural representations:** How are gender roles presented in the series? Are there any characters of color? Do minorities receive appropriate attention on the show?

5. **Conflicts:** What are the major conflicts that occur in the series? Is there an antagonist? If so, is the character round, flat, stock, or stereotyped? How do antagonists influence plot, narratives, and themes?

6. **Style:** What are some of the typical sets that are presented? Are these consistent with the characters' socioeconomic position? How would you describe the visual style? How does sound function (e.g., special effects, music)?

7. **Structure:** How are episodes usually structured as to plot?

8. **Tone:** What is the prevailing tone of the series (e.g., dramatic, suspenseful, humorous, mixture)? Do you detect a dominant ideology, or a bias, toward one political stance or toward certain issues? What characterizes the language?

9. **Themes/topics:** What are the recurring themes and topics of the series?

10. **Evaluation:** What do viewers like about the series? Dislike?

Application of Popular Culture and Literacy Principles to Matt Groening's *The Simpsons*

> *Although they are usually composed of stupid husbands, smug wives, and ill-mannered children, there is one thing you have to admire about the families in the TV serials—they don't waste their time watching TV.*
>
> —Valdez and Crow (1973: 141)

Valdez and Crow spoke for many 1970s critics regarding the general quality of television *situation comedies* (sitcoms). The genre did not seem to connect to real life at all. However, the attitude toward television viewing of sitcoms took a radical turn when an unlikely animated family took the country by storm—*The Simpsons* (Groening, 1989–2008).

The opening segment of every episode of *The Simpsons* portrays each member of the family eagerly rushing home to sit on the sofa and to watch television together. It may be that the Simpsons are the only sitcom family that makes the television set another member of the family. Ironically, one of the main targets of the show's satire is television, commercials, and mass media. As the longest running sitcom and the longest running animated series in television history, *The Simpsons* is a widely acknowledged icon of popular culture. It has won numerous Emmys and a Peabody Award, has been named the top television series of the twentieth century by *Time* magazine, and has seen its characters on the covers of numerous magazines for nearly 20 years. The series has also been a merchandising phenomenon, the characters' faces appearing on millions of tee shirts around the world. *The Simpsons Movie* (2007) was a blockbuster film.

There are many reasons given for the continuing popularity of the show, but one fact seems certain. *The Simpsons* is a collaborative effort—Matt Groening (pronounced GRAYning) created the cartoon family, and there are many directors, producers, writers, illustrators, and actors devoted to keeping the show fresh and funny. It takes from six to nine months to complete the animation for one episode, and each script goes through countless revisions. Viewers may be unaware of the behind-the-scenes commitment to excellence, but their consistent tuning in to the show speaks of the successful creativity of the entire crew.

1. Socioeconomics

The Simpsons represent a blue-collar family that sees itself as middle class and very typically American. (Homer once referred to his family as "upper lower middle class.") The Simpsons worry about their children's health and education, their community, and especially making ends meet. The Simpsons fit right in with everybody else in Springfield, USA, state unknown. The town is full of things American—an upscale shopping mall, taverns and small businesses, and a nuclear power plant that employs many of Springfield's citizens, including Homer Simpson. The only person set apart from the town is the billionaire plant owner, C. Montgomery Burns, the 104-year-old robber baron throwback.

2. The Main Characters

Homer began as an almost stock cartoonish character, a grumpy father who enjoyed strangling the ever-mischievous Bart. However, Homer soon became the show's protagonist. What's not to love about Homer? He likes to eat, to drink beer, and to watch television—all to excess. Homer begrudgingly attends church, prays when he is in big trouble, and succeeds in being a very lucky bumbler. Ironically, Homer mans the console for his (permanent) entry-level position as safety inspector at the Springfield Nuclear Power Plant. Homer will always be a 36-year-old balding and confused overweight man (donuts, Duff beers, and pork rinds), who, though an incompetent father, loves his wife and family without doubt.

Perpetually 34 years old, *Marge* sports a blue beehive hairdo and, like all of the Caucasian characters, has yellow skin. As stay-at-home mother of three, Marge makes occasional forays into other careers, such as carpenter, substitute teacher, and policeperson, but she always returns to homemaker. Although she tries to tame Homer's impulsive drives, he carries on with one foolhardy scheme after another (e.g., quitting the plant to work at his dream job as a bowling alley assistant; taking over the recently deceased ice-cream man's route).

Marge maintains the family's equilibrium, but is portrayed as very much a human with her own weaknesses. In "Life on the Fast Lane," a neglected Marge receives amorous attention from the lady's man Jacques, but Marge knows who she really is. By deciding not to meet with Jacques on the sly, Marge chooses Homer and heads for the power plant. Homer sweeps Marge off her feet, and (in one brief parody) he carries her in his arms with the theme song from the film *Officer and a Gentleman* (1982), "Up Where We Belong," playing for them just as it had played for the film's romantic couple.

Ten-year-old *Bart* is the anagram for *Brat*, and at first he was the show's naughty main character. Bart's spiky hair and ever-present skateboard mark him as a perpetually cool boy. Bart shows athletic ability but lacks the discipline to take it seriously. In some ways, he is a smaller version of Homer. But Bart is his own little guy who fulfills the archetypal trickster role: pulls practical jokes on Principal Skinner, leads the boys into misadventures, and teases his sister unmercifully.

Eight-year-old *Lisa*, the middle child, stands for idealized young people in an almost 1960s throwback. As a charter member of Springfield's Mensa group, Lisa remains loyal to her beliefs—vegetarianism, animal rights, and honesty, to list a few. Her feminism originates from her natural sense of justice and fair play. When the new Malibu Stacy doll finally spoke its first words, Lisa was horrified at its sexist, stereotypical content. In one of her articulate monologues, Lisa said, "Millions of girls will grow up thinking that this is the right way to act" (cited in Richmond and Coffman, 1997: 135). Lisa's solution was to convince the doll maker to create an empowered doll, Lisa Lionheart, which will "have the wisdom of Gertrude Stein and the wit of Cathy Guisewaite, the tenacity of Nina Totenberg and the common sense of Elizabeth Cady Stanton. And to top it off, the down-to-earth good looks of Eleanor Roosevelt!" (cited in Richmond and Coffman, 1997: 135). True to real life, the new doll is a commercial flop. The girls go for the newest but most familiar old Stacy.

One-year-old *Maggie* is known for the ever-present pacifier stuck in her mouth. She once spent a short time in the Ayn Rand School for Tots and has spoken only one word, "Daddy," which none of her family heard and which was spoken by actress Elizabeth Taylor (known for her Oscar role as Maggie in *Cat on a Hot Tin Roof* whose antagonist was "Big Daddy"), just one example of the show's layering of spoof, parody, and allusion.

3. Secondary Characters

The show's strengths and longevity can be attributed to its eccentric characters and to the celebrity voices who often speak their parts. Edna Krabappel (pronounced Krub APP'l) is the stereotypical experienced but always near the edge elementary school teacher. Principal Seymour Skinner is also stereotyped but is not the easygoing, friendly school official from old sitcoms. Instead, he takes joy in catching Bart break a school rule or in praising the school's cafeteria food, which the children clearly do not like. Caricatures include Comic Book Guy; Dr. Hibbert, a Dr. Huxtable/Bill Cosby clone; and philandering Mayor Quimby, whose voice sounds a lot like JFK's. Of the dozens of stock characters are Luigi the Italian chef and Sandwich Delivery Guy. Caricatures and stock characters perform important functions in a short animation, which needs every minute devoted to plot and dialogue; they are time savers, as viewers automatically know who and what they are.

4. Cultural Representations

The show has more male characters than female, but the characters are diverse in ethnicity. As owner of the Kwiki-Mart, Apu (a Hindu from India) quickly became an important secondary character, representing immigrants who truly believe in the American Dream. Homer's supervisor is the well-adjusted African American Carl. There are stereotypes or caricatures representing Italian Americans, Japanese Americans, Hispanic Americans, and an assortment of other ethnic characters, following the cartoon convention of illustrating recognizable, flat characters and in occasionally breaking politically incorrect expectations, although the show is clearly self-aware and it knows the audience is also aware that the show is counting on the audience to understand.

5. Conflicts

Mr. Burns is the most important antagonist on the show. As representative greedy capitalist, he finally pushed his brand of business ethics too far and was brought down by, of all people, Maggie Simpson, who accidentally shot Burns while he was reaching for her pacifier. Small-town squabbles fuel some episodes, such as problems at school, or communitywide worries, such as violence on television. Nothing is too minor (Ned Flanders' barbeque grill) or too major (ecological disaster) to become a conflict in this 22-minute series.

6. Style

The colorfully illustrated backdrops include the Simpson's living room and kitchen with stereotypical sitcom props, except that objects or decorations, such as storefront signs, are sometimes allusions to popular or elite culture or sight gags. High color matches the rapid pace of the dialogue and action. Homer drives a beat-up pink sedan that he will not give up. The series takes full advantage of the conventions of animation to move to more exotic locales (Japan, Australia, England) where Homer and Bart can cause mayhem on foreign soil. Music plays an important part in the series. The show has its own composers and orchestra and uses original songs to highlight an episode's topic.

7. Structure

The structure of the show is very important, especially the openers that include two important gags that viewers eagerly await. The first gag is variously called Bart's *atonement, chalkboard gags*, or *chalkboard punishment*, depicting Bart in front of an old-fashioned blackboard writing a single phrase over and over in white chalk (e.g., "Shooting paintballs is not an art form" and "I am not delightfully saucy"). There have been hundreds of these phrases, indicating that Mrs. Krabapple detains Bart every day after school as punishment for something he has said or done.

The second gag is the recurring but content-changing *sofa gag*. In the opening sequence, each Simpson scurries home to sit together on their sofa and immediately begin to watch television. Some sofa gags have also become legendary, including a parody of an Escher painting, the sofa as pop-up book or Etch-o-Sketch, and the family members as crash test dummies. There are hundreds of the sofa gags and many allusions to television, movies, literature, or popular culture iconic events (e.g., holidays, the Super Bowl).

8. Tone

The Simpsons is first and foremost a *parody* of situation comedies of the 1950–1980s when the American family was presented as ideal and father always knew best. A *parody* is the humorous imitation of a widely known work's style and content. The show has parodied movies, musicals, television shows, classics of literature, and sound tracks. The series also spoofs its own format of cartoons and cartoon history, especially the debate on the inherent violence in cartoons in the form of the show-within-the-show "Itchy and Scratchy." The primitively drawn cartoon, a favorite of Bart and Lisa, features a cat and mouse participating in increasingly more violent acts against each other. Even smart Lisa is easily drawn in by the show's violence. The attitude of the Simpsons (except for Marge) seems to be "Since it is just a cartoon, why take it seriously?"

As a show important to the success of Fox entertainment channel, the series mocks global corporate moguls (Rupert Murdoch owns Fox). The show targets consumerism in many ways. Krusty the Klown sells merchandise known for its poor quality, and Bart buys everything "Krusty" from his breakfast cereal to a flashlight. Episodes depict Springfield always in a buying mood. The Reverend Lovejoy worries every week about the collection plate.

The show's writers make fun of just about everything and everyone who is in a position of power and abuses that power in some form, the targets of classic satire. There are those who have objected to being spoofed (e.g., the country of Australia and a group of Catholics). The show did not poke fun of President George H.W. Bush until he denounced the series before a public meeting of church associates. The show's bias leans toward anything or anyone the writers believe is dishonest or manipulative within American society.

9. Themes

Because the show is a satire, its themes deal with irony: that things and people are not what they appear, that society is too easily taken in by con artists, propagandists, and dishonest authorities. Sometimes we take ourselves too seriously, the show often points out, especially if we become obsessive or pushy or try to control others. Since the war in Iraq, some verbal lines have been directed at the expense of the war or of its handling. However, in one episode Homer enlisted, feeling it was his duty to serve.

10. Evaluation

The Simpsons is fun to watch, and each show or rerun becomes a game of "name that allusion." The episodes reward viewers who are savvy in popular culture and in the classics, as fans show delight when they catch the allusions that the writers have so carefully planted.

POPULAR CULTURE AND FILMS

Young people have seen hundreds of movies by the time they reach secondary school and may have settled on a favorite genre. Film genres come and go in popularity, often peaking for several years and then virtually disappearing, such as the American western. By approaching film from the standpoint of genre, young people can discuss a film in relation to others within the same kind.

Discussion of a Movie Through Popular Culture

Young people may consider the following questions for discussion of a movie (adapted from Costanzo, 2004: 79).

1. Where do movies of this kind usually take place (i.e., setting)?
2. Who are the characters one expects to find in this genre (e.g., main characters, secondary, and stereotypes)?
3. What stories does this genre usually tell (e.g., narrative formula, central conflict, threat and resolution, standard plot devices)?

4. What are some of the scenes one comes to expect in this genre (e.g., important moments, typical events)?
5. What properties (props) does the genre use (e.g., costumes, weapons, vehicles, icons of the genre)?
6. What makes the visual style of the genre, and of this movie in particular, unique (e.g., décor, framing, camera work, lighting, color)?
7. What does one expect on the sound track of this genre (e.g., music, sound effects, typical dialogue)?
8. How does this film rate within its genre? What do audiences like about this film? Dislike?

Application of Film Genre to Niki Caro's *Whale Rider*

Directed and written by Niki Caro (2002), *Whale Rider* is a coming-of-age film about a Maori girl whose birth sets events into motion that would change her people forever.

1. *Setting.* Coming-of-age movies can take place anywhere in the world, but the plot usually begins in or near the main character's home. This movie is set on the small island of Whangara, New Zealand, in contemporary time.
2. *Main characters.* The main character in the majority of coming-of-age films is a boy. However, this movie features Paikea Apirana, a 12-year-old girl. For a girl to come of age, she needs to challenge her parents or other adults who may try to make her conform to their ideas. Pai's grandfather, Koro, as chief of his people, cares only about finding a boy to become the next chief, because Pai's twin brother died at birth. Although Koro loves Pai, he cannot accept her as an equal to the boys. Because his eldest son does not want to be the leader, Koro is forced to look outside the family for another firstborn son to train. Pai's father Porourangi has become a recognized artist and sculptor in Europe and has a fiancée who is white, all of which Koro does not approve. The major conflict of the film is the battle between two stubborn people, Koro and Pai, the first who represents the old way (only men can lead, and they must be firstborn sons), the second who represents the new way (the best leader shares the power).
3. *Plot.* Coming of age for boys involves the familiar circular heroic journey, but a girl's initiation may not involve the same kind of journey. Pai must make her journey inward as she struggles with herself to remain strong and courageous in the face of Koro's stubborn rejection of her because she is a girl. To him, she represents an unknown future (girls as leaders), which he sees as somewhat his enemy because his job is to preserve the ancient past. Pai is also physically strong, as she practices Maori warrior skills on the sly with her uncle Rawiri and listens in on Koro's sacred

instructions to the boys. Time after time Koro catches her and becomes angry with her. Somehow she knows that what she is doing is right. She never blames him; the fault lies with the old ways. She respects and understands his responsibility as leader more than anyone else in Whangara, including her beloved Nanny.

4. *Scenes*: The protagonist must take a final giant step toward independence. Sometimes this may be physically dangerous. At this movie's climax, a group of whales found beached and dying brings the entire community together as old and young alike work in a driving rain storm to save the sacred animals. Even the young people who had abandoned the ancient ways join to assist the elders and to save the whales. But it is only Pai who can save them. She has been communicating with them for some time, and after everybody leaves the beach, Pai gently touches the lead whale and climbs atop it as if she belonged there. The great whale turns back toward the sea with Pai riding it as it dives deeper and deeper. She is ready to die, she says, and disappears from view.

5. *Props*: Pai's Maori culture comes alive when she participates in a program where the girls dance wearing traditional Maori costumes and makeup. The Maori hold several objects as sacred icons—the carved whale's tooth that Koro wears around his neck (*reiputa*), the warrior's weapon (*taiha*), and the wood carving of the ancestor Paikea riding the whale. After Pai is found alive, the movie ends with a dramatic celebration of Pai's boat (finally finished by her father) being pushed to sea with men *and* women at the oars in honor of their new leader, Pai. Many are in traditional costumes, and all are chanting together.

6. *Visual style*: The incorporation of footage of live whales lends authenticity to the setting. Manmade whales were constructed for the beached scenes and are photographed to look real (through rain, quick shots, shadowed lighting). At several key moments the camera centers on Koro and Pai together, such as the final scene when she wears his *reiputa* as the new wise leader. Koro has come to terms with his conflict. Pai was the only youth, after all, who had genuinely wanted to learn the lessons he was teaching to the less-than-inspired boys.

7. *Sound track*: The film's original sound track was composed using traditional instruments and subtle techniques, such as the scene when Pai was riding the whale and diving deeper. At that climactic moment, the sound went almost silent, highlighting only what Pai could have heard under the water, just her and the whale, no music, only a few bubbles.

8. *Audience reception*: This coming-of-age movie with a female protagonist delivers an honest, simple story that evokes an unsentimental emotional response. The film received two major audience awards (Sundance and

Toronto) and an Oscar nomination for Keisha Castle-Hughes as Pai. It is a beautifully filmed story rated PG-13 that rivals familiar American stories with its universal theme. In a voice-over, Pai says, "I am not a prophet, but I know that our people will keep going forward all together, with all of our strength."

POPULAR CULTURE AND GRAPHIC NOVELS

Graphic novels are books whose format combines sequential art (cartoon panels) and text (word balloons) to tell a story that can stand alone as a single work. Comic books, by contrast, are shorter ephemera that usually tell one 16-page episode in a story arc. If the single comic issues are collected in a trade paperback under one title, the compilation is considered a graphic novel. However, except for superhero genre, most graphic novels originate as a complete story with an end. They are in fact novels. Creating graphic novels requires time and imagination as well as collaboration among many specialists besides author and illustrator, such as cover coordinators, inkers, and letterers.

For those unfamiliar with graphic novels, the word *graphic* may suggest violent or even lurid content. But *Merriam-Webster's* (2003) definition of *graphic* is "evoking a clear lifelike picture," thus indicating no pejorative denotation for the word. These longer narratives may be referred to as *comics*, and, generally speaking, the terms *graphic novels* and *comics* are used synonymously. More importantly, all graphic novels are not necessarily novels (fiction) but include titles in all genres. However, no matter the genre, most graphic novels are true narratives and do tell a story. Indeed, the more accurate term for this format is *graphic narrative*.

Developing a graphic novel collection has several advantages. As an achievable advocacy goal, giving young people "permission" to read comics supports and respects their choices and validates their responses to texts. Research on the benefits of reading graphic narratives continues to show positive results. In *The Power of Reading: Insights from the Research*, Stephen D. Krashen (2004: 102) writes, "[L]ong-term comic book readers do as much book reading as non-comic book readers. . . , and the results of several studies suggest they do more." Krashen (2004: 103) adds, "Comic books can play an important role in helping readers progress to the level where they can read and understand challenging texts." By reading one comic book per day, a young person would read "well over a half million words a year, half the average yearly volume of middle-class children" (p. 97). YAs who are avid fans of graphic novels spread the word about their favorite titles, thereby encouraging their friends to visit a library that selects and displays a graphic novel collection.

Parents also recognize the value of graphic novels. For example, Jerome Weeks, newspaper columnist and book reviewer, heard that his seventh-grade daughter won first place in her school's academic bowl. Weeks was surprised when she told him how she had prepared for the competition. His daughter had become a fan of Larry Gonick's (1991) history series, *The Cartoon History of the United States*. Weeks (2003: 10) notes, "Whoever first thought of using comic books to convey nonfiction will get a nice, big reward from me. Such books have intrigued my daughter with facts and history. I wish there were tons of these books for kids." In fact, along with the host of fiction titles, there are many excellent graphic nonfiction works geared for elementary, middle school, and high school readers.

Francisca Goldsmith (2002: 986) notes that graphic novels "invite critical discussion and analysis" and provide an opportunity for students to develop higher order thinking skills. Goldsmith's invitation to critical evaluation is supported by the legitimacy afforded to the genre by the National Book Foundation Award nomination of Gene Yang's (2006) *American Born Chinese*, the first graphic novel to be so honored by the foundation.

Every year fans of science fiction, fantasy, comics, and graphic novels attend Comic-Con, or the Comic Convention, held in San Diego, California. During these conventions, Hollywood writers and producers occasionally attended. It soon became clear to them that the wide popularity of the graphic narrative could provide a rich source for new story material for motion pictures. Although superhero comics have been made into films for several years, recent comics carried over to film are a testament to the power of story that lies within the pages of graphic novels. Without mentioning the many new superhero comics that have become movies, some graphic novels that became blockbuster films include the following:

Frank Miller's *300* (2007; directed by Jack Snyder)
Max Collins' *Road to Perdition* (2002; directed by Sam Mendes)
Frank Miller's *The Dark Night Returns* (2008; directed by Christopher Nolan)
Alan Moore's *V for Vendetta* (2006; directed by James McTeigue)
Alan Moore's *The League of Extraordinary Gentlemen* (2003; directed by Stephen Norrington)
Daniel Clowes' *Ghost World* (2001; directed by Terry Zwigoff)

Graphic Novels: Genre or Format?

YALSA's June 2002 preconference in Atlanta, "Getting Graphic @ Your Library," posed many questions about graphic novels: What are they? How should they be selected? What is the core secondary collection? However, one question seemed to be settled: Are graphic novels a *genre* or a *format*? Attendees were reminded by panelists and speakers that graphic novels were a format, not a genre. After all, there are titles in every genre represented in graphic novel format. A review of the literature, however, reveals that the question is less settled than may be

246 Critical Approaches to Young Adult Literature

thought. Some who refer to graphic novels *as a genre* include Kean (2003), Bilyeu (2004), Op de Beek (2004), Michaels (2004), Thompson (2007: 29), and Seyfried (2008). Some who refer to graphic novels *as a format* include Schwarz (2002), Reid (2002), Gorman (2008), Behler (2006), Brenner (2006), Campbell (2007), and Zvirin (2008).

If this difference of opinion were not enough to muddy the water, some critics refer to graphic novels as both genre and format (St. Lifer, 2002; McTaggart, 2005; Walliser, 2005; Baird and Jackson, 2007; Fialkoff, 2007). There is yet another group who refer to graphic novels as something other than a genre or a format. Michael Cart (2005: 1301) calls them "a literary art form." To some, graphic novels are a "category" (MacDonald, 2008: 34; Fleming, 2006: 26). Other labels include "a real and important literary niche unto themselves" (Michaels, 2004: 306) and "a new medium" (Campbell, 2007: 13).

Considering graphic novels to be a format might help promote them to those who are reluctant to give them a try. That is, audiobooks are a *format* (or medium) of fiction and nonfiction print books, and few would argue about their benefits to reader pleasure and circulation numbers. Like the medium it resembles (both are built on a storyboard), movies are a format (or medium), not a genre, in that many categories of films exist and compete for annual awards by their genre. It is tempting, however, to think of graphic novels as a genre while they are coming into their own. All graphic novels share comic conventions, techniques, terminology, and principles of sequential narration. By examining one of the finest examples of graphic novels, the debate over genre or format may be considered.

Response to Marjane Satrapi's Graphic Novel *Persepolis*

Marjane Satrapi's (2003) autobiography *Persepolis* shows the impact and influence that graphic narratives can bring to a factual story. Satrapi's book, set in the tumultuous years between the overthrow of the Shah of Iran and the Iran–Iraq War, is required reading for cadets of the class of 2006 at the United States Military Academy at West Point (Foroohar, 2005). Its choice is based in part on Satrapi's realistic portrayal of Iranians as individuals, her accurate description of Iran's religious history, and the "need for fresh ways to comment on the increasingly complex political and social issues of the day" (Foroohar, 2005).

Persepolis recalls Satrapi's life under two oppressive regimes and a major war. Marji's first ten years are spent in a progressive, well-educated, middle-class family. A bright, spirited girl, she comes of age after the Ayatollah gains power, and she rebels against his new set of strict religious laws that make no sense to her. In an early episode, immediately after their overly serious teacher announces that wearing of the veil is now compulsory, Marji and her friends are shown frolicking during recess, naively unaware of the dangers that lie ahead for them as female under the full control of an extremist regime.

Even as a little child Marji expected her parents to answer all of her questions: Why did her society have such rigid class boundaries? Why did the new state-sponsored religious schools teach the girls ideas that contradicted those in former textbooks without explanations? As a six-year-old whose goal was to become the first female prophet, Marji takes her religious faith seriously within a religiously complacent family. She writes her own "holy" book of rules following in the footsteps of her beloved Zarathustra. Her rule book highlights a precocious sense of social justice: "Everybody should have a car, all maids should eat at the table with others, and no old person should have to suffer," the favorite rule of her much-admired grandmother (p. 7). Marji chats nightly with God, who resembles Marx, she thinks, after she reads a comic book on famous philosophers.

After her Uncle Anoosh, a legendary Iranian revolutionary, returns home from exile, the two become fast friends and find comfort in each other's similarly rebellious natures. However, after Anoosh is arrested and executed, Marji repudiates God and orders him out of her life. Sad and angry, she cries, "And so I was lost, without any bearings" (p. 71), now bereft of her hero and her faith. One by one her beliefs, dreams, and goals evaporate under increasing oppression and the onset of war with Iraq. The universities are closed. Food and gas shortages plague their livelihood. Neighbors become spies. Hypocrites abound, Marji notices. The moral police (labeled "Guardians") accost her on the street for her "decadent" (e.g., Western) appearance. Families seek shelter in their basements during bombings. Her family tries to hold on to a few pleasures in life, such as tasting forbidden foods and drink, but they narrowly escape detection during one police intrusion, driving home the extremes to which the fanatical regime is willing to go to in order to enforce all restrictions.

She watches as friends and family members become exiles or victims of torture or execution. When she discovers her friend Neda's turquoise bracelet among the rubble after a bombing, she writes, "The bracelet was still attached to . . . I don't know what," followed by a silent panel of Marji's covering her eyes. The last panel of the vignette is drawn completely black. A caption indicates her thoughts: "No scream in the world could have relieved my suffering and my anger" (p. 142).

Following Neda's death, Marji says, "I was fourteen and a rebel. Nothing scared me anymore" (p. 143). Temperamentally curious, willful, and fearless, Marji enters full adolescence stronger and more outspoken than ever. After striking her cruel, abusive principal, Marji is expelled. Shortly after enrolling in a different school, she confronts her new teacher who informs the class there are no political prisoners under the Islamic Republic. Marji asserts, "We've gone from 300 prisoners under the Shah to 300,000 under your regime. How dare you lie to us like that?" (p. 144). Like observant teenagers the world over, Marji holds adults to very high standards of truthfulness, but in Iran her frank remarks come at a very high price.

Marji's parents realize she must leave Iran or she will inevitably put herself in mortal danger. To Marji such an idea is tantamount to desertion, or at least a cowardly act. Desperate to get through to her, Marji's mother angrily tells her exactly what happens to young girls who fall into the hands of the authorities. Because it is against the law to kill a virgin, "A Guardian of the revolution marries her and takes her virginity before executing her" (p. 145). By Iranian tradition, after the girl's execution her "husband" gives the parents a five dollar dowry "to make sure her awful fate is understood" (p. 146). With her mother's somber reality for young women in mind, Marji relents and departs for Europe alone and afraid.

Black-and-white drawings illustrate Marji's life, including scenes of family fun, pranks with friends, and adolescent concerns. But other scenes depict heinous acts of terrorism, such as the murder of Iranian citizens locked in a movie theater then deliberately set on fire, with the horror etched on each victim's face. In another panel, several 13-year-old boys, enticed into the army with "golden" keys to the kingdom, perish in a minefield explosion. The simple, woodcut-like drawings (resembling Russian nesting egg dolls) belie the book's complex theme of coming of age in the midst of great conflict. Marji's story transcends regional details to show the struggles of a child who tries to understand a society that runs counter to what she believes is morally right.

For *Persepolis* Satrapi received the Alex Award (in 2004), *Library Journal*'s Best Book of the Year (2004), the *New York Times* Notable Books of the Year (2003), and many other awards. Her *Persepolis 2* (2004) and *Embroideries* (2005) complete her autobiographical trilogy. In 2008 an animated movie from her graphic novels was released that tells Satrapi's story taken from *Persepolis 1* and *2*. The film was France's entry for the 2008 Academy Awards Best Foreign Film.

Popular Culture and Manga

One of the most popular forms of graphic narratives is *manga*, the Japanese word for comic book. There are manga titles and series in historical fiction, fantasy, biography, mystery, school life, and so forth. Japanese of all ages read manga and become lifetime readers of their favorite writers and illustrators. The universal appeal of these narratives derives in part from their stylized characters whose appearance and features indicate no specific nationality, ethnic group, or race. The characters often look almost androgynous, thus inviting readers of any gender. Manga's humor and adventure also account for its widespread popularity. Japan turned its manga into film earlier than comics became movies in the West, and they are called *anime*.

Criteria for Selecting and Evaluating Graphic Novels

To evaluate graphic narratives and manga by genre, librarians should use the same criteria recommended for evaluation of a specific genre (as detailed in

Chapter 4). Consideration of the quality of the art is important, and each criterion should be analyzed by the art and the text in each work. The annotations that conclude this chapter contain examples of works that successfully combine art and words to produce a new format that excites and informs young people.

ANNOTATED BIBLIOGRAPHY OF GRAPHIC NOVELS BY GENRE

Adventure

Robinson, James. 2002. *Leave It to Chance: A Shaman's Rain.* Orange, CA: Image Comics. Grades 3 and up.

Determined to prove she's ready to train as falconer protector, Chance and her dinky dragon sidekick confront shape-shifters, a kidnapping, Toad God, and goblins, along with evil politicians who plan to destroy the city she vows to defend. Chance's mystery adventure is appropriate for all ages. It fits well with a study of empowered female protagonists in other graphic narratives.

Biography

Brown, Chester. 2003. *Louis Riel: A Comic-Strip Biography.* Montreal, Canada: Drawn and Quarterly. Grades 9–12.

Reminiscent of American abolitionist John Brown, Canada's folk hero Louis Riel seeks justice for his Native people but fails. Later the rebels beg him to return to lead yet another insurrection soon doomed by betrayal, railroad barons, religious fanaticism, and madness. This thoroughly researched biography (e.g., extensive notes, maps, bibliography, and index) on a hero largely unknown in the United States can be used as a model for research on any charismatic or rebellious leader in world history. Young people can use graphic organizers to compare the leaders in such topics as time periods, reasons for rebellion, their opponents, the issues, and the outcomes.

Contemporary Realistic Fiction

Thompson, Craig. 2003. *Blankets: An Illustrated Novel.* Marietta, GA: Top Shelf. Adult book for YAs.

A teen struggles against his overbearing parents, school bullies, and prevailing attitudes that ridicule his drawing talent, but his first love makes him a quilt that comforts him as he moves toward independence. YAs can create a graphic organizer (such as an arc) that traces Craig's development from shy conformist to independent YA.

Fantasy

Smith, Jeff. 1996. *Bone: Out of Boneville.* Columbus, OH: Cartoon Books. Grades 5 and up.

Cast out of town by an angry mob, Fone Bone and two cousins become separated, forcing Fone to enter uncharted land where he makes friends with a dragon and a mother possum but is threatened by vicious rat creatures led by Kingdok and Death himself. This volume demonstrates a comic art technique that relies entirely on dialogue to tell the story (no captions or narrators to give background information). Young people could adapt a folktale, using the fast-moving technique of putting all the text in word balloons (dialogue) and omitting captions.

Folktale

Spiegelman, Art and Francoise Mouly, eds. 2000. *Folktales and Fairy Tale Funnies.* **New York: HarperCollins. All ages.**

Calling on artists to interpret, retell, or spoof traditional stories, Spiegelman and Mouly offer a variety from offbeat ghoulish spin-offs to fractured tales using old-fashioned or retro motifs, activity pages, and a "Road Rage" board game. This is the first volume of the "Little Lit" series that appeals to children and adults with its humorously imaginative retellings. In book circles, YAs can discuss how art and style affect a story whenever a folktale is recast in contemporary times.

Historical Fiction

Miller, Frank, and Lynn Varley. 1999. *300.* **Milwaukie, OR: Dark Horse Comics. Adult book for YAs.**

In 480 BCE, King Leonidas and his small band of Spartan warriors entrap King Xerxes's thousands of Persian soldiers within "The Hot Gates" corridor, turning the Battle of Thermopylae into a symbol of extraordinary courage. Miller and Varley's book portrays the origins of democracy and its behind-the-scenes politics as the great Spartan ruler is destroyed by a single Spartan spy. Readers can focus on the bold, powerful artwork in this oversized book to analyze and discuss how its style and format reinforce the book's history and theme of the brutality of war and the courage of a committed few.

Manga

Clamp. 2001. *Clover 1.* **Los Angeles, CA: TokyoPop. Grades 8–12.**

In this first of a four-part story, General Ko coerces Kazuhiko into delivering into his hands a beautiful young waif whose status as a four-leaf clover makes her invaluable to two powerful, warring parties. This understated, black and white minimalist styled manga stands out from most manga titles that are full of action and fast-paced dialogue. As young people complete the first volume they can discuss any unanswered questions and then return to the panel art and text to see if some of the answers lie within a closer second reading.

Mystery

Geary, Richard. 2003. *The Mystery of Mary Rogers.* **New York: NBM. Grades 9–12.**

Before the days of police departments, New York City in 1841 relied on its journalists to investigate the murder of Mary Rogers, whose case started a frenzy of competition for the most sensational headlines and exploited her life and death with tabloid theories in this true-crime mystery. Mary's death inspired Edgar Allan Poe (1938) to "solve" her murder by writing "The Mystery of Marie Roget" set in Paris. (In fact, her murder remains an unsolved case.) After reading Poe's story, students can create a graphic organizer that compares and contrasts Poe's version with Geary's version.

Nonfiction

Ottaviani, Jim. 2001. *Two-Fisted Science: Stories About Scientists.* **Ann Arbor, MI: G. T. Labs. Grades 9 and up.**

This book recounts the lives of several scientists. In the chapter on Richard Feynman (an energetic and witty professor of physics and a Nobel Prize winner), the scientist falls in love, loses a beloved wife, and assists in one of the most important assignments in United States history (the Manhattan Project at Los Alamos). His figure as a character connects to the stories of the other scientists (Galileo versus the Vatican, Niels Bohr, Einstein) in this anthology of scientists (written by Ottaviani but illustrated by different artists) who stood on the shoulders of giants. Each section concludes with notes and references. Readers interested in the history of science may pursue more background on a particular scientist, or they can discuss Galileo's story (he died blind and under house arrest in 1642), which ends in 1992—350 years after his death—when the Vatican officially apologized for censuring him.

Poetry

Edgar Allan Poe. "The Bells." 2001. Adapted by Rafael Nieves. *Rosebud Graphic Classics: Edgar Allan Poe.* **Mount Horeb, WI: Eureka. Grades 7 and up.**

"The Bells" is unabridged but narrated by Poe himself, who observes the tragic story-frame of a newly married girl who dies in a fire. Thus, using words and illustrations, Nieves creates a new and imaginative context for a classic poem. Young people can work in teams to brainstorm how a non-narrative favorite poem could be reset and illustrated as a graphic narrative.

Short Stories

Hirsch, Karen D., ed. 1997. *Mind Riot: Coming of Age in Comix.* **New York: Aladdin. Grades 7 and up.**

Skateboarding mayhem, shoplifting remorse, challenging bullies, and falling in love are a few of the subjects offered by different writers centered on life as a teenager. This is a good example in one volume of the wide variety of art, storytelling, and styles with a common theme in graphic narratives. Young people can select a favorite traditional short story and design a storyboard as a shared bulletin board display.

Wordless

Kochalka, James. 2000. *Monkey vs. Robot.* **Marietta, GA: Top Shelf. Grades 6 and up.**

Pitted against a factory of robots, the monkeys must fight for their existence against the more powerful and numerous machines. Using a palette of greens and white, this part fable, part allegory shows that the battle of nature versus machine continues to rage on and that nature seems to win in this episode. As environmental issues become more topical, YAs can create a poster inspired from the issues addressed in the graphic novel (e.g., industrial waste, destruction of rain forests, endangered species, and the paradoxical nature of progress).

REFERENCES AND SUGGESTIONS FOR FURTHER READING

Alvermann, Donna, and Margaret C. Hagood. 2000. "Critical Media Literacy: Research, Theory, and Practice in 'New Times.'" *Journal of Educational Research* 93, no. 3 (January–February): 193–206.

Baird, Zahra M., and Tracey Jackson. 2007. "Got Graphic? More Than Just Superheroes in Tights." *Children and Libraries* 5, no. 1 (Spring): 4–7.

Behler, Anne. 2006. "Getting Started with Graphic Novels." *Reference and User Services Quarterly* 46, no. 2 (Winter): 16–21.

Bilyeu, Suzanne. 2004. *Literary Cavalcade* 56, no. 8 (May): T-3.

Brenner, Robin. 2004. "The Lair." Available at: www.lair.com.

Brenner, Robin. 2004. "No Flying, No Tights: Reviewing Graphic Novels for Teens." Available at: www.noflyingnotights.com.

Brenner, Robin. 2004. "Sidekicks." Available at: www.noflyingnotights.com/sidekicks.

Brenner, Robin. 2006. "FAQs: Graphic Novels 101." *Horn Book* 82, no. 2 (March): 123–125.

Brill, J.M., D. Kim, and R.M. Branch. 2000. "Visual Literacy Defined." In *Exploring the Visual Future*, edited by R.E. Griffen, V.S. Williams, and J. Lee, pp. 9–15. Blacksburg, VA: The International Visual Literacy Association.

Campbell, Eddie. 2007. "What Is a Graphic Novel?" *World Literature Today* 81, no. 1 (March–April): 12–15.

Caro, Nikki. *Whale Rider*. Produced by Tim Sanders, John Barnett, and Frank Hubner. 105 min. NewMarket Films, 2002. DVD.

Cart, Michael. 2005. "A Graphic Novel Explosion." *Booklist* 101, no. 4 (March 15): 1301.

Costanzo, William V. 2004. *Great Films and How to Teach Them.* Urbana, IL: National Council of Teachers of English.

Fialkoff, Francine. 2007. "Turf Building." *Library Journal* 132, no. 5 (March 15): 8.

Fleming, Robert. 2006. "Beyond Funny." *Black Issues Book Review* 8, no. 4 (July–August): 26–29.

Foroohar, Rana. 2005. "Evolution of a Genre." *Newsweek International.* August 22, 2005. Available at: www.newsweek.com.

Goldsmith, Francisca. 2002. "YA Talk." *Booklist* 98, no. 12 (February): 986.

Gonick, Larry. 1991. *The Cartoon History of the United States.* New York: HarperPerennial.

Gorman, Michele. 2008. "Getting Graphic." *Library Media Connection* 26, no. 6 (March): 38.

Groening, Matt. 1989–2008. *The Simpsons.* Fox Television Entertainment.

Kean, Danuta. 2003. "Graphic Reading." *Bookseller* no. 5100 (October 24): 22–25.

Kellner, Douglas, and Jeff Share. 2005. "Toward Critical Media Literacy: Core Concepts, Debates, Organizations, and Policy." *Discourse: Studies in the Culture Politics of Education* 26, no. 3 (September): 369–386.

Krashen, Steven. 2004. *The Power of Reading: Insights from the Research.* Westport, CT: Heinemann.

MacDonald, Heidi. 2008. "Comics Class of '08." *Publisher's Weekly* 255, no. 18 (May 5): 34–36.

McTaggart, Jacquie. 2005. "Using Comics and Graphic Novels to Enchant Reluctant Readers." *Reading Today* 23, no. 2 (October–November): 46.

Merriam-Webster's Collegiate Dictionary, 11th ed. 2003. Springfield, MA: Merriam-Webster.

Michaels, Julia. 2004. "Pulp Fiction." *Horn Book* 80, no. (May–June): 299–306.

Op de Beek, Nathalie. 2004. "Growing a Genre." *Publisher's Weekly* 251, no. 49 (December 6): 29.

Poe, Edgar Allan. 1938. "The Mystery of Marie Roget." In *The Complete Tales and Poems of Edgar Allan Poe*, pp. 169–207. New York: Modern Library.

Reid, Calvin. 2002. "Press Launches iBooks." *Publisher's Weekly* 249, no. 45 (November 11): 15.

Richmond, Ray, and Antonia Coffman. 1997. *The Simpsons: A Complete Guide to Our Favorite Family*. New York: HarperPerennial.

Satrapi, Marjane. 2003. *Persepolis*. New York: Pantheon Books.

Schwarz, Gretchen E. 2002. "Graphic Novels for Multi-Cultural Literacies." *Journal of Adolescent and Adult Literacy* 46, no. 3 (November): 262–263.

Seyfried, Jonathan. 2008. "Graphic Novels as Educational Heavyweights." *Knowledge Quest* 36, no. 3 (January–February): 44–45.

St. Lifer, Evan. 2002. "Graphic Novels, Seriously." *School Library Journal* 48, no. 8 (August): 9.

Thoman, Elizabeth. 1999. "Skills and Strategies for Media Education." *Educational Leadership* 56, no. 5 (February): 50–54.

Thompson, Terry. 2007. "Embracing Reluctance." *Library Media Connection* 25, no. 4 (January): 29.

Valdez, Joan, and Jeanne Crow. 1973. *The Media Works*. New York: Cebco Pflaum.

Walliser, Karen. 2005. "Graphic Novels." *School Libraries of Canada* 25, no. 1: 18–23.

Weeks, Jerome. 2003. *Dallas Morning News*. "Books" (August 3): 29A.

Yang, Gene. 2006. *American Born Chinese*. New York: First Second.

Zvirin, Stephanie. 2008. "More on the Graphic Format." *Booklinks* 17, no. 5 (May): 12–13.

Chapter 12

Reader-Response Criticism

INTRODUCTION TO READER-RESPONSE CRITICISM

Reader-response criticism developed as a critical approach to literature from Louise Rosenblatt's (1938) transactional approach to reading. She chose the term *transaction* as a counterbalance to *interaction*, indicating the equal give and take between the reader and the text. She credits John Dewey for introducing the term *transaction* as an experiential concept appropriate to the social, the individual, and the creative acts of reading. She offered the transactional approach up to the world as "a defense of democracy" (Probst, 2005: 13), envisioning the individual reader as a unique contributor to the social dialogue that is democracy in action. Thus, Louise Rosenblatt's reader-response transactional theory has a place in every library.

To define the adult role in nurturing young readers' responses occurs at the risk of squelching a response altogether or, worse, subverting the response with bias and expectations. The response must occur in its own time by a reflective reader who is encouraged only to explore and imagine. The adult role in the process is a highly intuitive one that is better seen as an intention rather than a process or an outcome, which can be more elusive than the expectation that a horse led to water will drink or swim. An adult can intellectually place the young adult (YA) reader at the center of the text, yet more and less are often required to press toward a rewarding understanding of the work. One concrete approach may be to view the adult role in YA reader responses as a set of *progressive stances* through which the adult's distance to the reader diminishes:

1. *Invisible stance:* The YA reader reflects and interacts with peers as suggested in the following open-ended questions. These questions seek not to limit or define an interpretation but rather to expand the potential interpretations before textual judgments are formed.

255

   a. Group members share a "memory or story the [work] evoked," taking
      time to discuss the memories or stories" but without an obligation to tell
      more than they wish to tell.
   b. What do these individual stories "have in common? How do they differ?
      With what aspect of human experience do they all deal?"
   c. "Did the recalling and sharing of your own stories shed any light on the
      [work]? Did you see anything more clearly in the work as a result of
      telling and hearing the other stories? Did the discussion change your
      feelings about the work in any way?"
   d. "What were the pleasures or pains of the reading, the storytelling, and
      the subsequent discussion? Did you observe anything new about your-
      self, or if not new, then more clearly or in a new light?"
   e. "Did the activity provide you with any insight into the work? Did you
      find any satisfaction or pleasure in what you have learned about [the
      group's members]?"
   f. "... [S]hare your readings of the work, your stories, and your discussion
      with another discussion group. Do you observe any similarities or dif-
      ferences in the paths the two discussions followed?"
   g. "Finally, what inferences can you draw about the role of the reader in
      creating meaning from a text?" (adapted by Latrobe and Drury from
      Robert Probst, 2004: 21)

2. *Unobtrusive stance*: Young people are provided an opportunity to discuss
   their puzzlements and to scan the text, reconciling different impressions
   but not leaping to an interpretation.

3. *Collaborative stance*: YAs may independently reflect, with pencil in hand.
   Knowing the basic elements of literature (e.g., plot, character, setting) and
   their conventions, YAs should be self-directed to a conscious transaction
   with the text. In discussions with peers and adults, they may pose their own
   questions, seeking to justify a textual interpretation with their initial emotional response.

4. *Co-critical stance*: Readers are at the center of their engagement with the
   text, the context, the author, and other readers. They may have conversations with the adult (often in a prompting role) as well as peers, and yet it
   is the reader who identifies the issues to be considered and the critical
   lenses through which to examine them.

Thus, across these stances, true and honest response requires at first the
adult's respectful distance, and then the adult becomes more engaged as YAs'
responses become more analytical. However, these four stances are not a routine
but are offered as a way of looking at an adult's role in transactional reading.

An Adult Listener's Uncritical Response to an Audio Recording of Philip Pullman's *The Golden Compass*

Those who have the privilege to interact with YAs and their literature intuitively realize that they simultaneously experience YA literature on multiple levels: that of adult reader immersed in a story that may be more or less captivating; that of a YA of a certain developmental age, cultural context, or focused attention; and that of adult reader who is weighing how to promote the book with potential YA readers and how to encourage thoughtful responses after YA readers have finished a book and closed its covers. Such adults gain broad experience and wisdom over time but never can know a YA reading experience. Therefore, adult readers must trust the truth in their own reflections, such as the one in the following narrative in which an adult anonymous reader tells about his first encounter with Philip Pullman's (2004) *The Golden Compass*, heard as a CD audio recording:

> I am typically a reflective reader, but my personal reading was recently illuminated by my experiencing story in a different format. I had planned a road trip that included two 7–8 hour driving segments, and, as an afterthought to the planning, I took along *The Golden Compass* in audio format. The recording was a set of nine CD disks that I had purchased at the last minute from a bookstore. I knew about the work and its respected author, although fantasy is not my favorite genre. The cover art portrayed a young Lyra on the back of a polar bear. And, the nine disks were a mystery that held hope for an adventure yet dread of a series of seemingly disconnected magical events.
>
> The story began, and Philip Pullman was the narrator. He had a forceful voice, and the other readers' voices commanded attention and quickly led me into a story where a young Lyra was exploring a forbidden dining room at Oxford University. She miscalculated the risks of being discovered, by chance saw the apparent dispensing of a poison, possessed a chimera-like pet who was in the form of a moth, hid in a wardrobe which she briefly left to warn Lord Asriel about the poison, overheard his presentation about a strange dust in the north, and fell asleep before the end of the evening.
>
> As my car traveled with the traffic down the highway, I suspended disbelief for a fantasy that stretched across three volumes, that lacked a significant YA character, and that focused on a young girl, a variety of animals (daemons and otherwise), and an assortment of significant adult characters of mixed motives. I had entered a classic fantasy structure: an immature heroine from a mysterious ancestry and an uncertain mix of good and evil. With the novel's many significant adult characters, I came to understand why it had had a strong adult reading audience and could imagine that YAs would also be drawn into a world taken so seriously by the author and the adult characters yet not put off by the perspective of a child.
>
> I engaged and disengaged with the story as the disks were exchanged and as the trip itself intervened with stops along the way. I became more accustomed to the

UK English but missed not seeing the unfamiliar names in print, and I lacked a sense of the pacing of the story which unfolded outside numbered pages. Also, noteworthy language and events sped past my attention and were not tracked by a page corner folded or a note tucked between pages. Also, I developed an awareness that my interpretations of the story were shaped by its readers and that my interpretations of the setting increased in scope to include not only southern England and London but also a mythical North and a cosmos that allowed good and evil to compete in multiple dimensions.

Though aware of the characters' individual voices and emotions/attitudes, I did not imagine their visual images as clearly. Was that difference a function of the audio format? And, as the trip defined breaks in the story, I picked up the continuing threads with more effort as a listener than I usually did as a reader because I could not glance to the paragraph above or to previously marked passages for context or structure.

The conclusion of the recording extended past the long weekend road trip, covering several more days of brief trips around town. The brief trips altered the pace of my involvement as the recording drew to its ending, and, having driven through one red light, I realized that my attention to the text was less focused in town than on the highway.

Reflecting on the process of hearing the story (as opposed to decoding and imagining the story) seemed to offer an unexpected view on the traditional reading process. For example, the two central bears are delineated characters in my mind. One bear is beloved by Lyra, who tricks the second bear through his profound and hollow pride. Yet, I cannot spell or pronounce either bear's name. I cannot visualize any part of their names, which now exist for me only as jumbled syllables. And, despite this limited grasp of the text, I am more motivated to continue the second volume than to listen again to the recording or to read the text of the first volume. That is, I am emotionally satisfied with my understanding of the story and sufficiently motivated as reader to continue with the two later volumes in a different (print) format. And, I will always question what my first response to the work would have been if I had read, not listened to it. Or, was the superior quality of the audio format greater than the quiet words on the page?

Thus, I realize the text (even the "unabridged text") and the reader (even the same reader) are subject to many variables, and the same story revisited by the same reader becomes a revised story. (Anonymous. Reprinted with permission.)

Perspectives on the Reader in Reader-Response Theory

Louise Rosenblatt's position on reader and text remained in the background during the reign of New Criticism, or *formalism*, the work-itself-only theory. *Reader response* as an umbrella term began to be used during the 1970s to designate the different literary theories that developed as a reaction against New Criticism. As Walter Slatoff (1970: 50) wrote of the then-prevailing formalism, the reader had been "ignored" or "even defined out of existence." Slatoff (1970: 4) complained, "If one were to judge from the dominant modes of literary study and literary theory and from much of the teaching of literature, it would seem as though readers and the act or experience of reading were peripheral if not entirely irrelevant considerations." Within the academy, instructors began offering new theories that focused on readers, the nature of language itself, and the reading experience. Although the text was still front and center in some theories, either the reader or reading began to be considered important subjects for study and discussion. The switch of critical attention from the work itself to the reader/reading marked a major change in literary criticism and ultimately in pedagogy. Reader response became the focal point of those whose ideas were built on theoretical readers.

The first comprehensive empirical study to record and analyze reader responses was I.A. Richards' (1929) *Practical Criticism: A Study of Literary Judgment*. For years Richards had experimented with his undergraduate students by giving them several poems to read and to respond to. Richards presented each poem without its title or author's name, and with up-to-date spellings and punctuation to keep each poem free from any historical clues. Richards primarily wanted to find the right method for teaching students how to develop more discriminating tastes in their reading but was still surprised to discover "the astonishing variety of human responses" (p. 11). Ironically, it was the New Critics who took Richards' study and made it their own—close readings of literary works with few, if any, outside sources to guide readers as they analyzed and interpreted works while ignoring the reader response and the authorial intent.

One early theorist of reader response includes Wolfgang Iser, whose work was based in part on *phenomenology*, "the philosophical tendency which stresses the central role of the perceiver in determining [a text's] meaning" (Selden, 1986: 110). Iser (1974) proposed the idea of *The Implied Reader*, one who is active as he or she fills gaps, blanks, or inevitable omissions in any given text. For instance, when readers approach a short story written by Ernest Hemingway (1925, 1996) (e.g., "Indian Camp"), they may feel that something seems missing from the narrative, or, as in a frequently heard response, "Nothing *happens* in this story!" Iser's theory suggests that readers must fill in the gaps that Hemingway's style inevitably leaves. Knowledge about Iser's theory helps prepare YAs to be alert for Hemingway's "tip-of-the-iceberg" style of writing. Also important to Iser's theory is the idea of established conventions that signal, guide, and direct the implied reader through the many questions that can arise when reading a text. The reading process is "steered" by the text's "repertoire of familiar literary patterns and recurrent literary themes" (Iser, 1980: 62). Iser was among the first to emphasize the reader's role in literary criticism and in the instruction of literature.

Like Iser, Jonathan Culler (1980: 102) sees not a flesh-and-blood reader but a theoretical *competent reader*, one who exercises "implicit understanding of operations of literary discourse which tells one what to look for." The competent reader becomes skilled through years of participation in experiences in school where certain modes of reading are taught (Culler 1980: 104). In other words, young people learn how to read literature from their public school teachers and from their college instructors, all of whom provide opportunities for their students to practice and assimilate *the language* of reading literature. Culler (1987: 285) notes that a competent reader is guided by expectations, such as thematic unity in a poem, conventions, and other "interpretive requirements which the poem imposes upon him," putting the emphasis on the reader but also on the impositions of the text.

Stanley Fish shares Rosenblatt's belief that meaning is derived from the reading experience, a transaction between reader and text. However, he acknowledges (somewhat like Iser and Culler) that the reader is no ordinary reader. Instead, Fish (1980a: 167) identifies the *informed reader* as one whose response is dictated in part by his or her "*interpretive community.*" As a member of a reading community, an informed reader will bring certain assumptions that help to determine the meanings of texts. Seeing that reading is a very active event, Fish (1980b: 83) writes, "Somehow when we put a book down, we forget that while we were reading, it was moving (pages turning, lines receding into the past) and forget too that *we* were moving with it," thereby stressing the active nature of the transactional process.

THE YA COMMUNITY OF READERS

Young readers, somehow, glimpse not only in my novels but in those of other YA writers . . . things that echo in their own lives. . . . YA writers and their young readers are collaborators in a sense, joined in a partnership that sustains them both.

—Robert Cormier (1997: xxii)

Writers, secondary and college students and teachers, librarians, and publishers are all collaborators in the YA community of readers. The nature of the YA community remains a subject of debate along many lines, including, What is YA literature? Should YA authors have a theoretical YA in mind when they write? In consideration of reader-response theory, one scholar who remains aware of the flesh-and-blood reader along with the theoretical reader in constructing his reading model is Peter Rabinowitz. Although he does not address the subject of YA readers in his work, Rabinowitz's theory of reading applies to even the youngest readers. In *Before Reading: Narrative Conventions and the Politics of Interpretation*, Rabinowitz (1987) centers his theory on the learned strategies that readers bring with them at the starting point of their reading of a text. Rabinowitz (1987: 26–27) recognizes the complexity of interpretation, which he sees as "an intuitive mix of experience and faith, knowledge and hunch—plus a certain amount of luck."

Unlike New Critics and others who subscribe to the *intentional fallacy*, or the notion that it is an error to think that one can ever arrive at an author's intentional meaning, Rabinowitz (1987: 30) maintains, "The initial question most commonly asked of a literary text in our culture is, What is the author saying?" To answer this question, Rabinowitz believes that readers bring presuppositions to every text they read (hence the title, *Before Reading*) a prior knowledge of literary conventions and reading principles that influence a reader's interpretation and evaluation of texts. He believes that readers transform, or shape, a text as they respond to it, based in part on assumptions built on shared principles of reading.

Each reader also brings a varying amount of understanding of literary conventions to the reading of a work, and these conventions inform reading in complex ways. Rabinowitz maintains that literary conventions are the property of communities rather than individuals and that those conventions are socially constructed concepts available to both authors and readers. However, individuals still experience and interpret a work in their own ways. Young people who are avid readers of science fiction might not be able to verbalize the conventions of their favorite genre. But they know how to apply the implicit principles of the genre (along with the conventions they have gleaned from their reading of all other genres) before they even begin to read a science fiction novel.

PETER RABINOWITZ'S FOUR PRINCIPLES OF READING

In constructing his theory of reading, Rabinowitz (1987) arrived at four meta-rules, or underlying principles, that readers take into account as they transact with a text. Within each of the four principles he identifies a variety of more specific rules that further describe the reading principle. Generally, the principles move from concrete to abstract and from the beginning of a reading to the end. The four principles are

1. notice (p. 53),
2. signification (p. 76),
3. configuration (p. 110), and
4. coherence (p. 141).

Rabinowitz's goal is not to present an exhaustive or even a comprehensive model of the reading experience. Instead, his aim is to provide a tool for readers to use before, during, and after reading.

Principle of Notice

Rabinowitz says that interpretation starts with the most noticeable details of a work. He identifies the reader's paying attention to the most important details as the principle of *notice* (Rabinowitz, 1987: 53). There are far more details in a novel than a reader can keep track of. Do all of the details in a novel bear equal weight? In order to tame the large amount of features in a text, readers apply a hierarchy of importance to certain details. One way to achieve this hierarchy is to apply the principles of *privileged positions* wherein certain details gain special attention because of their placement in the text (p. 58). Privileged positions include

- the title of a work (or of a chapter or section) (p. 59),
- first and last sentences (p. 60),
- repetitions (p. 54),
- ruptures (disruptions) (p. 65), and
- extratextual features (epigraphs, cover, blurbs, typographical features) (p. 56).

The title of a book tells the reader which character (*When Zachary Beaver Came to Town*), which place (*145th Street*), and which time (*Fever, 1793*) to concentrate on. Some titles signal the mode or tone that a reader should expect (*The Earth, My Butt and Other Big Round Things*). Titles may allude to other books or authors and alert readers to possible thematic tie-ins. The contemporary mystery *The Curious Incident of the Dog in the Night-time* comes from a line that Sherlock Holmes speaks in the short story, "Silver Blaze," and to the protagonist Christopher's favorite author, Sir Arthur Conan Doyle. *Making up Megaboy* refers to the structure of the novel with its multiple (biased) points of view that make up, or "create," the protagonist who never tells his own story. Sometimes titles reverse expectations, such as *This Is What I Did*, wherein the protagonist reveals that his great sin was that he did *nothing*. Many titles signal a book's theme: *catalyst* is a term in chemistry, the protagonist Kate's favorite subject, but it is also the term given to a person who can change others in unexpected ways. Readers begin to make note of the places in the story where the title is repeated or variations of the title are given. Titles, then, can indicate where readers should concentrate their attention as well as provide a core around which to organize their (future or final) interpretation (p. 61).

By their very placement, first and last sentences (and beginnings and endings) ask for our attention. "Once upon a time" conveys a host of expectations on readers of all ages. In Brady Udall's (2001: 13) *The Miracle Life of Edgar Mint*, the narrator begins, "If I could tell you only one thing about my life it would be this: when I was seven years old the mailman ran over my head." Famous last lines include the narrator's (maddeningly) open-ended question in Terry Trueman's (2000: 114) *Stuck in Neutral*, "What will my dad do? Whatever it is, in another moment I'll be flying free. Either way, whatever he does, I'll be soaring." Laurie Halse Anderson's (1999) *Speak* shows how a first and a last sentence may create a frame for a story. The first sentence reads, "It is my first morning of high school. I have seven new notebooks, a skirt I hate, and a stomachache."

The last sentence reads, "'Me: Let me tell you about it,'" expressing the reader's relief along with Melinda's, as she has earned the right to tell her tale. Last sentences actually come into play as a scaffold in the final interpretation of the work as a whole (see later discussion of the principle of coherence), but, as in *Speak*, they may complete a frame around the narrative with a possible connection to the book's theme.

Repetitions of titles, objects, phrases, words, motifs, and so forth provide an author with a way to emphasize one idea over others. A reader notices the host of references to birds in Almond's (1999) *Skellig* (the eponymous birdlike creature), all ultimately tying in to the novel's rebirth theme. In Anderson's (2006) *The Astonishing Life of Octavian Nothing*, the twin themes of freedom and slavery remain in the forefront with repetitions of words or synonyms such as in posted notices of runaway slaves, a catalogue of torture instruments used on slaves, Octavian's "belonging" to all the scientists at the College and seen as another specimen for study, and notices of slave sales that emphasize the "fine" Negro specimens (p. 41) alongside fine horses.

Rabinowitz (1987) notes that readers tend to skim over smooth, even passages of text while any disruption calls for attention. He refers to this rule of notice as *rupture* when the story contains disruptions, changes, shifts, or breaks in genre conventions. Ruptures within a text may be straightforward and include such features as blatantly irrelevant details (p. 66) that later become relevant. If a character behaves or speaks inappropriately within the world of the narrative, readers will notice. Near the end of *The Astonishing Life of Octavian Nothing*, Dr. Trefusis refuses to give Octavian any tea while Gitney and Sharpe are drinking theirs, and the reader is surprised, as Trefusis is the only living character who has been kind to Octavian. Soon we learn that Trefusis has poisoned the tea, giving him and Octavian time to escape. Readers also attend to shifts or disruptions in the direction of the plot, of the narrator's point of view, and of a character's perspective (e.g., when a teacher jolts a YA protagonist out of a daydream by asking a question).

The *extratextual features* of a book, such as its cover, blurbs, and epigraph grab the reader's attention. The best covers do more than attract; they also signal genre, theme, and/or atmosphere. The format features of Tonya Hurley's (2008) *Ghostgirl* signal its genre, subgenre, mode, and subject with its small black coffin-shaped book (no dust jacket), with the center illustration of a black silhouette of a girl lying in a pink and white coffin, with a pink ribbon that says, "Rest in Popularity," trumpeting its satire of gothic stories about teenagers who die but then come to "life" to tell their story. Some younger readers might ignore an epigraph, but more experienced readers assume that the author has something important to say by placing a quotation in such a privileged position of notice. *Ghostgirl* begins with the well-known quotation from Oscar Wilde, "The only thing worse than being talked about is not being talked about," echoing Charlotte's main crisis, being invisible to the popular crowd.

Readers also pay attention to *typographical features* of a text (e.g., sections in italics, changes in fonts, illustrations). The use of typographical features and unusual layouts has become commonplace in contemporary YA literature with novels written in multiple formats (*Making up Megaboy*), novels in verse (*Out of the Dust*), novels in e-mails (*ttyl*), and genre blends (*Names Will Never Hurt Me*). When a text deviates from its genre, readers can be jolted by the change. The classic example is Emily Dickinson's poetry, a style in which readers expect a word that perfectly rhymes but instead they hear a startlingly near-rhyming word choice that demands their special attention.

Principle of Signification

The principle of *signification* tells readers how to deal with the details garnered from *notice* and how to designate larger meanings to those details (Rabinowitz, 1987: 44). Much of literary criticism consists of applying the principles of signification (p. 78). The principles of signification are

- figurative language (p. 78),
- source (who is speaking? how reliable is the speaker?) (p. 79), and
- snap moral judgments (p. 84).

Principles of *figurative language* include recognizing the significance of the metaphors, similes, and symbols that registered as important details with a reader. Most readers have had years of experience in identifying and in creating their own examples of figurative language and know that they usually point to major ideas in a literary work. In Alexie's (2007) *The Absolutely True Diary of a Part-time Indian*, the narrator Junior reveals, "My mother and father are the twin suns around which I orbit and my world would EXPLODE without them" (p. 11). He emphasizes the importance that art plays in his life when he says, "my cartoons are little lifeboats" (p. 7). In some cases, readers may observe possible metaphorical meanings in a character's name (Stephanie in *Seventeen: A Novel* stands for a modern day Greek goddess Persephone), in the name of a locale (*The Secret Garden*), or in the title of a work (*Shattering Glass*, with its ironic meanings of the protagonist's last name and in the construction and then destruction of his persona). Thus, readers have garnered details that suggest more than their literal meanings, and through signification they begin to designate metaphorical meanings to them.

Principles of *source* have to do with knowing who the narrator is or the speaker in a text (e.g., who is speaking in this passage?). There are principles that readers intuitively know that indicate when a change in speaker takes place. A story told in third person omniscient may occasionally shift to a limited third person revealing more about one specific character. Although some readers may sometimes not recognize all unreliable narrators, they eventually begin to sense that something is *definitely* wrong with first person narrator Keir Sarafian in Chris Lynch's (2005) *Inexcusable*, in part because Keir states again and again that he is not a bad person. Readers pick up on irony through exaggerations, statements that are obviously in error, and conflicts between the beliefs stated in a text and the beliefs reasonable people believe (Rabinowitz, 1987: 80). When Keir admits without remorse that his unnecessarily violent tackle left a player on the opposing football team paralyzed for life and Keir actually blames the victim, readers sense that he is not a reliable narrator.

Figuring out who are the "good guys" and who are the "bad guys" falls under the principle of *snap moral judgments* (p. 93). In the fictional world, as Rabinowitz writes, "Physical appearance can be assumed to stand metaphorically for inner quality . . . and the specific applications often echo and reinforce cultural norms" (pp. 86–87). Part of snap moral judgment includes what Rabinowitz calls *enchainment* (p. 89). It is appropriate to assume that the presence of one moral quality is linked to the presence of another that lies more or less in the same area of personality, and readers come to expect a range of behaviors from them (p. 90). For example, in YA literature bullies carry a bag full of enchained, or connected, traits and behaviors. The specifics vary, but, as in Jaime Adoff's (2004) *Names Will Never Hurt Me*, bullies have an exaggerated sense of their own importance (quarterback Ryan Duncan); they smack Kurt Reynolds on the back of the neck—hard—throughout the day, every day, and never get punished; and they taunt him by repeating the same insulting names like "Kurt is Dirt." Each clique or each character type carries a package of closely related assumed moral or ethical traits in the fictional world of school life.

YA authors may reverse conventional expectations with surprising behaviors that, of course, bring pleasure to the reader. After setting up at least three potential shooters within the course of the plot in *Names Will Never Hurt Me*, the author turns the tables on the reader when, with a gun in his hand, jock Ryan Duncan (not the emotionally scarred Kurt Reynolds who carries *something* in his gym bag that makes him feel safe) confronts his domineering father fully prepared to kill him. In Hoffman's (2003) *Stravaganza: City of Stars*, after the narrator tells the reader twice within 80 pages that the filly that can fly is definitely safe with Roderigo in Santa Fina, the reader expects that she will be stolen, as she is.

Although most people do not apply such assumptions in the real world, in the fictional realm readers put significance on a character's morality according to his or her physical features and behaviors. In YA literature, physical attractiveness and social success are often the traits found lacking (or self-perceived as lacking) in the protagonist whose story deals with the development of self-esteem. The skinny blonde cheerleader who is the protagonist in an adult genre novel is more likely to be the antagonist in a contemporary realistic YA novel.

Principle of Configuration

The principle of *configuration* governs the activities by which readers determine probability in a story (Rabinowitz, 1987: 112). Configuration helps readers to predict events, behaviors, and outcomes while reading a text. In other words, readers intuitively ask themselves how an episode is likely to be resolved or how the book is likely to turn out. Rabinowitz notes that, on the whole, novels are more or less predictable. More often than not, readers have a good sense of the general course of future events before they have gotten very far into a narrative in that the principles of configuration are highly genre specific (p. 113). Readers expect different outcomes in a gothic novel and in a contemporary realistic YA novel. Rabinowitz notes, "Many rules of configuration are so much a part of our intuitive understanding of literature that they seem almost trivial when made explicit" (p. 116). Additionally, readers expect certain events to occur in fiction that they would not expect to occur in real life. Broadly speaking, readers expect that "*some*thing will happen in a novel but they also expect that not just *any*thing can happen" in a novel (p. 117). The principles of configuration include

- undermining (p. 119),
- focus (p. 125), and
- action (p. 132).

The principles of *undermining* are evident even to very young readers. When a plot is going along too smoothly, readers expect for that stability to be overturned. If a character makes a boast or a claim of surety, readers justifiably predict the opposite will happen. In Schaefer's (1984) *Shane*, one of the ranchers calls Shane a coward for backing down from a fight and, although adversaries of the ranchers, many of the farmers agree. For the first half of the book, Shane stays out of trouble. The reader expects that Shane will prove them all wrong, as of course he does when he kills the villain in a gun fight. Claims of committing a perfect crime beg for a reversal in a reader's mind. If something is stated as being impossible or a sure thing, then a reader will expect the opposite to occur because of the principles of configuration.

Principles of *focus* come into play as readers narrow their attention toward a "central consciousness" in the narrative (Rabinowitz, 1987: 126) or the story's controlling point of view. The plethora of first-person point of view stories in YA novels makes it easy for readers to know where to focus their attention. But even if a YA novel is told using multiple narrators, the reader senses that the author has chosen to maintain a consciousness of multiplicity with the point being to see how each speaker sees things from different—sometimes opposite views—as in Julie's and Bryce's alternating perspectives as in Wendelin Van Draanen's (2001) *Flipped*. Additionally, a reader learns to recognize fairly quickly who the protagonist of a story is. Novels with more than one main character have become commonplace in YA literature, and readers have learned to focus on the characters who show up in the most dramatic scenes or who have received more attention. A reader also learns fairly quickly what the novel is likely to be about. For example, the opening sentence of Judy Blume's (1975: 1) *Forever* easily leads the reader to assume what the subject matter is likely to be: "Sybil Davison has a genius I.Q. and has been laid by at least six different guys."

Principles of *action* refer to the assumptions that readers activate when presented with two (or more) plot strands within the same text. In order for the narrative to be balanced, they assume that the plots "will eventually merge" (Rabinowitz, 1987: 132). In the graphic novel *American Born Chinese* (Yang, 2006), there are three subplots that do not fully reveal their connection until the novel's conclusion. Additionally, when readers encounter certain events, they expect certain consequences or results to occur. In a mystery readers expect justice. In a romance readers expect a happy couple. Rabinowitz (1987: 133) notes, "Readers have learned to expect literary events to come in patterns" of the *fictional* world's cause and effect. In *American Born Chinese*, Jin impulsively kisses his best friend's girl, and readers justifiably expect that he will pay for that serious moral error, as in fact he does, losing Wei-Chen's trust. When characters are clearly set up as friends or as foes, readers expect some resolution in the relationships to occur by the end of the narrative.

Philosophical comments or pithy statements of truth within a story often serve predictive purposes (Rabinowitz, 1987: 136). During one dramatic moment in *Octavian Nothing*, the boy's mother reads to him from Psalms 137, "By the rivers of Babylon," where the biblical captives had been ordered to entertain their captors with their music (like Octavian and his mother do) but all the while lamenting and mourning their exile from their land, a country that Octavian admits he knows nothing about (Anderson, 2006: 65–66). The book becomes a literary exploration of the meaning of freedom.

Principle of Coherence

The principle of *coherence* is applied after the reading of a work has been concluded and leads readers to bring together a work's various elements into a unified whole (Rabinowitz, 1987: 147). This includes the search for basic patterns and overarching meaning(s). Readers assume that a book is coherent and that any apparent problems in its construction are intentional (p. 147). The principles of coherence include

- insufficient information (p. 149),
- surplus information (p. 154), and
- naming, bundling, and thematizing (p. 158).

Principles of *insufficient information* have to do with making sense of the gaps and holes in a narrative that must be resolved. Gaps need to be filled in or dealt with before interpretation and evaluation can begin. Authors, of course, leave out anything that they consider unimportant; however, readers' perspectives on what is important may differ from an author's perspective (Rabinowitz, 1987: 149). In Robert Cormier's (1998) *Heroes*, Larry LaSalle's assault on Nicole is never called a rape, and the attack itself is described in very little detail because the narrator Francis cannot see the event. The only thing that the protagonist Francis says is, "What were they doing? But I knew what they were doing" (Cormier, 1998: 96). Readers also know what was taking place and fill in that gap by using the principle of coherence.

Principles of *surplus information* come into play after the reader has been left with too much to notice. Ordinarily, readers assume that (most) of the surplus is intentional and that they must "interpret it one way or another, transforming the text so that it is no longer excessive" (Rabinowitz, 1987: 154). But sometimes the surplus seems to have a metaphorical or figurative meaning, such as the many references to goats in Brad Land's memoir that add up to the more modern meaning of a scapegoat, any victim of irrational hostility.

Readers employ principles of *naming, bundling,* and *thematizing* as they identify the various story details that point toward one or more patterns and then naming them to arrive at meaning (p. 148). *Naming* is especially important in the process of interpretation, as it "serves to take the complex or unfamiliar and make it manageable by putting it in a category, increasing its apparent coherence by stressing some features and downplaying others" (p. 158). *Bundling* is the accumulation of all the details that seem disparate (different) and putting them into meaningful categories. *Parallelism* (repeated syntactical similarities) is an example of bundling. Sometimes readers discern parallel myth patterns, as Stephanie's coming of age in *Seventeen: A Novel* (Rosenberg, 2002) that follows the pattern of the myth of Persephone's journey into the underworld through the novel's chronological plot from fall to spring, the seasons symbolizing death to rebirth. The book's many details that fulfill the archetypal pattern include Stephanie's lover Denny, who resembles Hades, and her mother, who resembles the goddess Demeter. When Stephanie first sees Denny at school, like Hades, he "looms up beside her as if the ground had opened beneath his feet" (p. 3), paralleling Persephone's kidnapping by Hades. She learns that Denny's father "is rich and mighty, an Olympian. Which makes Denny the son of a god" (p. 8). Literary parallelism, however, does not need to be an exact match. To be a true parallel, only a few of the myth's details need to be similar to, or parallel with, the contemporary narrative.

Another technique of bundling occurs in the principle of *conclusive endings*. Readers expect to read the conclusion of a book in a special way from any other part of the book. Under the principle of coherence, a *conclusion* differs from an ending. A *conclusion* means "a summing up of the book's meaning" (Rabinowitz, 1987: 160). Readers assume that authors save their best for last and assign "a special value to the final pages of a text" (p. 160). With traditional tales comprising their first stories, young people expect a fable to end with that all-important moral and a fairy tale to end with a happily-ever-after. The conclusion of *Octavian Nothing* brings this first volume of the slave's story to an end: "I knew not what I ran toward; I knew not what freedom meant. . . . I thought on the word *freedom*, and could picture nothing that it might be, beyond freedom to die. . . . " (Anderson, 2006: 350), reinforcing the book's theme on the irony of the American Revolutionary War as a fight by the colonists against their "enslavement" by England while the same men were blind to the inhumane bondage of Africans that had made America an economic success.

For many years, YA literature subscribed to the principle of optimistic endings. Robert Cormier's (1974) *The Chocolate War* created controversy for its dark and grimly realistic ending, and readers in the YA community took sides over this break in convention. Although contemporary YA novels are more realistic, there are still few blatantly pessimistic conclusions. Readers expect conclusive endings, even if the ending is open. Following the principles of coherence, and in light of an open ending, readers simply reinterpret the work so that the ending serves as an appropriate conclusion. Rabinowitz (1987: 166) writes, "Readers take open endings and assume that open-ness itself is part of the point of the conclusion."

TAKING A CRITICAL STANCE IN READER RESPONSE

When considering the different ways to respond to literature, those who choose to take a critical stance can apply any of the approaches that are discussed in this book, or they can respond using an original idea of their own. Another possibility is to apply Rabinowitz's four reading principles to a book. The discussion that follows is based on a summary of Rabinowitz's model. No single work necessarily exhibits all of the textual elements that would activate the principles of notice, signification, configuration, and coherence. In addition, readers may activate rules at any point in the reading process and simultaneously in some cases. The discussion is presented separately for clarity and understanding.

After readers have completed their books, they may discuss some of the following as they take a critical stance in response to a literary work.

Summary of Rabinowitz's Model

1. **Principle of notice:** Do the book's epigraph, title, and first and last sentences (or opening and closing) gain the reader's attention? Are there certain details or descriptions that seem more important than others?
   a. Are there any textual disruptions, changes, shifts, or breaks in the book's genre conventions?
   b. Does the cover grab the reader's attention or seem important? Is the book an unusual size or format?
   c. What are the repetitions that occur frequently enough to signal the reader to be on the lookout for more of the same?
   d. Do the book's typographical features seem important (e.g., italics, changes in font, illustrations)?

2. **Principle of signification:**
   a. Does the text contain figurative language? Do any of the characters' names sound metaphorical? Are there any objects that might become symbolic because of their frequent mention?
   b. Does the narrator of the book remain the same? Are there shifts at any point that cause the reader to adjust and identify that change? What do other disruptions suggest?
   c. Who is the protagonist? How does the reader know this? Are there other major characters? Do their physical features lead to snap moral judgments about them?
   d. What are the motivations behind characters' actions? Does the plot seem plausible as far as cause and effect?

3. **Principle of configuration:**
   a. Has the author provided details that help to predict certain actions or events or to cause the reader to anticipate certain events, behaviors, and outcomes? Can just anything happen in this book, or are only certain things more likely to happen?
   b. Are references made that at first seem to be insignificant details but that later become important in the course of the action? Has a character made a boast, a promise, or other declaration of surety that does in fact reverse?

4. **Principle of coherence:**
   a. Are there gaps or things that seem missing in the plot that need to be resolved before a reader can make sense of the book? Are surplus details working into meaningful patterns?
   b. What are the details that can be bundled and named as a category that might point a reader toward an overarching theme? Are there patterns that have emerged? What does the story seem to add up to? What's it all about?
   c. Does the book end in a conclusive manner?

Application of Rabinowitz's Reading Principles to Lynne Rae Perkins's *Criss Cross*

It takes two people to make a book—a writer and a reader—and it's not clear-cut who is doing the giving and who is receiving. The roles of giver and receiver go back and forth like alternating current, when there is a connection.

—Lynne Rae Perkins (2006: 11)

The words of Lynne Rae Perkins, spoken during her Newbery Medal acceptance speech, indicate that she is a writer who grasps the concept of reader response. Her *Criss Cross* (Perkins, 2005) captures the feelings of young people as they move from childhood into adolescence. Those who own a copy of *Criss Cross* can be encouraged to make annotations as they read, including using post-its to write immediate responses to passages. With 38 titled chapters, it is easy to locate episodes. After completion, readers can be encouraged to return to their annotations and discuss or write a critical response. An example of such a written response follows.

1. Principle of Notice

Associations of the title, along with the dust jacket that depicts a girl with her fingers crossed behind her back, remind the reader of someone who is hoping for good luck. The opening sentence, "She wished something would happen" (p. 1) confirms that initial thought. The first chapter is titled "The Catch" and at first it refers to Debbie Pelbry's necklace, whose latch sometimes becomes loose. Besides the glitch in the necklace, the title also refers to the "loophole" in Debbie's wish: "Hoping it wasn't too late to tack on one more condition, she thought the word *soon*" (p. 4), revealing Debbie's desire for a connection with another person, regretting the day when she was a child and actually wished that everybody would just leave her alone.

Criss cross can also mean "to go or pass back and forth" (*Merriam-Webster's Collegiate Dictionary*, Eleventh Edition). As the story progresses, the lives of the characters intersect, cross paths by chance, barely touch each other, or experience brief moments of joy. On the page opposite the second title page is a black-and-white continuum titled "the spectrum of connectedness." For 0 percent it says, "No one is here—no one." In the middle, "people move back and forth in this area like molecules in a stream." At 100 percent it says, "No one is here—no one." Such an illustration trumpets the subject, and possibly theme, of the book.

The book's epigraph comes from Shakespeare's *A Midsummer Night's Dream*: "What thou seest when thou dost wake, / Do it for thy true-love take." Knowing that this is one of Shakespeare's comedies about the confusions and problems of young love makes one consider that love could (should?) be one of the subjects. Shakespeare's play is a brilliant weaving of confusions, of young couples falling in and out of love, and of the role that magic, spells, and fate can play in romance.

Shakespeare's comedy takes place during May Day activities. *Criss Cross* is set during late spring and through midsummer when the teenage characters spend more leisure time with each other. The reader should be alert to any characters in the novel whose description or actions parallel those in the play. The epigraph is spoken by jealous King Oberon who wants his Queen Titania to fall magically in love with the first person she sees when she awakes. A parallel occurs in the novel when Debbie Pelbry suddenly falls for football star Dan Persik (pp. 137–139).

The author's use of *fonts and formats* is significant. During one episode, Debbie reads plumbing instructions to her father as he is under the sink trying to repair a leak. The text emphasizes the ungrammatical sentences of the sheet with a bold font, "**Precise teeth are biting sharply the slippery oil to a grip**" (p. 66). Debbie says, "I like the way it sounds" (p. 66), words that make her laugh, indicating the first of several references that reveal her to be a girl with a keen awareness of words, a lover of languages and reading, and of communication in general, the latter something she does quite well until she tries to talk to handsome Dan Persik, whose locker is next to hers. In another chapter, Debbie tells Patty about a big change that had occurred with her in junior high school. To indicate that this is a flashback, the text is written in italics, suggesting that the event seems far in Debbie's past, a time when she and her best friend grew apart, but Debbie has resolved that sadness, its memory lingering but no longer hurting her (pp. 124–126).

One revealing shift in format occurs in Chapter 22 "*Wuthering Heights/Popular Mechanics*" which divides the pages into two columns. Debbie's thoughts on the love triangle in Emily Bronte's novel are displayed down the left-hand column of the page, while her neighbor Lenny's thoughts are displayed down the right-hand column. The two columns represent the physical and emotional separation that occurs between boys and girls at this stage in their lives. Lenny sees Debbie reading in her backyard and feels "a neighborly urge to go do something in his own backyard" (p. 201), but he forgets her almost immediately as he becomes engrossed in fiddling with his dirt bike. Debbie stops reading just long enough to notice Lenny's muscled arms but quickly returns to the love story.

Another shift in format occurs in "Conversation in the Night: Brilliant Eskimo Thoughts," which begins with a dialogue between characters identified only as "P." and "D." Because Phil had been a focus character in the previous chapter, the reader might think that the chat is between Debbie and Phil, until P. talks about once being "the tallest girl in class" (p. 87). Then, the reader might think it must be Patty and Debbie. In the middle of the chapter, there is a break (*rules of rupture*) in the narrative, with an icon separating the second section from the first. The initials no longer accompany the dialogue. Instead, "?:" introduces each speaker. The reader is now puzzled. Is this still Debbie and Patty? One character mentions Dan Persik, who in a previous chapter meets a pretty girl named Meadow. Could this be a conversation between Meadow and her friend Robin? However, the reader is foiled (fooled?) again, when the character mentions Dan's locker is next to hers. Aha! This *is* Debbie and Patty after all. Perhaps the question marks are there to emphasize that the dialogue is composed of many questions the girls ask each other, philosophical questions interspersed with everyday life questions about boys. The chapter also shows two girls connecting with each other. The topic of their conversation considers the philosophical notion of life's being like a domino effect, with any single action affecting every other action on the planet.

2. Principle of Signification

There are two protagonists among a group of ten YAs. Through their stories, the narrator focuses on Debbie and Hector as representatives of young people on the cusp of male and female sexual attraction. Debbie has a very common name for the time. On two different occasions two speakers mention, "There are a lot of Debbies" (pp. 149, 160). Later, Hector says that he knows only one Debbie, his friend for many years whom he sees—for one brief moment on a summer's evening—in a different way. For most of the narrative Hector has a crush on Meadow, but she tells him that he has an unusual name, "a word that means 'to bother people'" (p. 80), revealing her true character and her reaction to Hector. However, Hector points out that his name also refers to one of the heroes of the Trojan War, a reference that is one of many in the text that allude to characters and events reminiscent of Homer's Greek epics. When he leaves his first guitar lesson alone, Hector holds "his guitar case aloft, like a trophy" (p. 84), after contrasting himself to the jock Dan Persik earlier. Despite Hector's tentativeness about girls, he is the hero of his own story, ready to take on his opponent on the fantasy field of teenage romance.

Hector's opponent for Meadow's heart, Dan Persik, behaves at times like the stereotypical jock: he taunts the other boys, brags, and puts on a friendly face for all the girls. However, the narrator is not interested in portraying yet another dumb jock. Instead she humanizes him by portraying him as a work in progress. Out of the blue, the narrator says, Dan "wasn't really a donkey" (p. 140), alluding to Shakespeare's Nick Bottom, who was dressed in a donkey's head for his role in the tradesmen's play-within-the-play. Like Shakespeare's Nick, Dan is part conceited, part ignorant. The narrator recognizes that in high school society, Dan holds a special place, godlike, as if he were cast "under a spell" with a "magic jersey and a powerful potion of lucky genes and emerging hormones" (p. 140). The narrator informs us, "The spell gave him special powers. He was having a lot of fun with it. Who wouldn't?" (p. 140). Emphasizing Dan's comparison to Nick, the text includes an illustration of a donkey head on Persik's jersey. Dan cannot see that he sometimes acts like a donkey, but the omniscient narrator certainly can.

The narrator says that star athlete Dan must "somehow learn certain lessons, involving humility, compassion, respect, and independent thinking. . . . Actually, these are the same lessons everyone has to learn, but part of the spell was a blinder effect that made it a lot more difficult" (p. 141) for a favored young person to see himself honestly. After one episode when Dan treats the lonely, shy Russell with disdain, Dan's "stomach's burgeoning size crowded his heart, especially the underdeveloped kindness lobe" (pp. 251–252). The narrator concludes of Dan's behavior, "There was a barely perceptible subdermal movement near his tailbone. There was a slight bray in his voice. It was all still reversible" (p. 253), in part fulfilling his comparison with Shakespeare's donkey-headed character Nick Bottom. But the stereotypical arrogant jock, to the narrator, still has time to change, as he does in a chapter titled "Dan Persik's Progress" wherein he shows genuine interest in and concern for an injured Vietnam veteran (pp. 289–291).

The author uses *figurative language* to describe and allude to references from ancient Greece to create an archetypal, mythic realm of magic and nature as the backdrop for some episodes and characters. "In the Rhododendrons" is set in thick flowers and shrubs where Debbie and Patty—like pastoral nymphs—go to change into the clothes they really want to wear to a party. The narrator describes the girls as "Two Eves in the Garden of Eden" (p. 43). Debbie's mom "could not hear the siren call of the dragging jeans" (p. 45) which Debbie had so desperately wanted to buy in order to be on the cutting edge of fashion. As the girls undo the jean hems that they had earlier sewed to please their moms, they are described as being "like Penelope unraveling her weaving in the Odyssey, only backward and for different reasons" (p. 50). Of the little hideaway: "It felt very Arcadian, as if a shepherd might appear with a harp and some grapes" (p. 50). By using classical allusions, the narrator shows how primal but natural the girls' behavior and dreams really are as they dress themselves in the clothes that closer represent the older girls they believe themselves to be.

3. Principle of Configuration

Hector falls for the beautiful Meadow during his first guitar lesson and worries ceaselessly about how to ask her out and where he could possibly take her. His sister Rowanne gives him tips and advises him against some of his more imaginative ideas, such as taking Meadow to the closest thing to a "park" that his neighborhood has, a drainage ditch with trees and critters and a small stream. His fantasy imagines them together in nature, sharing the beauty of a spot away from the small town blandness of Seldem. His expectations for success with Meadow are high, while the reader can predict otherwise, in part because of the aggressive Dan Persik and his smooth way with all the girls. But it takes an embarrassing encounter at the city's festival to convince Hector that he does not stand a chance with Meadow. His intended connection with the girl of his dreams does not work out for him, and, although the reader hopes so much that it will, there is not much surprise when his dream of love with Meadow ends.

In another episode, Lenny asks Debbie on the spur of the moment if she would like to learn to drive a stick shift pickup truck. As a 14-year-old girl, Debbie sees this as an opportunity for adventure and talks herself into trying it. "It might be an emergency life skill a person should have" and "she might be sorry someday" if she ever needed to apply such a skill (p. 99). Under the principle of configuration, this lengthy episode raises reader expectations and heightens predictability of more to come. Indeed, many chapters later, Debbie rescues an elderly neighbor, who has gone into insulin shock, by driving the woman (in first gear only!) to the closest fire station for the town's only ambulance.

4. Principle of Coherence

The unifying element of the text is its third person omniscient (limited) point of view. Although many YA novels are written in first person and/or multiple first person narration, this text is not. Considering there are several young people's stories being told, why did Perkins choose this point of view? The reader can only speculate. It is possible this choice achieves what the text and its theme require—the exact distance of voice. First person tells as much as the author is willing to permit a character to reveal, including intimate thoughts. With an ensemble of ten characters who have known one another since childhood, *Criss Cross* shows both a broad look at the protagonists' lives and a fairly close look into their thoughts and reflections through Debbie's and Hector's third person limited perspectives. A third person narrator (when considering the theme of life's interconnections) can better focus on the events that show many characters intersecting with one another in everyday life than a first person narrator, who would depict a psychological slant of one character's obsessions or angst.

Another seemingly disparate element—Debbie's necklace—becomes, in the end, a symbol of the random nature of human contacts. Its route through the story takes many coincidental turns. The necklace is mentioned in the first chapter (privileged position), and its title, "Catch," alludes in part to Debbie's losing her necklace when she and Patty are changing clothes in the rhododendron bushes. A frisky chipmunk picks up the necklace and drops it in the grass of a nearby lawn. This seemingly unimportant incident is described at the very end of the chapter (p. 51) in another privileged position, thereby signaling that the reader needs to follow the progress of Debbie's necklace. It makes contact with two more characters (who lose or misplace it) before Dan Persik spots the necklace and thinks, "Maybe he could have some fun with this necklace, and he put it in his pocket" (p. 160). It is Dan's intent to embarrass Debbie with the necklace, but when he talks to her on the last of school to pull his prank, he discovers he has lost it.

The next chapter, "Where the Necklace Went," tells how the necklace (after making contact with three more characters) falls onto the asphalt ready to become melted and destroyed. That seems to be the end of the necklace, but the principle of configuration will not support such an expectation. By now, it is clear that the necklace is symbolic and in a way that relates to theme. At the end of the book, before a block party is to take place, while Hector crosses the street, he sees the gold necklace. He could barely make out the letters, *Debbie.* For him, there is only one Debbie. He picks it up, thinking he could give it to Debbie at the party as a joke that would make her laugh. Unlike the mean-spirited Dan, Hector thinks of turning the necklace into a shared surprise for his friend. At the end of the evening, when only a few people are left, Hector and Debbie sit together while he plays his guitar and sings. It is a beautiful midsummer evening with lightning bugs (sprites or fairies?) filling the night air with their charm. Hector remembers the necklace and shows it to Debbie, saying it is a gift "made especially" for her. He jokes to her, "I had cars drive over it" (p. 333). As he fixes the chain around her neck, they both sense a momentary connection. Almost like magic, the characters see each other in a different way. "Something should have happened.... Their paths crossed, but they missed each other" (p. 335). With a two-sentence paragraph, the narrator injects a witty line to round out the role of the necklace in its "attempts" to bring two young lovers together. "The hardworking necklace couldn't believe it. It let out an inaudible, exasperated gasp" (p. 336), a brilliant way to end a story that magically sees life is everywhere, including in ordinary objects.

The narrator makes her only first-person intrusion in the text in the conclusion. Knowing the honest, vulnerable nature of young people like Hector and Debbie, she writes, "Mistakes would have to be made. Maybe a lot of mistakes. It was okay. They can't hear me, but I want to tell them it's okay, they're doing just fine" (p. 337), bringing the novel to a satisfying conclusion.

ANNOTATED BIBLIOGRAPHY

Austen, Jane. 1811, 1996. *Sense and Sensibility.* **New York: Bantam. Classic.**

When the Dashwoods are forced out of their family's estate by the patriarchal inheritance laws of Regency England, older sisters Elinor and Marianne confront a social hierarchy that is binding on their fates and fortunes. A book's title holds a privileged position, and young people can search for more information on the historical meanings of this book's title and can be introduced to specialized handbooks, such as the *Princeton Encyclopedia of Poetry and Poetics* (1974). Young people can discuss how the nineteenth-century meanings of *sense* and *sensibility* differ from today's and the way that the meanings of words change over time.

Geras, Adele. 2000. *Troy*. New York: Harcourt. Grades 8–12.

The women and the working class of Troy speak about how life on the home front had its own battles, heroes, and villains during the Trojan War. YAs can take a *critical stance* by noting the book's creative use of point of view: third person limited omniscient through Helen and Andromache; protagonist Marpessa, the quiet one, who makes intricate weavings of myths that are described as if in her own words and set off in italics; The Gossips, or kitchen women, whose interspersed chats provide important details of everything going on; and the italicized sections that at times resemble a Greek chorus.

Grimes, Nikki. 2005. *Dark Sons*. New York: Hyperion. Grades 5–9.

Biblical Ishmael tells his story of being cast out by his father Abraham after the birth of Isaac, and contemporary urbanite Sam tells his story of feeling abandoned by his father James after a bitter divorce. Each character's story is written in a distinctive voice in free verse, and the stories contain parallel elements. YAs can construct a body biography split in half, illustrating the similarities and differences in the boys' lives.

Koertge, Ron. 2007. *Strays*. Cambridge, MA: Candlewick Press. Grades 7–10.

As Ted and a second passenger ride in a white van toward their new foster home, 15-year-old Ted begins his first-person account, "I don't know where I am." Having just lost his parents in a car wreck, Ted faces an emotionally complicated future that develops from the social isolation that he has always known; his story is one that includes believable, round YA characters who support, socialize, and educate him. Before reading the book, YAs can brainstorm and discuss the possible events that led to Ted's revelation that "I was so miserable in my other school that I fantasized about faking my death, then finding a veterinarian who takes care of exotic animals and offering to work for nothing. I'd put in twelve-hour days. I'd sleep on the floor" (p. 99).

Lynch, Chris. 2005. *Inexcusable*. New York: Simon Pulse. Grades 9–12.

After denying he's done anything wrong, explaining why things look bad but really aren't, and making excuses for his violent behavior, Keir Sarafian is forced to confront himself and his life truthfully, but tragically, for the first time. Keir sees himself as "a good guy"; therefore, he could not possibly have committed date rape against Gigi Boudakian, as she alleges. It eventually becomes clear that Keir is an unreliable narrator. Young people can discuss the point in the narrative when they first doubted Keir's reliability and the point where they felt sure that he was unreliable.

Sfar, Joann. 2007. *The Professor's Daughter*. Translated by Alexis Siegel; illustrated by Emmanuel Guibert. New York: First Second. Grades 7–12.

Lillian, the professor's elegant daughter, releases the mummified Pharaoh Imhotep IV for a Victorian afternoon in Kensington, where Imhotep recklessly assaults a man. When the victim seeks redress, Lillian accidentally poisons him as well as a policeman and lands in jail. What ensues in this 80-page graphic novella is a satire of Victorian society where the daughter and the mummy have much in common, e.g., each is a valuable possession of the professor, and their competing patriarchal fathers (the professor and the Imhotep III, also a mummy) have a shoot out. Imhotep IV and Lillian marry, have three children, blend into Victorian society, and visit the professor, who is on display as an Egyptian mummy in the British Museum. To prepare readers for a thoughtful reading experience with this graphic creation, a booktalk can focus on the work's cover art, challenging the novella's potential readers to imagine quietly how the apparent contradictions of time and place and relationship could be resolved in a satisfying tale.

Shivack, Nadia. 2007. *Inside Out: Portrait of an Eating Disorder*. New York: Atheneum. Grades 9–12.

The author's stark and painful story is a personal account of a 26-year struggle against anorexia and bulimia. The story is illustrated with surreal and fantastic sketches and is told through three narrative strands: text embedded in the sketches that tell the emotional tale of a life in chaos, a series of black boxes that relate her first person history of Ed (the eating disorder), and a series of gold boxes that contain facts about eating disorders (e.g., "Bulimia nervosa is frequently associated with symptoms of depression and changes in social adjustment" [n.p.]). This work is an example of the privacy that is inherently a significant aspect of reader response, and, while the work can be made accessible through multiple avenues (e.g., bibliographies, displays, booktalks), young people may prefer to read the work quietly and to reach out (for themselves or for others) as the author has.

Snicket, Lemony. 1999. *The Bad Beginning*. New York: Harper Collins. Grades 5 and up.

The first of 13 volumes in "A Series of Unfortunate Events" introduces the three Baudelaire orphans, whose parents' untimely death by fire places the children under the control of various adult guardians. The children instantly know when Violet, a gifted inventor, is thinking because she immediately ties up her long hair with a ribbon. Klaus, like a detective, can find important, lifesaving information whenever it is needed through his passion for reading. Toddler Sunny likes to bite things and observes the world from a perspective closer to the ground. Young people may discuss how the movie version (Silbering, 2004) compares to the series. The movie covers the first three books.

Talbot, Bryan. 1995. *The Tale of One Bad Rat*. Milwaukie, OR: Dark Horse. Grades 9–12.

On a cold Christmas Eve, Helen Potter runs away from her physically abusive father and emotionally distant mother and retraces the steps in the life of the only anchor she has ever had, author Beatrix Potter. Gaining emotional and physical strength from the English countryside and her kind employers at a country bed-and-breakfast, Helen confronts her parents and begins her road to full recovery. YAs who remember the stories and illustrations of Beatrix Potter will enjoy the many allusions to the author's life and works in this graphic novel (e.g., the protagonist Helen's employers are the McGregors).

Turner, Ann. 2000. *Learning to Swim: A Memoir*. New York: Scholastic. Grades 7–12.

A pleasant summer vacation at the beach turns into a horrific nightmare after Annie is subjected to repeated assaults by an older boy. Kevin threatens and frightens Annie to keep their secret—or else—but after her mother asks one question about Kevin, Annie breaks down and tells about her abuse. Young people can compare the handling of this sensitive topic in Turner's verse novel with Talbot's (1995) handling of the same topic in *The Tale of One Bad Rat*.

REFERENCES AND SUGGESTIONS FOR FURTHER READING

Adoff, Jaime. 2004. *Names Will Never Hurt Me*. New York: Dutton Children's.

Alexie, Sherman. 2007. *The Absolutely True Diary of a Part-time Indian*. Art by Ellen Forney. New York: Little, Brown.

Almond, David. 1999. *Skellig*. New York: Delacorte

Anderson, Laurie Halse. 1999. *Speak*. New York: Farrar, Straus, and Giroux.

Anderson, Laurie Halse. 2000. *Fever 1793*. New York: Simon and Schuster.

Anderson, Laurie Halse. 2002. *Catalyst*. New York: Viking Press.

Anderson, M.T. 2006. *The Astonishing Life of Octavian Nothing, Traitor to the Nation*, vol. 1, *The Pox Party*. Cambridge, MA: Candlewick.

Appleman, Deborah. 2000. *Critical Encounters in High School English: Teaching Literary Theory to Adolescents*. New York: Teachers College Press.

Blume, Judy. 1975. *Forever. . . . : A Novel*. Scarsdale, NY: Bradbury Press.

Burnett, Frances Hodgson. 1911. *The Secret Garden*. New York: F.A. Stokes.

Cormier, Robert. 1974. *The Chocolate War*. New York: Pantheon.

Cormier, Robert. 1997. "To the Student." In *Writers for Young Adults*, vol. 1, edited by Ted Hipple, pp. xix–xxii. New York: Scribner.

Cormier, Robert. 1998. *Heroes: A Novel*. New York: Delacorte.

Culler, Jonathan. 1980. "Literary Competence." In *Reader Response Criticism: From Formalism to Post-structuralism*, edited by Jane Tompkins, pp. 101–117. Baltimore, MD: Johns Hopkins University Press.

Culler, Jonathan. 1987. "Structuralism and Literature." In *Contexts for Criticism*, edited by Donald Keesey, pp. 277–286. Mountain View, CA: Mayfield Publishing.

Ellis, Ann Dee. 2007. *This Is What I Did*. New York: Little, Brown.

Fish, Stanley. 1980a. *Is There a Text in This Class?* Cambridge, MA: Harvard University Press.

Fish, Stanley. 1980b. "Literature in the Reader: Affective Stylistics." In *Reader Response: From Formalism to Post-structuralism*, edited by Jane Tompkins, pp. 70–100. Baltimore, MD: Johns Hopkins University Press.

Giles, Gail. 2002. *Shattering Glass*. Brookfield, CT: Roaring Brook Press.

Haddon, Mark. 2003. *The Curious Incident of the Dog in the Night-time*. New York: Doubleday.

Hemingway, Ernest. 1925, 1996. "Indian Camp." In *In Our Time*, pp. 13–19. New York: Simon and Schuster.

Hesse, Karen. 1997. *Out of the Dust*. New York: Scholastic.

Hoffman, Mary. 2003. *Stravaganza: City of Stars*. New York: Bloomsbury Publishing.

Holt, Kimberly Willis. 1999. *When Zachary Beaver Came to Town*. New York: Holt.

Hurley, Tonya. 2008. *Ghostgirl*. New York: Little, Brown Books.

Iser, Wolfgang. 1974. *The Implied Reader*. Baltimore, MD: Johns Hopkins University Press.

Iser, Wolfgang. 1980. "The Reader Process: A Phenomenological Approach." In *Reader Response Criticism: From Formalism to Post-structuralism*, edited by Jane Tompkins, pp. 50–69. Baltimore, MD: Johns Hopkins University Press.

Land, Brad. 2004. *Goat: A Memoir*. New York: Random House.

Lynch, Chris. 2005. *Inexcusable*. New York: Simon Pulse.

Mackler, Carolyn. 2003. *The Earth, My Butt, and Other, Big Round Things*. Cambridge, MA: Candlewick Press.

Myers, Walter Dean. 2000. *145th Street: Short Stories*. New York: Delacorte.

Myracle, Lauren. 2004. *ttyl*. New York: Amulet.

Perkins, Lynne Rae. 2005. *Criss Cross*. New York: Greenwillow Books.

Perkins, Lynne Rae. 2006. "Newbery Medal Acceptance Speech." *Children and Libraries* 4, no. 2 (Summer/Fall): 8–11.

Probst, Robert. 2004. *Response and Analysis: Teaching Literature in Secondary Schools*. Portsmouth, NH: Heinemann.

Probst, Robert. 2005. "In Memoriam: Louise M. Rosenblatt." *English Journal* 94, no. 5 (May): 11–14.

Pullman, Phillip. 2004. *The Golden Compass*. New York: Random House Audio.

Rabinowitz, Peter J. 1987. *Before Reading: Narrative Conventions and the Politics of Interpretation*. Columbus: Ohio State University Press.

Richards, I.A. 1929. *Practical Criticism: A Study of Literary Judgment*. New York: Harcourt, Brace and World.

Rosenberg, Liz. 2002. *Seventeen: A Novel in Prose Poems*. Chicago: Cricket.

Rosenblatt, Louise. 1938. *Literature as Exploration*. New York: Appleton-Century.

Schaefer, Jack. 1984. *Shane: The Critical Edition*. Lincoln: University of Nebraska Press.

Selden, Roman. 1986. *A Reader's Guide to Contemporary Literary Theory*. Lexington: University Press of Kentucky.

Silbering, Brad. 2004. *Lemony Snicket's A Series of Unfortunate Events*. Barry Sonenfield. 108 min. Paramount Pictures.

Slatoff, Walter. 1970. *With Respect to Reader: Dimensions of Literary Response*. Ithaca, NY: Cornell University Press.

Tompkins, Jane, ed. 1980. *Reader Response Criticism: From Formalism to Post-structuralism*. Baltimore, MD: Johns Hopkins University.

Trueman, Terry. 2000. *Stuck in Neutral*. Carmel, CA: Hampton Brown.

Udall, Barry. 2001. *The Miracle Life of Edgar Mint*. New York: W.W. Norton.

Van Draanen, Wendelin. 2001. *Flipped*. New York: Knopf.

Walter, Virginia. 1998. *Making up Megaboy*. Graphics by Katrina Roeckelein. New York: DK.

Yang, Gene Luen. 2006. *American Born Chinese*. New York: First Second.

Afterword

In this book, reader-response criticism is emphasized because, having been developed for young adults, it is especially attuned to their needs and interests. However, no single critical theory can illuminate all of young adults' reading. Their access to the full range of traditional critical approaches to literature is like having all the colors of the rainbow in one creative pallet. And, like the colors of a rainbow, the forms of literary criticism combine and blur into innumerable possibilities. Furthermore, like the rainbow, critical theories are boundless, and, although they may have many interpretations and combinations of interpretations, they offer a recurring shape and structure, enlightening reading and response. Wherever young adult readers' imaginations take them, their creative responses across the spectrum of critical theories enrich their reading pleasure and understanding and ensure literacy for lifelong learning.

Index

About the Authors

Kathy H. Latrobe is a professor at the School of Library and Information Studies at the University of Oklahoma where she has taught courses in library materials and services for young people since 1986. She has earned a BA, English; an MLIS; and a PhD, Education. She has over 25 years of teaching experience, including working with young people in classrooms and libraries in elementary, middle, and high schools. An active member of ALSC, YALSA, and AASL, Dr. Latrobe has served on the Newbery, the Carnegie, and the Margaret Edwards award committees as well as on the board of School Library Media Research Online.

Judy Drury received her BS and MEd in Language Arts and her MLIS from the University of Oklahoma. She has taught English in public and private middle and senior high schools. She was a high school library media specialist in Norman, Oklahoma, before her recent retirement.

CPSIA information can be obtained
at www.ICGtesting.com
Printed in the USA
FFOW01n0001161015
17746FF